Ethics, Wealth, and Salvation

A Study in Buddhist Social Ethics

Edited by
Russell F. Sizemore
& Donald K. Swearer

University of South Carolina Press

Published in Columbia, South Carolina, by the
University of South Carolina Press

First Paperback Printing 1992

Manufactured in the United States of America

Library of Congress Cataloging-in-Publication

Ethics, wealth, and salvation : a study in Buddhist social ethics /
edited by Russell F. Sizemore & Donald K. Swearer. — 1st ed.
p. cm. — (Studies in comparative religion)
Bibliography: p.
Includes index.
ISBN 0-87249-612-0
ISBN 0-87249-881-6 pbk.
1. Buddhist ethics. 2. Social ethics. 3. Wealth—religious aspects—Theravāda Buddhism. 4. Theravāda Buddhism—Doctrines. 5. Wealth, Ethics of. I. Sizemore, Russell F., 1954– II. Swearer, Donald K., 1934– III. Title: Ethics, wealth, and salvation. IV. Series: Studies in comparative religion (Columbia, S.C.)
BJ1289.E84 1989
294.3'568—dc20 89-14743
CIP

To John B. Carman

in appreciation for his support of comparative study
at the Center for the Study of World Religions

Contents

Series Editor's Preface

The comparative study of religion has come a long way from the time when it was chiefly concerned with literal comparisons between beliefs, doctrines and practices of religions according to set and often rigid categories. The categories were defined according to a variety of agendas, implicit or explicit, such as theological, anthropological, or philosophical.

Ethics, Wealth, and Salvation is a collection of essays in the relatively new field of comparative religious ethics. The field is "comparative" in that it seeks to be applicable across religious boundaries and it utilizes a variety of methods and approaches—sociological, textual-historical, anthropological, philosophical, symbolic, and others. This particular project is comparative also in its pioneering effort to bring scholars of diverse backgrounds, specializations, experiences, and interests to focus on Buddhist social philosophy and its relation to Buddhist faith in a variety of countries. Most of the contributors are Buddhologists of one kind or another, while the others are Western academic specialists in ethics with comparative interests.

The main focus of the book is wealth and its uses in various Buddhist texts and contexts, both lay and monastic. Comparisons are made both within and between Buddhist periods and places treated and between Buddhist and Western—especially Christian—ideas of wealth and ethics. The reader of this book will find George Bond's *The Buddhist Revival in Sri Lanka: Religious Tradition, Reinterpretation and Response* (1988) to be an interesting and informative companion in its detailed treatment of modern Buddhist movements and their implications for comparative studies in religion and ethics.

Ethics, Wealth, and Salvation is a pioneering, interdisciplinary project by some of the leading scholars both of Buddhism and comparative religious ethics. In keeping with the fundamental principles of this series, it provides original, technically sophisticated scholarship for a wide range of thoughtful readers, while inviting specialists to join in the emerging scholarly discourse it represents.

Frederick Mathewson Denny
Series Editor

Preface

Contemporary international politics have done a great deal to bring the arcane-sounding field of comparative religious ethics into new prominence. The ever-growing interdependence of nations and the significance of religious influences in international affairs make the importance of this area of inquiry increasingly obvious. Yet many obstacles must be overcome before the need for expertise will be translated into intellectual competence. Few areas are as troublesome for claims of objectivity as studies linking religion and morality, and cross-cultural research inevitably raises problems of precision, comparability, and intellectual bias. Historians, anthropologists, philosophers, and religious scholars, as well as policy makers, are likely to find this a difficult and confusing field for a long time to come.

The present volume arose out of a new effort to develop the field of comparative ethics in a balanced and purposeful fashion by drawing on scholars from a variety of disciplines and traditions. The essays collected here address the nature of Buddhist social ethics, in particular the specific moral issues associated with the acquisition and distribution of wealth. Although this topic may appear exotic, the essays raise concerns of remarkably broad significance. Questions about wealth and poverty lead naturally to the most basic issues of social existence and individual fulfillment, of obligations to self and others, and of the obligations of political leaders which justify their power.

Questions of this nature have been addressed within societies shaped by the Buddhist faith, but the social philosophy of Buddhism underlying them has received little scholarly attention. This volume proposes to explore the resources of the Theravāda tradition for dealing with such matters and to place these resources and these questions into a wider frame of reference shaped by historians of religion, ethicists, and philosophers. The social philosophy of Theravāda Buddhism in both its normative-doctrinal and its social-historical dimensions, exhibits certain tensions between the moral ideal of social and economic well-being and the religious ideal of individual salvation, which may imply an indifference to such well-being. These tensions are central to both the historical development of Theravāda Buddhism and recent reflections on method and interpretative approach in comparative religious ethics.

To pose a tension between individual salvation and social good is not an issue foreign to the Theravāda tradition; indeed, in doctrine and history Theravāda Buddhism has struggled with these notions in various ways. There are, for example, the tensions between the mundane (*lokiya*) and the transmundane (*lokuttara*) realms of being and acting, between kammic and nibbanic values, and between the ideals of world ruler (*cakkavatti*) and world renouncer (*sammasambuddha*), laity and monk. Concretely, in Theravāda history we find the ideal of monastic poverty coupled with monastery wealth, the paradox of worldly power joined with the perfections of moral virtue, the material benefits of meritorious acts symbiotically correlated with ascetic practice, frequent instances of monastic legitimation of government policies regarding national development, and even the ideals of non-attachment and equanimity validating programs of economic and social advancement. Comparatively speaking, these paradoxes, so fundamental to an understanding of Buddhist social ethics, are found in other systems of religious ethics as well and have led some scholars to argue that the tensions reflect two distinct realms of human endeavor—religion on the one hand and morality on the other.

As this volume amply demonstrates, however, even in regard to such a fundamentally ''worldly'' activity as the acquisition and distribution of wealth, distinctions between religion and morality cannot be readily defined. Consequently, the several perspectives represented by the authors of these essays combine to make the point that even a highly focused topic of study within a religious tradition—in this case, attitudes toward wealth—must necessarily be understood within the broader parameters of the religious system, including the tradition's world view, institutional/historical development, and socioeconomic context. Hence the lead essay by Phra Rājavaramuni, one of Thailand's most outstanding scholar-monks, places the discussion of Theravāda attitudes toward wealth and poverty within the total Theravāda religioethical system. The volume begins with this chapter not simply because it represents a voice from within the tradition itself, but because it stands as an exceptionally concise interpretation of the doctrinal foundations of Theravāda Buddhist ethics. In Chapter 2 Frank Reynolds, as a historian of religion, also argues for the internal coherence of religious traditions, insisting that a particular issue of Buddhist social ethics must be based on an understanding of the underlying and pervasive dhammic norms that integrate such polarities as non-attachment and the acquisition of wealth. Other essays, particularly those by John Strong (Chap. 5) and Nancy Falk (Chap. 6), use narratives of kings and lay donors who embody the central virtue of generosity (*dāna*) to show how the Theravāda tradition has symbolized the polarity of non-attachment and the acquisition of wealth.

Although no study of Buddhist social ethics can comprehensively address all of the tradition's historical, socioeconomic, and political aspects, several of these essays examine more specific effects of Buddhist faith on social practice. Buddhist attitudes toward wealth and poverty, embedded as they are in a Buddhist view of the world and history, have played a significant role within Buddhist institutional history and continue to inform Buddhists' behavior in the contemporary world. The essays by Steven Kemper (Chap. 7) and Charles Keyes (Chap. 8), in particular, move our study of Buddhist social ethics out of merely doctrinal and textual analysis into the areas of institutional history (monastic organization in Sri Lanka) and contemporary village life (Thai-Lao villagers in northeast Thailand).

The question of how Buddhist social ethics are to be interpreted also lies at the heart of this study. Is the analysis to be derived solely or largely in terms of the categories of the doctrinal and historical traditions of Theravāda Buddhism? Or are there legitimate cross-cultural and comparative interpretive perspectives, derived historically, as in the case of Robin Lovin's essay (Chap. 9), or philosophically, as in the contributions by Ronald Green (Chap. 10) and John Reeder (Chap. 11)? Some of these issues are focused by Russell Sizemore's reflections in Chapter 4 on the essays by Frank Reynolds and David Little (Chaps. 2 and 3).

As this collection makes abundantly clear, interpretive or methodological consensus does not come easily in this emerging field of comparative religious ethics. It may be, as Ronald Green suggests, that Theravāda Buddhist attitudes toward wealth are compatible with universal norms of distributive justice. But as John Reeder argues, these norms themselves have complex origins that may not be fully shared in Buddhism. Still others, such as Frank Reynolds, question the application of such universal categories altogether, especially when they are derived from western philosophical discourse and applied to an Asian religious tradition. But the debate, both explicit and implicit in this volume, has served to highlight the contribution that historians of religion and ethicists can make to the mutual enterprise of interpreting religious ethics. As we hope this volume demonstrates, the vitality of the parts can enhance our understanding of the whole. And the whole, we believe, is a significant contribution to the study of Buddhist ethics, as well as an important opening into the new field of comparative religious ethics.

Acknowledgments

The editors would like to express their thanks to the institutions and individuals who assisted in bringing the authors together and making this volume possible. We are grateful to the National Endowment for the Humanities and the Henry Luce Foundation for sponsoring the conferences at which many of these essays were first presented and for providing funds toward the resulting publications. Professor John Carman of the Center for the Study of World Religions at Harvard University was supportive throughout the enterprise. Andrew Rasanen and Lissa McCullough of the Center gave invaluable assistance in preparing the final manuscript. Our thanks also to Fred Denny for including this volume in the University of South Carolina Press Studies in Comparative Religion and to Kenneth Scott of the Press for advice and editorial assistance.

Ethics, Wealth, and Salvation

Introduction

Although the essays in this volume address Theravāda Buddhist attitudes toward wealth from different perspectives, there are several unifying themes. We turn now to a substantive consideration of six of them: The Principle of Non-Attachment and the Possession of Material Wealth, Instruction for Religious Salvation and Guidance for Ethics, The Social Effect of Individual Virtue, *Dāna*: The Concept of Religious Giving, The *Sangha* as a Social Power, and The Question of Universality: Equality, Justice and Individualism.

THE PRINCIPLE OF NON-ATTACHMENT AND THE POSSESSION OF MATERIAL WEALTH

It has at times been assumed that Buddhism's central principle of non-attachment and its call for renunciation of the mundane world entail a wholly negative view of the world and of wealth. This assumption, together with perhaps a subconscious borrowing of images from Christian monasticism and popular stereotypes, has led some observers to imagine that Buddhism is a religion of extreme asceticism. The next step in this orientation is a sharp contrasting of the asceticism of Buddhist monks on the one hand and the seemingly materialistic interest of the laity in securing more comfortable rebirths on the other, which gives rise to the idea that there are "two Buddhisms." All of the authors in this volume find this approach to Buddhism simplistic and misleading. They believe not only that Buddhism gives at least a provisional affirmation to material prosperity, but that there are many instances in which wealth is highly praised and there are many norms for handling wealth which intimately link lay and monastic society. Instead of a single-minded condemnation of wealth, according to the contributors, Theravāda Buddhism offers a "middle way," or sees the acquisition and renunciation of wealth in a dialectical relationship.

Both Reynolds and Rājavaramuni, for example, maintain that the principle of non-attachment is at the heart of Buddhist ethics and is especially relevant to the tradition's handling of wealth. But both reject a simple opposition between non-attachment and material prosperity. As

Reynolds puts it, non-attachment is the attitude that one has when seeing things as they truly are, that is, when one sees things according to the *dhamma*. To know the *dhamma*, to see things truly, is to recognize the self as a conditioned, temporal reality and to reject self-indulgent cravings as harmful illusions. Thus, a non-attached orientation toward life does not require a flat renunciation of all material possessions. Rather, it specifies an attitude to be cultivated and expresssed in whatever material condition one finds oneself. To be non-attached is to possess and use material things but not to be possessed or used by them. Therefore, the ideal of non-attachment applies all across Buddhist society, to layman and monk alike. Whereas the monk has adopted a lifestyle and discipline to single-mindedly advance his cultivation and practice of the *dhamma*, the layman is at a stage in which his best preparation for this path is to take up the responsibilities of the householder. For both, the practice of non-attachment in the performance of their activities will create a greater harmony with reality.

In Chapter 1 Rājavaramuni makes a similar point specifically about the concept of poverty. If to be "poor" means to have less than what one desires, it is always bad to be poor, and Buddhism recommends poverty to no one. After all, it is suffering (caused by frustrated desire) that enlightenment eliminates. In this way Buddhism regards poverty as a problem of improper desire or inappropriate attitude—the greed at work in craving or hoarding—rather than as a problem of material shortcomings. Buddhism's main concern is not with bounty or scarcity, but with the human response to these conditions. To be content with what one has, regardless of its material value, is an expression of wisdom, and such contentment is the natural accompaniment of the attitude of non-attachment. From this Buddhist point of view, then, material conditions are important only to the extent that they influence one's ability to cultivate non-attachment. Extreme scarcity will be bad if it stimulates greed and provokes acts of crime; economic sufficiency is good because it is conducive to spiritual growth and more generally to individual and social well-being. But apart from these qualifications, it is the adherent's attitude toward his wealth and not the amount of wealth he possesses that is determinative of the evaluation.

A corollary of this view is that moral scrutiny is shifted from questions of rightful possession (and from debate about the justice of the existing distribution) to questions of appropriate acquisition and use. As Rājavaramuni puts it: "It is not wealth that is praised or blamed, but the way one acquires and uses it." And, as dramatically portrayed in the Buddhist donor stories recounted by Strong and Falk, the goodness of a good act of material acquisition or use is a matter not so much of the consequences (although these are expected to be favorable) as in the manner in which it is done, that is, in its expression of the attitude of non-attachment. Thus the attitude of non-attachment is seen as completely compatible with and in fact required for virtuous acquisition of wealth.

A more free-flowing affirmation of wealth may be seen in the way material prosperity is paired with moral virtue in Buddhist legends and donor stories and in the Buddhist philosophy of *kamma* generally. The ideal societies depicted in Buddhist legends, for example, as Reynolds and Green relate them, enjoy a superabundance of material goods. The storytellers clearly delighted in providing the details of this wealth, and the prosperity of these societies is traced directly to their compliance with the *dhamma*. Similarly, as the stories analyzed by Strong and Falk show, wealthy kings and laymen are singled out for praise and emulation. Their wealth is portrayed as the result of their non-attached giving of previous wealth; their diligence and their success make them ideal exemplars for the laity. The same is true within the monastery: as Steven Kemper shows in his treatment of monastic reform, accomplished monks are deemed worthy of special benefits, and monks who are the recipients of large offerings are regarded as especially worthy. They must take care to remain non-attached to the prosperity their virtue creates, but who more than a monk is prepared to resist the temptations of abundance?

Thus, although Buddhism is unyielding in its condemnation of the attitude of craving or prizing wealth for self-gratification, it projects a vision of social order that sees a perfect harmony between virtue and prosperity. Specifically, the kammic system of reward and punishment identifies advances in spiritual accomplishment with improvements in material well-being. Whatever a person's station in this present life, acts of virtue will eventually be rewarded and the rewards will include material prosperity; vice will likewise be materially punished. Reynolds notes, "Dhammic actions always lead to a higher status in the hierarchy of cosmic and social existence and, therefore, to the possession and enjoyment of greater amounts of material wealth. . . . Actions violating dhammic norms will lead with equal certainty to a lower status in the hierarchy that orders the cosmos and society and therefore to increased increments of suffering, poverty, and hunger." The *dhamma* and the law of kammic retribution are thought to work together as a system of cosmic natural law—the most pious, most morally pure action is also the most practical, materially effective action.[1] For the individual, following the *dhamma* is not only morally the best and religiously the highest life; it is prudentially the wisest and ultimately the most profitable. And yet non-attachment is still the dominant motif: if self-serving greed becomes the motive for such a life, the virtue of even the best action will be lost. Craving destroys the merit of any action and so conformity to the dhammic code for the sake of gain is self-defeating.

As a result of these insights, Buddhism's basic orientation toward wealth includes a set of paradoxes. To live in accord with the *dhamma* will bring greater prosperity, but prosperity may spur craving. Although wealth is a mark of virtue and an appropriate reward for virtuous activity, it has no ultimate reality or value. As Reynolds points out, Buddhists recognize that every increase in wealth offers both the opportunity for renewed giving—a greater cultivation and expression of non-attachment—''*and* a temptation toward the kind of antidhammic self-indulgence that leads to increased entrapment in the web of worldly existence.'' These tensions give to Buddhist life and story a characteristic dynamic, concisely captured in Reynolds's story of the near-ideal Buddhist society: first, a flurry of virtuous activity brings reward. This reward causes the recipients to forget the wisdom that initiated their virtue. A lapse of virtue brings new experiences of suffering. Suffering once again evokes the basic truths of the Buddhist path. Virtue, reward, and temptation accompany wisdom and forgetfulness, and thus the moral of the lesson is the importance of mental discipline and remembering the nonessentiality of material wealth. When prosperity leads to forgetfulness and then to suffering, the basic truth of the *dhamma* and the principle of non-attachment are reaffirmed.

INSTRUCTION FOR RELIGIOUS SALVATION AND GUIDANCE FOR ETHICS

One could thus summarize the basic thrust of Theravāda teaching on wealth in four statements: First, craving is bad. *Craving* is an abbreviated term for the cluster of mental states and resulting actions that express ignorance about the true nature of the self and of reality. Second, wealth, if it can be gained and possessed without craving, is good. Or we could say wealth, if it is gained, possessed, and used in accord with dhammic norms, is good, for the *dhamma*'s rules portray the path of non-craving. Third, wealth is a sign of virtue. Because the law of *kamma* guarantees that each receives the fate merited by his/her acts and because wealth, being good, is a fit reward for meritorious action, prosperity is proof of virtue. And, of course, properly motivated meritorious behavior will eventually be rewarded with prosperity. Fourth, at the higher levels of virtue and wisdom, wealth is recognized as meaningless. This principle may be honored in the breach, as when forgetfulness of this truth leads to craving for more rewards and a downfall into suffering.

The most potent implications of this fourth paradoxical point are admirably portrayed in the Jōtika legend recounted by Reynolds. In that tale the evil king Ajātasattu expresses craving in his envy for Jōtika's wealth and his use of violent means to seize it. Jōtika's virtue is mirrored in his wealth, and his wealth is protected by his virtue. In the climax of the story Jōtika confronts Ajātasattu directly and proves decisively the power of virtue over unjust violence. Then, in the face of this triumph, in a second climax Jōtika renounces his fortune and declares his intention to enter the monastic life. In Buddhist stories of cxcmplary figures, great increases in wisdom, virtue, and wealth (as these are understood to be complementary) characteristically lead to a complete renunciation of material possessions and the subject's entering the *sangha* (the Buddhist monastic order). In such fashion—and this point can be found in nearly all of the stories recounted throughout the volume—the greatest of all lay accomplishments are portrayed as merely preparatory for the highest path of cultivating wisdom in the *sangha*. It is well to keep in mind, of course, that the authors of these texts were monks.

It is noteworthy that the morality of wealth is handled so completely in relation to the pursuit of salvation. The overriding, incomparable value of spiritual enlightenment seemingly determines all judgments made concerning wealth and poverty; the religiously preeminent virtue of non-attachment serves as the central ethical guide as well. All of the teaching appears to be addressed to the individual concerned about his or her own perfection in virtue. "What must I do to be saved?" is the question being answered, not "What should be the role and distribution of wealth in the community?"

The apparent priority of religious advancement over all other concerns in Buddhism may lead to a conflict between religious values and ethical responsibility. In the story of Prince Vessantara, for example, as recounted by John Strong, Vessantara's perfect generosity and personal acts of renunciation appear to be in tension with his responsibilities for his family. His own sacrifices, however well-intentioned, seem to have the effect of bringing pain to others. In an exchange on the matter between King Milinda and the Venerable Nāgasena, various resolutions of this tension are proposed, but none is completely persuasive. Similarly, in Nancy Falk's story about Anāthapiṇḍika and the household spirit there is an explicit conflict between Anāthapiṇḍika's heedless giving, which is praised, and the spirit's skepticism and prudence, which are vigorously condemned. The tradition itself is willing to consider that although such heedlessness is a religious virtue it could appear to be a moral vice.

It should be noted that there are some surprisingly close parallels between the heedlessness of Buddhist generosity and the self-sacrificing element in Christian notions of love, and nearly identical interaction between religious and moral elements. Particularly in the Gospel parables, the Kingdom of God is portrayed as a pearl of great price, worthy of the sacrifice of all other possessions.[2] Thematically, the infinite value of the individual soul in harmony with God matches the Buddhist valuing of *nibbāna*. Material wealth is similarly regarded as a dangerous attachment to the world which may hinder one's spiritual commitment, and the prudential motive is utterly condemned—"verily, these already have their reward." In both cases there is the possibility of conflict between religious purity and apparent moral responsibility, which is symbolized by the prudential claims of families.[3] And finally, both traditions show the tendency to collapse all ethical choice into a matter of virtuous character and religious piety: In his commentary *On the Epistle of John* St. Augustine says, "Love and do what you will"; in Buddhist terms, "Avoid craving and do what is necessary."

Such conflicts between religious ideals and commonplace moral expectations naturally raise the question of the relationship between religion and morality in Buddhism. One approach to such issues is pursued by David Little in Chapter 3. He notes that Buddhism's goal of *nibbāna* may engage altruistic or egoistic impulses on the part of individuals and that Buddhist religious beliefs about the ultimate status of the self, the operation of *kamma*, and of the importance of religious giving qualify what is otherwise a rather straightforward consequentialist ethic. Religious aspirations do overshadow any explicit endorsement of the values of social cooperation, and so Little concludes that finally the Theravāda ethic is justified on religious rather than moral grounds.[4] Strong's closing comment on the Vessantara story, incidentally, is perfectly consistent with this analysis: Vessantara is praised because "he did what he did for the sake of enlightenment. It is not that he 'loved [his wife and children] less, but Buddhahood more, that he renounced them all.' "

A contrasting reading of the Theravāda tradition may be found in the essay by Ronald Green (Chap. 10). Green argues that Buddhism's emphasis on selfless giving is necessary as a counterbalance to the typical tendency of human beings to justify for themselves more than their fair share of social goods. One could say that the example of Vessantara is a salutary, even if extreme, exhortation against greed and pride, necessary to counteract the natural course of human striving toward selfish and socially dangerous private accumulation. Thus, Green concludes that such admonitions demonstrate Buddhism's "basic acceptance" of the moral value of equality and allegiance to rational methods of social cooperation.

Readers will have to judge for themselves how effectively these divergent assessments correspond to Theravāda texts and history. It may be that Buddhists do find heedless generosity consistent with the prudential calculations of justice, as Green suggests, but only because they believe that the law of *kamma*, which Little stresses, guarantees that selfless acts will be rewarded and all will be as it should be. (In what ways such beliefs express commitment to the value of equality is a question we shall return to below.) And one must consider whether definitions of religion and morality which set religious and moral justifications in opposition are adequate. Depending on the definitions one adopts for these terms, radically different conclusions result. Since in some views Buddhist advice for conduct has nothing to do with social cooperation or welfare and is concerned only with individual salvation, it could be said that Buddhism is an example of a religion without ethics, or even a religion that repudiates ethics. Conversely, since Buddhism envisions an unbreakable link between seeing reality as it is and living as one should, one could conclude that Buddhism is uniquely practical and is, in fact, an example of the way religion and ethics can be completely merged.

We cannot sort out these definitions and contentions here, but a closely related question, essential to our study, is the relationship Buddhism envisions between individual perfection and social good, between the individual's spiritual welfare and the material welfare of the community.

THE SOCIAL EFFECT OF INDIVIDUAL VIRTUE

In the history of scholarship on Theravāda Buddhism the tradition's apparent focus on *individual* religious advancement has led some observers to suggest that Theravāda lacks a social ethic entirely or that there are "two Buddhisms," one for the monks and another for the laity. Does it make sense to say that Buddhism has a social ethic? Or is it exclusively a religion of individual virtuosi, who are purposefully isolated from all social relations? Does Buddhism have a social philosophy, or is its social influence merely the unintended result of its religious striving?

The contributors in this volume are agreed that Budddhism's social concerns are not simply incidental and that to deny this does justice neither to the complexity of Buddhist thought nor to its historical impact in Buddhist societies. It is appropriate, therefore, to ask how Buddhist social practices are integrated into the broader Buddhist world view and to see to what extent Theravāda Buddhist thought takes an interest in social welfare apart from religious advancement.

According to Phra Rājavaramuni in Chapter 1, scholars have been mistaken in regarding Buddhism as solely a religion of the monks. In his view Buddhism does take spiritual and social diversity seriously and extends its moral consideration to society as a whole. It does hold a vision of a cooperative society marked by spiritual and material reciprocity between the monastic establishment and the laity. This cooperative society is purposefully designed to provide the optimal social context necessary for the pursuit of salvation. The monastic establishment's primary function is to maintain the *dhamma* for the rest of society, although it also plays an important role in providing education, food, and housing for the destitute and the orphaned. In complementary fashion, the lay people are to provide material support for the monks (which is, of course, essential for the spread of the *dhamma*) and discharge their householder duties responsibly. Lay persons are also to cultivate what wisdom and discipline they can gain from their contact with the monks. Thus, there are principled reasons for why monks are to have daily contact with the rest of society.

One traditional way of thinking about the social context for spiritual development, suggested by Rājavaramuni, is in the Buddha's teaching on the significance of good friends. The Buddha taught that a person's acquaintances are vitally important in providing the conditions for spiritual advancement. These conditions include minimal material comfort, moral encouragement, and wise teaching. When Rājavaramuni examines the guidelines the tradition offers on relations between the monks and the laity and on relations among the laity, he finds a close correlation between these and the Buddhist ideals of friendship. Thus, a properly functioning society is a society of good friends—it provides its members with the prerequisites for salvation and becomes one more of Buddhism's "skillful means" in fostering enlightenment. In such fashion a Buddhist ideal for individual virtue and the Buddhist vision of social harmony are united in the single charge that all persons are to be as good friends.[5]

In Chapter 9 Robin Lovin draws on Rājavaramuni's description of Buddhist monasticism and society to make a comparison with Christian monastic forms and the accompanying social philosophies. Both Christianity and Buddhism, Lovin notes, lack intrinsic social theologies; unlike Islam, they did not have founders with preeminently political identities.

This lack turns out to be a strength of sorts, in that it gives Christianity and Buddhism great flexibility in adapting their interpersonal ideals and social aspirations to a variety of times, places, and political structures.[6] Yet Buddhism does show what should be recognized as an integrated social philosophy, Lovin argues, in the role the tradition assigns to the *sangha* in society.

Unlike the Christian monastics' complete withdrawal from society into self-sufficient communities, the Buddhist *sangha* is positioned to exercise a certain degree of selectivity in legitimating social and political practices. The spiritual and material exchange system of interdependence between monks and laity is perfectly in accord with Buddhist notions of how the *dhamma* is known and transmitted. The mediating role of the king between the *sangha* and mundane society signals a purposeful political strategy of adjustment and accomodation, reflecting a distinctively Buddhist understanding of the possibilities for social change and of the importance of social conditions for individuals' spiritual advancement. Because human ignorance is regarded as the basic source of suffering, because selfish illusions are thought to be overcome in the gradual advancement of spiritual knowledge, and furthermore, because the best social setting for spiritual advancement is established through the routine interaction of the *sangha*, the king, and the social order, Theravāda Buddhist societies have a religiously informed preference for a social philosophy of gradual reform with emphasis on religious education. This ameliorist approach, Lovin says, reflects a strategy of purification—of preserving an ideal social form in the monastery while maintaining regular contact with the rest of society.[7]

Lovin's approach to the relationship between religion and ethics in Buddhism is particularly noteworthy because he includes in the concept of a tradition's ethics not only its moral principles and aspirations, but also its way of understanding how the world works to encourage and inhibit such aspirations. This considerably broadens the role assigned to religious affirmations in ethical reasoning. By looking at the tradition's conception of human nature and destiny and its view of evil and fate in order to see how they have shaped a complementary strategy for preserving moral ideals, Lovin illuminates the interaction between the Theravāda world view and its ethos.[8]

It should be noted that within Rājavaramuni's interpretation Buddhism does possess a social philosophy, but once again the justification for social action is primarily religious. The instruction for action is based on a theory of what is conducive to salvation (for the entire society), not on an independent norm of social cooperation or nonreligious rationality.

One might say critically that Buddhism's single concern is with religious salvation, not social welfare. The material well-being of society's members pales in comparison to the supreme value of spiritual enlightenment. Lovin's point is that Buddhist social ideals are no less social for this religious justification, nor are they any less connected to traditional moral concerns of social harmony. Social welfare and religious advancement are not in conflict, and Buddhist methods for directing society envision their mutual achievement.

Similar conclusions can be drawn from Reynolds's comments in Chapter 2 on the unity of Buddhist society and the social action of the law of *kamma*. Because there is a "unity of the religiomoral, the societal, and the natural orders," any kind of appropriate dhammic action inevitably leads to an increase in the wealth of the community as well as the individual responsible. And, of course, the converse situation is regulated by the same law. A person who acts with self-indulgence and fails to give to others in the proper fashion undermines the dhammic order and subverts the social good. Hence there is a basis for *social* criticism against individuals who abuse their wealth and an explicit *social* benefit for properly used wealth. The virtuous man's *dhamma*-guided use of his wealth—whether he is a monk or a layman—not only brings benefits to himself, but also raises the kammic status of the community as a whole, bringing spiritual and material advancement.

As described by Reynolds and Rājavaramuni, the society envisioned by Buddhism is a thoroughly interdependent organic system. Drawing on the classic Buddhist doctrine of causation, both insist that individual and social virtue and welfare are linked as co-arising. It takes good individuals to create a good society, and a good society to create good individuals. A seeker who raises himself, raises his community. A seeker who advances spiritually does so in part because of the aid of his friends. As the seeker advances, his presence will aid others in their spiritual growth. And in this advancement religious development and moral virtue are completely identified.

These responses to the charge that Buddhism is exclusively individualistic are remarkable on two accounts. One is that they continue the link commented on earlier between material and spiritual advancement. The Buddhist path, requiring both individual striving and social cooperation, lies in ever-greater fulfillment of the *dhamma*, which is, in the scheme of things, accompanied by ever greater material prosperity. The good society—the morally advanced, materially prosperous, properly functioning society—may also be the most salvifically effective society.

Second, in these responses the law of kammic retribution is being expanded in a social way, and this expansion raises some fundamental questions about the individual's responsibility for his own destiny. The relationship between individual merit and destiny is, of course, the issue that the law of kammic retribution seemingly settles. The present order is thought to be perfectly just because each individual's fate follows from his or her own actions. But if individuals are solely responsible for their own destinies, how can it be that one is aided or restrained by the activities of others beyond one's own control?

It is not clear how far the tradition goes in answering this question. Even as he talks about the importance of the social context, Rājavaramuni is careful to stress that there are many things that the individual can do only for him or herself. Mental discipline and self-control are seemingly inseparable from the will of the individual concerned. And Rājavaramuni cites the point that "good training of oneself includes regulating one's associates." Presumably, he means to say that one is responsible for one's friends—in choosing them and in encouraging them, which in turn makes them better friends and better supporters for one's own spiritual development. Thus, presumably, one gets the community one deserves. So it seems that the final responsibility for spiritual advancement still lies on the shoulders of the individual.

It is clear that a complicated theory of causation will be required to resolve adequately the paradoxes of individual responsibility, social influences, and the justice of each individual destiny which Buddhism seeks to preserve. The Buddhist doctrine of co-arising and interdependence (*paṭicca samuppāda*) affirms that the quality of a society is the result of the virtue of all its members, and as each individual influences others for good or for evil, he or she will reap the reward of living in the society that results from all these influences. Thus, the way the society shapes the individual's destiny is seen as the result of the individual's own action, even though other beings are involved whose destinies are being shaped by their actions and responses.

The kammic system of retribution can give these paradoxes a very practical form. If all beings deserve their present fates on the basis of past actions, and the present distribution of burdens and benefits is just, why should anyone intervene to change the existing situation? According to the law of *kamma*, the man lying robbed and beaten in the ditch has received just what he deserves. Presumably as a result of past offenses, the poor and the destitute have their just deserts. It would seem that the appropriate response from the passerby would be to do nothing. Are there any grounds in Buddhist ethics for thinking that the passerby has an obligation toward the stricken victim?

Reynolds and Rājavaramuni would argue that to exercise compassion and assist someone in the midst of a sorry (though deserved) state is a meritorious action. Although the unfortunate may have no specific claim on the passerby, the virtue of compassion imposes on the passerby the obligation to lend what assistance he or she can. Such assistance will be all the more meritorious if the victim has no specific claim on the benefactor. It should be observed here that the ethical reasoning involved in this assessment does not invoke the principle of justice to require assistance or a transfer of wealth. It is the virtue of compassion or charity that is involved, the virtue of the individual giver that is at stake. This is in keeping with what we have seen before, that even as the prosperous and the destitute have what they have on the basis of the law of *kamma*, Buddhists also believe that how they respond to their wealth or lack of it is a crucial moral issue. The principle of *kamma* is complemented by the moral virtue of compassion (*karuṇā*).

In keeping with the law of *kamma*, since every destiny is truly just, there can be ultimately no instances of undeserved compassion.[9] The injured man who was later helped by the compassionate passerby did deserve to be beaten and abandoned, but he also deserved to be helped. From the point of view of the giver, however, the act of assistance is an act of charity. The benefactor has no obligation specifically toward the victim; he is merely acting from non-attachment and compassion to make an appropriate use of his wealth and power. On the other hand, from the point of view of the victim, his past behavior brought upon him this punishment but also this hope for the future. When the passerby responds to him as a good friend, he will deservedly be comforted materially and encouraged on the path to spiritual development. Thus the law of *kamma* remains unbroken, and at the same time the virtue of compassion is affirmed.

As the example above indicates, when the doctrine of kammic retribution is understood as an exceptionless moral explanation and justification for the present distribution of wealth and poverty in society, it undercuts moral criticism of that distribution per se. Consequently, Buddhists concerned with how to make their present society more just appeal not to a distribution of wealth corresponding more adequately to moral desert, but to the principle of non-attachment and virtues such as compassion and generosity. Present positions and circumstances are thought to be the justly deserved results of previous actions or lives according to the law of *kamma*. To be sure, Buddhists wish to understand better the workings of the present distribution and to raise the prosperity of society as a whole, but the kammic justice of the current distribution is already guaranteed.

Belief in the justice of the present distribution does not, however, lead to a completely static economic system. Norms exist for redistributing wealth in society, with rules governing the acquisition and use of wealth, and influential religious beliefs dictate the appropriate ways to raise the welfare of society as a whole. Not surprisingly, these norms for the most part focus on the virtue of the individual who gives away his or her wealth and on the individual and social *kamma* generated by such gifts.

DĀNA: THE CONCEPT OF RELIGIOUS GIVING

The giving of gifts to those in need, to one's family, and to the religious establishment is an extraordinarily prominent practice in Theravāda Buddhism. As Reynolds indicates, such giving in all forms is widely commended for its faithfulness to the *dhamma* and has predictable results: "the non-attachment of the giver is expressed and cultivated; and the merit of the giver is increased so that he or she will enjoy even greater wealth in the future." But as Reynolds notes, and the essays by Strong and Falk elaborate, there is a definite hierarchy concerning these forms of giving. According to the Theravāda texts, by far the most important form of giving, called *dāna*, is that directed to the Buddha and the *sangha*. In fact, we may go so far as to suggest that religious giving is of such importance in Buddhist thinking about wealth that *dāna* and not some concept of structural justice is the central concept in Buddhist social and political philosophy.

The practice of *dāna*—of providing material support to the Buddhist monastic establishment, whether by donating to individual monks on their alms rounds, financially supporting Buddhist monasteries, or offering monuments to the Buddha—is regarded as the most important and the most effective form of giving. For several reasons this is consistent with the basic perspective on wealth we have examined thus far. First, the concept of *dāna* echoes the Buddhist condemnation of craving and hoarding. Buddhism puts the greatest emphasis on cultivating and expressing the attitude of non-attachment; religious giving is thought to offer the best opportunity to express non-attachment and, accordingly, the best opportunity to win merit for the giver. Two common phrases convey this understanding. Buddhism recognizes a hierarchy of giving among "fields of merit." The more noble and accomplished the recipient of the gift—the higher the field of merit—the more the act of giving reflects non-attachment. Naturally, monks and the *sangha* generally are thought to be the worthiest of all recipients, and distinguished monks are especially fruitful of merit. The nobility of the recipient must be matched by the purity of the donor's attitude, and Buddhist texts on *dāna* speak of "the efficiency of the thought" in giving to mark the importance of giving with the proper attitude. Even a valuable gift given for selfish reasons brings the giver no benefit and may bring harm, but so also a small gift given selflessly is especially potent.

Second, the concept of *dāna* affirms that the amount of wealth possessed and its distribution is morally irrelevant compared to the orientation one has toward wealth and the way one uses it. In fact, because the effectiveness of a gift (in producing merit) is determined by the attitude with which it is given (the efficiency of the thought) and the virtue of the one to whom it is given (the field of merit), there can be an ironic contrast between the size of the gift and the amount of merit produced. In Strong's essay, for example, King Aśoka's gift of a piece of shriveled fruit results in the restoration of his power and wealth. Falk's essay offers similar stories, and she observes in her analysis of the "petty" donors of the Theravāda tradition that such dynamics bring the practice of *dāna* back within the reach of even the poor members of society.

A third point of consistency between the prominence of *dāna* and basic Theravāda attitudes toward wealth is an affirmation of the provisional value of material prosperity. Wealth used in appropriate ways is good, and properly used wealth will benefit both the individual and his or her community. As we have seen, the benefits of faithfulness to the *dhamma* are thought to accrue to the community as well as to the individual; this is especially the case with religious giving. Giving to the *sangha* is the most effective kind of giving *socially* because it materially aids in the spreading of the *dhamma*. The Buddhists' faith in the power of the *dhamma* assumes that the spread of the *dhamma* will raise the general virtue of the community and bring a corresponding increase in the community's material prosperity. As Reynolds puts it, "giving directed to the Buddha and the *sangha* is deemed to be the most crucial for the maintenance of the dhammic order in society and the natural world and, therefore, to the maintenance or enhancement of the society's wealth."

Accordingly, stories of Buddhist donors affirm that the law of *kamma* ensures a proper reward for all faithful gifts, that quite often the reward will be of additional wealth, and that the benefits that come to the individual will be accompanied by social improvements. In Falk's essay the more Anāthapiṇḍika gives, the more he receives and the more his community prospers. Similarly, Aśoka's giving, as described by Strong, is offered by the tradition as a model for social leadership for social improvement, not merely as the story of one individual in the pursuit of merit. The concept of *dāna* thus provides a perfect illustration of Buddhism's ability to link spiritual accomplishment, moral achievement, and material improvement, and its tendency to attach social progress to the religious advancement of individuals.

Finally, donor stories illustrating the concept of *dāna* also remind us that material prosperity is *only* of provisional value and that this must not be forgotten. A gift is most effective when the giver is least mindful of the reward, and gifts given for the hope of material return usually backfire in some way. Appropriately, it is most often the Buddha (or a representative monk) who speaks of the benefits to come and not the donors. The point of the reward is not to indulge the giver in future pleasures but to draw him or her ever closer to direct cultivation of the *dhamma*. Thus the final comment of many such donor stories is that even the greatest material rewards pale before the treasures of spiritual advancement.

With regard to this last point it should be observed that, contrary to first impressions, the concept of *dāna* serves to integrate the layman's striving for a better rebirth and the monk's search for *nibbāna*. One might expect the practice of *dāna* to reinforce the divisions between lay and monastic society, with one-sided giving by the laity in pursuit of merit, but the donor narratives go to some lengths to show the continuity between the achievement of high rebirth and the opportunity for more direct cultivation of spiritual wisdom. Chapter 5 in particular makes this point as Strong criticizes the notion of "two Buddhisms." There is a sense that it is necessary to become wealthy before one can authentically take the step of self-renunciation. Only the wealthy man who, through the practice of *dāna*, has experienced progressively greater wealth and successfully mastered it truly knows what it is that he is renouncing. In this sense one must reach the pinnacle of lay existence before one can get a glimpse of the jewels of higher knowledge. The ceremonies of *dāna* ritually evoke precisely this state of affairs: in the great kingly festivals of *dāna* the divisions between mortals and the gods and between commoners and royalty are explicitly overcome. The people mix with the king, the king mixes with the monks, and the mundane world is overlaid with the celestial; the ideal of non-attached generosity embodied in *dāna* bridges all religious and social distinctions. Similarly, as Strong points out, the term *dāna* is inflected in a variety of ways to apply to the material gifts of laity to the *sangha*, to individuals' gifts of themselves to the *sangha* (i.e., the entrance into monkhood), and to the monks' gifts of *dhamma* to the laity. In the rites commemorating initiation into adult society, for example, the individual ritually assumes the role of the king (who himself has mirrored the Buddha). The life of non-attachment, as a layman, a king, or a monk, is a life of *dāna*. Whether one gives money, oneself, or a teaching discourse on the truth, the quality of mind involved is the same.

If, as we have seen, support of the *sangha* is the most virtuous and soteriologically effective act for the individual and the most productive act on behalf of society, there is a complete and exceptionless identification of religious piety, individual interest, and social well-being. It is not that Buddhists believe that it is more important to make pious donations than to seek economic development. Rather, they believe that such donations are the most effective way to advance social concerns.[10] Non-Buddhists might regard Buddhists' generosity toward the *sangha* as a socially unproductive channel for wealth, but the practice of *dāna* is praised by Buddhists as the most prudent and pragmatic choice for investment. In the case of *dāna*, then, an appeal to the individual's hope of salvation has been fashioned into a social practice with vast implications. A not-surprising outcome is a continuous impetus for religious donations, resulting in a more-than-prosperous monastic establishment and, as Steven Kemper demonstrates, the development of norms to regulate this social power within the broader life of Buddhist society.

THE *SANGHA* AS A SOCIAL POWER

As we have already seen, the stories of wealthy donors and the basic principles of Theravāda giving lift up the *sangha*, the Buddhist monastic establishment, as the most potent recipient of believers' gifts and as the storehouse of the infinitely valuable *dhamma*. Not surprisingly, in some areas where Theravāda Buddhism has flourished, the practice of *dāna* has led to the accumulation of monastic wealth and the emergence of the *sangha* as an economic and social power in Buddhist society. Frequently, the *sangha* has been a large landholder as well as serving as the cultural and social center of Buddhist communities. This not only raises obvious difficulties for a religious order that defines itself in terms of non-attachment to the mundane material world, but also provides the *sangha* with significant influence in social and political affairs.

Many scholars have followed Max Weber (1958) in seeing the prosperity of the *sangha* as an ironic reversal of Buddhist religious ideals. The rise of monastic landlordism is regarded as a moral and spiritual failure, ironically produced by the piety of the laity. Certainly the image of world renouncers living in luxury has troubled Buddhist society over the ages, and there have been numerous instances of monastic reform to cope with excesses. Yet, again, one may ask whether monastic wealth truly runs counter to the ideal of non-attachment, whether devotion to the *dhamma* requires monastic poverty. Obviously, self-renunciation cannot be completely divorced from asceticism, but how much worldly success and comfort is consonant with spiritual power is not so clear. In Chapter 8 Keyes tells of the respect given to the highly ascetic monks of northeastern Thailand; their spiritual discipline reflects a widely held cultural ideal that has perhaps contributed to the rise of a Buddhist work ethic. On the other hand, Kemper's essay (Chap. 7) describes the suspicion that is attached to truly homeless monks, and he emphasizes the social approval and middle-class respectability accorded to prosperous monks.[11]

Historically, the so-called "domesticated," property-holding *sangha* has been a constant in some areas (e.g., Sri Lanka) and will continue to be a substantial force in Buddhist life. According to Kemper, the impulse for reform has not sought to do away with the domesticated *sangha* by reducing it to poverty or by restoring monks to an ideal of impoverished itinerancy. Rather, in keeping with the themes we have traced so far, reform attacks the abuse of wealth, not its possession. Theravāda's dialectical affirmation of wealth sets wide parameters for the *sangha*'s behavior, but there is always the general truth that it is not the amount so much as the way wealth is possessed and used that is subject to moral scrutiny.

When monks abuse their wealth by being personally attached to it, they blur the lines between monastic and lay society and undermine the *sangha*'s ability to maintain social order. One of the most far-reaching features of the practice of *dāna* is the resultant role of the *sangha* in providing moral legitimation to the prominent social institutions within Buddhist society. Naturally, monastic abuses of wealth destroy the moral authority this role requires, and the effects of such corruption are felt all across Buddhist society. When the monks are righteous and the *sangha*'s authority is unblemished, however, the practice of *dāna* creates a potent exchange relationship between the *sangha* and the king, the wealthy, and the upstanding members of the Buddhist community. To compare for a moment with Christian images, one may say that in theory the *sangha* holds the keys to the kingdom in politics and society as well as religion, roughly paralleling the power and the reach of the medieval Catholic Church in its synthesis between church and state. By means of the exchange relationship, the *sangha* is intimately involved in saying who deserves his or her wealth, who deserves to rule, and who may participate in adult society.

In the first place, the *sangha* is the source of social legitimation for those who have accumulated wealth beyond their fellows. The judgment of monks schooled in the *dhamma* is necessary to vindicate the worthiness and success of the prospering merchant. As Reynolds mentions in passing, a wealthy man must often demonstrate that his wealth was acquired in a meritorious fashion or at least that he will now use it in a non-attached way. This he does by means of (sometimes ostentatiously) giving gifts to the *sangha*.

Second, the *sangha* plays a central role in establishing the political legitimacy of the Buddhist king. The great festivals of *dāna* made famous by Aśoka perform much the same function as inaugural ceremonies in the West. The king demonstates his worthiness to rule by his support of the *sangha*, by his willingness to be advised by it, by his commitment to keep it pure, and finally by expressing ritually his desire to renounce his life and become a monk. The righteous king donates land to the order and establishes boundaries for the monasteries, and in return the *sangha* upholds the *dhamma* in the land and verifies the boundaries of the kingdom.

Third, the *sangha* is an essential agent in defining and transmitting the cultural values of lay society. In ceremonies paralleling the king's festivals of *dāna*, young men enter the *sangha* for a limited period of training and maturation. This "temporary" experience of monkhood is thought to prepare them for the responsibilities of adulthood. To enter the order, they ritually take on the trappings of the king, the symbols of wealth and royal power, and then discard them. During their time in the *sangha* they live as monks and are given instruction and discipline in the *dhamma*, completing their preparation to become responsible citizens. In such fashion their socialization into adult society is overlaid with a ritualized experience of the full spectrum of spiritual development.

And finally, relevant at even the lowest levels of society, the *sangha* possesses the treasury of merit necessary to improve one's spiritual and material destiny in this life and the next. By giving gifts to the *sangha* on behalf of oneself or on behalf of deceased loved ones, merit can be obtained by which to gain freedom from the suffering of a low birth in the realm of *samsāra*.[12] By virtue of the ideas inherent in the concept of *dāna* and the law of *kamma*, the *sangha* remains a pivotal force in controlling the individual's ultimate future.

Naturally, in practice the power of the *sangha* is something less than it is in theory. Moreover, the point of view considered in these essays is by and large that of the Buddhist monastic establishment, which understandably presents the *sangha*'s moral authority in the widest and most favorable perspective. Still, the most popular Buddhist legends, ceremonies, and practices do corroborate these ideal images of social interaction between the *sangha*, the king, and the laity.

In sum, then, though Buddhism does not criticize the present distribution of wealth on the grounds of just (i.e., kammic) deserts, it does possess moral strictures about the use of wealth. There are norms for redistributing wealth and visions of the well-ordered society which serve as guides in criticizing existing social arrangements. These norms have primarily to do with the practice of giving, or *dāna*, and the appeal to the higher principle of non-attachment. The focus is on the virtue of the giver and the dynamics of giving rather than on some generalized norm of structural justice, but it is recognized that individual choices and actions will have social consequences. Those who follow these norms can expect to be rewarded with increased prosperity at some point in the future, and their virtuous actions will raise the material level of their society. But the final religious point is that material prosperity is of little value compared to the treasure of the *dhamma*. Traditionally, in their social policy Buddhists have sought to maximize the spread of enlightenment, making the issue of the proper distribution of goods in society primarily a matter of aiding the organs of enlightenment—the *sangha*. So, too, the greatest achievements in the secular realm of society are regarded as merely preparatory for the cultivation of wisdom available in the *sangha*. It should be pointed out, however, that contemporary Buddhist interpreters criticize the focusing of *dāna* on the monastic order. By generalizing the notion of generosity and by interpreting moral action in terms of interdependent co-arising or mutuality instead of *kamma* some Theravadins have fashioned a theory of dhammic or Buddhist socialism (see, e.g., Buddhadhasa 1986).

THE QUESTION OF UNIVERSALITY: EQUALITY, JUSTICE, AND INDIVIDUALISM

A volume in the field of comparative ethics cannot avoid certain questions about the existence of universal moral norms. Are there any moral absolutes, any normative principles or ideals that extend across all cultural differences? The search for universal moral guidelines is not new, but it has been the subject of renewed interest in the West in a variety of intellectual disciplines, and the issues of wealth and economic justice have been near the center of concern. How do Buddhist reflections on wealth and poverty compare with analogous accounts in the modern West? Is it possible to show that one tradition or another has the best or the right perspective? Although there is no consensus on these questions even in the West, there are certain recurrent themes in contemporary conversations on these matters in comparative ethics.

The essays by Ronald M. Green and John P. Reeder in the final section of the volume offer the most direct and theoretical reflections on these questions. In both chapters issues of just distribution are linked to broader questions concerning the nature of moral discourse and political legitimacy. Their conclusions sharply diverge on how closely Theravadin attitudes toward social order parallel those of western liberalism. Green argues that the Buddhist tradition often displays conformity to the general framework for moral reasoning on justice developed by philosopher John Rawls; Reeder analyzes the convictions underlying Rawls's approach and concludes that it requires an individualism rejected by Buddhism. Green suggests that the criteria on which the Buddhist king's right to rule is grounded include the free consent of the governed. Reeder argues that the liberal justification of political power assumes a nonessentialist theory of the good, which copes with western pluralism by a studied neutrality toward the final ends of life. Equality under these circumstances entails equality of opportunity to pursue one's own ends apart from the beliefs of others, and this, he claims, is an ideal not shared by Buddhism. Where Green claims that Buddhism does display a foundational allegiance to the norm of equality in economic distribution, Reeder finds a mixture of hierarchical and egalitarian impulses. Some reasons behind their disagreements are explored in the introduction to Part V, but we may connect their questions with the rest of the volume by looking more closely at the notion of equality in several of the essays.

It does seem clear that some version of the principle of equality is operative in Buddhist attitudes toward wealth and poverty. One striking quality of the practice of *dāna* is how thoroughly the festivals of giving overturn the typical religious and social divisions of society. In the festival ceremonies described by Strong and Keyes, for example, gods and mortals, kings and commoners, monks and laity ritually experience intimate contact and exchange. The basic symbols of the Buddha legend, of wealth, divestment, and spiritual commitment, are employed in the rites marking initiation into adulthood, in the festivities of political accession, and in the ceremonies for induction into the *sangha*. Young boys ritually reenact the role of the king, who has reenacted the role of the Buddha, who serves as the model for all monks, who in turn serve as the model for all citizens. In the brief but powerful experiences of these various rites all stand equally before the *dhamma*, all share the goal of enlightenment, all acknowledge the ideal of non-attachment. And thus also the ideals of *dāna* unite the political and the religious orderings of society.

In similar fashion Falk's stories of male and female donors and rich and poor donors demonstrate an equality of religious opportunity and obligation across sexual and economic lines, and Green's analysis of the Aggañña Suttānta presents a distinctly egalitarian critique of the caste system. The Buddhist condemnation of pride and self-satisfaction over high rebirth and its admonition that one's wealth must be used selflessly both serve to assert a basic moral equality across all social lines. To recast a familiar Christian phrase in Buddhist terms, one may say that in the practice of *dāna* there is no slave or free, rich or poor, male or female, monk or laity—a righteous, non-attached act will bring merit, and even the smallest gift can bring a great reward.

Such equality before the law of *kamma* resembles the West's notion of procedural justice. The same procedure is followed equally for all, with full acceptance that the results may not be equal. There is equality of opportunity in the sense that the law of *kamma* treats all evenhandedly in rewarding virtue and punishing vice, and the determining essence of virtue (the attitude of non-attachment) is presumably an equal possibility for all. Any inequalities in rebirth are thought to be just, because similar cases are treated similarly. On this sort of equality, all the essays agree; the question is, what kind of responsibilities or exhortations does this form of justice establish for the state?

On the one side Rājavaramuni states that Buddhist social philosophy is concerned not with the amount of wealth one has, but with the way it is acquired and used. This sounds like a wholehearted endorsement of procedural justice and a complete rejection of any judgment made on the resultant distribution per se. The state is explicitly not charged with making the distribution of wealth in society more equal; it is charged with upholding Buddhist virtues in the manner of a "good friend." The state is itself an instrument of the law of *kamma*, reflecting the level of virtue of its citizens. The cosmic system of kammic justice cannot be thwarted by an evil ruler; rather, an evil ruler will be regarded as a fitting reward for the lack of virtue of the people.

Similarly, in the essays of Strong, Falk, Kemper, Lovin, and Keyes the state is not neutral toward the ends of life. Its job is not to provide all with equal means to pursue their own ends. The king displays his worthiness to rule by a public expression of non-attachment; in the great ceremonies of *dāna* he does this ritually and concretely (in giving gifts to the *sangha*) in ways that directly aid in the spread of the *dhamma*; he is charged with preserving the integrity of the monastic order; and in the broadest sense he plays the crucial role of mediator between the *dhamma*, as preserved by the monastic order, and the life of the laity. It seems that Buddhism provides an unambiguous rejection of the pluralistic society's conception of equality. It rejects state neutrality toward the ends of life and offers the *dhamma* as the truth that justifies state power, not the consent of the least well off in Buddhist society.

On the other hand, Green argues that Buddhism also displays acceptance of the principle of equality as applied to tangible restraint of material inequalities in the organization of society. The doctrine of *dāna*, he maintains, may be seen as the Buddhist way of acknowledging the need for private ownership, with its attendant inequalities, while restraining the wealthy by stressing the need for charity and selflessness. The fact that the giving is directed to a religious organization does not rule out its ethical/egalitarian character. Within Buddhist society the *sangha* represents a number of equalizing social tendencies (as the Strong and Falk chapters confirm); it has at times functioned as the welfare institution of last resort; and as we have seen, it is regarded as the key to·social advancement, material as well as spiritual. Moreover, Buddhist images of virtuous social orders do include the ideal of the king's ruling by universal consent, and state-sponsored reforms of the monastic order (as described by Kemper) have included attempts to restrain inequalities of power within monasteries.

Whereas the pluralistic approach concludes that political power must be grounded in the consent of the governed, it seems that Buddhism measures political authority by the ruler's allegiance to the *dhamma*. To judge from the chapter by Strong, for example, the king establishes his worthiness to rule by ritually entering the *sangha*. After he displays his willingness to renounce all of his power and possessions, the state redeems him from the order so as to reacquire his services as ruler. The result is a substantial gift to the *sangha* and a renewed vow of selflessness on the part of the king. One could easily conclude that popular consent has no place in this process. And yet Green is correct that Buddhist legends (particularly the Aggañña Suttānta) depict an image of ideal order in which all are equals and kings rule by popular acclaim. He could also point to the fact that when the state redeems the king from the *sangha* it is symbolically doing so on behalf of all its citizens. Clearly, a

Buddhist might argue that when ignorance is overcome and the *dhamma* is well known, all will freely consent to be ruled by a virtuous king.

There is, then, no definitive way to adjudicate between these conflicting interpretations of the Buddhist tradition. No simple relationship exists between the Theravāda vision of equality before the *dhamma* and an ideal of equal social power. After all, the festivals of *dāna* which provide a ritualized taste of equality with kings and gods do finally suggest an ideal of all united without social distinction even as they are justifying a hierarchical social order. This state of affairs should not be surprising. A tradition as multifaceted as Theravāda Buddhism will not produce straightforward and conclusive statements on such matters, and the notions of equality, consent, and rationality as they have been discussed in the West are themselves too complex to allow for simple applications to religious texts and symbols. Similarly, one is not bound to accept contemporary philosophy's separation of religion and morality and rationalist definitions of morality. Certainly those who differ with Green's reading of the Theravāda tradition do not need to conclude that Buddhism is in some way morally deficient.[13]

Perhaps the most balanced conclusion to be drawn is that, although the common problems of social cooperation provoke some reasonably common solutions, the variations of culture give these common solutions such a remarkably varied appearance that the diversity is as obvious as the unity. Before we can conclude that all share a certain idea or value, it will be necessary to unwind the webs of significance human beings have spun for their actions and feelings. Common ideals or principles receive distinctive interpretations in different religious traditions, and common virtues must adjust to diverse circumstances. If, as many of the authors suggest, the Theravāda tradition endorses primarily a virtue ethic centered on the attitude of non-attachment, the interpreter must consider the detailed elaborations into social arrangements, practices, and expectations that now contribute to the meaning of this principle. If, as Lovin suggests, the Theravāda political ethic is largely a secondary or tertiary phenomenon arising out of a more narrowly religious impulse, the interpreter must consider how the tradition has gone about reconciling its ideals with the stresses and strains of history and the limitations of politics. If we are to talk meaningfully about the parallels and divergences among different religious and cultural systems, there seems to be no escape from the "thick description" (Geertz 1973: Chap. 1) of the cultures we wish to compare.

Introduction

The field of comparative religious ethics is young enough that one may reasonably hope for future contributions to our thinking about the status of morality in cross-cultural encounters. Certainly continued descriptive study is necessary in order to grasp the complexity of moral values and their embodiment in the world's cultures, whatever the advances we hope to make toward a normative perspective. In any event, the case of Theravāda Buddhism in its attitudes toward wealth, poverty, and social order offers fascinating glimpses of how religious impulses and ideas can contribute to a cultural framework with vast social implications. Taken as a whole, we think, this volume makes a genuine contribution to the continuing process of descriptive study and, if one may say so, is a ''profitable'' exercise in cross-cultural investigation.

Part I.

BUDDHISM AND ETHICS

Introduction

Phra Rājavaramuni's essay represents an interpretation of Theravāda Buddhist ethics by a noted Thai monk-scholar. Although Rājavaramuni (recently elevated in monastic rank to Thepwēthi) has held administrative positions within the monastic order, he is regarded in Thailand primarily as a scholar of text and doctrine. His highly esteemed dictionary of Buddhist terms and interpretation of Buddhist thought (*Buddhadhamma*) place him in a rank with Vajirañānavarorosa, the greatest of the Thai monastic reformers in the modern period.

We begin with Rājavaramuni for several reasons. His exposition of the tradition serves as a point of reference for several of the other chapters. Rājavaramuni's perspective in this volume is unique in that he writes from within the tradition, from the standpoint of his own view as a Buddhist monk thoroughly grounded in the texts of Theravāda Buddhism. The essay, therefore, provides both a unique normative view and a very useful collection of canonical references for those interested in exploring the topic of Buddhist ethics within the Theravāda texts themselves. Finally, the author sets the two foci of the volume—wealth and poverty, and individual perfection and the social good—within the broad context of Buddhist ethics as a whole. Rājavaramuni, then, begins this study by addressing a general problem in the field of religious ethics: the relationship between the soteriological (individual perfection) and moral (social good) dimensions of a religious tradition, but he does so as a Buddhist monk interpreting a particular problem within the social-ethical dimensions of the tradition.

Rejecting the stereotypical view of Buddhism as a world-denying monasticism, Rājavaramuni argues that the tradition has consistently affirmed a balanced, middle-way view of interdependence between individual perfection and the social good, monk and laity. He stresses the importance of the categories of reciprocity and friendship within the Buddhist community as a whole and contends that the classical admonition of "taking oneself for a refuge" necessarily means "becoming dependable" within society. In the context of the monastic life the monk does not simply work toward his own salvation (*nibbāna*), but functions as teacher and moral exemplar within the broader community.

Accordingly, Rājavaramuni argues that the roles of monk and laity are distinct but interrelated. Both live and act in terms of a single, unified "system of Buddhist ethics," which Rājavaramuni describes in terms of principles or ideals (*dhamma*) and rules (*vinaya*). Both draw on aspects of the moral life (pre-*magga*) coupled with specific categories or stages in a developmental path (*magga*). Rājavaramuni's discussion of pre-*magga* and *magga* aspects of the moral life reflects his concern for the polarity of individual perfection and the social good. Thus, in general terms Rājavaramuni analyzes the moral life around social interaction ("association with good people") on the one hand and the development of mental awareness ("systematic attention and reflection") on the other. Likewise, the path of moral and spiritual development includes training rules (*sikkhā*), which build character and stipulate appropriate reactions, but which also promote mental awareness and insight. The distinction between lay and monastic ethics is as much a matter of context as it is of specific content. Thus, lay ethics emphasizes generosity (*dāna*)—the laity have material goods to give—whereas the monk has a responsibility to gain the wisdom (*adhipaññā*) associated with mental training (*adhicitta*) in order to fulfill his responsibilities as teacher and moral exemplar.

Consistent with this view of Buddhist ethics, Rājavaramuni argues that Buddhism takes a middle-way stance toward wealth. That one accumulates wealth is less of a moral problem than how one acquires and uses it. Furthermore, given the principle of mutual reciprocity at the heart of Buddhism's Middle Way, the person of wealth has the natural responsibility to be generous or to redistribute it. On the practical level generosity means lay support of the monastery; spiritually it expresses an attitude of non-grasping or unselfishness which leads to compassionate, generous, other-regarding attitudes and actions.

The system of Buddhist ethics, in short, integrates the highest good of the individual with the welfare of society, connects the mental development and exemplary character of the individual devotee with virtuous and harmonious social existence. Put in Buddhist terms, Rājavaramuni integrates the Four Sublime States of Mind (loving-kindness, compassion, sympathetic joy, equanimity) and the Four Bases of Social Harmony (charity, beneficial speech, acts of service, and impartiality).

1 Foundations of Buddhist Social Ethics

Phra Rājavaramuni

Although the ethics of Buddhism is widely discussed today, its treatment is frequently misconceived or lopsided, even when offered by Buddhist scholars. In order to gain a more accurate picture of Buddhist ethics, it would be helpful to avoid certain mistakes from the start.

First, Buddhism has been characterized by some people as an ascetic religion. In reality, asceticism was experimented with by the Buddha and later rejected by him before he attained enlightenment. As far as Buddhism is concerned, the meaning of the term is ambiguous and should not be used without qualification. Also, since the western term *monasticism* has been applied to the way of life and practice of the Buddhist *bhikkhu*s (Pāli), or monks, they have been misunderstood by many as living apart from society in isolation from the world. In principle, at least, a Buddhist monk cannot live even a single day without contact with lay people.

The way of life and practice of Buddhist monks, furthermore, have been mistaken by some interpreters as the whole content or the standard of Buddhist ethics, whereas in fact monks are only one part of the Buddhist community and their ethics are only one component of Buddhist ethical reflection. Buddhism is the religion or way of life not only of the monks, but of the laity as well.

A different sort of problem results from the history of Buddhist studies in the West. It seems that most of the books on the doctrinal aspect of Buddhism written by western scholars deal mainly, if not exclusively, with metaphysical and spiritual teachings, with the mind and meditation. Very few treat the daily-life ethics of the common people. It might be that Buddhist metaphysical and spiritual teachings are what make Buddhism unique or different from other religions and philosophical systems, or it might simply be that these writers are especially interested in such subjects. Whatever the case, this slant has lured many into thinking that Buddhism is merely an ethics of the mind and that it lacks concern for social and material welfare. Although Buddhism does emphasize the cultivation of certain mental states, it teaches that human existence consists of both mind and body, and it states flatly that a necessary degree of material and social well-being is a prerequisite for any spiritual progress.

It is common, furthermore, for scholars of Buddhism to confine themselves to the *dhamma*, or the doctrinal portions of Buddhism, whereas Buddhism in its entirety consists of the *dhamma* and the *vinaya*. In other words, the *dhamma*, or the doctrine, and the *vinaya*, or the discipline, make the whole of Buddhist ethics. The *dhamma* deals with ideals and principles, whereas the *vinaya* deals with rules and circumstances in which these ideals and principles are practiced and realized. The *vinaya* here denotes not only the monks' or nuns' discipline, but also the spirit of these rules and regulations. Without taking into consideration both of these components, the *dhamma* and the *vinaya*, no adequate idea of Buddhist ethics can be reached.

Some scholars tend to regard the traditional exposition of the teachings in the *Visuddhimagga* (the Path of Purification), authored by Buddhaghosa in the fifth century C.E., as the standard summary of Theravāda Buddhist ethics. The *Visuddhimagga*, however, is a standard text only for the *yogi*, or the monks, who are engaged in concentrated spiritual endeavour. Used exclusively, it provides an incomplete and misleading picture of Buddhist ethics. To avoid such misunderstandings, it is best to begin by remembering that the whole of Buddhist ethics is contained in the doctrine of the Middle Way and its prerequisites. This doctrine of the Middle Way teaches that both the extreme of asceticism and the extreme of sensual indulgence are to be avoided. It emphasizes that even the lives and practices of monks who live austerely should not be excessively ascetic, and the life of even the most lax Buddhist lay person should not be so pleasure-oriented as to become an object of attachment. These two extremes can be seen as the most individualistic and selfish ways of life, with their pursuers being overly concerned with either self-mortification or sense-gratification.[1] In avoiding these two extremes, the extent of the Middle Way is vast, wide, and very flexible, depending on such circumstances as one's point on the path and stage of maturity.

The extent of justifiable latitude in the Buddhist Middle Way applies also to the matter of the individual's responsibility for himself or herself and for the sharing of social relationships. There are some things that no other person or any external power can do for the individual, both in his or her everyday life, such as walking, eating, listening, and sleeping, and toward his or her spiritual perfection, such as the application of the mind to good or bad thoughts and the development of wisdom and insight. At the same time, there are many things for which one has to depend on others, one can do for others, and which others can do for someone else. Even with regard to individual perfection, there are many things that a good friend can do to help in the development of mental qualities, in meditation practice, and in the cultivation of wisdom by teaching, inducement, advice, and other skillful means.

The most basic point to be made about Buddhist social ethics is that in keeping with the Buddhist doctrine of dependent co-arising, individual betterment and perfection on the one hand and the social good on the other are fundamentally interrelated and interdependent. For example, a society in which all individual members are self-sufficient or self-sustaining can be called happy and secure to a large extent. Also, a secure and peaceful society is favorable to individual intellectual and spiritual pursuits. The Buddhist standpoint here is that a minimal amount of responsibility to oneself for betterment and perfection is required of all individuals, and at the same time they must maintain an appropriate degree of social responsibility. Beyond this minimal requirement, the range of variation in an individual's specific responsibilities is very wide, depending on his or her place in society, relationship to others, aptitude, and mental inclinations. Buddhist monks may be regarded as the most aloof from society of all Buddhists. They may be recruited from those people who love a peaceful and solitary life. The style of monastic life differs greatly, however, ranging from town monks who are in a close day-to-day relationship with all sorts of people, to forest monks who spend almost their whole lives in seclusion. Yet even the most solitary forest monks have to be in regular contact with and are responsible for the well-being of a community of monks. Moreover, the monks must also meet with villagers on their daily food rounds when they receive physical nourishment and in turn share their spiritual attainments by teaching the *dhamma*.

It is a natural impossibility that at any given time all people can be found at the same level of maturity or stage of development. But it is also a natural truth that people are educable. Accordingly, all people should have the opportunity to be trained and educated and they should be allowed to develop according to their training or education and their individual effort toward attainment and perfection. Thus the Buddhist community or society consists not merely of the monks alone but of the four assemblies of monks, nuns, lay male devotees, and lay female devotees. Monks and nuns on the one hand and lay people on the other lead different daily lives with different responsibilities and duties and enjoying different kinds of satisfactions. There is some variation in development among the monks and great variation among the lay people. This Buddhist principle of the Four Assemblies shows clearly that the monks and laity are intended to be seen as complementary sides of a single moral community (see, e.g., A.II.132; D.III.125). In sum, a moral community is diversity in unity. Harmonious diversities or variety make a complete whole. Hence monastic and lay groupings, not to speak of many minor ones, are intended to continue in harmony as necessary components of a society, and it is with their continuity that a good society is maintained.

SOCIAL RELATIONSHIPS AND RESPONSIBILITY

Within the Monastic Order

In comparison with society as a whole the *sangha*, or monastic fellowship, is a very small community. It is intended to be the completing segment of society. Relatively speaking, it is an independent community that points toward a transcendent aspect of life. Its essential task is to maintain the *dhamma* for the society. As mentioned above, Buddhist monks cannot live an absolutely solitary life because they are required by the discipline to maintain good relationships both among themselves and with the lay society. The lives of the monks bound to the *sangha* are regulated by the disciplinary rules so that they will live in concord and harmony, pay respect according to seniority in the *sangha*, divide all gains and acquisitions equally among the members, and decide all legal cases justly. The supreme authority remains in the hands of the *sangha* itself, or the meeting of the community. Even the most solitary monk has to attend the fortnightly meeting of the *sangha* and any meeting of the *sangha* convened for the performance of a formal act.[2] The spirit of the *vinaya* that is most stressed is the supremacy of the *sangha* as a whole and harmony within the order (see, e.g., A.III.330; A.V.74ff.). Causing schism in the order is viewed as one of the most heinous crimes (A.III.146). Historically, as the *sangha* grew larger, the Buddha himself held its voice in high regard (A.II.21). The ordination ceremonies today still represent this passing on of the authority of the Buddha through the order (Vin.I.27).

This emphasis on the *sangha* as a whole and its cooperative parts can be illustrated by the six virtues of fraternal living:

1. To be amiable in deed, openly and in private;
2. To be amiable in word, openly and in private;
3. To be amiable in thought, openly and in private;
4. To share any lawful gains with virtuous fellows;

5. To keep without blemish the rules of conduct along with one's fellows; openly and in private; and
6. To be endowed with right views along with one's fellows, openly and in private. (D.III.245; A.III.288f.)

The seven conditions of welfare are another good illustration:

1. To hold regular and frequent meetings;
2. To meet together in harmony, disperse in harmony, and do the business and duties of the order in harmony;
3. To introduce no revolutionary ordinance or break up established ordinance, but train oneself in accordance with the prescribed training rules;
4. To honor and respect those elders of long experience, the fathers and leaders of the order, and deem them worthy of listening to;
5. Not to fall under the influence of craving which arises;
6. To delight in forest retreat; and
7. To establish oneself in mindfulness, with this thought, "Let disciplined co-celibates who have not come, come hither, and let those that have already come live in comfort." (D.II.77; A.IV.20)

Although these virtues were originally intended for the monks, they have been recommended in the Thai Buddhist tradition for adaptation by the laity as well.

Between the Monks and the Laity

According to the *vinaya*, a monk is dependent on the lay people for food and other material necessities. The monks get their food for daily meals during the morning alms round, but they are sometimes invited to the houses of donors, or the latter may also present food to them at the monastery (e.g., Vin.I.58). This practice binds the monks' life to that of the lay society and keeps them in daily contact with lay people. As the Buddha himself says, "my livelihood is bound up with others" (A.V.87). Monks are exhorted to contemplate this fact again and again, so that they will be earnest both in their exertion for their individual perfection and in working for the good of the laity. The daily alms round reflects the reciprocal nature of the relationship between monks and laity (e.g., S.II.270), a reciprocity emphasized by the Buddha in these words:

> Monks, brahmins and householders are most helpful to you, since they support you with robe and bowl, with lodging and seat, medicines and necessaries for sickness. Ye, also, monks, are most help-

> ful to brahmins and householders, since ye teach them the *dhamma* that is lovely. . . . Thus, monks, this holy life is lived in mutual dependence, for ferrying across the flood, for the utter cessation of suffering. (It.111)

Monks perform this task for the good of lay society not only as an act of returning favors, but out of their own virtue of compassion for the people. Such compassion was stressed by the Buddha when he sent out his first group of disciples to teach the *dhamma* in the first year after his enlightenment: "Go, monks, on your journey, for the profit of the many, for the happiness of the many, out of compassion for the world, for the welfare, the profit, the happiness of gods and men" (Vin.I.20). The monks' task of working for the good of the people both as an act of compassion and in terms of the necessarily reciprocal nature of their relationship is also brought out in the Buddha's admonitions to the young layman Sigāla as reported in the *Sigālovāda-Sutta*:

> In five ways a clansman should minister to monks and priests as the upper quarter:
>
> 1. By kindly acts,
> 2. By kindly words,
> 3. By kindly thoughts,
> 4. By keeping open house to them,
> 5. By supplying them with their material needs.
>
> In six ways the monks and priests, thus ministered to as the upper quarter, show their love for him:
>
> 1. They keep him back from evil,
> 2. They encourage him to do good,
> 3. They feel for him with kindly thoughts,
> 4. They teach him what he has not heard before,
> 5. They correct and clarify what he has learnt,
> 6. They show him the way to heaven. (D.III.151)

Among the Laity

Whereas practical instructions for the regulation of the orders of monks and nuns are contained in a specific part of the Pāli canon called the *Vinaya Piṭaka*, for lay society there is no special collection of instructions as such. The Five Precepts of abstaining from killing, stealing, sexual misconduct, false speech, and taking intoxicants are accepted as the basic moral rules for lay people, but they do not form a part of a collection or code. Although the Buddha's admonitions in the *Sigālovāda-Sutta* are rendered by the Great Commentator, Buddhaghosa, as the Layman's Code of Discipline, they have been preserved as a *sutta* delivered to a specific person on only one occasion and are not framed as a general code of discipline for the laity. Similar moral instruction can be found scattered in other parts of the *Sutta-Piṭaka*. The ethical admonitions in the *sutta*s were thus given not as disciplinary rules enforced with authority as is the case with the *vinaya* of the monks. These facts support the conclusion that the wider lay society was so open to the changing circumstances of space and time that the monks did not consider it as a subject appropriate for fixed rules. Consequently, only some basic rules and general principles were stipulated. Beyond that, it should rest on the people subject to different circumstances to formulate detailed moral codes, based on those basic Buddhist rules and principles, and to suit them to their own society.

In the search for general principles the *Jātaka*s are a good source of Buddhist social ethics for lay people, but the teachings therein are scattered and unsystematic. Among other sources, the *Sigālovāda-Sutta*, attributed to the Buddha himself, can serve as a typical example of the Buddhist code of social ethics. The teachings in this *Sutta* consist of:

1. The avoidance of the four vices of conduct (corresponding to the first four of the Five Precepts).
2. Doing no evil out of the four prejudices that are caused by love, hatred, delusion, and fear.
3. Not following the six ways of squandering wealth, viz., addiction to intoxicants, roaming the streets at unseemly hours, frequenting shows, indulgence in gambling, association with bad companions, and the habit of idleness.
4. Knowledge of how to distinguish among the four false friends, viz., the out-and-out robber, the man who pays lip service, the flatterer, and the leader to destruction, and the four true friends, viz., the helper, the man who is the same in weal and woe, the good counselor, and the sympathizer.
5. The amassing of wealth and the fourfold division of money into one part for living and doing duties toward others, two parts for business, and one part for time of need.
6. The covering of the six quarters of human relationships and their attendant mutual responsibilities, viz., child-parent, pupil-teacher,

husband-wife, friend-friend, servants and workmen-master or employer, monk-layman.

7. The four bases of social harmony, viz., giving, kindly words, life of service, and impartial treatment and participation. (D.III.180–93)

What is worthy of special notice is the frequent mention the Buddha made of friendship and association. In the above *sutta* alone friendship and association can be found at least five times: association with bad companions as a way of squandering wealth, how to distinguish between false and true friends, the friend-friend relationship, the ways the monks and priest show their love for lay people, and the four bases of social harmony. Advice on friendship and stories illustrating the dynamics of good and bad social relationships can also be found in many parts of the *Jātakas*. Given this guidance and the oft-stressed advice on the importance of good friends in the development of the Noble Eightfold Path, we see that the theme of association with good friends and of a good social environment generally occupies a very important place in Buddhist ethics, both at the mundane social level and at the level of spiritual endeavor for individual perfection.[3]

On the one hand there is a close correspondence between the ways monks are to treat the laity and the image of a "friend of good counsel." And on the other hand there is a correlation between the four bases of social harmony and the ways lay people are to treat their friends. Friendship is thus the model for social harmony in the mundane sphere and the model for spiritual encouragement of the laity by the monks in the transmundane sphere. We might conclude that in Buddhist ethics everyone is a friend, meaning that everyone should be treated as a friend.

THE INTERDEPENDENCE OF INDIVIDUAL PERFECTION AND THE SOCIAL GOOD: MONKS, KINGS, AND LAITY

As mentioned earlier, individual perfection and the social good are interdependent. The society that is made up of people who can depend on themselves and are freed from attachment can be peaceful, stable, and secure to a large extent. Also, a peaceful, stable, and secure society is ideally favorable to the individual growth, development, and perfection of every person. If society is in turmoil, suffering from instability and insecurity, even the monks who are engaged in the task of individual perfection, not to speak of other more materialistic people, may have to stop or suspend their efforts. As the Pāli canon notes:

> Monks, there are these five unfavorable times for (spiritual) striving. What five? Herein a monk is old. . . . A monk is ill. . . . There is a famine. . . . Fear is about, perils of robbers, and the country folk mount their carts and drive away. . . . Again, monks, the Order is rent; then there is reviling . . . accusation. . . . Monks, there are these five favorable times for (spiritual) striving. What five? Herein a monk is young. . . . A monk has health and well-being. . . . There is no famine and crops are good, food is easy to get. . . . Men dwell in friendly fellowship together. . . . Again, monks, the Order dwells in friendly fellowship together. . . . (A.III.65f.; cf. A.III.103)

There are some things which no one else can do for the individual and for which one has to be responsible to oneself. Every individual, however, also acts directly or indirectly for the benefit of other people. Each person should take some responsibility for the good of his or her society, for maintaining the society in a condition favorable to the common well-being, development, and perfection. The practice of responsibility varies among different individuals according to the extent, degree, and character of the actions, depending on various factors including the mental inclinations and free choices of the individuals themselves. However, every person is at least responsible to the society for his or her own wellbeing and perfection in order to make himself or herself a good constituent of a good society. It is at this point that the Buddhist principles of being a refuge to oneself (*attanātha*) and of training, taming, or educating (*dama*) are required.

One should be a refuge to oneself. In order to be a refuge to oneself, one must make oneself dependable. To make oneself dependable, one has to train oneself in virtue, learning, energy, mindfulness, in the development of wisdom, and so on. One should also associate with good people, should be amenable to correction, and should readily give a helping hand in the affairs of one's fellows in the community.[4] At this point individual responsibility to oneself and good social relationships are closely related or interdependent. To be able to help others, furthermore, one must be dependable and have an inner strength and stability. Again we turn to the Pāli texts:

> How, monks, guarding oneself, does one guard others? By practice, by development, by continuous exercise; in this way, monks, one guarding oneself also guards others. And how, monks, guarding others, does one guard oneself? By tolerance, by nonviolence,

by having a mind full of loving-kindness, by care; in this way, monks, one guarding others also guards oneself. (S.V.169)

When the monks of the most seclusion-loving type go out on their daily alms rounds, they come into contact with the lay society. When they teach the *dhamma* to the villagers, every stage of their progress in individual perfection benefits society. In other words, effort toward individual perfection and acting for the social good proceed together. Moreover, the donated food generally benefits not only the monks, but also a number of people who come to seek shelter in the monasteries. This tradition is said to have originated at the time of the Buddha, and in the course of time monasteries have become places where the destitute, orphans, and students live, obtain sufficient food, and receive moral and educational training from the monks.[5] It may be desirable to improve or modify this tradition to suit the current circumstances, but in any case it affords an example of the monks' contribution to the well-being of society.

For the monks, responsibility for the social good is mainly exercised through teaching the common people how to live good lives and how to conduct themselves as good members of the society, through the counseling of rulers and administrators to help them conform to virtue and to act for the benefit of the people, and through their own rightful conduct and practice toward individual perfection. On a practical level much of this responsibility for social welfare is mediated through political leaders, who traditionally carry a special burden for connecting the principles of the *dhamma* to the requirements of everyday life. Rulers and administrators are obligated to put the virtues and duties expected of them into actual practice for the benefit of the people and to make a good society favorable to the individual development and perfection of every member.

In the Thai Buddhist tradition the king is to observe and possess four sets of Buddhist virtues and qualities. The first set is called the *Dasa Rājadhamma* (*Ten Virtues of the King*): namely, charity, high moral character, self-sacrifice, integrity, gentleness, austerity (or non-indulgence), non-anger, non-oppression, tolerance, and non-deviation from the norm (J.V.378). These virtues are the best known and the most emphasized of the four sets of royal virtues.

The second set is called the Twelvefold *Cakkavattivatta* and consists of the twelve duties of the Universal Ruler as enumerated in the *Cakkavatti-Sutta*: the provision of right watch, ward, and protection for one's own folk and the armed forces, for the nobles, for the royal dependents, for brahmins and householders, for townspeople and villagers, for monks and priests, for beasts and birds, prevention and suppression of unrighteous deeds, distribution of wealth to the poor, frequenting and seeking counsels from monks and the religious, abstention from unlawful sexual desire, and abstention from unrighteously coveting others' property.[6]

The third set, the Fourfold *Rājasangahavatthu* (four royal acts making for social integration), consists of shrewdness in agricultural promotion (*sassamedha*), shrewdness in the encouragement of government officials (*purisamedha*), binding the people's hearts by vocational promotion (*sammāpāsa*), and kindly beneficial words (*vājapeyya*).[7]

The fourth set, the Fivefold *Khattiyabala* (five strengths of a monarch), requires strength of arms, of wealth, of ministers, of royal ancestry, and of wisdom. Of these five the last, strength of wisdom, is regarded as the most important quality (JA.V.120).

What is especially noteworthy about these virtues and duties is the emphasis on the absence of poverty. Poverty is regarded as the main source of crime and disorder as well as greed (D.III.65; D.III.92). This absence of poverty, the accumulation of wealth or economic sufficiency, is a prerequisite for a happy, secure, and stable society, favorable to individual development and perfection. It is required of the ruler to see to it that this desirable state of affairs prevails in his country.

Individuals as members of society are responsible both for their individual perfection and for the good of society through individual development and well-being and through helpful social relationships. People should first strive to be economically, intellectually, and morally dependable in order to be good members of society. To achieve this, many among the following selected virtues may be observed:

The Four Virtues Leading to Temporal Welfare

1. To be endowed with energy, industry, and skill in management,
2. To be endowed with attentiveness,
3. To associate with good people,
4. To have a balanced livelihood. (A.IV.281)

The Four Virtues Leading to Prosperity

1. To live in a good environment,
2. To associate with good people,
3. To aspire and direct oneself in the right way,
4. To have prepared oneself with good background. (D.III.276; A.II.32)

The Four Virtues for a Good Lay Life

1. Truth and honesty,
2. Training and adjustment,
3. Tolerance and forbearance,
4. Liberality. (S.I.215; Sn.189)

The Fourfold Deserved Bliss of a Layman

1. Bliss of ownership,
2. Bliss of enjoyment,
3. Bliss of debtlessness,
4. Bliss of blamelessness. (A.II.69)

The Four Virtues Leading to Spiritual Welfare

1. To be endowed with confidence,
2. To be endowed with morality,
3. To be endowed with generosity or charity,
4. To be endowed with wisdom. (A.IV.284)

On the social side, the individual should maintain good social relationships with other people and make his or her contribution to the maintenance and encouragement of a happy and favorable society by practicing such virtues as the Four Bases of Social Harmony or the Four Principles of Social Integration (*sanghavatthu*): giving, distribution, and charity; kindly and beneficial words; rendering of services; and equality, impartiality, and participation.[8]

ATTITUDES TOWARD POVERTY AND WEALTH

The term *poverty* may sometimes be misleading. The familiar Buddhist concepts are rather contentment (*santuṭṭhi*) or limited desires (*appicchatā*). Poverty (*daliddiya*) is in no place praised or encouraged in Buddhism. The Buddha says, "Poverty is a suffering in the world for a layman." He also says, "Woeful in the world is poverty and debt" (A.III.350, 352). Though monks should be contented and have few wishes, poverty is never encouraged even for the monks.

The possession of wealth by a king or even an average layman is often praised and encouraged in the Pāli canon. In other words, wealth is something to be amassed or sought after. Among the Buddha's lay disciples, the better known, the most helpful, and the often praised were mostly wealthy persons such as Anāthapiṇḍika. For the monks, though they are not expected to seek wealth, to be a frequent recipient of offerings can be regarded as a good qualification. Two monks may be equal in other qualifications and virtues, but the one who receives more offerings is praised. Even the Buddha praised a monk who was foremost in receiving offerings: "Chief among my disciples who are obtainers of offerings is Sivali" (A.I.24). However, these remarks must be qualified and further clarified.

The main theme in these texts is that it is not wealth that is praised or blamed, but the way one acquires and uses it. For the monks, as mentioned above, it is not acquisition as such that is blamed, nor poverty that is praised. The things that are blamed are greed for gain, stinginess, clinging, attachment to gain, and hoarding of wealth. Acquisition is acceptable if it is helpful in the practice of the Noble Path or if it benefits one's fellow members of the order. This does not mean that monks are encouraged to own possessions. Insofar as it is allowable by the *vinaya*, or monastic code, gain is justifiable if the possessions belong to the *sangha* or the community. But if a monk is rich in personal possessions, it is evidence of his greed and attachment and therefore he cannot be said to conform to Buddhist principles. The right practice is to own nothing except the basic requisites of life. Here the question is not one of being rich or poor, but of having few personal cares, easy mobility, the spirit of contentment, and few wishes, and as the monk's life is dependent for material sustenance on other people, of making oneself easy to support. With high mobility and almost no personal cares, monks can devote most of their time and energy to their work, whether for their individual perfection or for the social good. Thus, it is contentment and paucity of wishes accompanied by commitment to the development of good and the abandonment of evil that is praised. Even contentment and paucity of wishes are to be qualified, that is, they must be accompanied by effort and diligence, and not by passivity and idleness. In other words, for a monk it can be good to gain many possessions, but not to own or hoard them. It is good rather to gain much and to give it away.

The above conclusions have been drawn from such sayings in the Pāli canon as:

> Monks, possessed of five qualities the way of an elder monk is to the advantage of many folk, for the happiness of many folk, for the good of many folk; it is to the advantage and happiness of devas and men. Of what five?
>
> There is the elder, time-honored and long gone forth; well-known, renowned, with a great following of householders and those gone forth; a receiver of the requisites: the robe, alms, lodging, and medicaments for sickness; who is learned, has a retentive and

well-stored mind, and those Dhammas, lovely . . . are by him fully understood in theory; and he is a right viewer with an unperverted vision. He turns away many folk from what is not the true Dhamma and sets them in the true Dhamma. . . . (A.III.115)

Four Ariyan lineages; herein, brethren, a monk is content with whatever robes (he may have), commends contentment of this kind, and does not try to gain robes in improper, unsuitable ways. And he is not dismayed if he gain no robe, but when he has gained one, he is not greedy, nor infatuated, nor overwhelmed. Seeing the danger therein and understanding its object he makes use of it. Yet does he not exalt himself because of his contentment with any robes, nor does he disparage others. Whoso, brethren, is skilled herein, not slothful, but mindful and helpful, this monk is one who stands firm in the primeval, ancient Ariyan lineage. Then, again, the monk is content with whatever almsfood . . . with whatever lodging. . . . Lastly, brethren, the monk delights in abandoning (evil) and delights in developing (good). . . . (D.III.224; A.II.27)

Furthermore, brethren, he is content with whatever necessaries, whether it be robes, alms, lodging, medicines, and provision against sickness. Furthermore, brethren, he is continually stirring up effort to eliminate bad qualities, making dogged and vigorous progress in good things, never throwing off the burden. (D.III.266, 290; A.V.23)

The monk is content with a robe sufficient to protect the body, with almsfood enough for his belly's need. Wherever he may go he just takes these with him. Just as, for instance, a bird upon the wing, wherever he may fly, just flies with the load of his wings. (E.g., A.II.209)

Monks, this holy life is not lived to cheat or cajole people. It is not for getting gain, profit, or notoriety. It is not concerned with a flood of gossip nor with the idea of "let folk know me as so-and-so." Nay, monks, this holy life is lived for the sake of self-restraint, of abandoning (evil), of dispassionateness, of the cessation of suffering. (A.II.24)

Monks, these four qualities are according to the true Dhamma. What four? Regard for the true Dhamma, not for wrath; regard for the true Dhamma, not for hypocrisy; regard for the true Dhamma, not for gain; regard for the true Dhamma, not for honors. (A.II.47, 84)

Harsh, monks, is gain, honor, and fame, severe and rough, being a stumbling block to the attainment of the supreme safety (of

Nibbāna). Therefore, monks, let you train yourselves: we shall let go the arisen gain, honor, and fame, and the arisen gain, honor, and fame will not stand overwhelming our minds. . . .

For one whether being honored or not whose collected mind does not waver, him the wise call a worthy man. (S.II.232)

One is the road that leads to wealth, another the road that leads to Nibbāna. If the Bhikkhu, the disciple of the Buddha, has learnt this, he will not yearn for honor, he will foster solitude. (Dh.75)

Wealth destroys the foolish, though not those who search for the Goal. (Dh. 355)

For the laity, as mentioned earlier, there is no instance in which poverty is encouraged. On the contrary, many Pāli passages exhort lay people to seek and amass wealth in a rightful way. Among the advantages or good results of good *karma*, one is to be wealthy.[9] What is blamed as evil in connection with wealth is to earn it in a dishonest and unlawful way. Worthy of blame also is the one who, having earned wealth, becomes enslaved through clinging and attachment to it and incurs suffering because of it. No less evil and blameworthy than the unlawful earning of wealth is to accumulate riches and, out of stinginess, not to spend them for the benefit and well-being of oneself, one's dependents, and other people. Again, it is also evil if one squanders wealth foolishly or indulgently or uses it to cause suffering to other people:

And what, Ujjaya, is achievement of diligence? Herein, by whatsoever activity a clansman make his living, whether by the plough, by trading or by cattle-herding, by archery or in royal service, or by any of the crafts—he is deft and tireless; gifted with an inquiring turn of mind into ways and means, he is able to arrange and carry out his job. This is called achievement of diligence. (A.IV.285)

And what is the bliss of wealth? Herein, housefather, a clansman by means of wealth acquired by energetic striving, amassed by strength of arm, won by sweat, lawful and lawfully gotten, both enjoys his wealth and does good deeds therewith. (A.II.68)

Herein, housefather, with the wealth acquired by energetic striving . . . and lawfully gotten, the Ariyan disciple makes himself happy and cheerful, he rightly contrives happiness, and makes his mother and father, his children and wife, his servants and workmen, his friends and comrades cheerful and happy, he rightly contrives happiness. This, housefather, is the first opportunity seized by him, turned to merit and fittingly made use of. (A.II.67; cf. A.III.45)

Monks, if people knew, as I know, the ripening of sharing gifts, they would not enjoy their use without sharing them, nor would the taint of stinginess stand obsessing the heart. Even if it were their last bit, their last morsel of food, they would not enjoy its use without sharing it, if there were anyone to receive it. (It.18)

Like waters fresh lying in savage region
Where none can drink, running to waste and barren,
Such is the wealth gained by a man of base mind.
On self he spends nothing, nor aught he gives.
The wise, the strong-minded, who has won riches,
He useth them, thereby fulfills his duties.
His troop of kin fostering, noble-hearted, blameless, at death
faring to heav'nly mansion. (S.I.90)
The misers do not go to heaven; fools do not
praise liberality. (Dh.177)

Thus, good and praiseworthy wealthy people are those who seek wealth in a rightful way and use it for the good and happiness of both themselves and others. Accordingly, the Buddha's lay disciples, being wealthy, liberally devoted much or most of their wealth to the support of the *sangha* and to the alleviation of the suffering and poverty of others. For example, the millionaire Anāthapiṇḍika is said in the Commentary on the *Dhammapada* to have spent a large amount of money every day to feed hundreds of monks as well as hundreds of the poor.[10] Of course, in an ideal society under an able and righteous ruler or under a righteous and effective administration, there will be no poor people, as all people will be at least self-sufficient, and monks will be the only community set apart by intention to be sustained with the material surplus of the lay society.

A true Buddhist lay person not only seeks wealth lawfully and spends it for the good, but also enjoys spiritual freedom, not being attached to it, infatuated with or enslaved by that wealth. At this point the mundane and the transmundane intersect. The Buddha classifies lay people or the enjoyers of sense-pleasure into various classes according to lawful and unlawful means of seeking wealth, the spending or not spending of wealth for the good and happiness of oneself or others and for the performing of good deeds, and the attitude of greed and attachment or wisdom and spiritual freedom in dealing with wealth. The last, which the Buddha calls the best, the greatest, and the noblest, is praiseworthy in four respects. Such a person enjoys life on both the mundane and the transmundane planes as follows:

Mundane

1. Seeking wealth lawfully and unarbitrarily,
2. Making oneself happy and cheerful,
3. Sharing with others and doing meritorious deeds.

Transmundane

4. Making use of one's wealth without greed and longing, without infatuation, heedful of danger and possessed of the insight that sustains spiritual freedom.[11]

This person is indeed an Ariyan or Noble Disciple, that is, one who has made great progress toward individual perfection. Of much significance, moreover, is the compatibility between the mundane and the transmundane spheres of life which combine to form the integral whole of Buddhist ethics in which the transmundane acts as the completing part.

In spite of its great ethical utility, however, too much importance should not be given to wealth. The limitation of its utility in relation to the realization of the goal of *nibbāna*, furthermore, should also be recognized. Though on the mundane level poverty is something to be avoided, a poor person is not deprived of all means to act for the good of himself or herself and for the good of society. The ten ways of doing good or making merit begin with giving, but they also include moral conduct, the development of mental qualities and wisdom, the rendering of services, and the teaching of the *dhamma*. Because of poverty, people may be too preoccupied with the mere struggle for survival and thus cannot do anything for their own perfection. They may even cause trouble to society and difficulty for other people in their effort toward their own perfection. But when basic living needs are satisfied, if one is mentally qualified and makes the effort, nothing can hinder one from realizing one's individual perfection. Wealth as a resource for achieving the social good can help create favorable circumstances for realizing individual perfection, but ultimately it is mental maturity and wisdom, not wealth, that bring about the realization of this perfection. Wealth mistreated and misused not only obstructs individual development, but can also be detrimental to the social good. A wealthy man can do much more either for the better or for the worse of the social good than a poor man. The wealth of a good man is also the wealth of the society. It is, therefore, conducive to the social good and thus becomes a resource for all the members of that society. In other words, acquiring wealth is acceptable if, at the same time, it promotes the well-being of a community or society. But if one's wealth grows at the expense of the well-being of the community, that wealth is harmful and becomes a problem to be overcome. If personal wealth is not the wealth of society and is not conducive to the social good, the society may have to seek other means of ownership and distribution of wealth to ensure the social good and the resourcefulness of wealth for both individual development and perfection of all members of the society.

In short, the Buddhist attitude toward wealth is the same as that toward power, fame, and honor. This is clearly expressed in the words of the great Buddhist king, Aśoka, in his Edict X, ''King Piyadorshi, the beloved of the gods, does not consider prestige and glory as of any great meaning unless he desires prestige and glory for this purpose, that people may attend to the teaching of the *dhamma* and that they may abide by the practices of the *dhamma*.''

THE SYSTEM OF BUDDHIST ETHICS

Buddhist social ethics will be understood more adequately if we understand its place in the whole system of Buddhist ethics. As mentioned earlier, the whole of Buddhist ethics is based in the Noble Eightfold Path and its prerequisites. The Noble Eightfold Path is well known, but what are its prerequisites? In the Buddha's own words: ''Monks, there are these two conditions for the arising of right view. What two? These are inducement by others and systematic attention'' (A.I.87; cf. M.I.294).

The first condition, or factor, is generally represented by association with good people or having good friends (*kalyāṇamittatā*) and is regarded as the external or environmental factor, whereas the second is the internal or personal one. The importance of these two factors as prerequisites of the Eightfold Path is often stressed:

> Just as, monks, the dawn is the forerunner, the harbinger, of the arising of the sun, so friendship with good people is the forerunner, the harbinger, of the arising of the Ariyan eightfold way. (S.V.28, 30)
>
> Just as, monks, the dawn is the forerunner, the harbinger, of the arising of the sun, so systematic attention is the forerunner, the harbinger, of the arising of the Ariyan eightfold way. (S.V.29, 31)

As the Noble Eightfold Path, or the Ariyan Eightfold Way, is known as the *magga*, we may term these two prerequisites of the Path the *pre-magga factors*. The system may then be outlined as follows:

Pre-magga

1. Association with good people (*kalyāṇamittatā*)
2. Systematic attention or reflection (*yonisomanisikāra*)

Magga

Paññā (wisdom)	1. Right View (*sammā-diṭṭhi*)
	2. Right Thought (*sammā-saṅkappa*)
Sīla (morality)	3. Right Speech (*sammā-vācā*)
	4. Right Action (*sammā-kammanta*)
	5. Right Livelihood (*sammā-ajīva*)
Samādhi	6. Right Effort (*sammā-vāyāma*)
(mental discipline)	7. Right Mindfulness (*sammā-sati*)
	8. Right Concentration (*sammā-samādhi*)

The eight *magga* factors are segments of the individual's path toward perfection, and the two pre-*magga* factors are the means by which the individual deals with the world and environment. The *magga* factors are classified into the three categories of *paññā* (wisdom), *sīla* (morality), and *samādhi* (mental discipline). The category of *paññā* includes especially an enlightened world view based on insight into the impermanent, conflicting, and not-self nature of things, and the dependent origination of all phenomena, that is, that all changes are subject to causes and conditions. Buddhist ethics is rooted in knowledge and effort based on this knowledge, not accidentalism or fatalism. This *paññā*, or wisdom, serves as the keystone. The category of *samādhi* consists in the development of mental qualities and is responsible for the earnestness, resolution, and steady progress in treading the ethical path. The third category of *sīla*, or morality, is an expression of social responsibility on the part of the individual. The two pre-*magga* factors indicate the conditions for the arising and the support for the development of all the *magga* factors. Though the *sīla* factors of Right Speech, Right Action, and Right Livelihood are directly concerned with society, they are of the character of social responsibility of the individual toward society rather than vice versa. The two pre-*magga* factors, on the contrary, deal with the influence and effect the world and society can have on the individual. They stress what one can get from one's environment, natural and social, through one's dealings and relations with it. Of these two pre-*magga* factors, emphasis is here placed on the first, that is, association with good people.

As mentioned earlier, the importance of friendship with the good is stressed in Buddhism both at the level of individual perfection and at the level of the daily life of the common people:

> It is the whole, not the half, of the holy life—this friendship, this association, this intimacy with the good. Of a monk who is a friend, an associate, an intimate of the good we may expect this—that he will develop the Ariyan eightfold way, that he will make much of the Ariyan eightfold way.
>
> Owing to me who is a good friend, beings who are subject to birth . . . to old age . . . to death . . . to sorrow, lamentation, pain, grief and despair, become free from (these things). (S.V.2)
>
> Some friends are bottle-comrades; some are they
> Who (to your face) dear friend! dear friend! will say.
> Who proves a comrade in your hour of need,
> Him may ye rightly call a friend indeed. (D.III.184)
>
> Not to follow fools, to associate with the wise, to honor those who are worthy of honor, this is the highest blessing. To live in a place of favorable environment . . . , this is the highest blessing. (Kh.V.3; Sn.259)

Thus, association with the good embodied in good people is a prerequisite of the good life not only in Buddhist social ethics, but in Buddhist thought and practice more generally. We can say that in Buddhist social ethics a good society is a society of good friends, or a society in which people are good friends to one another.[12]

Training (*sikkhā*) for further progress in morality, mental discipline, and wisdom is especially prescribed for the monks and is usually known as the Threefold Training, namely, *adhisīla-sikkhā* (training in higher morality), *adhicitta-sikkhā* (training in higher mentality), and *adhipaññā-sikkhā* (training in higher wisdom) (e.g., A.I.229).

To the laity, however, the triad of giving, liberality, or charity (*dāna*), morality (*sīla*), and mental development (*bhāvanā*) is more widely taught in Theravāda countries such as Thailand as the popular Buddhist practices, or ways of making merit. In the Pāli canon it is also stated in synonymous terms as the triad of giving, self-control regarding other beings, and taming, refinement, improvement, or development. These are collectively called the three bases of meritorious action (*puññakiriyāvatthu*), or the threefold training in the good (*puñña-sikkhā*) (It.15, 51). They may be called the lay version of the Threefold Training, as they are merely a restatement or rearrangement of the first monastic triad to suit the laity.

The difference between the two versions of the Buddhist training lies in the points of emphasis. In the monks' version the emphasis is placed on individual perfection, whereas in the laymen's the social aspects of life are given a more important place, as lay people are expected to be more concerned with good social relationships and more concrete actions for social good. Thus, moral conduct (*sīla*), the single factor of the monks' general social responsibility, is in the lay version split into the explicit and more tangible social acts of giving (*dāna*), and virtuous conduct (*sīla*). The two inner and more individual factors of training in higher mentality (*samādhi*) and that in higher wisdom (*paññā*) are, for the laity, broadly stated in the single more generalized factor of mental development (*bhāvanā*). Again, mental development on the part of the laity, with its focus on the cultivation of loving-kindness, together with giving and virtuous conduct, is mainly intended for bringing about happiness in the realization of a world free from malice (It.15, 51). Moreover, as the monks' triad lacks an explicit factor of giving or charity, it is a corruption for a monk to accumulate wealth, whereas the layman's industrious amassing of wealth is to be justified and glorified by the factor of giving, benevolence, or charity.

Another way to summarize Buddhist ethics as a system is to speak of Buddhism as *dhamma-vinaya*, or the doctrine and the discipline. The *dhamma* consists in the domain of ideas, ideals, truths, and principles, while the *vinaya* covers the domain of legislation, regulation, and social organization. As far as social ethics is concerned, the *vinaya* is of great importance, as it deals especially with social life and the putting of ideas, ideals, and principles into practice. The *dhamma* is a natural law and as such enters directly into the developmental process of the individual. The *vinaya*, by contrast, is human law, being laid down for the good of society. The *vinaya* is consistent with the *dhamma* as the social good is compatible with individual perfection; the rightful *vinaya* has to be based on the *dhamma* just as what is good for society is favorable also to individual development and perfection.

The *vinaya* for the monkhood has been fixed and rather closed, but that for lay society is, to a large extent, left open for temporal regulation to suit the specific time and place. The *vinaya* for the community of monks has been laid down by the Buddha. The *vinaya* for the laity is left open for able and righteous people like enlightened monarchs to formulate based on the general ideas and principles enunciated by the Buddha. In principle, this lay *vinaya* should enjoin the kind of social organization that maintains a society of "good friends" in which people live together for their mutual benefit, where all environmental conditions are favorable to the individual development and perfection.

Four aspects of Buddhist thought and practice of special relevance to a consideration of Theravāda ethics should, furthermore, be emphasized:

I. *General standards and criteria*

a. The *criteria of means* can be represented by the three fundamental admonitions of the Buddha, viz.,
   1. Not to do any evil
   2. To cultivate good
   3. To purify the mind

b. The *criteria of goals* can be represented by two sets of three goals, or benefits, that people should realize as fully as possible taking into account differing personal circumstances. The first set of goals comprises:
   1. The goals or benefits for the here and now, or temporal welfare (*diṭṭhadhammikattha*), e.g., wealth, health, honor, position, good name, good friends, and happy family life
   2. The goals or benefits for the beyond, or spiritual welfare (*samparāyikattha*), i.e., peace and happiness of mind, a blameless life, and confidence regarding future lives
   3. The highest good, or the final goal (*paramattha*), i.e., the supreme peace, bliss, and freedom of *nibbāna*[13]

   And the second comprises:
   1. One's own welfare (*attattha*)
   2. Others' welfare (*parattha*)
   3. Welfare of both oneself and others (*ubhayattha*)[14]

II. *The relationship between mental and character virtues or virtuous acts.*

(Ignorance of this interconnection can lead to confusion and inappropriate action. This can be illustrated by two sets of virtues which occupy a central place in Buddhist social ethics.[15])

a. The first of these sets is that of the Four Sublime States of Mind (*brahma-vihāra*):
   1. Loving-kindness (*mettā*)
   2. Compassion (*karuṇā*)
   3. Sympathetic joy (*muditā*)
   4. Equanimity (*upekkhā*) (D.II.196; D.III.220)

b. And the second set, the Four Bases of Social Harmony, or the Four Principles of Social Integration (*sangaha-vatthu*), consists of:
   1. Giving, distribution, and charity (*dāna*)
   2. Kindly and beneficial words (*piyavācā*)

3. Acts of help or service (*atthacariyā*)
4. Equality, impartiality, and participation (*samānattatā*) (D.III.152, 232; A.II.32, 248; A.IV.218, 363)

III. *The centrality of the virtue of mindfulness.* A virtue that plays a focal role in Buddhist ethics is *appamāda*, rendered as *heedfulness, diligence*, and *earnestness.* It is found among the last words attributed to the Buddha: "All component things are subject to decay, work out (the goal or one's own and others' benefits) with earnestness" (D.II.120). It is also regarded as the basis or common ground of all virtues (S.V.44). Traditionally, it is defined as the presence of mindfulness (*sati*) (e.g., D.A.I.104). In fact, it can be seen as a combination of mindfulness and effort, energy, or exertion (*viriya*). In a sermon to the king of Kosala the Buddha enjoined this virtue of mindful exertion as part of the practice of having good friends for the good and security of his country (S.I.86–87). This virtue may be defined as responsibility for the good. It should be brought into a more prominent place in considering the nature of Buddhist social ethics.

IV. *The issue of motivation.* There are, in short, two kinds of desire or motivation (*chanda*). One is wholesome and the other is unwholesome. The former is called the desire for the good or the desire to do good (*kusala-chanda, dhamma-chanda*, or *kusala-dhammachanda*) (A.III.440). The latter is the better-known *taṇhā* or *akusala-chanda*, which can be defined as the desire for indulgence or the desire to gratify the self, often rendered as *craving. Kusala-chanda*, or wholesome desire, is encouraged in Buddhist ethics (as in the Four Bases of Success, D.III. 221). The two kinds of desire should be clearly distinguished from each other, and the wholesome one should be studied more closely, brought into prominence, and encouraged.

CONCLUSION

The foundations of Buddhist social ethics can be schematized in the following diagram, which outlines the whole system of Buddhist ethics:

paññā	Enlightened world view (based on insight into *anicca, dukkha, anattā*, and *paṭicca-samuppāda*—the keystone of the system)	
magga	*samādhi*	Development of mental qualities (basis for virtues of outward expression)

	sīla	Moral responsibility toward others and society (virtues of outward expression or action)
	yoniso-manasikāra	Mental attitude toward environment
pre-*magga*	*kalyāṇamitta*	Influence from a good social environment and good social relationships

dhamma
With stress on mind and the individual, bridging the transmundane, and involving personal maturity.

vinaya
With stress on the environment, physical circumstances, society, and the surrounding system. Centered on the mundane world and involving the social order.

Within this picture of Buddhist social ethics, the following three points deserve special emphasis:

1. The Buddhist ethical system is composed of the *magga* and pre-*magga* factors, and it is in the latter, especially in the first factor of good external influences or good association, that the principal theme of Buddhist social ethics can be found. The concept of *kalyāṇamittatā* (having good friends) should, thus, be more fully studied. In combination with the category of morality in the *magga*, it is the heart of Buddhist social ethics.

2. There is an essential relationship between the virtues that are qualities of the mind and the virtues for outward action. The former are the source and basis of the latter. In Buddhist terminology both kinds of virtues belong to the threefold training (*sikkhā*) or the three categories of the *magga* factors, the former being the category of mental discipline (*adhicitta*) and the latter the category of morality (*adhisīla*). The category of mental discipline is related in turn to the category of wisdom (*adhipaññā*), which is the mainstay and keystone of Buddhist ethics.

3. The *dhamma* as natural law and the *vinaya* as human law are complementary parts of the Buddhist ethical system. In the *dhamma* the individual has responsibility for his or her own development, whereas through the *vinaya* the community or society offers sanctions and rules to regulate the actions of individuals. With the *vinaya* the Buddha puts people into reciprocal or interdependent relationships, and with the *dhamma*

the individual's internal independence and freedom are to be attained and retained in the world of mutual dependence.

In Buddhist ethics individual perfection and social good are interdependent and inseparable. Even the monks, who are the most devoted to individual perfection, depend on the lay people for material necessities. These, in turn, can be readily and adequately supplied only by a secure and peaceful society, which the monks must help to maintain. At the highest level only the Buddha and the *pacceka-Buddha* (a self-enlightened Buddha) can be self-enlightened through their own wise, systematic reflection. Other people have to depend on the inducement, instigation, and instruction of good friends. Therefore, every average person has to maintain good relationships with others and has some responsibility to maintain the community or society in a favorable state. Conversely, the closer to perfection men and women are, the better they know what is really good for society and the better they can act for the good of society.

In Buddhist ethics wealth is only a means, not an end. It is a question not of the polarities of wealth and poverty, but of how to deal with wealth and when to be independent or freed from wealth. As long and as far as wealth is necessary as a resource, it should be used for achieving social well-being and, thus, for providing favorable circumstances for the individual development of all members of the society. As long as wealth is used in this way, it does not matter to whom it belongs, whether the individual, community, or society. Wealth can rightfully be personal as long as the wealthy person acts as a provider or resource of wealth for society or as a field where wealth grows for the benefit of one's fellows. Without such a value, wealth is useless, the wealthy man is worthless, and the accumulation of wealth becomes evil. Wealth remains of merely instrumental value. In the community of monks, those who are disseminators of individual perfection for the good of all and whose material necessities are supplied by the lay society, life is to be lived independently of wealth. This shows that training for the realization of the goal (*nibbāna*) may depend directly or indirectly on wealth, but its realization proper is independent of it. Here also we can see a relationship between individual perfection and social good: by being used without attachment and for the benefit of oneself and others, wealth improves social welfare, thus contributing to individual perfection, which in turn leads to a greater social good.

Part II.

SOCIAL ETHICS AND SALVATION

Problems of Interpretation

Introduction

The second section of this volume contains essays that set out a general understanding of the relationship between material prosperity and religious salvation as envisioned in Theravāda Buddhism. Implicitly raised in this section is the question of how a tradition's purely religious aspirations and doctrines—its instruction and hope for salvation, its views of history and fate and the human condition—can relate to or shape its practical guidance for life and the structure of society. This question in turn is connected to the issue of how religious guidance for conduct is related to reason as it has been interpreted in the West.

In Chapter 2 Frank Reynolds provides a general discussion of Buddhism's central concept of *dhamma* (variously translated as *truth*, *norm*, or *law*) in relation to wealth and renunciation, and traces out some of the specific dhammic norms associated with the acquisition and use of wealth. He argues that Buddhism's basic orientation toward wealth is best seen as a middle way between asceticism and self-indulgence and as a virtue ethic emphasizing cultivation of the attitude of non-attachment. He describes a provisional affirmation of material prosperity together with wariness about its corrupting influence and lack of ultimate importance. This provisional affirmation is substantial, however. In the Buddhist perspective the law of *kamma* ensures that religious piety, moral behavior, and material prosperity are mutually supportive and that the accumulation of merit will at some point in the future be rewarded with the possession of wealth. Further, this law operates on both an individual and a societal level, so that the virtuous *cakkavatti* king will unfailingly establish a peaceful and prosperous realm.

Reynolds also describes the basic relationship between the Buddhist monastic establishment and lay society and discusses the various types of religious giving prized by Buddhists. Like Rājavaramuni, he sees a total Buddhist social philosophy that strives to maximize conformity with the *dhamma* under the present conditions. This philosophy offers different guidance for people in various stages of religious accomplishment, even as it is unified by its central theme of non-attachment. Thus Reynolds suggests that the Buddhist lay ethic, which calls for sober economic activity, avoidance of irresponsible expenditures, and frequent religious giving, is an appropriate expression of the layman's present capacity and potential for religious advancement, even as it also resonates with the growth of a middle-class merchant ethos.

In Chapter 3 David Little attempts to restate Reynolds's observations and conclusions in the language of philosophical ethics and argues that such an approach can help explain many of Buddhism's distinctive historical features. Little holds that the pursuit of *ṉibbāna* (the Buddhist state of enlightenment) dominates Theravāda Buddhist moral reasoning, giving Buddhist moral arguments a consequentialist tilt and wealth a merely instrumental value. As a result he asks whether this goal is pursued only for oneself, or if the enlightenment of all humankind is the justifying end in Buddhist ethics. Reynolds emphasizes the *dhamma*, the fundamental law of reality and determinative guide for Buddhist behavior as the primary influence on Buddhist moral reasoning, whereas Little focuses on the goal of Buddhist striving. In Chapter 4 Russell Sizemore argues that this disagreement is itself a clue about the complexity and dynamic nature of religious traditions as they provide moral guidance.

Little also argues that the law of *kamma*, with its all-encompassing explanation of existing inequalities, tends to do away with Buddhist perplexity over the plight of the poor. Buddhist emphasis on the virtue of charity tends to outweigh interest in justice, and so ethical reflection is shifted away from evaluation of the existing distribution of wealth. Further, the accompanying emphasis on *religious* giving, as conducive to salvation, contrasts sharply with the West's Puritan impulse toward the creation of new wealth. This difference, Little suggests, may have a central role in illuminating the economic histories of Buddhist cultures.

Both Reynolds and Little also scrutinize the methods employed in the newly developing field of comparative ethics. Sizemore analyzes the debate between them over approaches to this field and attempts to locate the dispute within the growth of the field in general. He argues that the field has been marked not only by divergent interests and orientations, but also by conflicting conceptions of religion and models of human knowledge. Whereas Reynolds envisions moral reasoning as inseparably informed by religious sensibilities, Little operates out of a philosophical approach that contrasts religious and moral reasoning. Sizemore notes that these differences become apparent as each side struggles with the paradoxes typical of religious life. Although he contends that the disagreement will not be resolved by the arguments of either essay, he suggests that there are certain openings for a working synthesis which will allow both approaches to bear fruit.

2 Ethics and Wealth in Theravāda Buddhism

A Study in Comparative Religious Ethics

Frank E. Reynolds

The history of religions has an ambiguous relationship to the study of religious ethics. Clearly, religious ethics is a characteristic mode of religious expression and, as such, falls within the purview of historians of religion. Yet throughout the history of the discipline scholars in the field have displayed little interest in pursuing the study of ethical expressions.

Among the variety of reasons that might be adduced to explain this anomaly, two may be singled out. The first is that in the early stages in the development of the discipline, when its characteristic emphases and problematics were being formulated, scholars in the field were very conscious of the danger, closely associated with the liberalism of the late nineteenth century, that religion would be reduced to its ethical dimension. Taking their stand against this kind of reductionism, these scholars tended to separate religion from ethics and to leave the study of ethics to those in other fields. The second reason, related to the first, is that ethics in the western academic world has, in recent years, been closely associated with Kantian or neo-Kantian formalism. Since this kind of formalism is a part of the rationalistic tendency of modern western thought which historians have tended to challenge and reject, the study of ethics has been seen within the discipline as irrelevant, uninteresting, or both.

A point has now been reached, however, when the reticence of historians of religion to study religious ethics can and should be overcome. The tendency to reduce religion to ethics is no longer a significant threat to the field of history of religions. And the near monopoly held by Kantian and neo-Kantian formalists on the terminology and concepts associated with ethics has broken down. Thus, the way has been paved for historians of religion to lay aside their inherited prejudices and begin to engage the study of religious ethics.

The question that is immediately raised concerns methodology. How should historians of religion, operating within the parameters of their own discipline, engage in the study of comparative religious ethics? This is not the place for an extended discussion of the many complex and interesting questions that are involved.[1] But it may be worthwhile to emphasize several basic points.

The first point is that historians of religion, when they become involved in the study of comparative religious ethics, direct their attention to ethical expressions that are religious in character. The interpretation of ethical expressions found outside the orbit of religion is left to others.

Second, historians of religion operate with a conception of religious ethics that is broad and flexible. They take within their ken, at least in principle, all those religious expressions that have been historically influential in guiding human conduct within the traditions they study. Some of those expressions may be "theoretical" and some may be "practical"; some may involve modes of rationality quite commensurate with those to which we are accustomed in the modern West, whereas others may use modes of rationality that are different from ours.

Third, historians of religion emphasize the need to place the study of the ethics of any religious tradition within the context of a holistic understanding of that tradition. This does not involve any presumption that the distinctive configuration of elements that constitutes each tradition renders that tradition so unique that conceptual categories cannot be used cross-culturally, or that cross-cultural comparisons are not possible. But it does mean that the distinctive configurations of elements that constitute each tradition must be taken very seriously into account when the interpretation of any particular element is being considered.

Fourth, historians of religion take, as the starting point of their investigations, many different kinds of "texts." They are concerned with both scriptural texts and popular texts, with mythic texts and discursive texts, and with rituals and spiritual disciplines that can be read as texts.

Finally, historians of religion who take up the task of comparative religious ethics are self-conscious about the significance of the choices they make regarding the materials they study and the kind of interpretations they generate. They do not become so enmeshed in abstract theoretical discussions that they are distracted from their empirical research and their responsibilities as practicing historians. But they are sensitive to the implications of the presuppositions and categories they use and to the intellectual and social implications of the conclusions they reach.

THE PRIMACY OF *DHAMMA* IN THERAVĀDA BUDDHIST ETHICS

Scholars involved in the study of religion and culture have become increasingly aware of the pitfalls that are inevitably involved in the attempt to characterize the "essence" of whole traditions. Traditions, most especially great traditions like Theravāda Buddhism, are much too complex and stretch over much too broad a span of time to be summarized in simple terms. This is true at the level of mythology and doctrine, at the level of ritual and community life, and also at the level of religious ethics. But despite the fact that there is no defining and enduring "essence" of Theravāda Buddhism (or of any other tradition, for that matter), it is still possible to generate a basic set of formulations concerning Theravāda ethics which hold at many levels and persist with some consistency through the long course of Theravāda history. In order to tease out these formulations as they impinge on issues related to wealth, it will be necessary to begin by setting forth three basic presuppositions concerning the Theravāda tradition in general and the Theravāda notion of *dhamma* in particular.

The first basic assumption is that the *dhamma* (variously translated as *truth, norm, law*, etc.) provides a religioethical "center of gravity" for Theravāda Buddhism. Within the context of the classical Theravāda orientation it is the *dhamma* that constitutes the structure and the dynamics of all reality, including both the phenomenal world and salvation itself. The *dhamma* is also the normative truth that establishes guidelines for all forms of action that Theravadins approve or commend. All other Theravāda norms for action are expressions of *dhamma*, are subservient to it, or are in one way or another correlated with it.

My second basic assumption is that the *dhamma* is a sacred reality that can be understood only through the study of a variety of genres of Theravāda expression. These genres include foundational myths such as the various Buddhist cosmogonies and hagiographical accounts of the lives of the Founder; secondary narratives such as sacred histories, and stories regarding saints and other lesser figures; discursive teachings contained in dialogues and sermons; and more sophisticated systematic and philosophical discussions as well. They also include sacred activities through which ethical conceptions are expressed and reinforced—notably various kinds of ritual performance and spiritual discipline.

My third assumption is that for Theravadins the *dhamma* is itself a very complex and dynamic reality. Thus, the aspect of the *dhamma* that is thought to be manifest in an era of harmony and well-being may be quite different from the aspect of the *dhamma* that is thought to be manifest in an era characterized by conflict and degeneration. The *dhamma* may be considered relevant in one way in cosmic eras or portions of cosmic eras when no Buddha has appeared, and in another way in eras such as ours when a Buddha has appeared and his religion is being practiced. Within Buddhist society the *dhamma* may apply in one form to the monastic community and in another form to the laity. Moreover, Theravadins have always recognized that the import of the *dhamma* in particular situations is highly problematic and that a continuing process of interpretation is required.

A full statement and defense of these basic assumptions concerning the centrality of the *dhamma* in Theravāda religion and ethics, the variety of genres through which Theravadins have expressed different and sometimes divergent dhammic conceptions, and the flexibility of dhammic norms in relation to various existential situations would require a great deal more explication and argument. In the present context, however, I will refrain from pursuing such matters in any direct or explicit way.[2] Rather, I will move directly to a discussion of the specific dhammic principles that have been central to traditional Theravāda attitudes toward wealth.

BASIC PRINCIPLES

In western academic and popular consciousness the Theravāda Buddhist conception of *dhamma* has traditionally been associated almost exclusively with the idea of renunciation, and it has been assumed that the idea of renunciation entails a wholly negative evaluation of wealth. Recently, a more extended reading of Theravāda texts, as well as an increased emphasis on the study of Theravāda societies, has shown that this is a very one-sided characterization. The fact is that Theravāda interpretations of *dhamma* have, from the very beginning, incorporated a more or less positive valorization of wealth, including material resources, monetary resources, goods, and services. This attitude was present in the teachings of the Buddha himself, at least as far as we can discern them. It was certainly present in the teachings that were developed in the early Buddhist community whose members were—it must be remembered—drawn largely from the upper strata of society and included a significant number of well-to-do merchants. This same relatively positive dhammic valorization of wealth has remained in the foreground throughout the history of the Theravāda tradition in Sri Lanka and in Southeast Asia. And it continues to hold a prominent place in contemporary Theravāda thought and life.

The relationships that have pertained among the Theravāda notions of *dhamma*, renunciation, non-attachment, and wealth are very complex.[3] Interpretations have varied during the course of Theravāda history, and different viewpoints have been maintained by different groups within the

Theravāda community. This complexity notwithstanding, it is possible to discern three basic principles that inform the whole. The first highlights the positive valorization of non-attachment. The second highlights the positive valorization of wealth. The third specifies the ambivalence involved in the relationship between non-attachment on the one hand and wealth on the other.

The first principle affirms that all dhammic norms commend actions that are intended to express and cultivate non-attachment, including non-attachment to wealth. This strong emphasis on the centrality of non-attachment is perhaps most evident in the case of the norms that regulate the life of the monks. These include those norms that regulate monastic rituals, among them the important biweekly confession known as the *pāṭimokkha*. They include the norms that regulate the meditative disciplines that are, for some at least, a part of the monastic vocation. And they include the rules and regulations that govern the ordinary round of monastic activities. This emphasis on the centrality of non-attachment can also be discerned in the norms set forth to guide the life of the laity. These include the norms that regulate ethically oriented ritual activity, especially the ritually structured giving of gifts. They include the norms that guide the meditation practices that are specifically commended to the laity. And they also include the moral precepts that give direction to the moral life of laymen and laywomen—for example, the five dhammic precepts against killing, stealing, lying, sexual misconduct, and the use of intoxicants.

The second principle—the one that highlights the Theravadins' positive valorization of wealth—affirms that adherence to dhammic norms is conducive to the production of wealth. Again, this principle pertains in different ways in different contexts. In various mythic accounts of ideal societies adherence to the five dhammic precepts is presented as a crucial determining factor in the life of communities that enjoy a superabundance of wealth and well-being. Some accounts, such as those describing the primordial period that existed under the rule of the first king (Mahasammata, or Great Elect) or the times when a universal monarch (*cakkavatti*) reigns over the world, emphasize the moral purity of the king both in itself and in terms of its pervasive influence in society. Other accounts, such as those describing the beginning of the cosmic cycle and the kind of life that is lived in the fabulous northern continent of Uttarakuru, emphasize the moral purity of the populace as a whole. For our purposes the crucial point is that in both cases the myths portray an intrinsic connection between adherence to dhammic norms on the one hand and the wealth and well-being of the community on the other.

The intimate ties that presumably bind dhammic activity and material prosperity are also set forth in the Theravāda stories and teachings that deal with Buddhist societies in which both a Buddhist monastic community and a lay community are present. In these stories and teachings it is either presumed or maintained that the actions commended to the monks for their own spiritual benefit constitute a kind of pure behavior that, because of the unity of the religiomoral, the societal and the natural orders, also works to ensure the wealth of the community. In societies in which the *vinaya* (the collection of rules attributed to the Buddha which govern the behavior of individual monks and the proper ordering of the life of the monasic community) is properly observed and the level of path attainment is high, group life will be harmonious, the rhythms of nature will be properly maintained, and prosperity will prevail. In societies in which the monks violate the strictures of the *vinaya* and fail to practice the path the Buddha taught, group life will become fractious, the rhythms of nature will become unpredictable and destructive, and—as a part of the same antidhammic process—wealth and prosperity will disappear.

For the laity the teachings and stories illustrating the ties that bind dhammic activity and material prosperity place a strong emphasis on the faithfulness of the rulers in following a set of precepts called the *rājādhamma* (the *dhamma* of the kings). Consider, for example, the classic sermon that constitutes the central passage in the very important compendium of Theravāda teaching, the *Three Worlds according to King Ruang* (Reynolds and Reynolds 1982: 148–54). This sermon, preached by the great *cakkavatti* king at the moment immediately following his peaceful conquest of the kings of the four quarters of the universe, sets forth the dhammic responsibilities that these lesser kings are admonished to exercise in order to establish justice and prosperity in their respective realms. The great *cakkavatti* king (who, it is said, teaches in the same way that a Buddha would teach) begins by instructing the lesser kings who observe the *rājādhamma* and to love all subjects—princes, courtiers, and common people, both slaves and free—with equal intensity. He sets forth each of the five basic precepts and goes on to interpret each of them with specific reference to the responsibilities of governance. He then takes up the issue of taxation, emphasizing that the ruler should never take more than ten percent of the crop that his subjects produce, that he should take even less in times of drought and special difficulty, and that he should never increase his levies beyond the level established by his predecessors. The great *cakkavatti* king warns the lesser rulers against requiring their subjects to provide excessive labor for royal purposes; he insists that the elderly be exempted from royal service. The rulers, he admonishes, should provide from their treasuries loans without interest for those who wish to engage in commerce and trade, and they should refrain from taxing the profits. They should be quick to reward those who do well in the performance of public good, and they should be generous to their courtiers, to their families, and to the brahmins and monks residing within their territory.

According to the great *cakkavatti* king, the dhammic behavior of the lesser kings and rulers will ensure the prosperity of their realms:

> If any ruler, while he reigns, acts righteously and does righteous things, the common people, the slaves and the free men will live peacefully and happily, will have stability and balance, and will enjoy good fortune and prosperity; and this is because of the accumulation of merit of the one who is the lord above all. Rice and water, plus fish and other food, the ten thousand measures of gems and ornaments, the nine kinds of gems, silver, gold, clothing and garments of silk will all be available in abundance. The rain from the sky, which is regulated by the *devatā* (one of the kinds of deities in the traditional Buddhist cosmos), will fall appropriately in accordance with the season, not too little and not too much. The rice in the fields and the fish in the water will never be ruined by drought or damaged by rain. For another thing, the days, nights, years, and months will never be irregular. Also the guardian *devatā* who are present to guard and protect the towns and cities will do so because they respect the rulers and kings who act righteously in accordance with *dhamma*. In the case of any king who acts wrongly and does what is not in accord with the *dhamma*, the pattern of rainfall, which is regulated by the *devatā*, will be distorted. If the people cultivate the fields, the crops will be brought to ruin and will perish as a result of drought or flood. For another thing, fruits and plants that grow above the ground and ordinarily have a nutritive essence and a good and delicious taste will, instead, have these things disappear and be destroyed; and when the nutritive essence sinks completely under the ground the trunks of the trees and the stems will lose their healthy look. The sun, the wind, the moon and the stars will not be appropriate for the seasons as was the case before. This is because the rulers and kings do things that are not righteous; the *devatā* strongly hate and despise those unrighteous kings, and do not wish to look at their faces—even if they look at them they never look at their faces, and generally they look only out of the corner of their eyes. (Reynolds and Reynolds 1982: 153)

In addition to the dhammic activities of kings, the dhammic actions of other laymen and laywomen are recognized as contributing to social harmony, to a supportive natural environment, and to the economic prosperity that is associated with a properly ordered natural and social world. This is true whether these dhammic activities are seen within a macrosocial context, in which they are taken to be correlated with the actions of a good king, or in a microsocial context such as a village, in which royal themes play a more limited role. In either case general lay support for the monastic community and the brahmins, the adherence of the laity to the five basic precepts, and the laity's maintenance of proper social activities and relationships are all considered to be components essential for the maintenance of natural order, the cultivation of social well-being, and the attainment of economic prosperity for the community as a whole.

What is especially interesting and distinctive about the connection the Theravadins make between dhammic norms and the production of wealth is the fact that the monastic norms and the royal/lay norms are so structured that the actions they commend establish a system of exchange between the monks and the laity that has a double significance. At the ritual level it is believed that this exchange actualizes an ideal order in which the full benefits of dhammic activity, including an abundance of wealth, are enjoyed by the entire community. At the level of ordinary life it is believed that this same exchange ensures the maintenance of as much of that order and abundance as is possible under the prevailing historical conditions.[4]

The actions and exchanges commended by dhammic norms are thought to be conducive not only to the wealth of the community, but simultaneously to the wealth of the individuals who perform them. Those few individuals who have advanced to the higher stages of the path have, to be sure, a special position. They are usually members of the monastic order (the *sangha*), within which (ideally and symbolically at least) the monks are relatively equal in status and the possession and enjoyment of material wealth is limited to a very moderate level. What is more, these spiritually advanced individuals can be expected to remain within the *sangha* until they reach the final nibbānic goal. However, in the case of most monks, laymen, and laywomen, dhammic actions are expected to generate for each individual who performs them a greater abundance of material wealth, either in this life or in a future life. This occurs, in the Theravāda view, in accordance with the law of *kamma*—a law that structures reality so that dhammic and antidhammic actions always have a predictable effect in determining one's future position in the sociocosmic hierarchy that constitutes ordinary *samsāric* reality. According to the Theravadins, the law of *kamma* operates in such a way that dhammic actions always lead to a higher status in the hierarchy of cosmic and social existence and, therefore, to the possession and enjoyment of greater amounts of material wealth. Conversely, kammic retribution ensures that actions violating dhammic norms will lead with equal certainty to a lower status in the hierarchy that orders the cosmos and society and, therefore, to increased increments of suffering, poverty and hunger.

The correlation between the accumulation of good *kamma* (popularly known as merit, *puñña*) and the possession of wealth is vividly illustrated in a well-known story of an encounter between an evil king named Ajātasattu and a meritorious rich man named Jōtika. According to the story, Ajātasattu was envious of the great wealth possessed by Jōtika and sent his powerful army to confiscate it. By virtue of Jōtika's great merit, however, Ajātasattu's troops were miraculously repulsed. Hearing that Jōtika was meditating in a nearby monastery, the evil king immediately went to confront him personally and demand his wealth. Jōtika extended his hand to Ajātasattu and invited his adversary to remove the magnificent jeweled rings that were on his fingers. But despite Ajātasattu's great strength and frenzied efforts, he could not do so. After the king had given up in frustration, Jōtika instructed him to place his handkerchief on the ground; the rich man hung his hand over the handkerchief, and all of the rings dropped onto it. Jōtika then informed the king that since his wealth had come to him by virtue of his great merit, it could not be taken away by force. Having made his point, he proceeded to demonstrate his own non-attachment by declaring his intention to renounce his fortune and enter the order of monks (Reynolds and Reynolds 1982: 197–99).

The last of the three principles—the one concerning the relationship between wealth that is possessed and further adherence to dhammic norms—affirms that such wealth may serve either as a vehicle for achieving greater adherence to dhammic norms *or* as a factor that inhibits such adherence. At the lower economic levels the emphasis is on the positive value of wealth in relation to further dhammic activity. Theravadins have traditionally believed that a basic level of economic well-being is necessary to encourage and support the practice of the *dhamma*, both within the *sangha* and within the society as a whole. Beyond this, Theravadins have affirmed that extra increments of wealth may play either a positive or a negative role. They may play a positive role insofar as they provide the context and substance for even greater expressions and cultivations of non-attachment. But they may also play a negative role by evoking the attachment that generates kammic retribution and inhibits the practice of the Buddhist path.

This ambivalence concerning the role of wealth in the soteriological process has led to efforts to delineate a kind of economic middle way that could maximize the possibilities for continued dhammic activity. An example of the idealization of this economic middle way is found in a fascinating Theravāda account of the events that will lead to the coming of the future Buddha Metteya. According to this account, the period prior to the coming of Metteya will be marked by the gradual evolution of an ideal society in which wealth and well-being will be at their zenith. However, at this point in the cycle of cosmic and social evolution, conditions will be so favorable and so pleasurable that human beings will forget the reality and the causes of suffering. Consequently, personal and social well-being will decline until a point is reached at which people, though they remain in a relatively harmonious and prosperous environment, once again become conscious of the reality of suffering and of death. It is at this point that the soteriologically appropriate conditions will obtain and Metteya will descend into the world to lead the populace to the attainment of *nibbāna*.[5]

This same ambivalence has been evident in relation to individuals as well. From one point of view the higher positions in the cosmic hierarchy—those situated in the divine realms where the amount of affluence and pleasure is greatest—are considered to be the best. But from another, more profound perspective the human realm is preferred since it is recognized that it is only from the somewhat lower human level, where the amount of affluence and pleasure is more limited, that the attainment of salvation is possible. The immediate, existential relevance of this cosmological formulation becomes evident when we recognize that the divinities are quite explicitly homologized with royalty, whereas the human level is quite explicitly associated with people who enjoy a moderate level of wealth and well-being. Thus, it is affirmed that whereas royalty may have the greatest amount of enjoyment and pleasure, it is the people who enjoy a moderate level of wealth and well-being who hold a position that is soteriologically the most advantageous. Like the people living at the time of the coming of Metteya, they have sufficient wealth to make the practice of the Buddhist path a practical possibility at the same time that they are sufficiently aware of the reality of suffering and death that they are motivated to undertake its rigors.[6]

Despite such Theravāda efforts to delineate and symbolize an economic middle way, the problematic relationship between the possession of wealth and further dhammic activity has never been fully resolved. Wealth always provides both an opportunity for a new expression and cultivation of non-attachment *and* a temptation toward the kind of antidhammic self-indulgence that leads to increased entrapment in the web of worldly existence. To put the same point a bit differently, the problematic presented by the possession of wealth has remained for Theravāda practitioners a primary locus for religious and ethical decision.

ISSUES AND ADAPTATIONS

Throughout the course of their history Theravadins have employed these principles as they have confronted the problems and possibilities related to wealth. On the basis of these principles they have dealt with specific questions of how wealth can be acquired, managed, and expended in accordance with the dhammic norms. On the same basis they have developed particular strategies through which the possession and enjoyment of wealth can be justified or condemned. There has, of course, been considerable diversity in the way the issues have been approached and resolved. However, certain characteristic and persistent themes can be identified. These appear in one form in the context of the monastic community and in a related but different form in relation to the laity.

Within the monastic order the basic orientation toward wealth was established very early, probably during the lifetime of the Buddha himself. This orientation was fully articulated during the early centuries of Buddhist history and was embedded in the canonical *vinaya* (the monastic rules of discipline), including both the section that contains the rules for guiding the behavior of the individual monks and the section that sets forth the procedures for managing the affairs of the community. At the most basic level the *vinaya* specifically prohibits the monks from gaining wealth—even the minimum amount needed for subsistence—by engaging in any kind of work. The monks' privilege and responsibility is to practice the path the Buddha has taught and in so doing to maintain the purity of the community he has established. What the monks need in terms of food, clothing, and shelter is to be provided by gifts freely given by lay supporters.

During the early centuries of Buddhist history these gifts seem to have served the purpose for which they were originally prescribed—support for the nonascetic but moderate lifestyle that the Buddha exemplified in his own life and commended to his monastic followers. Gradually, however, the system began to generate a new kind of situation, one not envisioned at the outset. As the Theravāda tradition developed, the monastic order emerged as an important social institution, first in India and Sri Lanka and later in Southeast Asia. Through the reception of gifts, including those from kings and other highly placed persons, the *sangha* eventually became a wealthy community exercising control over a great deal of land, goods, and human services. This practice led to serious problems concerning the proper use of this wealth by the community as a whole and by individual monks. These issues have led to a continuing series of disagreements and controversies.

I cannot here recount the history of these disagreements and controversies.[7] However, a few comments may be relevant and useful. On the one hand, those Theravadins who have justified monastic wealth and the new modes of acquiring, managing, and expending it have consistently engaged in a process of interpreting the *vinaya* in a way that both legitimates and regulates the new practices. In addition, they have maintained that monastic wealth, properly used in accordance with the tradition of *vinaya* commentary, can play an effective role in advancing the well-being of the community and the spread of the religion. On the other hand, those Theravadins who have taken the opposing position, condemning what they have considered to be excessive monastic wealth and the new modes of acquiring and expending it, have also drawn on traditional material to make their case. They have held to a more literal interpretation of the canonical texts forbidding monastic wealth; they have also maintained that increased wealth and economic activity in the monastic community stimulates attachment and is, therefore, detrimental both to the soteriological progress of the monks and to the proper functioning of the dhammic order.

In various Theravāda countries there has been a continuing, cyclic oscillation between periods of monastic accumulation supported by the justification of monastic wealth and periods of monastic reform accompanied by the condemnation of monastic wealth. It is not surprising that the accumulation and justification of monastic wealth has often come to the fore in situations in which the monastic leadership has been closely affiliated, often by kinship, with the political and economic elite. It is also not surprising that monastic reforms and the condemnations of monastic wealth have often been initiated and supported by kings seeking to return monastic lands to the tax rolls.

Among the laity the religioethical issues involved in the ways wealth is acquired, the ways it is managed and expended, and justified and condemned have arisen and been dealt with in many quite different modes. But, again, patterns are clearly discernible. For example, the responsibility of the laity to engage in economically productive work has been consistently recognized and encouraged. The primary Theravāda norm associated with this productive activity has been that such work be carried out in accordance with the five basic dhammic precepts, especially the three that prohibit killing, stealing, and lying. Theravadins have traditionally maintained that those who earn their living without killing, stealing, or lying facilitate the dhammic ordering of society will be personally rewarded in accordance with the law of *kamma*. Conversely, those who earn their living in ways that do involve killing, stealing, or lying will undermine the dhammic ordering of society will suffer for their misdeeds, if not in this life then in the next.

In Theravāda ethics for the laity great importance has always been attached not only to proper ways of acquiring wealth, but also to the appropriate management and expenditure of wealth. It is rather surprising, but nevertheless true, that a primary element in this aspect of lay ethics has been articulated in commentaries on the last of the five most basic dhammic precepts—the one that prohibits the use of intoxicants. In these commentaries we find a strongly critical attitude not only toward intoxication as such, but also toward irresponsible or wasteful expenditures of any kind. The tenor is unmistakably bourgeois, and it is hard to resist the hypothesis that this attitude is closely correlated with the affinity that seems to have existed between early Buddhism and the merchant class. As Theravāda Buddhism became established in Sri Lanka and Southeast Asia, its special affinity with merchants became less pronounced. However, the early antipathy to irresponsible and wasteful expenditure has never been completely lost.

The Theravadins, as a counterpoint to their encouragement of honest economic activity and their normative antipathy to irresponsible expenditure and waste, have placed a strong emphasis on the virtue of generosity. The canonical and postcanonical literature of Buddhism is filled with admonitions to the laity concerning the giving of wealth and with stories that recount the benefits that flow therefrom. Perhaps the best-known and most-recited story in all of Theravāda literature, rivaling in many respects the classical account of the life of Gotama Buddha, is the story of the great exemplar of giving and generosity—King Vessantara. Presented as an account of the Buddha in his last life prior to his birth as Gotama, this story has traditionally been chanted and dramatized in festivals all across the Theravāda world. It tells of Vessantara's cultivation of the virtue of generosity through his giving up of his kingdom and all of his material wealth and, even beyond that, of his giving away of his beautiful wife and his children. Clearly, the story conveys the notion that it was through these heroic acts of giving that the future Buddha completed the spiritual preparation that qualified him for his ultimate life as the enlightened sage who served as the great teacher for all humanity.[8] Also, the most famous and praised of the lay followers of the Buddha are the givers of vast amounts of wealth. In this context one thinks of famous contemporaries of the Buddha, such as Anāthapiṇḍika, the paradigmatic lay giver who presented the great Jetavana monastery to the Buddha. One also thinks of famous kings and other lay patrons of later times such as King Aśoka, who according to the legendary accounts ultimately gave all of his vast possessions to the *sangha*.[9]

Throughout Theravāda history different forms of lay giving have been identified and commended. Theravāda practitioners have recognized a very diffused giving directed to anyone who might request it (see, for example, the story of Vessantara referred to above). In some cases they have advocated generosity to those for whom the giver has some special social responsibility, as, for example, the *cakkavatti*'s exhortation to the lesser kings and rulers summarized in the previous section. In still other cases they have focused attention on the giving of wealth to the Buddha in the form of offerings made to his relics, enshrined in *thūpa*s and images, or to the *sangha*. In each of these three types of giving the effects are structurally similar. The dhammic order of society and nature is supported, the non-attachment of the giver is expressed and cultivated, and the merit of the giver is increased so that he or she will enjoy even greater wealth in the future. In extreme situations like those associated with Anāthapiṇḍika and Aśoka, in which generosity seems to deplete or even exhaust the wealth of the giver, it is held that an especially high degree of affluence will be enjoyed in a future life.

The Theravāda texts quite consistently imply that the three types of giving are ordered hierarchically. Diffused giving and giving to one's family or entourage are good and efficacious, both socially and individually. But clearly the most important and effective type of giving is that directed to the Buddha and/or the *sangha*. According to the traditional Theravāda teaching, the effectiveness of a gift is to a very considerable extent dependent on the worthiness of the recipient, and the Buddha and the *sangha* are, of course, without comparison, the most worthy recipients. Thus, giving directed to the Buddha and the *sangha* is deemed to be the most crucial for the maintenance of the dhammic order in society and the natural world and, therefore, to the maintenance or enhancement of the society's wealth. It is also believed that this kind of giving generates for the individual giver the greatest amount of kammic reward.

Within the Theravāda tradition the justification and condemnation of lay wealth has been closely correlated with judgments concerning both the way the wealth has been acquired and the way it is spent. Since the kammic regulation of the hierarchy of wealth operates in long-range rather than short-range terms, the legitimacy of the wealth possessed by any particular individual at any particular time can become—and often has become—a matter of serious dispute. Those who seek to establish the legitimacy of their wealth must convince the community that it has been acquired by virtue of meritorious activity done in the past and that it has been more immediately earned in ways that are in accord with the precepts. As a supplement to this kind of apologetic, or as an alternative to it in situations in which the immorality involved in the acquisition of the wealth cannot be denied, the possessors of wealth must convince the community that they have achieved a level of non-attachment and generosity that ensures that they will spend what they have acquired in accord with dhammic norms. Thus it is that among Theravadins the need to establish the legitimacy of one's wealth has been one of the more obvious motivations for the construction of reliquary *thūpa*s devoted to the Buddha, the sponsorship of festivals honoring the *dhamma*, and the ostentatious giving of gifts to the *sangha*. On the other hand, those who challenge the legitimacy of the wealth possessed by another must convince the community that this wealth has been acquired by immoral means. Even more important, they must convince the community that the wealthy person is acting with the kind of self-indulgent craving that undermines dhammic order and subverts the social good. It was this sort of critique that was leveled against many wealthy rulers and landlords in various Theravāda countries during the premodern period, and these same criticisms are often brought to bear against the economic elite in the Theravāda world today.

CONTEMPORARY PROBLEMATICS

Over the past century or so the classical Theravāda tradition has encountered a new kind of challenge and opportunity. New ideas and institutions introduced into the various Theravāda countries have established, for some Theravadins at least, new understandings of the limitations and possibilities of human activity and new conceptions of a just social order. In this situation new ethical issues have arisen and new ethical guidelines have been generated.

The new influences associated with modernity have seriously challenged the traditional Theravāda conception of a single dhammic order encompassing the soteriological process, the social order, *and* the natural order. Thus, the traditional belief that dhammic activity in the religiomoral realm will ensure the proper functioning of nature, and will, therefore, contribute to economic prosperity, has been undermined. With the weakening of this correlation, one of the most important traditional connections between ethical norms and economic well-being has been severed.

Some Theravadins who have been affected by the breakdown in the conception of a comprehensive and unified dhammic order have responded conservatively. Their response has involved the reassertion of the traditional norms in ways that highlight their soteriological efficacy, their contribution to social order and stability, and their contribution, through their positive social impact, to communal prosperity and well-being. Those who have taken this position have reaffirmed the traditional emphasis on the specifically religious purity of monastic behavior and, along with it, a more or less exclusive focus on the traditional roles of the monks as exemplars and teachers of the *dhamma*. In regard to the laity, these somewhat modernized but conservative Theravadins have reaffirmed the primacy traditionally given to the laity's responsibility to support the monks and to the giving of gifts in specifically religious contexts.

Other Theravadins have taken a more liberal stance. These reform-oriented Theravadins have affirmed that Buddhists have an ethical responsibility to take a more direct role in the process of modernization that presumably leads, in its own way, to the attainment of economic prosperity. Those who have taken this kind of position have insisted that contemporary monks, in order to fulfill their ethical obligation to foster "the welfare of the many," should become actively engaged in the work of modern-style community development. And they have insisted that the laity has a similar responsibility in relation to development. For example, many of the liberal reformers have reinterpreted the norms associated with expenditures of wealth and the giving of gifts in such a way that excessive expenditures and giving in specifically religious contexts has been discouraged. What has been encouraged in their stead are new kinds of religiously motivated expenditures that are intended to make very direct and immediate contributions to the cause of social and economic progress.

Another aspect of modernity that has made a significant impact in the Theravāda world is the rise of conceptions of human equality and egalitarian modes of social and economic justice. Since these modernist notions are quite different from the classical Theravāda conceptions of a definitive cosmic-social hierarchy, those Theravadins who have been influenced by them have been forced to reevaluate the received tradition. Once again the new patterns that have emerged can be classified along a continuum that runs from conservative to liberal and reformist.

Conservative Theravadins influenced by modernist ideas of human equality and egalitarian justice have rejected the cosmological grounding of the traditional hierarchy of status and wealth but have continued to recognize both the traditional and more recent forms of hierarchy as conventional patterns necessary for the maintenance of cultural decorum, social order, and economic stability. Some of these conservatives have sought to mitigate the rigidities and blatant injustices related to the hierarchical ordering of wealth and privilege and have supported changes in the direction of more egalitarian ideals, both in the *sangha* and in the society as a whole. But they have resisted efforts to initiate any really basic moves toward structural innovation.

Many of the more liberal Theravadins have, however, taken a strongly reformist position. They have retrieved and emphasized the more egalitarian strands of the *vinaya* tradition related to the *sangha*. They have contended that the relatively egalitarian pattern that the *vinaya* prescribes for the monastic order implies the goal of a more egalitarian pattern for the society as a whole. They have made a concerted effort to retrieve other similar egalitarian ideals, including those expressed in the myths of primordial times and in certain versions of the myth of the coming of the Buddha Metteya. In recent years certain of the Theravāda reformers have gone on to formulate what they consider to be a specifically Theravadin philosophy of development that highlights the ideals of self-restraint, non-attachment, and social justice conceived in an essentially egalitarian mode. What is more, some of these reformers have organized, on the basis of the religioethical position they have developed, international, national, and village-level movements designed to embody and generate the social and economic reforms they advocate.[10]

In each of the areas where Theravāda Buddhism has traditionally been established, the character of contemporary transformation has been different. Two basic patterns can, however, be differentiated. In Cambodia and Laos the classical Theravāda orientation, including the orientation toward wealth, remained for many decades relatively impervious to modernist influences. Then, partially as a result of the tradition's own inflexibility, it was violently displaced by a Communist ideology that viewed Theravāda Buddhism as a form of false consciousness functioning to legitimate an old order that had become thoroughly identified with economic stagnation and injustice. In Sri Lanka, Burma, and Thailand the Theravadins have also had their share of inflexible traditionalists and a number of radical, anti-Buddhist revolutionaries. But these communities have over the years produced a large number of somewhat modernized conservatives and a goodly number of liberal-minded reformers as well. The resulting diversity and flexibility has enabled the tradition to adjust without losing its identity. As a result, in these countries the Theravadins and their attitudes toward the acquisition, management, and expenditure of wealth continue to exert a significant influence.

3 Ethical Analysis and Wealth in Theravāda Buddhism:

A Response to Frank Reynolds

David Little

When confronted with controversy, such as appears to exist between the "ethicists" and the "comparativists" (or historians of religion) over the comparative study of religious ethics, it is well to resist taking things at face value. As the discussions proceed, specific exercises should be designed in order to ascertain whether the conflict in approach and analysis is in fact as deep and pervasive as is alleged. I propose to design and perform such an exercise in response to Frank Reynolds's illuminating chapter, and I announce the results of the exercise in advance:

First, Reynolds's basic argument is readily translatable, without distortion, into the terms and categories familiar to ethicists, particularly as they are employed in Little and Twiss 1978. In fact, much that Reynolds says is fully compatible with the general analysis of Theravāda Buddhism in Little and Twiss 1978: chap. 8.

Second, some of Reynolds's observations suggest new resources and agenda items for the comparative study of religious ethics. They also suggest the need for some modification and further elaboration and clarification of the Little-Twiss interpretation of Theravāda Buddhism, although Reynolds's account in no way contradicts that interpretation.

Third, Reynolds's approach could usefully be supplemented, particularly for comparative analysis, by performing such an "ethical translation."[1] With the help of conventional ethical categories, we can ask some interesting questions about wealth and poverty in respect to the Theravāda tradition, identify points of contrast with other traditions, and perhaps locate some of the reasons for that contrast.

Fourth, there are a few points of alleged disagreement over theory, method, and approach that are not, on reflection, serious. There remains, however, one aspect of the discussion over theory that is of consequence. That is the issue of "holism."

The exercise, then, is simply to produce an "ethical translation" that supports these four conclusions.

AN ETHICAL TRANSLATION

In his account Reynolds makes clear that the question of the *justification* of wealth is significant for the Theravadins, and he is at pains to show how the "positive valorization of wealth" fits into the larger scheme of the Theravāda tradition.[2] To an important extent, his discussion is, in the terms of the Little-Twiss volume, an examination of the "structure of practical justification" of the Theravadins.

The specifics of his account never depart very far from that analysis. In the first place the Theravāda system is a "results-oriented" (or teleological-practical) system, according to which dhammic activity, if properly performed, leads ultimately to the highest goal of *nibbāna*. Achieving this goal is, of course, the basic point of adopting the Theravāda way of life, for it signifies the condition of complete non-attachment, or the renunciation of the self as an object of attachment, which is the ultimate state of overcoming all suffering.

Reynolds rightly refers to the ambivalence toward wealth that, given this outlook, characteristically exists among Theravadins. On the one hand, physical wealth is, like all coveted material objects, the occasion for desire and attachment, and, as such, of no ultimate worth. Indeed, attainment of nibbāna utterly precludes prizing wealth—or anything else, for that matter. As the *Dhammapada* has it: "There is no satisfying lusts, even by a shower of gold pieces; he that knows that lusts have a short taste and cause pain, he is wise; even in heavenly pleasures he finds no satisfaction; the disciple who is fully awakened delights only in the destruction of all desires" (Müller 1965: 51).

On the other hand, wealth does have a certain value, although a highly provisional and instrumental one. Reynolds makes this plain: "Theravadins have clearly affirmed that extra increments of wealth may play either a positive or a negative role. They may play a positive role *insofar as they provide the context and substance for even greater expressions and cultivations of non-attachment*" (emphasis added).

As Reynolds's example of the story of Jōtika and King Ajātasattu illustrates, Jōtika's great wealth affords an opportunity for proving his non-attachment by a supreme act of voluntary divestiture. In short, wealth is to be accumulated as a means for demonstrating selflessness through displays of appropriate generosity. As long as one views wealth in this provisional and instrumental way, it is legitimate to observe the dhammic prescriptions in order to acquire, according to the law of kammic retribution, "a greater abundance of material wealth, either in this life or in a future life."

Reynolds is perhaps not as precise as he might be concerning the attention given to self and other in acting to generate wealth, either in this incarnation or in the next. He suggests that in the mythic accounts of the ideal societies pure adherence to the *dhamma* yields "a superabundance of wealth and well-being." Furthermore, the proper performance of monastic requirements "works to assure the wealth of the community," "because of the unity of the religiomoral, the societal, and the natural orders." He continues: "The actions commended by dhammic norms are thought to be conducive not only to the wealth of the community, but simultaneously to the wealth of the individuals who perform them." And he and Clifford (1980: 62) elaborate the same point elsewhere:

> As related in the Agganna *sutta*, the monks constitute the perfect primordial humans, while the laity constitute the resplendent power of the natural world order. As a result of the monk's pure and selfless action, the laity prosper, they bear children, they enjoy successful and abundant harvests, they own healthy livestock, and so on. The monks, for their part, offer themselves selflessly to the pure *dhamma* and, as a result, the *dhamma* of world order flourishes, thereby enabling the laity to continue to support the monks in their ascetic and renunciative endeavor.

It is likely we should understand these statements as implying that the proper Theravadin, who has, of course, the correctly ambivalent attitude toward wealth, ought to act, among other reasons, so as to make wealth possible for others as well as for himself or herself. That is, part of being selfless is to encourage selflessness in others, and since possessing wealth can be, as Reynolds shows, an opportunity for expressing selflessness, it is benevolent to seek to provide others, as well as oneself, with the opportunities that wealth occasions. So exhibited, this material exemplifies, in the terminology of ethical study, a religiously qualified form of extrapersonal (or altruistic) teleology.[3]

It is teleological, as we have already noted, because all prescribed attitudes and actions are finally justified with reference to attaining *nibbāna*, the end of all suffering. It is extrapersonal (or altruistic) because the underlying normative assumption is that right action consists in maximizing the welfare (and minimizing the suffering) of all beings, including all human persons, by helping them to achieve their final end. Accordingly, it is fully in keeping with the extrapersonal spirit of the Theravāda system for the monks to observe the *dhamma* in the hope that the laity may thereby be made prosperous, so that the laity, in turn, may themselves be more generous and selfless and thus make ''soteriological progress.''

Finally, it is religiously qualified in that the attainment of the sacred goal, *nibbāna*, eclipses, in the last analysis, the material world, including all sentient beings, and of course all objects of gratification, such as wealth. We emphasize, as Reynolds does, that this objective does *not* efface the significance (or ''positive valorization'') of the material world, including wealth. But it does most certainly relegate it to having a provisional and instrumental function. In a word, the world, including wealth, is a grand ''proving ground'' toward a supernatural outcome.

In connection with this point the system is also religiously qualified in the sense that the prescribed patterns of generosity are governed by a belief in the *superiority of religious giving*, of giving, that is, to religiously elevated persons and communities, namely the monks and the *sangha*. We shall make more of this below.

ADDITIONAL ITEMS FOR STUDY

Reynolds's discussion of wealth and poverty brings forward a very important aspect of Theravāda practical thought, to which students of ethics, along with others, need to give much attention. No one can consult, for example, the *Book of Discipline* or accounts of later developments in respect to economic life among the Theravadins (e.g. Gunawardana 1979) without marking the abiding concern over the acquisition, management, and expenditure of wealth. All current efforts toward the comparative study of religious ethics stand in need of investigations of this sort.

Moreover, as Reynolds rightly emphasizes, such efforts must also attend to bodies or ''genres'' of literature and practice beyond the classical texts and learned commentaries and treatises. Reynolds's allusions to ritual, myth, and stories are all highly instructive. (The Little-Twiss effort, for example, would be deeply enriched by investigating such material.)

Reynolds's discussion of ''the primacy of *dhamma*'' does suggest a modification of the Little-Twiss interpretation. Our description of the Theravāda notion of ''sacred authority'' ought to be broadened to include the *dhamma*.[4] According to Reynolds, ''the *dhamma* (variously translated as *truth, norm, law,* etc.) provides a religio-ethical 'center of gravity' for Theravāda Buddhism. Within the context of the classical Theravāda orientation it is the *dhamma* that constitutes the structure and dynamics of all reality, including both the phenomenal world and salvation itself. The *dhamma* is also the normative truth that establishes guidelines for all forms of action that Theravadins approve or commend.''

This description of *dhamma* appears to conform in important respects to our defining characteristics of ''sacred authority'': special distinctiveness, special prominence, and determinativeness in regard to practice (Little and Twiss 1978: 59–60). Such a revision is completely acceptable, as long, of course, as *nibbāna*, the ''supreme *dhamma* and the locus of salvation itself,'' is fully appreciated.

So understood, this revision, or rather extension, of the application of the notion of sacred authority to Theravāda teaching would broaden our understanding of the kind of ''religious qualification'' that is imposed upon the basic norms of Theravāda practical thought, namely, extrapersonal teleology. Accordingly, the dhammic teachings themselves would be understood to be specially authoritative because they constitute the *exclusive means* for achieving *nibbāna*. They comprise, as the *Sutta-Nipata* has it, ''the excellent Dhamma leading to *nibbāna* to the greatest benefit (for all)'' (Müller 1965: 39).

This point about *dhamma* leads to a further clarification and elaboration of the kind of basic teleological norm that is characteristic of Theravāda practical thought. Though we do not include or make use of the distinction in our book, it is conventional in the study of ethics to distinguish between *extrinsic* and *intrinsic* forms of teleology. This distinction refers to the relationship between means and ends in a given teleological system. ''An extrinsic means is one which is itself not constituent of the end, and its only value derives from the fact that it is a cause of the end's coming into being'' (Ladd 1957: 167). An example is Bentham's brand of utilitarianism, in which attitudes and acts are held to be good or bad depending variously on the yield of pleasure or pain. ''Intrinsic means are, on the other hand, constitutive elements in the end'' (Ladd 1957: 168). Aristotle's eudaemonism is an example. The designated end is in part made up of, and is consistent with, only certain kinds of attitudes and actions.

It seems clear, on Reynolds's account, that Theravāda teleology is of the intrinsic sort. This is, I take it, what Reynolds means when he says that ''the *dhamma* . . . constitutes the structure and dynamics of all reality, including both the phenomenal world and salvation itself.'' That the way of life prescribed by the *dhamma*, including certain dispositions and meditative practices, is (in part) *constitutive* of the harmonious function of ''ordinary reality,'' as well as the attainment of salvation, is of course what is decisive in ascribing the label of intrinsic teleology to Theravāda thought.

CROSS-CULTURAL ETHICAL COMPARISONS

Even if the "ethical translation" performed above is, as I believe it to be, convincing and thoroughly compatible with the basic arguments of Reynolds's essay, one is still entitled to wonder whether there is any particular advantage to casting the material in the way the "ethicist" persists in doing. Two responses come to mind, one defensive and the second more offensive in character.

First, if the exercise is successful, we have some evidence for doubting that the divide between the ethicists and the historians is, at least at certain important points, as big as is often assumed. Second, by employing the conventional categories for the study of practical reasoning, we are readily able to place Theravāda reflections on wealth and poverty into a cross-cultural comparative framework that reveals differences of the greatest significance and, at the same time, a way of locating and accounting for the differences.

For example, the Theravadins appear to exhibit nothing comparable to the western theological and philosophical traditions' cogitation and controversy over distributive justice and intense perplexity over the plight of the poor. There is, apparently, no similar Theravadin literature on distributive problems, nor is it the poor as such who are for the Theravadins the primary objects of beneficence. One important reason (no doubt among others) for this remarkable difference in emphasis and outlook is related to the nature of the practical system of Theravāda Buddhism as revealed by the Little-Twiss framework. The Theravadins already presuppose a distributive system of cosmic proportions keyed to an intrinsic brand of teleology. According to the law of *kamma*, wealth and poverty, in any given instance, are the respective consequences of complying or not complying with the prescriptions of the *dhamma*. Accordingly, wealth and poverty are, speaking generally, assumed to be distributed justly—that is, on the basis of dhammic performance in a previous life. In a word, the Theravadins assume a cosmic distributive system determined on the basis of "just deserts."

There is, to be sure, what might be called the "lag-time" problem that is posed by Reynolds's example of the wealthy person of doubtful virtue. Naturally, if there is any question of the probity, according to dhammic standards, of a given rich person, then on the logic of the system, the legitimacy (as well as the chances for long-term retention) of that person's wealth is in jeopardy.

But what is most interesting and most revealing in Reynolds's account is the provision available to the wealthy person for rectifying his or her predicament:

> Possessors of wealth must convince the community that they have achieved a level of non-attachment and generosity that ensures that they will spend what they have acquired in accord with dhammic norms. Thus it is that among Theravadins the need to establish the legitimacy of one's wealth has been one of the more obvious motivations for the construction of reliquary *thūpas* devoted to the Buddha, the sponsorship of festivals honoring the *dhamma*, and the ostentatious giving of gifts to the *sangha*.

Our attention is drawn here to the basic and pervasive belief in the superiority of religious giving, which is thoroughly consistent with the sort of practical system Theravāda Buddhism is and which also explains the relatively moderate attention that is devoted to the poor in the Theravadin tradition.[5]

As Reynolds points out, "clearly the most important and effective type of giving is that directed to the Buddha and/or the *sangha*." The underlying reason, of course, is that the system is finally religiously qualified in the way we designated above. The ultimate (religious) objective is to achieve non-attachment in all things and, thereby, overcome attachment to the self, others, material objects, and so on. If, therefore, one gives to religious persons and communities, one approximates more closely the ultimate objective of nibbanic non-attachment. One thereby acts in greater conformity with the requirements of *dhamma* and can properly expect one's just deserts as the result.

There is a related reason for the superiority of acts of religious giving. It is surely the emphasis placed in the tradition on the priority of teaching as the way to enlightenment and, consequently, to ultimate happiness for all (see Aronson 1980: 17). If it is true that the happiness of all is maximized to the degree that all conform to the *dhamma*, acts that promote the spread of the *dhamma* by means of facilitating the work of the monks are acts of superior worth.

We may add a brief response—pertinent in this context—to Reynolds's passing reference to the "unmistakably bourgeois" character of the Theravāda economic ethic. He calls attention to the aversion to waste and the preference for "honest economic activity," phrases that suggest, in part, Max Weber's famous discussion of the Protestant ethic. However correct these references are, a crucial distinguishing feature remains between the Theravadin and the Puritan economic ethic. It is precisely the emphasis in the Theravāda tradition on the superiority of religious giving and the systematic lack of such an emphasis among the Puritans. As Spiro (1970: 460) points out, the comparative consequences for economic development have been striking.

> For the Puritan, who has already been predestined for salvation or damnation, successful economic action—if Weber is correct—provides him with the proof that he is one of the elect, and savings are to be reinvested to create further wealth—for the greater glory of God. For the Buddhist, whose salvation is problematic, successful economic action is a prerequisite to enhancing his chances of salvation, and savings are to be spent on *dana* [religious giving]. . . . For the Buddhist, the proof of salvation is to be found, not in accumulating and creating new wealth, but in giving it away in the form of *dana*.

I have intentionally reserved comment on the methodological questions until my exercise could be completed. Rather than speak in the air about the large questions of theory and approach, I wanted first to exhibit in some detail what one kind of ethicist, at least, does when he turns his hand to interpreting the observations of a historian of religion.

Most of what I have tried to do to this point is aimed at demonstrating that the suspicion and skepticism toward the conventional study of ethics that seems to animate many historians of religion and others is itself open to question. If I have succeeded in showing that my first major conclusion is correct—that Reynolds's basic argument is readily translatable without distortion into the terms and categories familiar to ethicists, it is pointless to go on acting as though some absolute and unbridgeable divide existed between ethicists and historians of religion. My exercise does not, of course, prove that there are never important differences of approach, objective, and interest, but it does suggest that we need to get down to specific cases in order to find out just where those points are. I am more and more convinced that purely abstract theoretical discussions are next to useless.

Three related issues bear mentioning here. First, assuming the translation has worked, we shall have no choice but to give careful attention to definitions of basic terms such as *religion* and *morality.* We have seen that the Theravāda system is, inferring from Reynolds's account, a religiously qualified one. Accordingly, we shall need clearer and fuller specifications of just what we mean when we say that (see, for example, Little and Twiss 1978: Chaps. 1–3). This is by no means an ethicist's quibble. Reynolds himself makes important distinctions among the basic terms: when historians of religion get involved in the study of comparative religious ethics, he says, they "direct their attention to ethical expressions that are religious in character. The interpretation of ethical expressions that are found outside the orbit of religion is left to others." But he does not go very far toward indicating what he means by the terms. It is not helpful to advocate being "broad and flexible" without showing the inadequacies of proposed definitions and substituting and defending, in some detail, one's own.

Our second conclusion demonstrated that, in the sort of dialogue this interchange represents, ethicists have much to learn from historians of religion. Ethicists need to be prompted to consider bodies of literature and practice that are quite independent of official scriptures and discourses and often better reflect the "lived experience" of religious traditions. Moreover, the analytical and reconstructive efforts of ethicists must stand open to correction and revision in the light of the insights and investigations of specialists, much as our observations about *dhamma* were altered in the light of Reynolds's essay and our discussion of wealth deeply illuminated and informed by it.

Our third conclusion suggested that historians of religion have, in turn, something to learn from ethicists. It is useful to view religious materials in terms of categories that make them readily available to cross-cultural comparison, as long, of course, as the categories do not do violence to those materials. We made several suggestions that seem worth pursuing in respect to distributive justice, attitudes toward the poor, and economic activity.

On these points of approach and method, I believe, the two sides have a good deal in common. But one aspect of Reynolds's approach—and a very significant one—is not so easily accommodated. It has to do with what Reynolds means by the "holistic understanding" (Reynolds 1980: 130) of religious ethics, a term that in his essay in this volume apparently implies the following: "the distinctive configurations of elements that constitute each tradition must be taken very seriously into account when the interpretation of any particular element is being considered."[6]

THE ISSUE OF HOLISM

To begin with, serious theoretical problems with holism have been skillfully laid out and dissected by D. C. Phillips (1976) and as a consequence of his work, now require rebuttal if such a method is going to continue to hold up its head. Most critical is the problem of establishing in the first place just what constitutes the tradition as a whole.

For example, one is struck in Reynolds's essay by the lack of attention to historical variation and divergence within the Theravāda tradition, as, for instance, Gunawardana (1979: 77–78) exhibits. Reynolds's generalizations about the tradition as a whole would be strengthened by more careful and detailed comparative textual exegesis, together with comparative analysis of the changing social and historical contexts in which the variations take place. In other words, undertaking to characterize a religious tradition as a whole, and to study it accordingly, is itself a substantial endeavor. Claims about such things and reasons for selecting one set of generalizations rather than another must be carefully argued for; they may not be assumed.

In any case, even if a certain kind of holistic approach is useful (and that needs to be demonstrated), it is not clear why it must exclude more limited studies of particular periods and aspects of religious traditions, depending on the interest and concern of the investigator. Indeed, we have endeavored to show in the above exercise that a holistic approach is not necessarily at odds with the more delimited concerns of the conventional ethicist.

4 Comparative Religious Ethics as a Field:

Faith, Culture, and Reason in Ethics

Russell F. Sizemore

Within the modern era the field of religious ethics has been notoriously difficult to define in its relationship to philosophical ethics, philosophy of religion, and philosophy in general. It should come as no surprise, then, that the emergence of comparative religious ethics as a subfield of inquiry has occasioned a similar discussion over the nature of religion and its relationship to philosophical reason and has been marked by a corresponding disagreement over methodology. Although preoccupation with methodology is certainly foolish, in the case of comparative religious ethics methodological reflection combined with case studies should prove to be a productive investigation for religious studies generally. For it promises to add a measure of concreteness to the previous more theoretical debate, and in doing so it provides an area of application that may be used to test, so to speak, the different perspectives that the abstract debate has occasioned.

In the present volume the debate over methodology in comparative religious ethics is represented by the essays of Frank Reynolds and David Little (Chaps. 2 and 3). Both directly address methodological questions in preparation for their substantive analyses, and both are self-consciously working to overcome the split in the field marked by the "ethicists" and the "historians."[1] Reynolds contends that a new "religiohistorical" approach is now emerging; Little argues that the split has been overdrawn and that the language of philosophical ethics can faithfully encapsulate the historians' observations. In this essay I shall argue that these two solutions restate rather than resolve the controversy.

In spite of the debate's seriousness and duration, part of the problem has been that the two sides' arguments have not been directly engaged with one another and the lines of contention need clarification. While historians have been arguing about how knowledge is to be gained, ethicists have been disputing about what form the answers should take and about what should count as an answer in the field of religious ethics. The deeper problem that lurks behind this discussion, as I suggested above, is the question of how the field of comparative ethics is to be defined in its subject matter and basic orientation as an academic discipline. Unfortunately, this debate can be settled only by arbitrary academic convention or by adopting as absolute one or the other of two disputed conceptions of human knowing now being discussed in contemporary philosophy. Accordingly, I shall argue that the best resolution is to adopt a broad definition of the field that allows both sets of interests and orientations to be recognized as appropriate and both sets of practitioners to be recognized as members. In closing I will suggest that there are some channels by which the different interests of the two sides might be combined and point to some openings for this sort of synthesis in the essay by David Little.

HERMENEUTICS AND INTEREST: WHAT IS THE OBJECT OF STUDY?

One persistent theme in the debate represented by Reynolds and Little has to do with how one is to go about the reading of religious texts. What is required, in the way of scholarly research and intuitive engagement, to make sense of such texts? How does one uncover what it is that a text, or some other feature in a religious tradition, has to say about a given topic in ethics?

The issue is one of hermeneutics, and the historians have in mind a pragmatic theory of meaning in the tradition of Max Weber: the scholar must see the world from within the tradition under study—Weber's notion of *Verstehen*—and the scholar must look to see how the tradition's beliefs have been put into practice. Only in examining the historical embodiment of a particular religious faith, the historians might say, can one see how ideas ostensibly removed from matters of conduct have in fact shaped the tradition's pattern of social life. The ethicists' methodological sin, from the historians' point of view, is their attempt to reconstruct a code or systematic ethic from a single text, or material drawn from a single type of source, divorced from its world view, historical context, and communal embodiment.

Reynolds speaks to this point for the historians in his comments about interpreting the Theravāda conception of the *dhamma*: to understand any particular idea or doctrine in a tradition one must examine a variety of the tradition's genres of religious expression. The scholar must consider foundational myths, sacred narratives and histories, ritual and devotional activity, even methods of pastoral counseling, as well as systematic philosophical discourses and explicit moral codes, to get at a tradition's beliefs and views. One has to come to terms with a tradition's religious life and affections, its distinctive vision and characteristic patterns of sensibility, in order to grasp any specific feature, such as its ethic. And, ideally, the scholar should also be familiar with the historical and geographical diversity of a tradition in order to be able to separate the more permanent and influential elements from the transient and trivial.

The historians' ideal sets a standard that is perhaps unreachable, and yet as guidance for understanding what a tradition has to say on a particular subject, it would be hard to argue against the desire for breadth in source material and historical awareness. Over the course of the debate this point seems to have gained general acceptance. David Little, for example, in his present response to Reynolds's essay, and speaking generally for the ethicists, agrees wholeheartedly with the value of attending to sources beyond the classical texts. He welcomes the assistance of the historians to bring forward the best sources of a tradition's "lived experience." And he invites the corrections and revisions they have to offer on the basis of greater historical familiarity with these traditions. In this both sides freely acknowledge the historical complexity of religious traditions, and so, on this hermeneutical matter, there seems to be no conflict at all.

One related question, however, which Little raises, does seem to apply to method at this level. The point of disagreement at the level of hermeneutics, if there is one, has to do with the degree of the historians' attachment to the view known as *holism*.

Reynolds asserts that the study of the ethics of any religious tradition must be placed "within the context of a holistic understanding of that tradition." By this I think he means the need for placing individual religious expressions into their historical and interpretative settings, the point just described and which Little accepts. Reynolds is careful to avoid claiming that religious traditions possess central, unchanging essences making them so unique that cross-cultural studies are rendered impossible. But he does go fairly far along in disallowing the study of any element of a tradition in isolation from the rest, and this means that broad generalizations about a tradition as a whole will be required whenever any facet of the tradition is under study. Again, Reynolds's summary comments about the *dhamma* at the outset of his essay illustrate this point. Thus, it seems the historians are at least tempted by the stronger version of holism which holds that any given utterance, principle, or exemplary figure within a religious tradition can be described only in connection with a characterization of the tradition as a whole. Little rightly points out that holism in this stronger form has been seriously criticized and that the generalizations required to support such a method make for a substantial if not impossible endeavor. His closing comment on this matter, which more or less sums up the ethicists' response to the historians' hermeneutical contentions, is that although the ideal of breadth is surely sound it does not forbid more limited studies of particular periods, practices, or concepts, subject as these are to correction by specialists in a tradition. Such focused analyses ironically may be more faithful to a tradition's historical diversity than an approach that depends upon broad generalizations.

Although we cannot resolve the theoretical debate over holism here, Little's warnings are surely well taken. Both historians and ethicists have reason to be wary of generalizations, much as they seek them. It will be interesting to note at a later point, however, that Little's own attempts to characterize the Theravāda ethical system invite the same sort of scrutiny and concern. At that point we may be able to reach a more profitable resolution of the issues raised by attempts to characterize whole traditions.

So much for the argument of the historians and the ethicists' present acquiescence in these hermeneutical matters. On the other side of the debate the issue at stake is not so much how to interpret a text as it is about the appropriate conceptual categories for analyzing what one finds. On this side ethicists have pressed for the importance of clear definitions of religion and ethics and for rigorous analytical categories. There is, they argue, no escaping from the western background that western scholars bring to their work and no alternative to independent conceptual analysis if one is going to get to the heart of a tradition's ethics. The point is to be self-conscious about the categories one employs. The problem with the historians, from the ethicists' point of view, is that although they may be well informed about their traditions they are insufficiently discriminating in their observations and unfamiliar with the questions and issues of ethics.

Along this line, David Little, in this volume, contends that there is no great divide between the historians and the ethicists, but then he goes on to argue for the need for an "ethical translation" of the historians' findings to make them useful for comparative study. Little claims that "by employing the conventional categories for the study of practical reasoning, we are readily able to place Theravāda reflection on wealth and poverty into a cross-cultural comparative framework that reveals differences of the greatest significance and, at the same time, a way of locating and accounting for the differences."

As with the historians' appeal for historical breadth, no one is likely to argue against the need for clarity and focused definitions. Nor does the question of the western bias of interpretative categories seem to be insurmountable. Reynolds accepts the western academic tradition as an appropriate place to develop the field of comparative ethics, and he calls for heightened self-consciousness from historians concerning the questions they ask and the modes of rationality they assume. Once again it would appear that the debate is easily resolved, with each side yielding to the strengths of the other.

But here the appearance of unanimity is deceptive. The gap between the historians and the ethicists is not really about insufficient allegiance to the virtues of clarity, or even about the cultural imperialism of using categories provided by western thought. The problem is that they have different questions to put to their material. They disagree over what it is that they should be clear about, over the sorts of categories that are required for the studies they want to do. They disagree over the object of the field as a discipline.

The historians, whether or not they put it in these terms, tend to conceive of the field of religious ethics as the intersection of religious thought and historical sociology. The object of the field is to illuminate how a given tradition has shaped its adherents' conduct, in aspiration and historical embodiment. The general point of the discipline is to uncover the relationship between conduct and religious faith or, more broadly, between *faith and culture*. Here, the content of a tradition's faith, particularly its behavioral guidance, is compared with its cultural context. By contrast, the ethicists conceive of the field of religious ethics primarily as the intersection of moral philosophy and the philosophy of religion. The general object of the field as they see it is to illuminate the relationship between *faith and reason*, within religious traditions, as these have guided conduct. Thus, for example, two of the most influential volumes on this subject by ethicists, Ronald Green's *Religious Reason* (1978) and Little and Twiss's *Comparative Religious Ethics: A New Method* (1978), in spite of their differences, agree that the point of comparative ethics is first of all to compare the *forms* of practical reasoning employed by religious traditions. The content of the traditions is clearly a secondary matter. How, they have asked, in a given tradition does religious reasoning about conduct relate to moral (i.e., irreligiously rational) and prudential reasoning about conduct? Given their shared view that the essence of a religious ethic is the sort of reasoning it provides to its adherents in thinking about their conduct, the point of comparative study is to see how different traditions illuminate the general relationships among religion, morality, and reason.[2]

So it is that Little's "comparative framework" employs the terms and categories of his chosen field and puts attention on the issues of interest to that field. These issues are not necessarily the same as what the historians have in mind when they set out to do comparative ethics. Unfortunately, this dispute over the appropriate object of study has been concealed by the hermeneutical questions described above and dispute over professional expertise. As historians, for a variety of reasons, found the ethicists' case studies unsatisfying, their objections too often suggested that the problem was simply the ethicists' inadequate acquaintance with the traditions under study. Ethicists interpreted the historians' dissatisfaction as an expression of their unfamiliarity with western philosophical ethics. In fact, the fundamental methodological divide was the participants' interests in different issues.

THE STATUS OF MORAL REASON: A DISAGREEMENT OVER EPISTEMOLOGY

Can the divide between the historians and the ethicists be bridged? Or if the two positions are mutually exclusive, is there a right answer about what should be the object of the field of comparative ethics? It is possible to accept both answers and regard the differences we have observed as simply variations of personal interest. We could say that one group is counting the nutrients in a meal, the other is describing the spices and the taste; a comprehensive approach includes both sets of questions. This solution suggests that the best strategy for the field at present is to move beyond methodological arguments and allow case studies to focus whatever debate persists. As a more or less diplomatic solution to the divisions in the field, this resolution has much to recommend it.

Still, the participants in the debate have generally felt that something more was at stake than an individual preference in subject matter. Arguments on both sides of this issue have suggested that one of these approaches ought to be pursued (and that the contrary approach ought not to be pursued) because to do otherwise was to violate the standards of good scholarship and to distort the subject matter at hand. Each group regarded its own conception of the field as the most apt, or even as obligatory, because of more deeply held conceptions concerning the nature of religion, ethics, and human knowledge.

Looking to the deeper intellectual underpinnings of the two approaches, we find a reflection of a current dispute in the philosophy of knowledge. Essentially, the two sides mirror the empiricist and the formalist epistemological orientations. Ethicists follow the formalists in regarding morality as an epistemologically autonomous human enterprise, an approach that makes it worthwhile to compare religion and morality with respect to rationality. *Moral* reasoning is seen as a distinctive employment of reason for guiding behavior, separate, for example, from prudence and aesthetics. Accordingly, formalist-inspired moral philosophy in this century has been largely concerned with working out how this form of guidance is related to other uses of reason. Religious ethics in turn has been largely concerned with sorting out how religion compares with these other action-guiding institutions.[3] Subsequently, comparative religious ethics as conducted by ethicists trained in philosophical ethics has played the role of proving ground for the ethicists' concepts of religion, morality, and reason.

The historians side more with followers of Hume and Hegel who look with suspicion upon talk of autonomous reason. They see the ethicists' approach as part of a general ''flight from authority'' in reason and morality which can sustain itself only by ignoring history and cultural diversity.[4] The historians tend to argue for the culturally embedded quality of all knowledge, including moral knowledge. Hence they see the very concept of rationality as itself a social construct and the diverse forms of behavioral guidance, which the ethicists want to distinguish, as all part of the seamless web of a culture's ethos. Reynolds's ''holism,'' his refusal to separate ethics from metaphysics and aesthetics, is grounded in his view that moral sensibilities are inseparable from the way one makes sense of the world. Subsequently, comparative religious ethics as conducted by the historians is an attempt to trace out the social and cultural components of the world's diverse ways of ordering thought and conduct.

Rightly or wrongly, these basic loyalties tempt the ethicists to accuse the historians of flirting with relativism and having an insufficient allegiance to rationality. In turn, the historians see the ethicists as pandering to an arrogant notion of reason and a disparaging conception of the religious life. The ethicists' and historians' divergent interests are to some extent inseparable from these conflicting conceptions of reason, religion, and morality. Thus, if pursued persistently, the methodological debate in comparative ethics leads to some of the most basic controversies in philosophical and moral epistemology. And these discussions in turn shape the status given to religious studies as part of the curriculum in the secular academy.

One could attempt to settle the debate in religious ethics by showing one of these underlying positions to be compelling. But, given the fact that the epistemological dispute is still unresolved in philosophical circles, this sort of settlement by students in religion does not seem to be forthcoming. It would also be a strange thing to ask students of religion to become full-blooded philosophers and masters of epistemology as a prerequisite for their work in religious ethics. But until some progress is made, practitioners on both sides of the question must resist the temptation to pretend that the issue is already settled. The twentieth-century dominance of the formalists thus cannot be used as proof of the ethicists' view, nor can the recent appearance of several highly respected philosophers on the empiricist side be taken as proof of the historians' claims.

Thus we have a difference that cannot be ignored but that cannot at present be resolved. It is still possible, however, to adopt a broad enough conception of the discipline to allow for both orientations. This follows the diplomatic solution mentioned above. The point is that scholars can disagree over which approach within the field is the most profitable without suggesting that those who take the opposing view have failed to meet minimal standards of the discipline. This requires that each side recognize the contributions of the other side as at least worthy of consideration and good-faith dispute. In the final analysis each group will be judged on its ability to illuminate the tradition under study and to show its bearing on matters of general significance. Each side's success in doing so may be taken as additional support for its epistemological orientation. Thus, as the field of philosophy includes both empiricists and formalists and the field of political science includes both natural-law theorists and their critics, so the field of comparative religious ethics can include both empiricist and formalist historians and ethicists.

FORMS OF REASONING AND SOTERIOLOGICAL BELIEFS: OPENINGS FOR A SYNTHESIS

If case studies in comparative ethics are the testing ground for the methodological assumptions and epistemological foundations we have discussed, it may be illuminating to take a closer look at David Little's essay as an example of how some of the debate's divergent concerns can be brought together. Although Little structures his chapter as an argument for the suitability of his own approach, I would like to suggest that his conclusions push beyond the limits of his method, perhaps more than he realizes. There are hints in his analysis of a more comprehensive and more integrated conception of the field. In particular, the extent to which he is drawn in practice to employ Theravāda religious concepts and not just formal reasoning to explain Theravāda's historical impact indicates the beginnings of a synthesis of the divergent interests of the two approaches we have been considering.

In a passage cited above, Little claims that his framework reveals, locates, and accounts for the most significant and distinctive elements of the Theravāda tradition. The point of his "ethical translation" is to prove that there is no serious conflict between the historians and the ethicists and to show the way that the historians' material on one tradition can be prepared for comparison with other traditions. His implicit claim is that his categories really are penetrating enough to ground both sets of interests, philosophical and sociological. But if we examine closely the evidence he presents for this claim we may discover some methodological tensions.

In the language of his ethical translation Little characterizes Theravāda Buddhist ethical reasoning as a "kind of 'religious qualification' that is imposed upon the basic norms of Theravāda practical thought, namely, extrapersonal teleology." According to Little, Buddhist reasoning is teleological because all prescribed attitudes and actions are justified on the basis of their furthering the goal of attaining *nibbāna*. It is extrapersonal because this goal extends to maximizing the welfare of all beings, not just the agent alone. And it is of the intrinsic sort of teleology because the means toward this goal (attitudes and action in accord with the *dhamma*) are intrinsically related to the goal (since *nibbāna* is, in a sense, the complete expression of the *dhamma*).

Little observes in a note and in several places in his discussion that this final categorization of Buddhist ethics has come with some difficulty. In his earlier book, with S. B. Twiss, Little offered three possible Buddhist patterns of ethical reasoning (Little and Twiss 1978: Chap. 8). His citation of Aronson's "hybrid" validating pattern similarly acknowledges the presence in Buddhism of several different forms of teleological reasoning. Part of the difficulty here has to do with the interplay between egoistic and altruistic elements in Buddhist ethics. If the goal of *nibbāna* is adopted only for oneself, the system has an egoistic tilt; if this orientation toward the self is qualified, by metaphysical convictions or by adopting the goal of *nibbāna* for all beings, the system is altruistic. Little's current view is that the altruistic classification provides, "all things considered, the most satisfactory description."

But one could also ask whether the tradition is as decidedly teleological as these studies have claimed. Although *nibbāna* is clearly the aim of existence for Buddhists, it is not so clear that all Buddhists think of their attitudes and actions as being justified by the progress they make toward that goal. As Little himself notes in talking about the *dhamma* and in describing intrinsic forms of teleological reasoning, Buddhists also understand their actions in terms of dhammic rules and as ultimately justified by their consonance with the most fundamental structure of reality (which is what the *dhamma* is about). These features of Buddhist reasoning suggest a deontological rationale for behavior: what makes an act right is that it is done with right-mindfulness (i.e., with correct awareness of the true nature of things). Such right acts will also advance the actor, and presumably his society, toward *nibbāna*, but the act's rightness is due to its consonance with reality, not its salvific efficacy.[5]

Incidentally, a similar combination of forms of reasoning obtains in Christianity, and perhaps in all religious traditions. The Christian aim of existence, the Kingdom of God, may, too, serve as the goal for all ethical striving and similarly establish a teleological form of reasoning. Or, as in Buddhism, the right act may be seen as right because of its consonance with natural law, with revealed law, or with the commandment to love, even as the adherent assumes that the right act will also further the Kingdom. Similarly, although it does make sense to distinguish egoistic and altruistic utterances in Theravāda Buddhism, it is generally problematic to use these categories with religious ethics, since, again, most religious traditions rather prominently employ a paradoxical identification of self-negation and self-fulfillment.[6]

The interesting point here is not that one of Little's characterizations of Buddhist moral reasoning is the right one and the others are mistaken, nor even that one of these characterizations is the best and most generally accurate. What we see in these diverse characterizations of Buddhism are indications of distinctive tensions within the tradition. Presumably, these tensions are reflected in the diverse ways that different Buddhists talk about why such and such an action is the right thing to do. Some Buddhists do sound just as Little says they should, as extrapersonal teleologists, justifying every action in terms of its contribution to the goal of *nibbāna* for all beings. Others speak of *nibbāna* as only a personal accomplishment and seem to be egocentric teleologists. Still others see Buddhism as a deontological system, or they find both tendencies in their Buddhist faith. If the scholar were to attempt to characterize the tradition as a whole, he or she would be poorly served by having to select just one classification. A far more penetrating approach would be to identify the pivotal contentions—the salient religious beliefs, the determinative interpretations of various aspects of their tradition—that, for several different Buddhists, shape their readings of moral situations and decide these issues of ethical reasoning one way or the other.[7]

At this point the debate over holism has a point. At its best, the historians' commitment to holism was, ironically, the conviction that broader studies of a tradition across its history would be bound to draw out these sorts of tensions. Their claim was that this web of tensions—"the tradition as a whole"—had to be kept in mind when examining any particular proponent within a tradition. To arrive at a single characterization of a whole tradition from limited sources was clearly dangerous. This would be the sort of excess simplification for which holism has been rightly criticized, by Little and others, although here Little himself seems in danger of falling into this trap. But, of course, there is no need to characterize Buddhism or any other religious tradition as exclusively employing one particular type of ethical reasoning. Presumably, the point of descriptive work and the value of a system of classification such as Little proposes is the ability to locate and focus the diversity that is present within any given tradition in preparation for making comparisons with other traditions. At any rate, the ability to discriminate within a tradition seems an essential first step if one is going to be able to select fruitful candidates for comparison.

If it is true that a single characterization of a tradition's ethical reasoning is not necessary, there is still the question of what sort of characterization is the most helpful. The categories developed by Little and Twiss are drawn from philosophical ethics and are largely formal. They primarily scrutinize and describe the form of reasoning or practical justification employed by a tradition rather than the tradition's moral content or underlying religious ideas. But in my view what is most significant about Little's essay is the extent to which he is drawn beyond such limits in trying to demonstrate his method's value.

In his characterization of Theravāda Buddhist reasoning as extrapersonal teleological, Little also says that it was "religiously qualified." Buddhist ethical reasoning, he notes, was qualified by the religious belief that attainment of *nibbāna* eclipsed any ultimate value for the material world, and of course wealth, and was qualified by the belief that religious giving—giving to religiously elevated persons and institutions—is superior in spiritual and material benefits produced. When Little turns to demonstrate the usefulness of his conclusions, it is these religious beliefs and other aspects of the Buddhist world view—and not the debated points about which form of teleology Buddhism employs—that carry the weight.

For example, Little observes that the Theravāda tradition seems to lack the West's "cogitation and controversy over distributive justice" and its "intense perplexity over the plight of the poor." The value of his method, Little says, is that it places Theravadin reflection on wealth and poverty into a cross-cultural comparative framework that can locate and account for such differences with the West. But no ethical translation is in evidence in the most important reason he provides for this particular difference: "according to the law of *kamma*, wealth and poverty, in any given instance, are the respective consequences of complying or not complying with the prescriptions of the *dhamma*. Accordingly, wealth and poverty are, speaking generally, assumed to be distributed justly—that is, on the basis of dhammic performance in a previous life." In other words, Theravadins lack debate about how to make society more just because their belief in *kamma* guarantees that the present distribution is just.

Again, in commenting upon the differences between Buddhist and Puritan economic activity, Little observes that the Buddhist's belief in the superiority of religious giving in the gaining of his salvation, as compared to the Puritan's duty to create new wealth in living out his salvation, has been at least partly responsible for the different economic histories of these cultures. Thus, the "crucial distinguishing feature" dividing the Theravāda economic ethos and the Puritan work ethic is not to be found in the forms of ethical reasoning these traditions employ, but rather in their particular religious beliefs about salvation and the workings of fate.

Little's evidence for his method actually and ironically reflects not so much the need for an ethical translation into formal categories, as the importance of a tradition's soteriological beliefs for its ethics. At least this is so if in a tradition's "ethics" we mean to include the way the religious tradition has shaped its adherents' social history. The point is not that Little's method is deficient but rather that it naturally leads us back to the content of the tradition's beliefs about salvation and its vision of cosmic order. The categories of philosophical ethics may be able to bring to the surface the logical tensions within a religious tradition, as Little claims, but his essay also suggests that it is often the way such categories are religiously qualified that is of the greatest interest. When the method is doing its job, it uncovers diverse forms of reasoning, which, rather than calling for some singular resolution, are clues to a tradition's internal options and determinative ambiguities.

In the final analysis, then, the debate between the ethicists and the historians calls us back to the most fundamental questions concerning the autonomy of reason as it has developed in the West and the role of religion in culture. These do not have to be antagonistic concerns. In fact, there is an easily cited precedent for their both being at the heart of religious studies masterfully pursued: Max Weber's work on the rise of instrumental rationality combined a keen interest in the sociological conditions of western rationality with a penetrating grasp of the impact of religious ideas on social organization. Little's own indebtedness to Weber is perhaps in part responsible for making his work go as far as it does in combining the interests and methods of the two approaches.[8]

What such a Weberian synthesis would say about the epistemological controversy mentioned above will be left to the reader's own reflections. One only hopes that it will not require another Weber to reunite historical breadth and philosophical acuity in the field of comparative religious ethics.

Part III.

WEALTH AND CHARITY

The Ethics of *Dāna*

Introduction

The following essays by John Strong and Nancy Auer Falk focus on the concept of *dāna* (giving, charity, generosity, liberality). Like most seminal terms in religious and ethical thought, *dāna* in Theravāda Buddhism possesses several different but related meanings. *Dāna* can refer to a character trait or *virtue*, a mode or type of *action*, or imply an esteemed cultural *value*. One who has a generous or giving nature, one who has a "danic" nature, helps others in an unstinting manner without regard to personal reward or benefit. Naturally, such a moral ideal also has practical consequences within traditional Theravāda cultures: patrons are to take care of the clients who serve them; masters are responsible for the material well-being of servants; hospitality conventions are ungrudgingly generous; and, in particular, those who produce and possess, that is the Buddhist laity, are to support those who do not produce and possess, that is, the Buddhist monastic establishment (*sangha*). The monastic establishment reciprocates this material support (*āmisadāna*) with another form of *dāna*—*dhammadāna*—the spiritual gifts represented by the Buddha's path (*magga*) which monks convey as teachers and, ideally, as exemplars.

Dāna, as an ethical concept, rests on the fundamental Theravāda view of things as differentiated and mutually interdependent (*paṭicca samuppāda*). Paradoxically, *dāna* also couples the religious ideal of selfless, uncalculating action with the assumption that generosity will be rewarded, if not in the present then in some future existence. In more specifically Buddhistic terms, *dāna* not only combines aspects of virtue, action, and value, but also integrates two differing validational concepts, *nibbāna* and *kamma*. *Nibbāna*, the Buddha's enlightenment, points to that which is beyond cause, calculation, reward; *kamma*, by contrast, stipulates a moral law of cause and effect or reward and punishment. *Dāna* bridges the two concepts. The dimensions of selflessness and non-attachment associated with generosity are nibbanic, but the expectation that generous deeds will be rewarded is kammic. *Dāna*, furthermore, incorporates both religious/monastic and moral/lay dimensions of Theravāda institutional life. The dhammic dimension of generosity (*dhammadāna*) is monastic whereas the material (*āmisadāna*) aspect is usually interpreted as lay support of the monastic order.

The chapters by Strong and Falk make the above points abundantly clear and in doing so focus our attention on the way in which the classical Theravāda Buddhist tradition viewed wealth: how it is to be acquired and used, how the well-off are to regard their wealth, and how the social uses of wealth are related to the individual's pursuit of perfection or salvation. The essays also serve to make an obvious but often overlooked point about the form of ethical instruction within classical Theravāda Buddhism. Moral ideals and action guides were conveyed at public meetings in stories, usually about moral exemplars like Vessantara, Aśoka, Anāthapiṇḍika, and Visākhā. These public meetings were and continue to be held at the quarters of the waxing and waning moon, especially during the period of the monastic Rains Retreat (*vassa*) from mid-July to mid-October. The stories in this section which form the basis of the discussion of charity (*dāna*) should be seen, therefore, as a popular oral literature; even when written down, they were intended to be read by monks to lay people within the context of a public meeting. The oral, narrative format had a practical intent. It made the instruction more interesting and easier to remember, especially for a largely illiterate lay audience; it contextualized moral ideals and action guides, making them appear attainable rather than removed from everyday life; and it brought together monk and lay person in a single, interdependent community.

John Strong's essay, Chapter 5, introduces the ideal of *dāna* by recounting the most popular story in Theravāda Buddhism outside the legend of the Prince Siddhattha's renunciation and eventual attainment of Buddhahood, namely, the *Jātaka* tale of Prince Vessantara's inexhaustible generosity. Vessantara's liberality led to his banishment from the capital of Sivi, his testing while exiled to a forest hermitage, and his eventual restoration—a narrative structure similar to the hero-legend of the Buddha. This parallelism, Strong argues, serves to emphasize the value of non-attachment, thereby bridging ideals of monastic and lay moral excellence. Strong uses another noted exemplar of *dāna*, Anāthapiṇḍika (one of the major figures also discussed by Nancy Falk), as a contrasting model of generosity, one that illustrates the value of devotion to the Buddha and the *sangha* and the promise of a better rebirth rather than enlightenment. Strong contends that the life of King Aśoka, popularized in the Sanskrit *Aśokāvadāna*, combines both models of generosity.

Within the Theravāda Buddhist tradition Aśoka has been revered for his personal virtue, the justice and equity of his rule, and his support of Buddhist monkhood. The *Aśokāvadāna* celebrates Aśoka's generosity toward the *sangha* by recounting the details of the *pañcavārṣika*, a ritual event held every five years during which the monarch makes a nearly incalculable material contribution to the monastic establishment. Strong's analysis of the *pañcavārṣika* and other *dāna* rituals associated with the Aśoka legend in various Sanskrit, Pāli, and Chinese Buddhist texts, and his linkage of these events with the practice of gift-giving in northern Thailand, Burma, and Laos on the occasion of temporary ordination into the monkhood, provide a fascinating insight into Theravāda moral values and ritual generally.

On a practical level, charity provides for the material well-being of the recipient. Charity toward the monastic order expresses devotion to the Buddha and the *sangha* and, furthermore, will result in a reward or restitution. The *pañcavārṣika* ceremony dramatizes this point symbolically: Aśoka gives everything to the monkhood, including himself; he is then "bought back," or redeemed, by his ministers for a donation of an additional four hundred thousand gold pieces. Strong contends that this giving of oneself to the monastic order provides more than an opportunity for further *dāna*. It blurs the distinction between lay and monastic communities: one not only gives away material things; one gives away oneself, that is, one joins the *sangha*, symbolically as in the case of the *pañcavārṣika* or literally in temporary ordination. One then returns to the lay life transformed, prepared to lead a responsible life as a married householder but with the knowledge of something more: monastic experience adds mastery of body and mind, and thus enables action without heedlessness, yet the ritual itself has given a foretaste of that ultimate aim of Buddhist existence in which conventional social and religious distinctions—between king and commoner, god (*deva*) and human—are transcended.

The Aśoka legends and the rituals of *dāna* demonstrate the complexity of the Theravāda understanding of charity or generous giving, an interweaving of the moral and religious, monastic and lay dimensions of the tradition. In a literal reading of the text *dāna* means material gift or donation, especially to the monastic order. As an action guide *dāna* condones the acquisition of wealth when coupled with virtue and generosity, as in the case of Aśoka. In Theravāda Buddhism wealth and generosity are reciprocally related. Without wealth generosity is limited, but without generosity the personal benefit of wealth, whether kammic or nibbanic, is lost. Ultimately, however, as the concluding stories of Aśoka make clear, a gift of small proportions outweighs the power of an entire royal treasury when it leads to "sovereignty over the mind."

Wealth and Charity

The theme of giving beyond all ordinary expectation and calculation or of giving to one's utmost limit (and beyond) which occurs at the end of the Aśoka legend is echoed in the canonical and commentarial tales of Anāthapiṇḍika and Visākhā analyzed by Nancy Falk in Chapter 6. Falk observes that the canonical accounts differentiate the type of *dāna* represented by the two figures. Anāthapiṇḍika, the wealthy merchant, makes a spectacular donation to the Buddha and his disciples. He buys a piece of land to be used as a monastic residence during the Rains Retreat from Prince Jeta of Savatthi for one hundred thousand pieces of gold. Visākhā, a devoted housewife, makes smaller gifts that meet the day-to-day needs of the monks. Falk argues that Visākhā's example legitimates the effectiveness of commonplace forms of *dāna*, the kind of charity available to ordinary people. Yet in the commentaries, Falk points out, Anāthapiṇḍika and Visākhā become a matched pair. This means that Visākhā, too, makes spectacular donations to the *sangha*, thus broadening the role open to women in holding prominent positions in lay society.

The stories of Vessantara and Aśoka, Anāthapiṇḍika and Visākhā differ, to be sure, but they share a set of assumptions about wealth and charity. As the reversals in the Vessantara, Aśoka, and Anāthapiṇḍika stories make abundantly clear, economic status is subject to the vagaries of time and fortune. Attachment to material possessions, therefore, can lead only to unhappiness (*dukkha*). True generosity is a good in itself, then, not primarily because of its beneficial consequences either for the receiver or the giver (although the tales make clear that such consequences inevitably accrue), but because giving expresses non-attachment, and non-attachment overcomes *dukkha*. Thus, we can understand why the wealthy, as in the case of Visākhā, will donate or give away their most prized possessions, or why Anāthapiṇḍika gives without limit and the subject of his funeral sermon is non-grasping. From this perspective *āmisadāna* (the gift of material things) and *dhammadāna* (the gift of *dhamma*) are but two sides of the same coin.

The stories analyzed by John Strong and Nancy Falk offer no program for the redistribution of wealth. Rather, they were meant to provide exemplars of lay people—high and low, male and female—who would inspire the listeners of these tales not only to be generous, but to develop the same attitude toward life ideally acquired by their monastic counterparts. *Dāna*, then, can be interpreted as a character trait acquired through the discipline of giving, much as a monk acquired an understanding of the *dhamma* through the discipline of meditation.

5 Rich Man, Poor Man, *Bhikkhu*, King:

Quinquennial Festival and the Nature of *Dāna*

John S. Strong

The practice of giving (*dāna*) has always been one of the hallmarks of Buddhist moral conduct. Although it does not figure among the Five Precepts (restraint from killing, stealing, illicit sex, lying, and drinking), it heads the postcanonical list of the Ten Good Deeds (*dasa kusala kamma*), which has been widely influential and popular in the Theravāda tradition (Gombrich 1971: 73–74).[1] Dāna has two basic forms: *āmisadāna*—the gift of material goods such as food and clothing, usually made by lay persons—and *dhammadāna*—the gift of *dhamma* usually (but, as we shall see, not always) consisting of sermons or teachings given by monks (Woodward 1932: 81; cf. Morris 1885: 91).

Buddhist tradition abounds with stories of "great givers" whose deeds of generosity serve even today as models for emulation or admiration. King Aśoka is one such paradigm. By way of introduction, however, it may be helpful to examine two others: Vessantara, whose story is found in the most popular of all the *Jātaka*, or tales of the Buddha's former lives, and Anāthapiṇḍika, who was one of the great early lay supporters of the Buddha.

The story of Vessantara is a sort of epic of *dāna* in which the *bodhisatta* (Prince Vessantara) is portrayed as one who was willing, in his quest for Buddhahood, to give away everything that was asked of him. His magic white elephant, his wealth, his kingdom, even (and especially) his children and his wife—all are willingly sacrificed to a succession of different characters who request them (Cone and Gombrich 1977: 3–96; cf. Fausbøll 1896: 479–93).

It is not difficult to understand Vessantara's immense appeal in the Buddhist world. He is, of course, a paradigm of perfect generosity and renunciation, but perhaps more importantly, he bridges the two careers that are commonly open to Buddhists: he manages to become a monk while remaining a layman. He never actually joins the *sangha* (monastic community) because there was no Buddhist community in his time, but he does give up his royal position, his home and his family, and much like a Buddhist monk, he ''wanders forth'' to a homeless life. It is not surprising, therefore, that in the Theravāda world his career should have become one of the models for that of the Buddhist monk (see Cone and Gombrich 1977: xxvi, and Swearer 1976: 41). Significantly, however, Vessantara accomplishes all this through the practice of *dāna*, the giving of material things characteristic of the lay life. There is an important correlation, then, in the Vessantara story, between the perfection of a layman's generosity and the monastic career.

The tale of Vessantara also raises certain ethical questions, however, and the Buddhist tradition has not been blind to them. In the semicanonical *Questions of King Milinda*, for instance, Milinda points out that Vessantara's *dāna*, though perhaps worthy of admiration, brought grief and considerable suffering upon Vessantara's own children, who were abused by the evil Brahmin to whom they were given. Milinda then pointedly asks the Venerable Nāgasena: ''What has the man who seeks to gain merit to do with bringing sorrow on others?'' (Rhys Davids 1894: 115; cf. Trenckner 1880: 275). Nāgasena is at some pains to answer. He agrees that good deeds may sometimes lead to suffering for others, but affirms that they make merit nonetheless, and he seeks to justify this with two quick and not very convincing examples: rushing a man who is sick or crippled by bullock cart to a place where he can get help is a meritorious deed, but it inflicts pain on the bullocks (Rhys Davids 1894: 117; cf. Trenckner 1880: 276–77). Or again, a king who gives out, as a gift, money he has obtained through taxation still makes merit, even though his taxes harass the people (Rhys Davids 1894: 118; cf. Trenckner 1880: 277). Just so, we are to believe, Vessantara's actions were meritorious even though his wife and children suffered because of them. Anyhow, Nāgasena adds, as though not altogether certain of his argument, the wife willingly consented to Vessantara's deeds and (he thinks) the children would have if they had been old enough. Moreover, the positive ending of the story—the fact that the family is eventually reunited and lives happily ever after—mitigates their suffering. And, in any case, the blame for their suffering should not be placed on Vessantara but on the cruel Brahmin Jūjaka, who should not have asked for the children in the first place! (Rhys Davids 1894: 114–32; cf. Trenckner 1880: 274–84).

Fortunately for Nāgasena, King Milinda is no ethicist and does not seek to poke holes in any of these arguments. Behind all this, however, is the real justification for Vessantara's actions. He did what he did for the sake of enlightenment. It is not that he ''loved [his wife and children] less, but Buddhahood more, that he renounced them all,'' and in this context "giving exceedingly is praised, applauded, and approved by the wise" (Rhys Davids 1894: 119, 125; cf. Trenckner 1880: 278, 281).

In the figure of Anāthapiṇḍika we seem to have a rather different model of *dāna*. For one thing, unlike Vessantara, he is living at the time of the Buddha. He, therefore, has available to him a potent field of merit—the Buddha and his community (the *sangha*)—which is "worthy of support" and toward which he can direct his *dāna*.

This difference in context should not be underestimated. It may be that in Vessantara we have a Buddhist model for how one should act when there are no Buddhists around (or perhaps towards non-Buddhists), whereas in Anāthapiṇḍika we have a model of how one should act toward Buddhists—most fully represented by members of the monastic community. Perhaps as a result of this, Anāthapiṇḍika appears to be moved less by a quest for Buddhahood than by his devotion to the Buddha and the monastic order (see Burlingame 1921: 147; cf. Norman 1906: 5). He generously and willingly sponsors the Buddhist cause. His most famous act of *dāna* is his gift to the Buddha of the Jetavana monastery, which he purchases by covering the site entirely with gold pieces! (Rhys Davids and Oldenberg 1885: 187–89.) More routinely, he is said to have provided food and other necessities, on a daily basis, for two thousand monks (Burlingame 1921: 147; cf. Norman 1906: 5).[2]

The very lavishness of these acts suggests that part of the attraction of the Anāthapiṇḍika paradigm is not simply his generosity but his wealth. Clearly, in the Buddhist tradition Anāthapiṇḍika is a great layman not only because he is a great donor, but also because he is very rich. The two qualities in fact, go hand in hand: the more Anāthapiṇḍika gives, the richer he seems, and the doctrine of *kamma* ensures that he will not get any poorer, at least in his future lives.

We seem to have, then, in Anāthapiṇḍika and Vessantara two distinct models of *dāna*, one motivated by desire for enlightenment and the other guided by a spirit of devotion to the Buddha and the *sangha* and a desire for a better rebirth. In the rest of this essay I would like to suggest that these two models are by no means contradictory and that, in fact, they should be viewed as mutually dependent. Indeed, as we shall see, they are neatly combined in the figure of yet another great Buddhist model of *dāna*, the Indian Emperor Aśoka.

AŚOKA'S GREAT QUINQUENNIAL FESTIVAL

Aśoka is best known to us today through the edicts and rock inscriptions with which he dotted the Indian countryside (see Bloch 1950 and

Nikam and McKeon 1959). Traditionally, however, in Buddhist lands it is not this "historical" Aśoka who has been famous but the "legendary" Aśoka whose great deeds in support of the Buddhist religion became a model for Buddhist kings everywhere (see Strong 1983: 5). In what follows, I shall examine one of these "great deeds," Aśoka's Quinquennial Festival of *dāna* (Sanskrit, *pañcavārṣika*), an account of which is given in the Sanskrit version of the Aśoka legend, the *Aśokāvadāna* (Mukhopadhyaya 1963: 94–103). Although this tradition does not appear in the Sinhalese chronicles and other standard Pāli treatments of the Aśoka story, it was not without influence in Southeast Asia, and as we shall see, it does inform the Theravāda practice of *dāna* and is very illuminating about the nature of giving in the Buddhist tradition as a whole.

Toward the end of the *Aśokāvadāna* King Aśoka, having already built eighty-four thousand *stūpa*s to house the Buddha's relics and having performed other notable acts of piety, announces his intention to hold a great Quinquennial Festival. Though there is some debate among scholars as to just what such a festival involved, the consensus appears to be that it was an especially extravagant ceremony of *dāna*, generally sponsored by a king[3] for the benefit of the entire *sangha* and held every five (*pañca*) years (*varṣa*) or paid for with funds that had accumulated over a five-year period (Lamotte 1958: 66).

In any case, in the *Aśokāvadāna* Aśoka, anticipating the entertainment of a large number of monks, prepares vast quantities of food, drink, perfumes, garlands, money, and cloth for them as offerings. He then climbs to the roof of his palace and ritually invites members of the *sangha* to come from all four directions to attend his festival. Almost instantaneously (i.e., certainly miraculously), three hundred thousand monks gather and seat themselves in front of him. When the assembly is complete, Aśoka proceeds to serve all the monks, from the most senior elder to the most junior novice, with his own hand, as though he were an ordinary layman, and he personally makes a donation of robes to the entire community. He then declares his desire to offer one hundred thousand pieces of gold to the *sangha* (Mukhopadhyaya 1963: 100).

At this point there occurs a curious and rather comic "potlatch" scene in which Aśoka's young son, Kunāla, who is standing next to his father, holds up two fingers, indicating to the crowd that he will double the amount of this offering. The crowd laughs and Aśoka is obliged to "outbid" his son; he triples his original offer, only to have Kunāla quadruple it. This goes on until finally Aśoka makes a total gift to the *sangha* of all his belongings as well as his concubines, his advisers, his family, and his self. He retains, however, possession of the state treasury:

My flourishing kingship
my harem, my ministers, my self,
and my own virtuous Kunāla—
all of these (except for the treasury)
I offer to the Sangha
which is a bowl of merit. (Mukhopadhyaya 1963: 101)

Two features of this *pañcavārṣika* deserve special comment. First of all, Aśoka progresses from rather ordinary gifts of food and robes to the giving of himself and his son. Such a gift was considered in the Buddhist tradition to be qualitatively a different kind of *dāna*. For example, in the Sinhalese legend of Aśoka as it is contained in the *Mahāvaṃsa* Aśoka also makes lavish material gifts to the *sangha* after celebrating the construction of the eighty-four thousand *stūpa*s.[4] When he finishes he is quite proud of himself, but Moggaliputta Tissa, the leader of the *sangha*, tells him that though he has now become a giver of material things to the community (*paccayadāyaka*) he has not yet become a "kinsman of the religion" (*sāsanadāyaka*). For this, a special kind of *dāna* is required: Aśoka must give his son, Mahinda, to the *sangha* as a monk (Geiger 1960: 42–43; cf. Geiger 1958: 47).[5]

The same point emerges from a similar story preserved in the Chinese version of the Aśoka legend. There, moreover, this special kind of *dāna* that goes beyond the gift of material goods is specifically identified as a gift of *dhamma* (*dhammadāna*), even though it is not a sermon or teaching and the gift is not being offered by a monk. The story is as follows: the elder Śānakavāsa, while still a layman, goes to sea as a merchant and makes a fortune. Upon his return he tells Ānanda, the Buddha's disciple, that he wishes to hold a *pañcavārṣika* in honor of the *sangha*. After doling out all the wealth he has accumulated over a five-year period, he is commended by Ānanda, who, however, informs him that now that he has made a gift of material goods he should go on to make a gift of *dhamma*. "How do I do that?" enquires Śānakavāsa. "By joining the *sangha*," replies Ānanda. So Śānakavāsa, wishing to accomplish this highest kind of *dāna*, becomes a monk and eventually goes on to become one of the patriarchs of the Northern Buddhist tradition (Przyluski 1923: 335).

These stories are noteworthy because they indicate that, at least in certain circles, embarking on a monastic career, that is, a quest for enlightenment, was considered as itself an act of *dāna*, even though it was a different kind of *dāna* than the giving of material goods. It seems safe to conclude, therefore, that Aśoka, in his *pañcavārṣika* offering of his self and his son to the *sangha*, is at least symbolically giving up the lay life and joining the Buddhist order.

The second interesting feature to be retained from the description of Aśoka's *pañcavārṣika* is the role played by the state in the quinquennial festival. In giving his self and his son to the *sangha*, Aśoka, nevertheless, refrains from making a donation of the state treasury. This exclusion of the treasury from what is otherwise an unlimited gift is significant, for it ensures the continued separation of *sangha* and state whatever else Aśoka does. It also enables the ministers of state, who steadfastly represent the interest of the government, to buy Aśoka back again (despite the fact that they, too, have supposedly just been given to the *sangha*). Indeed, in what follows in our story Aśoka's ministers soon dispense four hundred thousand pieces of gold from the reserved state treasury and thereby redeem from the monks the king, his kingship, his wives, and his son (Mukhopadhyaya 1963: 103–4).

Aśoka's *pañcavārṣika* thus involves more than a great donation culminating in the dedication of self to the *sangha*; it also includes a return to and renewal of the kingship and the king by means of *dāna*. Having renounced his kingship and his self, Aśoka is then redeemed by his ministers and finds he can start afresh as a new king, a new self.

This symbolic transformation of the self is stated even more dramatically in an episode of the *Lokapaññatti*, a noncanonical Pāli text widely influential in Burma and Northern Thailand. In it Aśoka celebrates a great festival in honor of the Buddha's reliquaries. As his culminating offering, however, he does not give his son to the *sangha*, nor does he become a monk himself. Instead he has his body wrapped in cotton, soaked in oil, and set on fire. In other words, he prepares his body as though for cremation and goes ahead and lights it. In his absorption and devotion to the Three Jewels (the Buddha, the *dhamma* and the *sangha*), however, his flesh is not consumed. In fact, he does not even feel the flames, and loudly praising the glories of the Buddha, he burns for seven days, a human lamp-offering. At the end of this period he bathes, dons his royal ornaments, circumambulates the *stūpa*, and returns, born again, to his kingship (Denis 1977: 152).[6]

There is more involved in this renunciation and renewal of the self and of kingship, however, than the symbolism of death and rebirth. In order to explore further the meaning of Aśoka's festival and, more generally, the nature of *dāna*, it will be helpful to examine a few other Indian examples of the *pañcavārṣika*.

INDRA'S *PAÑCAVĀRṢIKA*

Perhaps the earliest Buddhist reference to the quinquennial festival occurs in the *Avadānaśataka*, a Sarvāstivādin anthology of one hundred Buddhist legends. Chapter 16 of that work is entitled "Pañcavārṣika"; it recounts that while the Buddha was residing at the Veṇuvana in Rājagaha his evil-minded cousin Devadatta persuaded King Ajātasattu to issue an edict forbidding anyone from seeing the Blessed One or giving alms to him or any of his monks. Forced to obey, the people of the town were very distraught. They loudly lamented being cut off from the Buddha and feared that, unable to obtain alms, he would soon depart for some other place and leave them without spiritual support (Feer 1891: 72; cf. Vaidya 1958: 40).

Their cries of woe, however, soon caught the attention of the god Indra (Sakka), who promptly came down from his heaven and declared to the good lay people of the city that given the situation *he* would provide the Buddha and the *sangha* with all their requisites. This he offered to do for a total of five years (*pañca-varṣa*), a period then reduced by the Buddha, for ritual purposes, to five days (Feer 1891: 72–73; cf. Vaidya 1958: 40).

Indra's first act, interestingly, is to transform the Veṇuvana, by means of his divine powers, into a great heavenly palace of the gods. It is in this divine milieu that he proceeds, accompanied by thousands of *deva*s, to wait on the *sangha* personally and to serve food to the monks with his own hand. The splendor of the occasion is such that the populace, witnessing all this from a distance, becomes very eager to participate and forces King Ajātasattu to rescind his order. Then "people and gods together greatly honored the Blessed One." The Buddha preached a sermon, and "upon hearing the *dhamma* many gods and human beings came to see the truth" (Feer 1891: 74; cf. Vaidya 1958: 41).

Various comments can be made about this *pañcavārṣika* festival. One of the most striking things about it, at first glance, is that it serves the purpose of breaking down the normal barriers separating humans and gods (*deva*s). The festival is instigated by Indra, king of the *deva*s, who openly proclaims it to the people of the town. Furthermore, the *deva*s and the humans make merit together at the festival by praising the Buddha and listening to his sermon in the setting of the Veṇuvana, which for the ritual has been magically transformed into a heavenly place. It would seem, then, at least in the context of the Quinquennial Festival, that the ritual of *dāna* has as one of its immediate correlatives an experiencing of the presence of the gods. One is reminded here of a curious and much-discussed passage of the Aśokan edicts in which Aśoka declares that, as a result of religious zeal towards the *sangha*, ''gods (devas) and humans who formerly were not mingled, have now become mingled'' (Bloch 1950: 146; cf. Nikam and McKeon 1959: 49; see also Filliozat 1967: 35–53).

As a long-range goal, of course, ''mingling with the gods'' (i.e., being in heaven) has always been recognized as one of the legitimate aims of Buddhists engaged in *dāna* and other merit-making activities. If they are diligent in their generosity they will in a future lifetime be reborn among the gods. What is striking about Indra's *pañcavārṣika*, however, is that this mingling is portrayed as an immediate experience for the people of Rājagaha. Not only are they mixing with deities, but the ritual milieu in which their *dāna* takes place is transformed for the ceremony into a sort of heaven.[7] All of this, of course, is temporary; it lasts only for the duration of the festival. But it does represent, perhaps, an experiential foretaste of rebirth as a *deva*, something that should take place in time as a kammic result of the good deed of *dāna*.

How are we to relate this to Aśoka's *pañcavārṣika*, in which no mention is made of the presence of the gods or of heaven? First of all, it is important to remember that the word ''*deva*'' in India is commonly applied not only to gods but to kings. The ''commingling of *deva*s and people,'' therefore, can just as easily refer to a situation in which it is not the *deva* (god) Indra who is present with humans in the *pañcavārṣika*, but the *deva* (king) Aśoka.

This is, in fact, precisely the way in which Jean Filliozat has suggested we should read the Aśokan edict referred to above. What is new about Aśoka (even the historical Aśoka) is that unlike other kings (*deva*s) of his time, he is in contact with—he mixes with—ordinary individuals (Filliozat 1967: 45).

Filliozat makes this point even more literally by referring to a story in Buddhaghosa's *Commentary on the Vinaya* and in the *Mahāvaṃsa* in which Aśoka, welcoming the great elder Moggaliputta Tissa, respectfully touches him with his right hand. At that instant the king's guards unsheath their swords, declaring they will strike off the elder's head, for to touch the king, even his hand, is a crime punishable by death. Aśoka, however, restrains them, for his relationship with the *sangha* is a new kind of relationship, one characterized by the touching of *deva*s (i.e., kings) and men (Filliozat 1967: 47; cf. Geiger 1960: 47n.1). One might very well read, in this same light, our texts' insistence on the fact that, at their respective *pañcavārṣika*s, Indra and Aśoka served the members of the *sangha* personally, ''with their own hands,'' that is, they came into actual contact with them.

We have now seen several features of the *pañcavārṣika.* Putting them in a more structured order, we may say that (1) the *pañcavārṣika* involves the lavish giving of material goods to the *sangha.* (2) The display and giving of all this wealth call to mind the glories of kings and deities, so that in one way or another the act of *dāna* involves an experience of divinity or royalty, that is, a breaking down of the barriers between *deva*s and humans. (3) This experience appears to be transformative, for it stimulates in the donor a resolve for a new kind of *dāna*—a total dhammic gift of one's self to the *sangha* which, we have suggested, is equivalent to embarking on a monastic career. (4) Nonetheless, at the same time, this dhammic gift of the self to the *sangha* occasions a restitution of the donor's previous status and wealth—a restitution that, moreover, involves a rebirth and renewal of the individual.

HARṢA'S *PAÑCAVĀRṢIKA*

This pattern may be confirmed and further illuminated by the examination of one more example of a quinquennial festival, that which was celebrated by the great Indian emperor Harṣa (seventh century A.D.). The Chinese Buddhist pilgrim Hsüan Tsang, who was present at Harṣa's festival, has left us a fairly detailed account of its proceedings (Watters 1961: 364; see also Grousset 1971: 204–7; Mookerji 1965: Chap. 3). The ceremonies were attended by several hundred thousand persons. They took place on the great ''Plain of Alms-giving'' at Prayāga (Allahabad), an ancient Hindu and Buddhist place for *dāna* and pilgrimage at the confluence of the Jumna and the Ganges.[8] There an immense dining hall was built to feed the ten thousand Buddhist monks who had assembled for the occasion. Dozens of huts were constructed to contain the vast quantities of gold, silver, and precious jewels to be given away, and hundreds of sheds were built to store the cloth to be distributed. Over the next few weeks all of these items were given away by Harṣa and his vassal *rājas*. They gave them not only to the *sangha*, but also to the Brahmins and non-Buddhist ''heretics'' and to the masses of the poor (Grousset 1971: 204–6).

Thus far, then, we have the first stage in the *pañcavārṣika* pattern described above. This display and donation, however, also involve a commingling of humans and *deva*s, indicated not only by King Harṣa's personal participation in the ceremonies but also by the erection and worship of images of the Buddha and of various deities at the special site.

All of this inspires in Harṣa a new kind of *dāna*, one clearly corresponding to Aśoka's dedication of himself to the *sangha* but which is, in its form, a bit different from Aśoka's. René Grousset (1971: 206) has described the scene:

> This Indian fairy-tale of the Festival of Alms-Giving—the "Festival of Salvation" as the Buddhists called it—ended with a curious scene. Harsha, the poet-king, was seized with a kind of fever of charity. Like the Viśvantara [Vessantara] of Buddhist legend . . . [he] resolved to strip himself utterly: The clothes he was wearing, his necklaces, his earrings, his bracelets, the garland of his diadem, the pearls that adorned his throat and the carbuncle that blazed at the crest of his hair, all this Harsha gave in alms, keeping nothing back . . . . He then asked his sister to bring him a worn and common robe and dressing himself in this, he went to worship before the Buddha . . . [where] he abandoned himself to transports of joy: "Before," he cried, "while amassing all this wealth, I lived in constant fear of never finding a storeroom solid enough to keep it in. But now that I have spread it in alms upon the field of happiness I regard it as forever preserved!"

This self-divestment of the king as part of an act of *dāna* is a specific feature of the *pañcavārṣika* we have not encountered before, though its symbolism is already familiar to us. By giving away his royal robes, ornaments, and crown, Harṣa, like Aśoka, is giving away his kingship, for these are nothing less than the symbols of his sovereignty. At the same time, however, he is recalling the legend of another divestment—that of the Buddha, who took off his royal ornaments and exchanged his princely garb for a hunter's garment (the prototype of the monastic robe) as he set out on his quest for *nibbāna*. This event, in turn, as we shall soon see, became the model for the Theravāda ordination ceremony with its ritual forsaking of royal symbols at the time a candidate enters into monkhood and dons the yellow robe.

The "worn common robe" that Harṣa receives from his sister is not actually stated to be a monastic garment (theoretically made of "dust-heap rags"), but that is certainly the implication, and in an identical divestment ceremony carried out by the Chinese Buddhist emperor Liang Wu-ti (another monarch who consciously modeled himself after Aśoka), the garment put on by the king is explicitly said to be a monk's robe (Lévi and Chavannes 1916: 42 n.1; cf. Ch'en 1964: 125). Once again, therefore, we can see that the *pañcavārṣika* as a whole is not only an occasion for lavish giving; it is a ceremony in which, as a result of that giving, the king enters (at least temporarily) the Buddhist order and embarks (at least symbolically) on the path to *nibbāna.*

With Harṣa, however, as with Aśoka, this very commitment to the monastic enterprise has another effect: it makes for the renewal of his status and restoration of his kingship. For unlike the Buddha, and unlike ordinary monks who actually become ordained, the kings who ritually join the *sangha* in their *pañcavārṣika* do not remain monks long. They are monks for only a moment. Indeed, Harṣa's vassals, like Aśoka's ministers, soon collect large sums of cash (taxes) with which they redeem his royal ornaments and garments and buy him back from the *sangha* (Grousset 1971: 207). The same is true, we might add, of Liang Wu-ti, whose ministers soon ransom him back with a ''billion pieces of gold'' (Lévi and Chavannes 1916: 42n.1). In each case the effect is symbolically to link the willingness of the king to enter the *sangha* with his worthiness to rule.

DĀNA AND BUDDHIST INITIATION

The concept of *dāna* and the taking of monastic vows are linked to renewal and transformation in another important instance. The temporary nature of the kings' monkhood recalls the custom of Buddhist initiation which is widely practiced in Theravāda countries, especially in Burma and Thailand. In this ceremony laymen (in Burma, for example, they are often young boys around the age of puberty) enter the *sangha* for a while and then return to their lay life. They may remain in the monastery for only the period of the monsoon (approximately mid-July to mid-October) or for a few weeks, or even just overnight, but the ritual marks their abandoning the world and giving up of themselves to the *sangha.* It is an important part of growing up; afterward, they return as full members of the lay community (Spiro 1970: 234–47; Htin Aung 1962: 115–24).

It is common to consider this initiation ceremony (Burmese: *shinbyu*) as an important rite of passage, but at the same time it should be viewed in the context of *dāna.* It is, in fact, in Burma, the most important of all the offerings a layman can make (Spiro 1970: 234), for in it a boy's parents or sponsors are giving their son (and in him themselves) to the monastic life, to a quest for enlightenment. They are making a gift of *dhamma.* The initiation includes, as does the *pañcavārṣika*, the symbolic giving up of royalty. Indeed, in the first part of the ceremony, the boy is dressed in full regalia, mounted on a horse or royal elephant, shaded with a royal umbrella, and, to the sound of a solemn royal march, taken on a procession through the town or village. This ''sovereignty'' is then forsaken in the second part of the ceremony when the regalia are taken off and exchanged for the yellow "dust-heap" robes of a monk (Htin Aung 1962: 116).

Because of its obvious symbolic significance, it has been usual to focus, in this ceremony, on the giving up of the royal garments and other regalia. But just as striking, perhaps, in the context of traditional Theravāda culture, is the putting on of the regalia in the first place. As Maung Htin Aung has pointed out, in traditional Burmese society getting dressed as a prince or king was, for ordinary men and boys, against the law. "The king insisted that the difference between himself . . . and the rest of his people . . . should be clearly marked. . . . To wear a dress in imitation of the king's regalia and the robes of his officials was treason, certain to be punished with instant death" (Htin Aung 1962: 118–19).

Clearly, we have here a situation comparable to that mentioned above, in which the Elder Moggaliputta Tissa was threatened with having his head chopped off when his hand came into physical contact with that of King Aśoka. But just as this physical contact was allowed in the case of Aśoka's merit-making ceremonies, so too the impersonation of the king is allowed in the initiation ceremony. In fact, as Htin Aung points out (1962: 119), the boy going through the *shin-byu* initiation was specifically exempt from the law in this regard. Once again, then, we see how, in the midst of a festival of *dāna*, the traditional barriers that separated ordinary people from *deva*s (kings, gods) break down.

At the same time, a new dimension of this symbolism emerges. Kingship (*deva*hood) is not only something to be given up: it also represents the fullness of lay life. To give up kingship (or divinity), therefore, is equivalent to giving up the self in its highest development in the worlds (*loka*) of humans and gods, for the renunciation of anything less than *deva*hood would not be a total giving up of the self and hence would not involve a total commitment to the monastic life and the quest for *nibbāna*. This is one of the reasons why the example of the *dāna* of kings (Aśoka as well as other monarchs who perform the *pañcavārṣika*) has been such a powerful one in the Buddhist world. Aśoka is a paradigm not just for kings, but also for all lay persons aspiring to *nibbāna*.

AŚOKA'S GIFT OF HALF OF A MYROBALAN

With regard to Aśoka's relevance to the laity, however, one further fact about *dāna* must be noted. Not all acts of *dāna* are *pañcavārṣika*s or such grandiose affairs as initiation ceremonies. We need, therefore, to relate what we have seen thus far to more ordinary acts of giving made by more ordinary Buddhist lay persons. In order to do so, I would like to return once again to the Aśoka legend and examine one more story of *dāna*.

In the *Aśokavadāna*, toward the end of his life, Aśoka tallies up the offering he has made in support of the Buddhist religion and finds that, all told, he has given the equivalent of ninety-six koṭis of gold. This, according to the text, leaves him four koṭis shy of the one-hundred-koṭi record for *dāna* in a single lifetime set by Anāthapiṇḍika during the life of the Buddha (Mukhopadhyaya 1963: 126). Aśoka resolves to equal this sum, but unfortunately he is old, sick, and dying, and his time is running out. He starts drawing, therefore, on the state treasury and making donations from it to the *sangha*. This violation of the *pañcavārṣika* ritual (which exempts the treasury from *dāna*) immediately worries Aśoka's ministers, for it threatens in a more than ritual fashion the kingship itself. This time it may not be possible to buy the kingdom back. For the good of the state, therefore, the ministers carry out a mini coup d'état, persuading Sampadin (Aśoka's grandson and heir apparent) to forbid the treasurer to dispense any more state funds to the *sangha* (Mukhopadhyaya 1963: 127–28).

This measure, however, does not stop Aśoka. Although his access to the treasury is restricted, he still can give away the personal possessions of the royal household. In a frenzy of *dāna* not unlike Harṣa's, he starts sending to the monks the gold plates on which his meals are served. The ministers find out about this, however, and start serving him on silver plates. When Aśoka gives these away, too, they serve him on copper plates, and then on clay plates, and so on and so forth until Aśoka, desperate to equal Anāthapiṇḍika's record before he dies, is left with nothing at all except half of a myrobalan (*āmalaka*), a tiny, astringent, though reputedly medicinal, fruit (Mukhopadhyaya 1963: 128–30).

This myrobalan becomes the symbol of Aśoka's destitution as well as of the ultimate vagaries of wealth and kingship. From having been a great monarch and munificent patron of the *sangha*, the king has become powerless and poorer than the poorest. And yet he unhesitatingly offers the myrobalan to the *sangha* and with it he sends a message:

> A great donor, the Lord of men,
> the eminent Maurya Aśoka,
> has gone from being Lord of Jambudīpa
> to being Lord of half a myrobalan.
> Today this Lord of the Earth,
> his sovereignty stolen by his servants,

presents this gift of just half a myrobalan,
as though reproving the common folk
whose hearts are puffed up
with a passion for enjoying great splendor.
(Mukhopadhyaya 1963: 131)

The myrobalan is then cut up, put into a gruel, and distributed to the monks.

With this gift the *pañcavārṣika* paradigm has come down to earth. Now not only is Aśoka a model of *dāna* for great kings who have lavish wealth to give away, but he is also a model for ordinary lay persons. After all, what Buddhist cannot afford to give to the *sangha* at least half of one myrobalan?

Yet this myrobalan is shown to be just as effective a gift as vast amounts of wealth, for it results in Aśoka's achieving kingship once again. Just as Aśoka originally acquired his royal status because of an apparently equally worthless gift of a handful of dirt to the Buddha in a previous life (see Mukhopadhyaya 1963: 31–34), so he now regains his usurped powers because of this very ordinary gift of a myrobalan. Indeed, immediately upon offering the fruit, Aśoka turns to his prime minister and says, "Tell me, Rādhagupta, who is now Lord of the Earth?" and Rādhagupta replies, "Your majesty is Lord of the Earth" (Mukhopadhyaya 1963: 131).

The passage is significant not only because it attests to Aśoka's regaining of his sovereignty; it also demonstrates how great things (*deva*-hood, the fulfillment of lay life) can be achieved by very ordinary acts of *dāna*, and once those "great things" have been attained, they can then be given up for the sake of enlightenment. Thus, Aśoka's gift of the myrobalan and recovery of his kingship set the stage for a final total gift to the *sangha*. "Struggling to his feet," we are told, "King Aśoka gazed around at the points of the compass and said, making an *añjali* [obeisance] in the direction of the *sangha*: 'Except for the State Treasury, I now present the whole Earth, surrounded, by the ocean, to the Community of the Blessed One's disciples' " (Mukhopadhyaya 1963: 131).

This, then, is Aśoka's final act of *dāna*. It is essentially a repetition of part of the *pañcavārṣika*, made possible, however, by a very ordinary gift of a myrobalan. And like the *pañcavārṣika* it involves a commitment of the self to the *sangha*, to the quest for enlightenment. Aśoka's last words make this perfectly clear: "Because I gave it with faith," he declares, "I would obtain as the fruit of this gift something which cannot be stolen, which is honored by the Āryas and safe from all agitation: sovereignty over the mind'' (Mukhopadhyaya 1963: 132).

It is not clear in the text whether Aśoka ever achieves this new form of sovereignty. Only his future lives will tell. What is clear, however, is the status he retains here on earth. After his death his ministers take it upon themselves to install his grandson, Sampadin, on the throne. They cannot do so, however, until they get the kingship back from the *sangha*, for even though Aśoka is dead, his last deed (giving away the kingdom) still holds. They are forced to ransom the royalty back, therefore, at the going price of four *koṭis* of gold, which they dispense from the reserved state treasury. This completes the *pañcavārṣika* ritual, but it does something else as well, for with this final payment to the *sangha* Aśoka's lifetime gift now totals exactly one hundred *koṭis*, and this, posthumously, makes him the equal of Anāthapiṇḍika, the greatest lay donor of all times (Mukhopadhyaya 1963: 132–33).

CONCLUSION

It is sometimes claimed that the quest for enlightenment is basically divorced from the operations of *kamma* and the desire for a better rebirth and that there are, to use Melford Spiro's terms, two Buddhisms—a nibbanic one oriented toward ending rebirth which emphasizes monkhood and meditation, and a kammatic one, which is satisfied with achieving a better rebirth and oriented toward the laity and merit-making (Spiro 1970: Chaps. 2–5).[9] The texts we have examined, however, suggest that, at least in acts of *dāna*, these two dimensions of Buddhist life are inextricably interwoven. Of course, like Aśoka, one must give away *deva*hood, that is, kingship or rebirth in heaven, before one can commit oneself totally to enlightenment; but one must also, like Aśoka, achieve *deva*hood before one can renounce it.

The paradigmatic pattern of the life of a Buddha—any Buddha—should have made this clear long ago. All *bodhisatta*s become *deva*s (often several times) before they become Buddhas. In fact, *deva*hood is what they give up in order to become enlightened; in his final existence Gotama was born as a prince (*deva*) and had the option of becoming a great king (*cakkavatti*) only to renounce it for the monastic life. And the future Buddha Metteyya is now a *deva* in Tuṣita heaven, biding his time before giving up his divinity. The quest for Buddhahood is thus inevitably involved with attaining and giving up *deva*hood, and both of these acts are intimately linked to *dāna*, as the gift of goods and the dhammic giving of oneself.

Dāna, therefore, is an act that is kammatic and nibbanic at the same time. It is the act by which one gains a better rebirth; it is the act by which one renounces the fullness of mundane life brought by high birth. In fact, in this context these two dimensions of Buddhist practice are so closely interconnected that, even though *nibbāna* remains the ultimate goal of Buddhism, one should probably speak of *dāna* as having provisionally a dual teleology—for *deva*hood/*nibbāna*.

Even at the most mundane level of lay-giving this nibbanic quality is not completely eclipsed. As is well known, every act of giving, either to the Buddha or to the *sangha*, ends, when properly performed, with a statement of goals or "earnest wish" (*patthanā*) (Gombrich 1971: 217). In its simplest form this is a wish that the donors, as a result of their gift, may in their future lives enjoy human and divine bliss and then attain *nibbāna* by being reborn at the time and place of the Buddha Metteyya (Gombrich 1971: 218). Aśoka's own wish in giving the half a myrobalan takes a similar form. This does not mean, as some have suggested, that the goals of *nibbāna* and heaven are confused in the minds of Theravāda lay persons. It does, however, imply that the merit-makers' *path* to these two goals is for all practical purposes one and the same.[10]

There is more at work here, however, than mere hope for future goals. Sometimes the wishes that accompany acts of merit are quite colorful and the donor may noticeably dwell on the blessings that are expected. The description of the goals to be attained may be so glowingly detailed and enthusiastic that one suspects it provides immediate anticipatory joy and delight at the prospect of these rewards.[11] There is, in other words, in the ritual of stating one's wish, a taste of things to come. This, as we have seen, was also true in the paradigmatic examples of the *dāna* of King Aśoka and others. The commingling of *deva*s and humans in the *pañcavārṣika* and the dressing up of the boy in the *shinbyu* initiation ceremony are both illustrations of the way in which *dāna* not only eventually leads to a better rebirth (in heaven or as a king) but gives an immediate foretaste of that life.

At the same time, the act of *dāna* also gives a foretaste of renunciation, for the goal of enlightenment demands that the enjoyment of these rewards must also be given away. Thus Aśoka, as we have seen, gives away his kingship and kingdom to the *sangha*—an act that dedicates him to the monastic order, at least temporarily. The same pattern can be found in the initiation ceremony in which the boy renounces his "royalty" for the monastic life and may be detected in that portion of the earnest wish aiming at *nibbāna* and which, as Richard Gombrich has put it, is an ''epiphenomen[on] of the pure thoughts of a man who, by reason of those thoughts, is advancing spiritually'' (Gombrich 1971: 220–21).

In all of these cases, of course, once the ritual is over, there is a return to the status quo ante. But it is a status quo ante that has been transformed and renewed; to be sure, neither heaven nor *nibbāna* has been attained, but both of them have been anticipated, and this anticipation can only reinvigorate the merit-maker and his commitment to further acts of *dāna*.

6 Exemplary Donors of the Pāli Tradition

Nancy Auer Falk

Inculcating virtue by citing its paragons is a practice common to all of the world's great religions. Christians are reared with stories of biblical heroes and saints; Muslims scrutinize the *sunna* of the Prophet. The traditions of South Asia, rich in storytelling of all kinds, teem with models of praiseworthy (and blameworthy) behavior. Such stories are recounted to children by parents and grandparents or other family members, enacted by players on festal occasions, and painted, sculpted, or inlaid on the walls of religious structures; in modern times they have made their way into movies and comic books. They constitute, in short, a sizable component of the cultural atmosphere—so much so, in fact, that they furnish one of the principal vehicles of instruction in *dhamma*, that is, appropriate action.

The Theravāda Buddhist tradition shares with other paths parented in South Asia this propensity to concretize and communicate its norms for appropriate action by telling stories of exemplary figures.[1] These stories have formed a living oral tradition for Buddhism's twenty-five hundred years, but many have also been recorded in the Pāli literary tradition. Some have made their way into the canonical literature itself; others were preserved in the commentarial tradition collated and rewritten in Pāli after the fifth century C.E.[2]

Because the donation of wealth constitutes a significant component of prescribed action in the lay community, to whom the storytelling tradition is often principally addressed, donors are often cited as paradigmatic figures in Pāli stories. Stories about exemplary donors—their overall character, their resources, their motivations and actual gifts, the recipients, and finally the kammic results—all can furnish an important index to Theravāda evaluations of wealth and expectations concerning its appropriate uses.

In the following essay I intend to examine a sampling of these stories, to discover what they can tell us about the evaluations and appropriate uses of wealth. My findings are consistent with those of Rājavaramuni and Reynolds in this volume. Although precept and story do not always completely agree with one another in the Buddhist tradition, they tend to do so in their assessment of wealth: wealth is a hindrance when it generates the craving that perpetuates human suffering, but it is a positive good when used for the proper purposes with the appropriate attitudes. In this context "used for the proper purposes" can be construed to mean giving to the Buddha and/or his community, and "with the appropriate attitude" can be construed as giving selflessly and joyfully, with no regrets or stinting, and without an express regard for the gift's kammic outcome. This assessment, however, requires one important reservation: the good inherent in the proper use of such wealth in such stories is perceived to be kammic—that is, it produces good fortune and/or a rebirth in heaven.

The Theravāda tradition has preserved a plethora of donor stories of diverse forms and functions. The stories may be divided into at least four types, according to the status and resources of the donors.

1. *Stories of the bodhisatta as donor.* The Buddha is, of course, the ultimate paradigm for all constructive modes of human action. Once he has undergone the sequence of renunciations that enable his breakthrough to full enlightenment, he has nothing left to give except *dhamma* (which is, however, the best of offerings).[3] During his *bodhisatta* career, however, he has possessions and he offers them freely—most notably during his next-to-final birth as Vessantara. This legendary king, whose story is very well known in Theravāda countries, gives everything away, including his kingdom's rain-producing elephant and his wife and children.[4]

2. *Stories of royal (post-Enlightenment) donors.* Vessantara was, as I have noted, a king—and thus, de facto of the class of the royal donors. But other kings of the Buddha's era and beyond have also been celebrated as donors worthy of emulation. Local rulers appear as prominent donors already in the canonical texts (most notably Bimbisāra of Magadha and Pasenadi of Kosala). In the older literature they are not sharply distinguished from other celebrated donors. However, this pattern changes with later commentarial and legendary material, in which the king is held up as first among givers. The first of the first, closest in approximation to Vessantara, is without a doubt the emperor Aśoka, whose accomplishments have been discussed in the previous chapter of this volume.

3. *Stories of wealthy, nonroyal donors.* Although canonical accounts of the Buddha's teaching career largely focus on the life and concerns of the monastic community, nonetheless mention is made of a number of prominent lay supporters. Those whose names are most often repeated, with legends that continue to grow in the oral tradition, are wealthy

donors who offer substantial portions of their resources to feed, clothe, and shelter the wandering and mendicant community of Buddhist monks and nuns. These wealthy donors are members of a number of social groups, ranging from court retainers and professionals, such as the royal physician, Jīvaka of Rajagāha, to well-established courtesans, such as the beautiful and celebrated Ambapalī of Vesali. Perhaps the two most famous are from merchant families of the thriving trade center of Sāvatthi: the merchant-householder Sudatta, who became better known by the honorific name Anāthapiṇḍika, ''he who gives food to the poor and powerless,'' and the great laywoman Visākhā, also known as Migāramātā. The Buddha himself is said to have designated these two ''chief among male and female almsgivers.''[5]

4. *Stories of small-scale donors.* Over and above the tales of the great canonical donors, distinguished by their unstinting generosity and overall commitment to the Buddha and his renunciant order, Pāli literature preserves countless stories of small offerings whose donors' names may be preserved only in connection with their single, modest gifts. Unlike the wealthy donors, some of whose monasteries at least have been independently validated as real historical structures,[6] these small-scale donors for the most part appear as figures of legend. Furthermore, stories of this nature tend to be far less interested in the donor himself or herself than in the gift that is offered, the circumstances that call it forth, the recipient, and the fruit of the offering. That is to say, they are more explicitly geared to the problem of the appropriate forms and rewards of giving.

Of these four categories the last two are perhaps the most intriguing because their examples could most readily be emulated by members of the Buddhist lay community. The stories of the wealthy afforded examples to lay followers who often had, in fact, grown wealthy during times of an expanding South Asian economy.[7] At the same time, the accounts of far more modest efforts detailed the options that remained available to those whose reserves were slimmer.

In order to illuminate the teaching on wealth most accessible to emulation by members of the Buddhist lay community, my analysis will deal with stories from the last two categories. First, I shall examine at some length the legendary cycles of the wealthy Sāvatthi donors Anāthapiṇḍika and Visākhā as recorded in the Pāli canon and its later commentaries.[8] The stories of the two great donors change over time, and a substantial part of their interest lies in the way they are subtly reshaped to be brought into increased parallelism with each other; the two cycles seem to have consciously developed their respective donors as matched examples of a "perfect" male and female donor pair. Second, and far more briefly, I shall summarize stories of humble donations from two minor Pāli collections to show what sorts of models were proffered for more popular, and poorer, consumption.

ANĀTHAPIṆḌIKA: THE CANONICAL ACCOUNTS

Anāthapiṇḍika is identified in canonical texts as a merchant of the *seṭṭhi* category: the precise meaning of this term has not been determined, but it indicates, at minimum, considerable wealth.[9] He was not merely wealthy, but also highly respected; it is said that "the householder Anāthapiṇḍika had many friends, many companions, his word carried weight" (Cv 6.4.8; *BD* 5, 221).[10]

He had already won his reputation for generosity and his honorific name Anāthapiṇḍika before his conversion to Buddhism, which occurred when he was an adult and a well-established trader. The Vinaya's Cullavagga tells the story. Anāthapiṇḍika has taken a routine business trip to Rajagāha, capital of the kingdom of Magadha, which borders his own home state of Kosala. Arriving at the home of a brother-in-law (also a *seṭṭhi*), with whom he plans to stay, he finds the family in the midst of busy preparations; the Buddha and his community have been invited for a meal on the following day. Anāthapiṇḍika himself becomes so excited at the news that a Buddha has arisen in the world that he wakes three times during the night hallucinating that daylight has come.[11] The day at last breaks, and the merchant goes forth to see the Enlightened Being, not waiting for the visit in his brother-in-law's home. He himself invites the Buddha and his followers for a meal at his brother-in-law's residence on the following day.

At this meal, his first donation, Anāthapiṇḍika requests the privilege of making a gift that will be far greater. He wishes to offer a *vassāvasa*, a dwelling for the use of the Buddha and renunciant community during the annual rainy-season retreat. It will be located in his own town of Sāvatthi, a place that the Buddha has never visited; its acceptance will mean, by implication, that the citizens of Sāvatthi will have the Buddha and his community accessible to them during the entire four months' season when Buddhist renunciants were restricted to a single location, a longstanding custom of religious wanderers as well as the emerging rule of Buddhist order. The Buddha replies, "But householder, Truth-finders delight in empty places," thus implying that an acceptable dwelling must be located in such an "empty place" (Cv 6.4.7; *BD* 5, 221). Anāthapiṇḍika accedes, and the intended gift is tacitly accepted.

Now the merchant's task has been set out for him. He must locate and purchase a suitable "empty place" near Sāvatthi—far enough from the centers of ordinary human activity to be quiet and suitable for meditation, yet near enough so that Sāvatthi citizens can reach it for gift-giving and instruction. He determines that Prince Jeta's *vana*, or grove, will be an ideal spot and asks Jeta to name a price. The prince, unwilling to sell, cites an impossibly high price of one hundred thousand gold coins. Anāthapiṇḍika brings the coins in wagons and has the floor of the grove spread with them.[12] When the coins fail to cover the entire surface, he sends for more gold. But Jeta intervenes, greatly impressed by Anāthapiṇḍika's willingness to part with his wealth for this project. He claims the remaining space for a building of his own, to be dedicated to the renunciant community along with the monastic complex that Anāthapiṇḍika now has constructed.[13] This complex retains its original name, Jetavana, as well as acquiring the new name Anāthapiṇḍikārama, Anāthapiṇḍika's monastery. It is usually identified by both names in the texts, in which it is the locale of many of the Buddha's discourses.[14]

In later years the merchant himself receives a number of these discourses; some admonish him to complement his giving with a broader range of commonly prescribed lay activities. He is told, for example, in a passage from the Anguttara-Nikāya:

> Householder, you have served the Order of monks with gifts of the requisites: the robe, alms, lodging and medicine for sickness—but you must not just be satisfied with the thought: "We have served the Order with gifts of requisites." Wherefore, householder, train yourself thus: "Come now, let us, from time to time, enter and abide in the zest that comes from seclusion." (A 5.176.2–3; *GS* 3, 152)

Another discourse warns him of the "fivefold guilty dread" occasioned by violating the five moral precepts (A 9.27; *GS* 4, 272/S 1.12.41.1; *KS* 2, 47/S 5.55.28; *KS* 5, 333); yet another stresses the importance of guarding one's thoughts (AN 3.105–6; *GS* 1, 240–41).

Still, Anāthapiṇḍika's primary identity is that of a wealthy donor (A 1.14.6; *GS* 1, 23); hence we are not surprised to discover that he also receives a number of the Pāli canon's most important discourses on the subjects of wealth and giving. He is told of the four forms of householders' "bliss": gain, wealth, debtlessness, and blamelessness (A 4.62; *GS* 2, 77). He learns how wealth should be acquired and used: the best wealth-seeker will pursue his wealth lawfully and not through arbitrary action; he will share his wealth with others and use it to perform meritorious deeds; he will enjoy his wealth without greed, offense, or infatuation and will remain heedful of the danger that it presents (i.e., the temptation to attachment); and he will remain alive to the necessity of pursuing his own salvation (A 10.91.23; *GS* 5, 123–24).

Furthermore, he is told that the wealthy man should make himself happy and secure, together with his family, servants, workmen, and friends. He should carry on the traditional Indian fivefold offering to relatives, guests, ancestors, the king, and guardian spirits; but he should also give to brāhmans and religious recluses (*samaṇa*; the term includes Buddhist monks [A 4.61.10–13; *GS* 2, 75–76]). Giving food to "those who live on others' alms" is especially meritorious and will bring "long and honored life wherever born" (A 4.53.3; *GS* 2, 72). To offer to the order of monks robes, alms-food, lodging, and aid and medicines for the sick is a "path which brings good repute and leads to heaven" (A 4.60.1). Among these recipient monks, two are especially worthy of donations, the one who is striving and the adept who is "upright in body, speech and mind"; these are called a *khettan*, "field of merit," a concept that has remained an important component of Buddhist evaluations of offerings (A 2.4.4; *GS* 1, 58). For merit increases with the worthiness of the recipient, an accomplished being of one of six categories: a person of right views, a once-returner, a non-returner, an *arahant*, a *paccekabuddha* (solitary Buddha), and a *tathāgata* (A 9.20.5; *GS* 4, 264–65). Furthermore, even a coarse gift to a being of superior stature will be fruitful as long as it is given respectfully and with one's own hand (A 9.20.3; *GS* 4, 262–67).

These teachings directed to Anāthapiṇḍika outline, in effect, a complete program of appropriate attitudes and works for the wealthy donor. Let us note that this program incorporates a promise of kammic rewards: he who gives food will enjoy "long and honored life, wherever born"; he who gives requisites will enjoy good repute and can anticipate heavenly rewards. It is noteworthy, I think, that the Buddha speaks of these rewards rather than Anāthapiṇḍika. Our paradigmatic donor never articulates any interest in the possible fruits of his generosity. Unlike donors of the Northern Buddhist literary tradition, he makes no *praṇidhāna*—no vow regarding the disposition of his offerings' merit.[15] He just gives, joyful in the chance to do so. In this, too, as in his liberality, he is an exemplary giver. For like any other path of human action, according to the Theravāda understanding, the best gift must reflect selfless rather than selfish motivations. Paradoxically, Anāthapiṇḍika would be less than a perfect giver if he gave for the sake of the rewards that, according to his Master, are derived from the gift.

Anāthapiṇḍika, nonetheless, is well rewarded, and we are assured of this by the final episode in the eminent householder's life. He is reborn as a *deva* in Tuṣita heaven. In addition to assuring the hearer that Anāthapiṇḍika has indeed won his just deserts, the story sets in perspective both the reward and the dying man's progress on the Buddhist path. As fortunate as Anāthapiṇḍika's wealth may be, the story implies, and as well as he may have used it, his accomplishment in giving bears little comparison with that of monks who have won insight into *dhamma*.

The story begins as Anāthapiṇḍika is suffering on his deathbed. He sends for Sāriputta, the monk most celebrated for wisdom; we are told that Sāriputta is the merchant's favorite. Preparing Anāthapiṇḍika for the death that seems imminent, Sāriputta offers a discourse on non-grasping. This is not, however, the sort of sermon on this subject that a monk would commonly have offered to the laity—that is, it is not addressed to the problem of grasping material possessions and comforts. Instead, it is a discourse on Sāriputta's specialty, *abhidhamma* (higher *dhamma*). Anāthapiṇḍika is told not to grasp after his feelings, his perceptions, his consciousness—in other words, after life itself.

Anāthapiṇḍika responds as if a whole new world has opened for him: "I have never yet heard reasoned talk (*dhamma*) like this" (M 143; *MLS* 3, 312–13). Sāriputta responds that such discourses are usually offered only to those who have "gone forth"—to which Anāthapiṇḍika rejoins an urgent plea that Sāriputta make such *dhamma* available to able lay persons also. But the point has already been made: the great donor is still only a beginner on the spiritual path—he has not even heard or imagined the higher dhammic insights.

The dying man expires, and the scene shifts to the Jetavana, where the former householder, now a radiant *deva*, appears in the night sky and recites the *gāthā* (stanza) that constitutes his final statement. He expresses his joy in seeing again the friendly grove that he had offered to the Buddha in the crowning accomplishment of his own life. But then he immediately denigrates the great wealth that had made possible the gift of the grove. Wealth means little, he suggests, when compared to the discipline and insight cultivated by the monks who reside in Jetavana. The monks should take wise Sāriputta as their model. The *gāthā* does not state it, but the implication is clear: the better example to emulate is the wise monk, not the donor (M 143; *MLS* 3, 309–15).

This final episode counteracts any tendency toward overassessment not only of Anāthapiṇḍika's achievements, but also of the contributions of any Buddhist donor. Yes, the generous donor is indeed worthy of praise, especially when he or she supplements giving with further moral practice. But giving is a small thing after all when compared with the achievements of a realized monk like Sāriputta. Anāthapiṇḍika and his female counterpart Visākhā are indeed good models for lay persons to follow. But one should never assume that, in emulating them, one will accomplish all.

The commentaries develop the legendary cycle of Anāthapiṇḍika further. But before we turn to these portrayals, let us examine the canonical portrait of Visākhā.

VISĀKHĀ: THE CANONICAL ACCOUNTS

Who was Visākhā? Canonical accounts also call her Migāramātā, "Migara's mother"; her son Migāra was a wealthy young merchant of Sāvatthi. Another son, Migajāla, appears to have been a Buddhist monk; this is surely one reason for her lively and continuing interest in the Buddhist community's welfare.[16]

Visākhā was primarily a housewife. Hence, appropriately, one of the only two discourses directed toward her[17] is a list of the effective housewife's duties: a woman wins power in this world and the next, she is told, by being capable in her work and in managing her servants; her ways are pleasing to her husband and she guards his wealth; she is accomplished in faith, virtue, almsgiving, and wisdom (A 8.49; *GS* 4, 178–80).

Visākhā seems to have been quite secure in her role and accustomed to wielding authority; she does not hesitate to chastise even the monks and nuns when their behavior appears to be improper. For example, she scolds the venerable monk Udāyin for sitting alone with a girl on a secluded seat (Sv Aniyata 1, 2; *BD* 1, 331, 337); she charges indiscretion when nuns are seen bathing naked at the same place as a group of prostitutes (see Sv Pācittiya 21; *BD* 3, 283; cf. Mv 8.15.11, *BD* 4, 418, where the same story receives a different interpretation); and she protests the *sangha*'s failure to ordain her nephew during the time of the *vassa* retreat (since the nephew has second thoughts and later changes his mind [Mv 3.13; *BD* 4, 508]).

Visākhā again shows her concern for propriety and for the *sangha*'s well-being when she approaches the Buddha to ask how she, as a lay supporter, should respond to a group of schismatic monks which is about to arrive in Sāvatthi.[18] Anāthapiṇḍika seeks the same advice, making this the sole narrative in the canonical literature in which the two most famous Sāvatthi lay persons appear together in the same story (Mv 10.5.8–9; *BD* 4, 508).

Although stories of the Buddha often place him at "the storied palace (*pāsāda*)" of Migāramātā (Visākhā) in the East Park (*pubbārama*), the canonical accounts themselves do not record a donation of this park or structure.[19] Rather, the offerings for which Visākhā is celebrated are small but thoughtful items and services that will ease the monastic community's day-to-day burdens. She asks for permission to offer a "cloth for wiping the face"—that is, a kind of handkerchief; permission is granted (Mv 8.18; *BD* 4, 421–22). She offers a small water jar (allowed), a broom (allowed), and a scrubber for use in bathing (denied) (Cv 5.22; *BD* 5, 179). Clearly most important, however, is her request for the "Eight Great Boons." This long and complex account begins as Visākhā, characteristically, prepares a meal for the Buddha and the monks. She sends a maid to summon them. But the last great rain of the *vassa* season has just begun, and the Buddha has sent the monks out naked to cool themselves in the downpour. When the maid sees them, she mistakes them for naked ascetics (Ājīvikas), and so the message goes undelivered. Although the situation is finally resolved, Visākhā determines that monks should not go naked in the rain again, for nakedness is "impure" and "disagreeable" (Mv 8.15.7; *BD* 4, 417). So she asks for permission to give rain-cloaks (the first "boon") and offers to provide seven other modest but perpetual services. She will provide food for monks newly arrived in town who do not yet know where to seek it (second boon). She will provide food for those who are about to leave so that they do not wear themselves out in advance of the journey, or lose time and get left behind while they go on begging rounds (third). She will provide food for the sick (fourth) as well as food for those who tend the sick (fifth) and (sixth) a supply of medicine. She will provide a constant supply of rice gruel, a substance credited elsewhere in the Vinaya with health-maintaining properties (seventh). And she will provide bathing-cloaks for the nuns (eighth)—here she repeats her objection, mentioned earlier, to nuns bathing naked (for the full eight boon story see Mv 8.15; *BD* 4, 413–20).

Thus Visākhā offers gifts of a type that women could hope to emulate. Even if their personal resources were small—as they often were in the patriarchal, patrilineal, and patrilocal societies in which these stories were first repeated[20]—women could look to the order's incidental needs and take care of strangers and the sick. Nor should we forget that women, for the most part, fed the monks and nuns on their daily begging rounds. And, in fact, the *gāthā* that concludes the Eight Boons story emphasizes its specific importance for women. The Buddha speaks, commending our model housewife for her offering:

> Whatever (woman[21]), much delighted, endowed with virtue,
> a disciple of the well-farer, food and drink
> Gives—having overcome avarice—the gift is heavenly,
> dispelling sorrow, bringing happiness; (and)
> She gains a deva-like span owing to the spotless, stainless way,
> She desiring merit, at ease, healthy,
> delights long in a heavenly company.
> (Mv 8.15.14; *BD* 4, 419.)

Had Visākhā overcome avarice? Yes, without a doubt. She has made an open-ended commitment; she will give whenever there is a need. Furthermore, she expresses no more interest in the *outcome* of her giving than Anāthapiṇḍika. She merely gives in joy at the chance to do so. What rewards does she obtain despite her distinterested attitude? She obtains an Indian woman's dream: lots of healthy offspring: "Now at that time Visākhā, Migāra's mother, had many children and many grandchildren. The children were healthy and the grandchildren were healthy and she was considered to be auspicious. People used to regale Visākhā first at sacrifices, festivals, and feasts" (Sv Aniyata; *BD* 1, 330–31). For the story of her rebirth as a *deva*-queen, we must, however, turn to the commentaries.

VISĀKHĀ AND ANĀTHAPIṆḌIKA: THE DHAMMAPADA AND JĀTAKA COMMENTARIES

I shall restrict my comments here primarily to materials from the Jātaka and Dhammapada commentaries, both because these compositions offer the most popular and widespread collections of tales about Buddhists of the early community and because they include a rich and convenient assemblage of Visākhā/Anāthapiṇḍika references.[22] The commentators, of course, knew the stories of the existing Pāli texts; in a number of cases they either refer to these or rework them into longer and more elaborate accounts. But they also tell new stories, and give the reworked narratives a new significance. We can loosely cluster these alterations and additions into four categories.

1. *Enhanced information about family ties and relationships.* In the case of Anāthapiṇḍika, this information largely takes the form of addi-

tional stories about his children, other relatives, servants, and other acquaintances. These seem to be told less to enhance our acquaintance with Anāthapiṇḍika per se than to emphasize the significance of their own central characters by establishing a connection with the famous layman. Visākhā, however, receives in effect a whole life story, and a new twist is given to her alternate name Migāramātā. Her paternal grandfather and parents are identified with the lay followers of the Aṅga country whose conversion is recounted in a Mahāvagga story (Mv 6.34; *BD* 4, 329–30). She is converted as a young girl, but later marries into a wealthy and respected, but heretical (Ājīvika), family of Sāvatthi. Of special note in this tale of her marriage is an extended description of her fabulous dowry, which consists of enormous amounts of money, gold, silver and copper vesels, silk garments, ghee, rice, and farm implements, as well as equally enormous numbers of cattle, slave girls, and servants. As the capstone, her father has goldsmiths fashion the "great creeper ornament (*mahālatāpasādhana*)," described as a head-to-foot combination cloak and adornment woven of silver thread and encrusted with gold and jewels wrought to generate the impression of a peacock dancing on Visākhā's head.

Although wealthy and of distinguished family and impeccable deportment, Visākhā runs into trouble when she criticizes her father-in-law's support of the Ajīvikas. Nonetheless, the charges that he brings against her are disproved, and she is finally allowed to entertain the Buddha, who effects the father-in-law's conversion. Once he has seen the light, the father-in-law, named Migāra, takes her breast in his mouth, declaring "Today henceforth you are my mother."

The story continues with a reference to Visākhā's eight boons and an extended account of how she came to construct and offer her "storied palace"; I shall return to this later. It also extends our canonical reference to her auspiciousness as mother—in fact, it cites word for word the same passage I quoted in the previous section and adds:

> And even as the crescent moon waxes great in the sky, even so did Visākhā wax great with sons and daughters. It is said that she had ten sons and ten daughters, and that each of these had ten sons and ten daughters, and that each of these had ten sons and ten daughters. Thus the children and grandchildren and greatgrandchildren in the line of direct descent from her numbered eight thousand four hundred and twenty persons. She herself lived to be a hundred and twenty years old, and yet there was not a single grey hair on her head; she always seemed to be about sixteen years old. (Dh 4.8; *BL* 2, 76)

In sum, even while living she was a very fortunate lady. She was also very, very rich and utterly faithful to the Buddha, even at the risk of incurring her in-laws' displeasure.

2. *Enhanced testimonials to intelligence and moral probity*. The account just cited portrays Visākhā as a most intelligent and upright woman. Anāthapiṇḍika similarly has a number of miscellaneous stories testifying to his status as an exemplary lay person as well as a great donor. It is interesting to note, in light of Reynolds's observations in Chapter 1 about the commentary's connection between drinking and wastefulness, that both figures have stories about their refusal to take liquor (on Visākhā, J 16.2; *J* 5, 5–6; also Dh 11.1; *BL* 2, 329–30; on Anāthapiṇḍika, J 1.6.3; *J* 2, 76). Although the stories themselves are very different from one another, it seems noteworthy, nonetheless, that these two persons were chosen to exemplify the virtue of sobriety.

3. *The pairing of Anāthapiṇḍika and Visākhā*. Perhaps it is of little significance that both Anāthapiṇḍika and Visākhā are "heroes" of tales about intoxication, but this is not the only time our stories pair them. For one thing, they are linked by marriage. The *Jātaka* commentary repeats an account from Anguttara-Nikāya which tells how the Buddha tamed Anāthapiṇḍika's recalcitrant new daughter-in-law by offering her a discourse on the seven kinds of wives (A 7.6.59b; *GS* 5, 56–8); it adds the important information that this girl, named Sujātā, was Visākhā's younger sister (J 3.2.9; *J* 239–40).

Another indication of the editorial process of pairing the two great donors may be seen in the citing of both names within a single account. They appear together as leaders of the Sāvatthi lay community. When a seed of the Bodhi tree is planted at the Jetavana, both attend the ceremony, along with King Pasenadi and a "great," but otherwise faceless, concourse (J 13.6.479; *J* 4, 142–43). When Visākhā is summoned to determine whether a pregnant nun could have conceived before leaving her husband to join the order, Anāthapiṇḍika and, again, the king are asked to witness (J 1.2.2; *J* 1, 36–8). When the Buddha leaves Sāvatthi to take up a forest retreat, Anāthapiṇḍika and Visākhā send for him on behalf of the lay followers who miss his presence (Dh 23.7; *BL* 3, 212). And when the heretic Cincā falsely accuses the Buddha of making her pregnant, she also claims that he has failed to ask the king or the two lay supporters to prepare the childbirth chamber for her (J 12.9; *J* 4, 116–17; also Dh 13.9; *BL* 3, 21).

Most often the commentators match accounts of the two wealthy donors' giving:

> Anāthapiṇḍika and Visākhā, the eminent female lay disciple, went regularly twice every day to wait upon the Tathāgata. Knowing that the young novices would expect alms from them, they never went empty-handed. Before breakfast they took food, both hard and soft; after breakfast they took the five medicaments and the eight beverages. (Dh 1.1; *BL* 1, 147)

> For every day two thousand monks take their meal in the house of Anāthapiṇḍika at Sāvatthi, a like number in the house of the eminent female lay disciple Visākhā . . . both of these lay disciples understand thoroughly the tastes of the Congregation of monks and know exactly what is the proper thing to do. (Dh 1.12; *BL* 1, 242–43)

> At Sāvatthi in the house of Anāthapiṇḍika there was always unfailing food for five hundred brethren, and the same with Visākhā and the king of Kosala. (J 12.2; *J* 4, 91)

> [A certain brother] came, it was said, from the country to Jetavana, and, after putting away his bowl and robe, he saluted the Master and inquired of the young novices, saying "sirs, who looks after the stranger Brethren that come to Sāvatthi?" "The treasurer Anāthapiṇḍika," they said, "and the great and holy lay sister Visākhā look after the order of the Brethren, and stand in the place of father and mother to them." (J 4.4.7; *J* 3, 78–79)

The final quotation is especially striking; it credits both our model donors with a function initially assigned to Visākhā alone—that is, providing meals for newly arrived strangers (cf. the story of Visākhā's eight boons). This treatment anticipates a final device by which the commentaries make the male and female donors parallel. Each receives a new story of a great donation that is to some exent a counterpart of the other's most celebrated offering in the canonical texts.

4. *The new, great donations.* I shall recount each story at some length, for each addresses our central interest in Anāthapiṇḍika and Visākhā as paradigmatic givers.

Story A: "Anāthapiṇḍika and the House-fairy." This story, told in both commentaries (J 1.4.10; *J* 1, 100–103; also Dh 9.4; *BL* 2, 268–71), is derived from a brief and puzzling reference to a coarse offering of broken rice grains and sour gruel that Anāthapiṇḍika admits to in Anguttara-Nikāya (A 9.20.1; *GS* 4, 262). The story has two foci: first, the merchant's brush with bankruptcy, triggered by a series of business reversals and his incessant giving, and second, the objection raised by a ''heretic'' guardian spirit of his house, who protests that he is wasting his money on the latter.

The story opens by assessing the scope of Anāthapiṇḍika's giving. He has given away fifty-four crores of gold, just for the Jetavana monastery; he waits on the Buddha every day, and never goes empty-handed. In the morning he takes rice-gruel; after breakfast he brings ghee, butter, honey, and raw sugar. Moreover, rice for five hundred brethren is always kept ready in his home. Meanwhile, a variety of forces erode his fortune. He lends money to other traders but never calls in the loans. Family treasure amounting to eighteen crores, which has been literally ''banked''—that is, buried in a riverbank—has been washed out by a storm and swept to sea.

At this point the worried house spirit approaches Anāthapiṇḍika's business manager. ''Tell him to tend to his business and get rid of the ascetic Gotama,'' she warns (free rendering); yet both manager and eldest son are afraid to deliver such a message to the merchant. Thus, the worthy Anāthapiṇḍika descends into poverty until he has nothing left to give but the broken rice and sour gruel. Finally, the spirit herself approaches Anāthapiṇḍika and launches into a bitter reproach for his ''waste.'' But for even suggesting that his gifts are improper, the merchant drives her from his home. The homeless and despondent spirit now goes to a sequence of gods for advice. All tell her that she has been wicked. The king of the gods, however, recommends a solution; she must go to the merchant's creditors and to the bottom of the sea and recover the missing portions of Anāthapiṇḍika's fortune. After she has done this, all ends happily, for Anāthapiṇḍika both restores her to her guardian's post and takes her to the Buddha, where she attains the first level of conversion.

Let us briefly note this story's three most salient points before returning to the story of Visākhā's monastery. First, Anāthapiṇḍika gives continuously; his giving matches in content and style the commitment to perpetual offering that Visākhā made with her eight great boons. Second, he gives without stinting; not even the prospective loss of his entire fortune can faze him. And third, like Vessantara, the ultimate donor of the *bodhisatta* career, he finds his fortunes restored after he has given everything away. Thus, also like Visākhā, he realizes some benefits of his offering even in his current lifetime.

Story B: ''Visākhā's gift of the Great Creeper Ornament.'' This story, which concludes the long biography of Visākhā in the Dhammapada commentary (this segment *BL* 2, 77–82), combines and expands two incomplete motifs of the canonical materials. The first is the frequent reference to Visākhā's "storied palace." The second is an obscure Vinaya narrative which tells how Visākhā accidentally left some jewelry behind after she had gone to pay her respects to the Buddha; in its Vinaya context the story justifies a rule that allowed monks to pick up and hold treasure if they were waiting for someone else to claim it (Sv Pācittiya 84.2–3; *BD* 3, 78–79).

The story begins with the incident from the Vinaya, but the "jewelry" is now converted into the great creeper ornament. As in the Vinaya version, Visākhā wears her ornament to a festival and then modestly takes it off and leaves it with a slave girl while she stops by to see the Buddha. Both she and the slave forget it, as before, and the famous disciple Ānanda puts it aside to keep it for her. Of course, Visākhā recalls her lapse soon thereafter. But when she learns, with great joy, that Ānanda has touched it—and therefore, after a fashion, has indicated "acceptance"—she determines that she will not recover her possession. This decision presents a problem, however, for the *sangha* has no use for a fabulously jeweled ornamental cloak. Visākhā tries to sell the ornament, intending to donate the price to the *sangha*, but she can find no one who can afford to buy it. Finally she ransoms it from her own resources, and with its equivalent value she purchases a site and constructs her two-storied, thousand-roomed *pāsāda*. As the structure nears completion, she also gives alms for four months. Further,

> on the last day she gave cloth for robes to the Congregation of the Monks, each novice receiving cloth for robes worth a hundred thousand pieces of money each. Last of all she gave medicines to the monks, filling the bowl of each monk. The treasure she spent in the giving of alms amounted to nine crores. Thus in all she spent twenty-seven crores of treasure in the Religion of the Buddha, nine crores for the site of the monastery, nine crores to build it, and nine crores for alms.

The account concludes: "No other woman gave away so much money as this woman who lived in the house of a heretic" (Dh 4.8; *BL* 2, 81).

Here, too, the salient points of the story can be quickly noted. Visākhā has given her tradition's most ambitious gift, the monastery. In doing so, she matches the donation for which Anāthapiṇḍika is most famous. To purchase the requisite property and to construct and furnish its structure, she surrenders what is surely her greatest treasure—namely the fabulous ornament her father had given her as the chef d'oeuvre of her dowry. In India, where this story most likely originated, a woman's dowry was the only category of wealth over which she had indisputable control. Its most valuable portion was jewelry, usually a woman's sole insurance against personal economic reverses. Furthermore, Indian women have been traditionally close to their fathers. Thus the gift of a dowry's prize piece, specially commissioned by an adoring father, was indeed an immense sacrifice, and any female giver would have recognized it as such. Nonetheless, Visākhā shows no regrets. Once the gift is accepted she never looks back—even though both "gift" and "acceptance" were strictly accidental. Her only concern is to find the means to bring her offering to completion.

In sum, by the time the commentaries were put into writing, the tradition had generated a matched pair of "perfect" male and female donors. Both were extremely wealthy, but both used their wealth in the best possible way, without attachment, without stinting. Each offered the two most significant categories of gifts that their tradition could imagine. Both were, in addition, pious, moral, and sober. That is to say, both were exemplary lay persons as well as ideal donors.

Why the emphasis on pairing? It may have been prompted by little more than an impulse to make the two "best" donors complete in their character and their roster of offerings. But it is interesting to note that the revised version in effect denies that any gift is more appropriate for male or female. Even a woman can offer a monastery if appropriate resources are available. Even a man should try to supplement an occasional spectacular contribution with continuing devoted attention to the community's day-to-day needs.

However, even while it "perfected" the Anāthapiṇḍika and Visākhā cycles, the tradition was generating problems for itself. The legendary great disciples became *too* perfect; few ordinary people had at their disposal wealth that could even approach what the two dispensed so freely. Yet their stories demonstrated clearly that their gifts had been the principal source of their good fortune. What, then, was the merit of the small gifts that most Buddhists were capable of making? In what sense, that is to say, could lay followers of limited means hope to approximate the accomplishments of the two great merchant donors?

THE PETTY DONORS OF THE VIMĀNAVATTHU AND PETAVATTHU COLLECTIONS

The Pāli tradition's most extensive collection of stories of small donations may be found in two minor anthologies of *gāthā* (verse) and commentarial material, called Vimānavatthu ("stories of mansions") and

Petavatthu ("stories of the departed").[23] The question of the merit of small gifts is raised explicitly in the commentarial tradition itself:

> While the Blessed One was dwelling at Sāvatthi, in Jetavana at the monastery of Anāthapiṇḍika, after King Pasenadi of Kosala had given for seven days the Unparalleled Almsgiving for the Order of Monks with the Buddha at its head, and Anāthapiṇḍika, the great banker, had given alms for three days to conform to the (king's) gift, and the great laywoman follower, Visākhā, had given great alms likewise, news of the Unparalleled Almsgiving became known all over Jambudīpa. The people everywhere raised the question, "Does almsgiving become productive of great fruit only when it is liberality of such a magnificent sort as this, or is it rather when it is liberality in accordance with one's means?"
>
> When the monks heard of this discussion they told the Blessed One. The Blessed One said, "Not merely by efficiency of the gift does giving become especially productive of great fruit, but rather through the efficiency of the thought and efficiency of the field of those to whom the alms are given. Therefore even so little as a handful of rice-beans or a piece of rag or a spread of grass or leaves or a gall-nut in decomposing (cattle-) urine bestowed with devout heart upon a person who is worthy of receiving a gift of devotion will be of great fruit, of great splendour and of great pervasiveness." (V 1.1; *SM* 1–2)

Most of the Buddha's response should be familiar to us. We have heard it before in the discourses on giving delivered to Anāthapiṇḍika in Anguttara-Nikāya. The only novelty is the explicit assertion that small gifts offered in accordance with one's means are of comparable efficacy with large ones, assuming that they are given with the proper attitude and to an appropriate "field." The stories of the petty donors convert this assertion into example—with one significant twist: they stress far more emphatically than any stories we have encountered so far the glorious rewards that accrue to the donor.

The Vimānavatthu is the simpler of the collections; it also holds the larger component of donor stories. Its stories are formulaic; with some minor variations in format, all of them are essentially the same. A radiant *deva* inhabits a splendid mansion in one or another of popular Buddhism's several heavens.[24] An observer, usually a distinguished *arahant*, comes along and asks how she or he came to this estate (the majority of Vimānavatthu's *deva*s and donors are female). The *deva* responds. Out of eighty-five stories, sixty attribute the heavenly circumstances *solely* to some sort of offering; an additional fourteen cite a panoply of virtues—usually standards of lay moral practice—which include habitual offering. Only eleven stories cite a practice or virtue that does *not* include offering—and in five of these cases the practice cited is some sort of unspecified "homage." Offerings and/or homage are directed to individual, ordinary monks (*bhikku*s); to elders (*thera*s or *arahant*s), to the Buddha, to "solitary Buddhas" (*paccekabuddha*), to Buddhas of the past, and to their *thūpa*s (funerary monuments). As a general rule of thumb, the better the recipient's field of merit, the more dramatic the reward; thus the collection includes several stories of persons who are headed toward hell, but a single donation to an *arahant* or Buddha sends them off in a far more glorious and comfortable direction. Gifts are given "joyfully," or "with a devout mind."

Almost inevitably, moreover, there is some direct correlation between the nature of the gift and the specific circumstances the giver has achieved. Those who give water, for example, are situated in mansions surrounded by fragrant lotus ponds. However, as in the stories of Anāthapiṇḍika and Visākhā cited earlier, the accounts rarely cite any stated intention to achieve a particular outcome. Only in one instance does a *devī* indicate that she has specifically resolved to attain her heavenly location.[25] But the context of her statement is ironic; her effort was mistaken:

> I heard that Nandana was desirable;
> and a resolution arose within me
> Having put my thoughts on that place,
> I have been reborn in Nandana.
> I did not heed the words of the teacher—the Buddha,
> the sun's kinsman.
> Because I put my thoughts on what was low,
> I am now repenting. (V 24; author's translation)

The commentary on this stanza marks the *devī* as a former laywoman of upright and generous habit who had "entered the stream" during a former lifetime—that is to say, she had achieved the first level of insight on the Buddhist path. For her, heaven is a lesser achievement. Having resolved to reach heaven, she has won it; but had she not thus been trapped by this limited ambition, she might have attained a far more worthy condition. Here again we recognize a characteristically Therāvadin ambiguity toward the positive fruit of moral behavior and giving: left unspecified, the appropriate fruit comes automatically; and it is well worth winning. But to seek a specific reward for oneself dilutes the power of the action.

In one specific type of situation, however, it is perfectly proper to stipulate a purpose for one's gift. This exception is exemplified not in Vimānavatthu stories, but in those of its companion volume the Petavatthu.

On the surface, the majority of the Petavatthu's stories seem to invert the tales of Vimānavatthu. They are accounts of departed humans who have been reborn as the type of being that is known as *peta*. The condition of *peta* is not a desirable state. The denizens of the Petavatthu are ugly and often naked; they inhabit unpleasant places; although always hungry and thirsty, they cannot eat or drink (the characteristic condition of *peta*s in the classical Indian tradition). Along this line are the so-called Mansion *peta*s, who because of past lives that were generally good, but marred by some evil action, now spend a part of each day in heavenly enjoyment, but also a part in the *peta*'s usual misery. Naturally, the *peta*s' condition is a product of their *kamma*, just like the condition of the *deva*s in Vimānavatthu. In most cases their misery is a product of moral failings; in many cases the specific failing is the refusal to give a gift in circumstances when one was due.

Many of the Petavatthu stories, however, offer an entirely new context for gift giving. A person now living may offer a gift as a means of delivering *peta*s from their suffering. "Let someone make an offering and designate its merit for me," they beg the pitying observer who meets them. And once the act is accomplished, the *peta*s are immediately transformed: a gift of robes brings them clothing, an offering of food and water brings an equivalent to them, together with the longed-for capacity to enjoy it. Their bodies become beautiful and they relocate in heaven.

Such giving for others is, in its own way, a selfless use of wealth. A gift for the *peta*s happens to be a very good device for fulfilling the needs of one's departed, not-so-pious parent or son or daughter; indeed, in many of these stories the *peta* sends its request for redemption to a surviving child. The gift to redeem the *peta*s has no precedent, to my best knowledge, in any older section of the canon, but here it becomes canonical.[26] And this practice did become influential in Buddhist gift-giving patterns, as attested by many Buddhist donors' inscriptions stipulating that the gift they commemorate was offered "for the sake of my father and mother."[27]

CONCLUSION

Even though Theravāda Buddhism celebrated a renunciant ideal requiring its most intense practitioners to divest themselves of possessions, it also maintained a lively interest in wealth and its proper uses. This interest is specified not only through precepts, but also through stories of ideal wealth-users—that is, donors. These storied donors occupy every imaginable station in life from *bodhisatta* to king to merchant to beggar, and they come in both sexes. All give whatever they can, and they give without clinging; they may contemplate what the gift will accomplish for others, but they preferably show no interest in its potential fruits for themselves. A gift presented with the proper attitude to an appropriate recipient will nonetheless produce rich benefit in this world and/or the next. And although a small gift given well may bring as rich a reward as a large one, happy indeed is the donor whose resources will allow him or her to emulate Anāthapiṇḍika or Visākhā. Nonetheless, even the donor who gives on such a munificent scale as these two supreme exemplars is not yet accomplishing the final aim of his or her religion. For all donors must supplement giving with self-control and other forms of recognized religiomoral practice. And, finally, as the donor's discipline progresses far enough to begin gathering the fruits of the Buddhist path, he or she will seek to emulate a different and superior model—a model such as the wise monk Sāriputta, whose praises Anāthapiṇḍika sang in his final *gāthā*.

Part IV.

CONTEXTS OF BUDDHIST MORAL AND RELIGIOUS VALUES

Introduction

The three following essays move our study of Buddhist social ethics into specific historical, cultural, and comparative contexts. In Chapter 7 Steven Kemper uses the two major Sinhalese Buddhist chronicles, the *Mahāvaṃsa* and *Cūlavaṃsa*, codes of monastic regulation (*katikāvatas*), and his knowledge of contemporary monastic Buddhism in Sri Lanka to analyze how Sinhalese Buddhists have dealt with monastic wealth. In Chapter 8 Charles Keyes draws on more than twenty years of research in Thailand to interpret the changes of modernity in the lives of Buddhists in Ban Nǫng Tųn, a village in the northeastern region of the country. Keyes analyzes the challenge of these changes to the villagers' traditional Buddhist world view and the modifications they have made to their behavior in the light of these changes. In Chapter 9 Robin Lovin draws on the tradition as interpreted by Rājavaramuni and uses the tools of Max Weber and Ernst Troeltsch to construct a comparative interpretation of Theravāda Buddhist monasticism in relation to Christian monasticism. Although Lovin focuses on institutional Buddhism, his essay is explicitly more theoretical in intent, making it an appropriate conclusion to this section and a transition to the broad theoretical and comparative concerns of the essays by Ronald Green and John Reeder in Part V.

Kemper and Keyes agree that Buddhist social ethics should be approached not as projected embodiments of doctrinal ideals, but as a study of how Buddhists actually behave and interpret their behavior. In his analysis of the problem of wealth as an issue in Theravāda Buddhist social ethics Kemper comes to the following conclusions regarding the Sinhalese monastic order's acquisition of property and the periodic attempts on the part of Sinhalese Buddhist monarchs to reform the *sangha*. First, the problem of wealth was not its possession but how it was used; wealth should never become an end in itself but rather should contribute toward soteriological ends—the cultivation of non-attachment and the production of merit (*puñña*). Second, royal reforms of monastic wealth were aimed not at dispossessing wealthy monasteries, but at disciplining corrupt and immoral monks and establishing grounds for the disciplined use of property. Third, reforms tended to break up individual concentrations of monastic wealth, thereby encouraging more unity among monks through dispersing the control of property. Finally, in Sri Lanka landed wealth was interpreted as a positive good both morally and politically because it was the mediating vehicle by which the monastic order and the state exchanged and shared political power and moral legitimacy.

In agreement with the other studies in this volume, Kemper finds that the Buddhist middle way does not reject wealth as inherently evil, but seeks to balance wealth and non-attachment through justifying the acquisition of wealth—by either monk or lay person—and then enjoining that it either be given away or used in a disciplined and appropriate manner. The *dāna* exemplars described in Part III and such Sinhalese Buddhist monarchs as Devānampiyatissa (250–210 B.C.E.) illustrate the first charge; the royal *sangha* reforms reported in the Sinhalese Buddhist chronicles and the *katikāvata*s (codes of monastic regulation) illustrate the second.

The Buddhist chronicles laud kings who increase the wealth of the land and give lavish gifts to the *sangha*, and praise monks who increase the prosperity of the monastic order. Donations of land and its disciplined use are considered important signs of spiritual cultivation and accomplishment by both kings and monks. Thus, Kemper's findings support the contention made by Rājavaramuni, Reynolds, and others that lay and monastic communities have a common moral ideal. Kemper argues that the evidence from Sinhalese Buddhist sources challenges Weber's contention that the accumulation of monastic wealth means the moral and spiritual failure of Buddhism's goal of world renunciation or radical striving for salvation. On the basis of his sources Kemper contends that wealth undermines the social function of the *sangha* only when it affects the *sangha*'s capacity to guide the king, to exemplify good Buddhist behavior, and to serve as a field of merit. Kemper's claim that the moral courses of the renouncer and the lay person differed not so much in the amount of wealth but in a higher level of self-control is supported by the fact that by the sixth century C.E. the *sangha* in Sri Lanka was the largest landholder on the island.

Keyes's study of Buddhist "practical morality" in northeastern Thailand comes to a similar conclusion in regard to attitudes toward the acquisition and use of wealth, but it does so within a very different historical, cultural, and sociological context. Keyes examines the ways in which the Thai-Lao villagers of Ban Nọng Tụn respond to the challenge to their traditional Buddhist world view and rural agrarian ethos brought on by the development of the modern Thai nation-state: the omnipresence of central Thai government bureaucrats; a national educational system in which the medium of instruction is central Thai rather than the northeastern dialect; the intrusive and pervasive influence of central Thai urban values and culture through radio, television, and employment opportunities; the change from a subsistence to a market economy. Reactions to these pressures range from open appropriation to a self-defensive sense of unique regional identity to mediation between traditional and modern ways of thinking and acting.

Keyes contends that, despite efforts on the part of the government to promote Buddhism and the monarchy as symbols of national unity, religious and secular spheres of meaning have grown apart. He argues that, although cultural change has not undermined the basic premise of the Buddhist moral view, it has undermined the givenness of the ethos based on this premise. In particular, Keyes examines two different but related developments: the emergence of a Thai-Lao trader/merchant class and a conservative Buddhist movement (Dhamma Group/*Mū Tham*).

Unlike the traditional rice farmer or official/master, the Thai-Lao trader/merchant has an ambiguous status in the Buddhist moral hierarchy. He has acquired his wealth by nontraditional means, may be more oriented toward the interests of his family and business than toward the village, and may be critical of traditional village behavior. Villagers have an ambivalent attitude toward the trader/merchant as a consequence, respecting him for his financial success and power, but criticizing him for not acquiring or expending his wealth in ways consistent with the cultural ethos.

Keyes observes that the typical trader/merchant continues to hold a traditional attitude toward wealth, that is, that it can provide this-worldly happiness but cannot eliminate *dukkha* (suffering), thus producing a sort of Weberian "inner-worldly asceticism." This ethic combines the Buddhist ideal of non-attachment with the desire to improve this-worldly living standards. That is, it applies the idea of restraint, as associated with the traditional male and female initiation rites, to economic activity. The ideal Buddhist trader/merchant becomes a person who works hard, saves, and lives an upright life, faithfully observing the traditional Buddhist moral precepts such as avoidance of gambling, stealing, and so on.

Concomitant with the rise of a merchant class has been the emergence of a conservative, pietistic Buddhist movement sometimes called *Mū Tham* (*dhamma* group). Being "ordained in the *dhamma*," that is, becoming a member of the *Mū Tham*, works to legitimate the "inner-worldly asceticism" of the trader/merchant class within the changed cultural ethos of the northeastern village. This development, Keyes suggests, is a fundamentalist type of movement that arose in a "transformed world" where moral action no longer simply flows from common sense and where villagers confront circumstances in which they find they must make conscious moral choices. The *Mū Tham* movement strives to actualize in a self-conscious way Buddhist moral ideals, especially the foundational principle of restraint, as a part of the current Thai-Lao cultural ethos. In these ways Keyes's study of a rural Buddhist community in northeastern Thailand illuminates concretely how the practical morality of Theravāda Buddhism has been broadened and transformed to meet the cultural, social, and economic challenges to traditional village life which have accompanied the creation of the modern Thai nation-state.

In the third essay in this section Robin Lovin develops an interpretation of Buddhist monasticism in relation to Christian monasticism—or more particularly, a comparison of what Lovin characterizes as Buddhist and Christian "strategies for change"—in terms of the polarity of individual perfection and the social good. Lovin distinguishes his approach from a Weber or Troeltsch church/sect/mysticism typology, which consigns Buddhism to an extreme form of mysticism, and from a wholly secular view which considers the social good or public life to be the most serious human endeavor. He argues, in contrast to the latter, that Buddhist and Christian monasticism both promote strategies for change which incorporate individual salvation-seeking *and* the pursuit of the social good. Unlike Weber, Lovin contends that Buddhist social ethics (like Christian social ethics) cannot simply be interpreted as the effects of religious beliefs on society as it exists, but "has to do with the way people organize themselves to maintain and observe the precepts that mark their lives as Buddhists." Kemper and Keyes would certainly agree with this assertion.

Although Lovin distinguishes his approach to Buddhist and Christian monasticism from that of Max Weber and Ernst Troeltsch, like them he develops a typological interpretation. His analysis of Buddhist monasticism leads him to conclude that the most appropriate category for interpreting Buddhist strategies for the pursuit of individual perfection on the one hand and the social good on the other is "purification." He reaches this conclusion on the grounds of the Theravāda doctrine of interdependent co-arising, the complex and interdependent relationship between monk, laity, and king, and the nature and function of the *sangha* in Buddhist society. In particular, he argues that the monastic establishment represents an independent community that points toward a transcendent aspect of life but also maintains the *dhamma* for society. The independence of the *sangha*, Lovin contends, is not based on renunciation of society's achievements, but rather is necessary if the society is to understand and assess its achievements in relation to the uncompromised *dhamma*, the fundamental law of individual development and perfection. For example, though material prosperity is valued, the monk teaches that it is not an unconditional good. In this equation the monastic order, often assisted by the king as a kind of mediator between monk and laity, plays a purifying role.

Lovin contends that Christian monasticism as represented by Benedictine monks differs in two basic ways from Buddhist monasticism. In the first place, it is an institutional embodiment of an eschatological Christianity that rejected the importance of worldly success. Second, the Benedictine rule promoted the development of self-sufficient communities that actually attenuated the everyday ties between the monastery and society. Consequently, Lovin argues that in Christian monasticism the suspicion of wealth, leisure, and human companionship, combined with the material independence secured by monastic labor, precluded positive assessment of economic prosperity which the Buddhist monastic strategy presumes. He concludes, therefore, that Benedictine monasticism envisioned a radical transformation of the social order as its strategy for social change rather than a gradual purification of society brought about by the exemplary role of the *sangha*.

7 Wealth and Reformation in Sinhalese Buddhist Monasticism

Steven Kemper

Anthropologists have always made their living by invoking the charms of the particular and calling colleagues in other disciplines back to the social context of evaluation. Nowadays everyone else seems to be urging this argument, including moral philosophers. As Alasdair MacIntyre (1981: 22) puts the case,

> A moral philosophy . . . characteristically presupposes a sociology. For every moral philosophy offers explicitly or implicitly at least a partial conceptual analysis of the relationship of an agent to his or her reasons, motives, intentions and actions, and in so doing generally presupposes some claim that these concepts are embodied or at least can be embodied in the real social world. Even Kant, who sometimes seems to restrict moral agency to the inner realm of the noumenal, implies otherwise in his writings on law, history, and politics. Thus it would be a decisive refutation of a moral philosophy to show that moral agency on its own account of the matter could never be socially embodied; and it also follows that we have not yet fully understood the claims of any moral philosophy until we have spelled out what its social embodiment would be.

The anthropologist does not need to call the moral philosopher back to the social context. MacIntyre, at least, is already there.

But the anthropologist ought to insist upon two things. First, the comparative study of moral judgment must begin not by considering how other societies treat "serious" problems, but by considering what problems are locally regarded as serious and why. Second, the anthropologist should insist that it is one thing to examine a moral philosophy by considering what its social realization could or would be, as MacIntyre recommends, but quite another to understand what its social realization has been. The social embodiment a moral philosophy presupposes is not always the one it gets. In this essay I want to discuss the way Sinhalese Buddhists have actually dealt with monastic wealth, by examining several historical moments when events have drawn religious ideals into real situations. I will focus on Buddhist social institutions, as much as these can be recovered from the historical record. This approach provides a view of everyday Buddhist life and morality that is different in important ways from that which emerges by starting with doctrine and imagining the embodiment of doctrinal ideals.

The historical sources that make it possible to discuss the historical treatment of monastic wealth have distinct difficulties. The history of early Sri Lanka comes to us from sources—the *Mahāvaṃsa* and the *Cūlavaṃsa*—that are didactic accounts of a privileged relationship between the Sinhalese state and the Buddhist religion. These sacred histories have themselves been shaped by the normative picture favored by the dominant monks and ascendant political tradition. Much of what we can know of early Sri Lanka we can know only within the parameters of this relationship—the way the Theravāda monkhood has guided one king after another along the path of righteousness, the way those kings have showered righteous monks with charity, the steadfast way Theravāda monks have defended the authentic teachings of the Buddha against heretical monks. These interwoven political, religious, and moral impulses make it impossible to distill a purely ethical evaluation of monastic wealth. Still, the histories are consistent in their evaluation of monastic wealth and its problems. The abuse of wealth by Sinhalese monks has been a matter not of their possessing wealth, which is quite acceptable, but of their using wealth in ways that destroy the distinction between monastic society and lay society. I want to explore this thesis in three contexts: the *Mahāvaṃsa* and *Cūlavaṃsa* treatments of both lay and monastic wealth, in monastic reform as perceived in the *katikāvatas* (codes of regulation for monks), and in present-day Sinhalese conceptions of renunciation and monastic character.

WEALTH IN THE SACRED HISTORIES

The *Mahāvaṃsa* and *Cūlavaṃsa* never scorn wealth, but they condemn wealth as an end in itself. Wealth's virtue rests in its potential contribution toward soteriological progress, the cultivation of non-attachment, and organizing Sinhalese society in a way that produces great amounts of merit.[1] One copes with the value of non-attachment and the fact of wealth not by eschewing wealth altogether but by having it and giving it away, or having it and using it wisely. The king who converts Sri Lanka to Buddhism, Devānampiyatissa (250–210 B.C.), is the paradigmatic example. His merit—even before he accepts Buddhism—is so great that his consecration prompts events that are both extraordinary and the rightful expression of his merit:

> In the whole isle of Lanka treasures and jewels that had been buried deep rose up to the surface of the earth. . . . Pearls of the eight kinds . . . came forth out of the ocean and lay upon the shore in heaps. All this was the effect of Devanampiyatissa's merit. Sapphires, beryl, ruby, these gems and many jewels and those pearls and those bamboo-stems they brought, all in the same week, to the king. (*Mhv*. 11.8 – 17)

But Devānampiyatissa immediately gives his riches away, saying, "My friend Dhammāśoka and nobody else is worthy to have these priceless treasures; I will send them to him as a gift" (*Mhv*. 11.18). That first gift, a gift of wealth (*amisadāna*), prompts countergifts from Aśoka. He dispatches an assortment of auspicious and rare things "needful for consecrating a king," but he also sends an incomparably more valuable gift, knowledge of the Buddha's teachings (*dhammadāna*).

Kings are obliged not only to use wealth wisely but also to increase it. The greater the amount of available wealth, the greater the potential for doing good with it and for cultivating the virtue of non-attachment.[2] After having reunited the various parts of the island, parts of which his own father had recovered from Tamil usurpers, Parākkramabāhu II (1236 – 1270) explained to his sons their duties:

> Dear ones, harken to my words: there are here in the world these three (kinds) of sons: the low kind, those of like kind, those of higher kind. Now those who know not how to enjoy at its true worth the wealth of their parents which has come to them as a family heritage, but destroy it, as monkeys a wreath of flowers, and now live without wealth—the pious ancients have called "sons of a low kind." But those who enjoy such possessions as they have received them in like manner as their fathers, protecting them as a family heritage, these ye must know are the "(sons) of like kind." But yet another kind I name—those who besides the possessions taken over as family heritage, acquire thereto many other possessions and as prudent people enjoy in happiness—these are known as the "sons of higher kind." (*Cv*. II 87.18 – 22)

The message is not that wealth comes to those who act meritoriously, but that rank comes to those who "acquire many other possessions."

While producing increase, putting down evildoers, and protecting the honest among the laity, the king carries out similar responsibilities toward the monastic order. He must not only support the order materially; he must also mark out those monks who have themselves brought about the prosperity of the order. The *Cūlavaṃsa* speaks of Parākkamabāhu's son Vijayabāhu thus:

> Thereupon the King granted the rank of a Grand Master, the rank of a Chief Thera, the rank of a Grand Thera, and the rank of Parivena-Thera to such (*bhikkhus*) who because they had brought about the prosperity of the Order, deserved to receive this or that rank. Then having bestowed on them the eight articles of use, fair, worthy of a king, to the value of a thousand [gold pieces], and also to the other ascetics in succession, costly articles of use, he sent many remaining articles of use to *bhikkhus* settled in the Pandu and Cola countries. (II 89.64–68)

Prosperity presumably does not mean merely material development but the increase of learning, righteousness, and social order as well. Increase inside or outside the monastic order is affirmed and rewarded by the giving of more wealth. If a man has created prosperity, he deserves rank, whether he is a "son of a higher kind" or a monk.

The *Mahāvaṃsa* and *Cūlavaṃsa* also recount many occasions on which kings give lavish gifts (warm baths, pleasant gardens) to monks (*Mhv.* 5.180, 14.46–47, 15.15–17 and 31). The more accomplished the monk, the more lavish the gift (*Mhv.* 24.21–22, n.2; *Cv.* 1.44–47). Sometimes a high-ranking monk is rewarded with a gift, and scholarly monks are given "specially high revenues" (*Cv.* I 48.142): "The many scholars who came from Jambudīpa and who were worthy of a gift, the mighty Monarch who was a hero in giving, gladdened with gifts of money" (*Cv.* I 60.19–20). Merit deserves to be recognized, and wealth is a legitimate medium for its recognition: "For the thera named Sariputta who persevered firmly in the discipline, [Parakkamabahu I] ceded a vast (and) glorious *pāsāda* [residence] with rooms, terraces, and chambers" (*Cv.* II 81.35–37 and 100.192). Ascetics are treated no differently:

> Also he had built in the suburb called Rajavesibhujanga the Isipatana-vihara which was a delight for ascetics. There (there was) one relic shrine and three three-storeyed image houses with costly images and resplendent with brightly coloured painting, further a two-storeyed pasada whose ornaments called forth delight, two

> long pasadas and four gate-buildings, eight small pasadas, a sermon house, a cloister as well as eight fire-houses and six privies, a fine bathing-house wholly of stone, and a boundary wall and a garden which belonged to the bhikkhu community. (*Cv.* II 78.79–83)

The splendor of these gifts, of course, serves the rhetorical purposes of the writers of the *Mahāvaṃsa*, but that is not all there is to it. The magnificence of the gifts is meant as testimony to the importance of spiritual cultivation and accomplishment. All right-acting monks deserve support. As Vijayabāhu II (1232–1236) says: "*Bhikkhus* and *sāmaṇera*s who study the Tipitika in faith and lead in every way the pious life must never be troubled about their livelihood. They shall come to the gate of my house and receive whatever articles of use they are in need of" (*Cv.* 81.52–54). But over and above mere support, monks who achieve more deserve more. Monks who can teach difficult subjects such as logic and grammar deserve salaries, in addition to maintenance (Rahula 1956: 161n.2). Monks regarded as spiritually advanced attract even more attention, and throughout the *Mahāvaṃsa* wealth seems to be the rightful medium for recognizing merit. By virtue of that merit, monks ought to be able to possess wealth without being seduced by it.

This emphasis on giving takes several forms. Kings and lay people give material gifts; monks give the gift of *dhamma*. By being a "field of merit" the monks make possible the soteriological progress of those who support them. Sometimes individuals give themselves over to the monkhood and then liberate themselves by buying themselves back from the monastery. The donor gets the merit of both giving the initial gift—self-donation is considered a form of "taking refuge"—and of freeing someone from slavery; the monastery gets the price of liberation (Rahula 1956: 148–49). Kings also have given themselves over to the monkhood and at times to other people. But the grandest thing the king can give to the *sangha* is the state itself, as an act of reverence. This transfer was enacted several times in early Sinhalese history by the king's handing the royal umbrella, the Indic symbol of sovereignty, to the monks.[3]

Inevitably, such gift-giving has a contractual character, and customs stipulate who should give what and how it should be done. Some of these transactions are quite complex, but what is clear is this: with the exception of the gift of the royal umbrella (the symbol of kingly authority), all material gifts to the *sangha* are retained by the order and cannot be reclaimed by the state. A *vihāra* (temple), for example, once given cannot be reclaimed.[4] To support the monks who reside in the monasteries, paddy lands and coconut gardens will be given as supplementary gifts.

And, like the *vihāra*, these lands cannot be reclaimed. The long-term effect, of course, is that considerable amounts of profitable land accumulate in the hands of a group of world renouncers. It has been estimated that by the fourth century A.D., the monastic establishment had become the largest single landlord in the island.

Most students of Buddhism have treated this material accumulation as the historical consequence of two conflicting moralities. Indeed, that is the paradox implied by the Weberian account of the historical evolution of early Buddhism's radical spirituality. Weber treats the historical career of Buddhism as the logical consequence of everyone's acting morally: by taking the moral course and practicing non-attachment through giving, kings and lay people unintentionally undermine the renunciation of those who have renounced the household life entirely. World renunciation is eclipsed by monastic landlordism, and this accumulation of monastic wealth is regarded as a moral and spiritual failure.[5]

The sacred histories put the rise of monastic wealth in a different light. They regard monastic wealth as problematic only when abused. And the seriousness of this problem derives from the way that the abuse of wealth undermines the social function of the *sangha*—its capacity to guide the king, to exemplify good Buddhist behavior, and to serve as a field of merit. The chief symptom of the monks' abuse of wealth is a reduction in the difference between the moral course of the renouncer and that of the lay person. Monks start to engage in behavior acceptable for laymen but not for them. The proper difference depends not upon the laity's having wealth and monks not, but, however much the wealth—and generally the more the better—upon the higher level of self-control and discipline expected of Theravāda monks.[6] Monks, in short, should be well supported but non-attached.

Consequently, the sacred histories speak of reformation being aimed not at wealthy monks, but at "undisciplined," "corrupt," "immoral" ones (see table in note 10). The desired quality is discipline, not poverty. The two qualities that the Buddha commended as identifying a monk as a dependable leader were virtue and discipline, not asceticism (Rahula 1956: 171). From the start it is self-discipline, not poverty, that differentiates a monk from the laity and makes him a worthy recipient of gifts. When a monk falls into corruption the political and moral structure of the society falls too. Accordingly, the prohibition against the monks' casual interacting with lay people develops from the anxiety that such interaction will lead to the monks' becoming like lay people. Thus, when the *Mahāvaṃsa* recounts the first expulsion of a monk from the monkhood (it occurred during the reign of Vattagāmaṇī [89–77 B.C.]), the cause was his mingling with the families of lay people (*Mhv.* 33.95, but see also Gunawardana 1979: 24).

Reformation has often come at times when the monkhood is on the edge of extinction, either because the order contains fewer than the five members necessary for its ordaining more members or because the monasteries have been abandoned, razed, or deprived of property. Under these conditions the state will hardly reform the monastic order by taking things away from the monks. Instead, the king must bring more monks into the *sangha* by holding ordinations or by restoring monasteries and endowing them with land. Under more favorable material conditions, reform entails unifying the monks, improving their behavior, and removing lay people from monasteries. In neither case does the state force poverty on the monks.

The power of the ruler to reform the *sangha* is complemented by the *sangha*'s role in legitimating the power of the state. Gift exchange is an essential vehicle for both the king and his clerics. Thus, when Mahinda and his retinue bring Buddhism to the island, they establish the religion by the act of tracing an emblematic boundary (*sīmā*) within which Theravāda monks perform ecclesiastical acts. In doing so they incorporate and make sacred the preeminent city of the state.[7] The rituals of exchange continue, for the establishment of monastic lands is emblematic of the establishment of the *dhamma* within the kingdom as a whole.[8] After the monks acknowledge that they can properly accept a dwelling place (*ārāma*), Devānampiyatissa offers them a park:

> It is well, said the king, and taking a splendid vase he poured water (in token) of giving, over the hand of the thera Mahinda with the words: "This Mahamegha-park do I give to the brotherhood." As the water fell on the ground, the great earth quaked. And the protector of the earth asked the [thera]: "Wherefore does the earth quake?" And he replied: "Because the doctrine is (from henceforth) founded in the island." (*Mhv.* 15.24–26)

As the thera Mahinda and Devānampiyatissa walk about the capital, the monk scatters flowers at various spots where monastic buildings will be located—a place for ecclesiastical acts, a room for warm baths, the site of the Bodhi tree, a place where gifts will be distributed, a refectory, the site of the great relic mound. Each time a place is given over to Buddhism, the earth quakes. At last Devānampiyatissa asks, "Does the doctrine of the Conqueror stand, sir?" and Mahinda replies, "Not yet . . . only, O lord of nations, when the boundaries are established here for the *uposatha*-ceremony (the recitation of monastic rules) and the other acts (of religion) . . . shall the doctrine stand'' (15.180–81).

On the one hand, land ensures the continuity of the monkhood, for as long as monks have land they need not worry about their livelihood. And as long as the monkhood survives, the *dhamma* survives. On the other hand, the king's protection of the *sangha*'s wealth and virtue demonstrates his right to rule. Landed wealth thus serves as the mediating vehicle by which the *sangha* and the state share political power and moral legitimacy. Kings establish and maintain sacred boundaries within monasteries to affirm this commonality. When the evil king Mahasena wishes to recover the Mahāvihāra from its resident monks and give it to Jetavana-vihāra monks, he does not expel them (for they have already fled), nor does he simply appropriate the monasteries. First he ''removed the boundaries.'' In so doing he does not desecrate or desacralize the sacred area, rather he breaks the connection between the Mahāvihāra monks and the state. Kings, in other words, deny the relationship between themselves and groups of monks by denying those monks their rights in land. Monks can break the relationship, too. But they do so not by returning land but by refusing alms, a result accomplished by inverting the alms bowl (*patta-nikkujjana*). In each case the connection is broken by denying the exchange relationship.

Formally, these gifts of land are given over to the monastic order at large. Like other gifts, land is *sanghika* (belonging to the monkhood as a whole). But in practice monasteries and attached lands are often given to a sect (*nikāya*) and to a particular monk.[9]

> After building the vihāra called Kurunda destined for the whole Order (of *bhikkhu*s) . . . [he] granted it to Mahasiva as his dwelling and in addition to it revenues, honours and distinctions and a hundred monastery attendants. Near to it he built the Ambilapassava-vihāra and granted the village of this name to the Ascetics of the Thera School. To the Unnavalli-vihāra he granted the far-famed village of Ratana . . . . (*Cv*. I 42.15–19)

In other instances (*Cv*. I 25.25 and 45.53) a monastery is given to a specific monk, who promptly gives it over to the order. One Grand Thera (*Cv*. I 42.25) acts thus, handing over a monastery to sixty-four *bhikkhu*s who practiced yoga, because ''he no longer possessed wishes.'' But monasteries and lands are not returned to the state. To do so would violate the covenanted relationship. The inviolability of the revenues produced by these properties becomes a public understanding by the tenth century, when King Mahinda IV has it engraved in stone: ''Kings shall in the future take no revenues for themselves out of the revenues of the *Order*'' (*Cv.* I 54.28).

WEALTH AND REFORMATION

I have argued that monastic wealth is seen as a positive good, morally and politically in the Sinhalese chronicles, and that the ''serious'' moral issue has been its undisciplined use. I turn now to the matter of reformation in the face of such misuse. In doing so I want to raise the possibility that the primary impulse of reformation has been to put corrupt monks back on the right course by taking wealth away from them as individuals, but not from the monastic order generally. Most often reform has taken the path of creating greater equality of wealth among the monks, not of impoverishing them.

The importance of reformation in Theravāda Buddhism does not need a full rehearsal. In early Sinhalese history reformation served to purge the Buddhist sects of heretical beliefs; later on, when Theravāda had prevailed, reformation removed not heretical monks but corrupt ones. The initiative for reform lay with the king, who acted in conjunction with favored monks. The king expelled corrupted monks and, thenceforth, lent his authority to the writing of codes of conduct (*dhammakamena* or *katikāvata*), which spelled out rule by rule the proper behavior expected of the monks who remained in the order. Reformation was not only the king's prerogative, it was his responsibility and essential for maintaining his legitimacy. In so acting, the king enhanced his status as a Buddhist leader, which he acted out on more routine occasions by financially supporting monastic establishments and celebrations, by appointing monks to ecclesiastical offices, and by arbitrating monastic disputes. Ultimately, the king controlled those who entered the order and the donation of land to the monkhood by lay people. Reformative situations reveal the peculiarity of the king's position: the man who was expected to reform the *sangha* and maintain its purity was only a layman and, thus, of a relatively inferior sacred status. In keeping with the king's ambivalent position, the codes of conduct he proposed have a contractual character. The etymology of the word *katikāvata* suggests that these codes were more like agreements between king and monkhood than royal legislation (Ratanapala 1971: 6).

The *Mahāvaṃsa* and *Cūlavaṃsa* speak of some thirteen reforms in the course of one hundred twenty-five kingly reigns from the Anuradhapura period to the conquest of Kandy in 1815 (see table of reformation periods in note 10); the establishing of the Amarapura and Rāmañña during the British occupation may be counted as reformations, although they are rather different social phenomena.[10]

On the matter of reform, the sacred histories are nothing if not terse. Little or no comment is directed to the impact of reform on monastic wealth. We might expect from the Burmese example that reformation in Sri Lanka was an occasion for the state to reclaim monastic land for its own purposes, to return the monkhood to a condition in which the temptations of property are minimized, and to replenish the state's treasury (cf. Aung Thwin 1979). But there are only a few examples of a Sinhalese king who takes wealth away from the monkhood, and these intrusions were prompted not by reformative purposes but by the undisguised need to raise revenue for making war.[11] Generally, reform left the amount of monastic wealth unchanged, although monks could be expelled and new ones installed in their monasteries. Because reformation does not disturb monastic property, the routine system of property holding has great continuity, and the survival of monastic lines seems to suffer more from the rise and fall of various Sinhalese kingdoms than from reformation.

One crucial component of the monastic property holding-system is the body of traditions concerning succession for the monks administering property. Generally, it was the case that the lines of descent evolved in such a way that control over monastic property ended up in the hands of successively smaller groups of monks. The first caves given to early Sinhalese monks were given over to the "*sangha* of the four quarters, living and dead," and gifts to the monkhood have this same nominal character to the present day. But by the early medieval period (ninth to thirteenth centuries), effective management of property belonged to the monks of one of the constituent groups (*nikāya*) of the *sangha*, and narrower traditions of property holding followed (Gunawardana 1979: 57–94). By the tenth century the rule of *siṣyā paramparāva* (student descent) was stipulated for at least some monasteries. Their control was vested in those monks who were students of previous incumbents.[12] By the fourteenth century, some monasteries came to be vested in certain families, a custom known as *sivuru paramparāva*. The incumbencies of such monasteries had to be taken up by sons of a certain family, perhaps because of a remembered act of charity of the family. Both of these rules continue in force to the present, although Sri Lankan courts presume that every monastery is held under the rules of *siṣyā paramparāva* unless the contrary is proved. Because of these lines of descent, certain monasteries in Sri Lanka have remained in the permanent control of particular monkly lines, passed down from teacher to student to that student's student over long periods of time. It is less clear that incumbencies have also been indivisible, but a series of colonial judicial decisions have so codified monastic law (see Kemper 1984: 401–27). At present, at least, secondary students have no authority over their monastery and no rights to its revenues, unless the chief student defrocks himself.

The only *katikāvata* that speaks of property holding directly is a *vihāra katikāvata* (a code for conduct intended for the administration not of the monkhood as a whole, but of the monks of a particular monastery) issued by Kirti Sri Rājasiṁha and the reformist monk Saranamkara in 1753. This code reiterates the place of *siṣyā paramparāva* under which the monastery had been held. But it also says that future gifts of lands and villages "should be divided into a number of portions equal to the number of *bhikkhus* assembled plus two," one extra portion going to the monastery itself, and another for the chief monk (Ratanapala 1971: 175–76).[13] If we can take this *vihāra katikāvata* as more than caprice or the king's solution to a local problem, its implication is important. It puts property rights into the hands of more monks, not fewer. Instead of returning monks to the homeless state, quite the opposite happens in this case: reform puts property in the hands of more monks, and not as the *sangha* or the *nikāya* as a whole, but as joint holders. At the same time, the original dedication of the monasteries is respected, and the chief monk is given a double portion, befitting his position. This code does not seem to envision either homelessness or complete equality, but it does diminish the high concentration of wealth in the hands of a few.

Records from the early period of British occupation reveal another generalization about how property was held by Buddhist monks. *Siṣyā paramparāva* was the most common rule of succession, although several cases of dedications from that period apply the rule rather differently from its modern form. The Bambave monastery and its attached lands were given in 1759 to Urulawatte Dhammasiddhi to be passed on to one of his pupils "suited for a religious life, not addicted to material gain, disciplined and just" (Dewaraja 1972: 111–12). Kirti Sri Rājasiṁha gave the Kelaṇiya monastery in 1779 to Mapitigama Buddharakhita "so that he and one of his pupils, the most worthy and learned in the holy *vinaya* and *dhamma*, in succession shall preserve this holy place" (Woodhouse 1917–18: 183 n.7). The Alut Vihāra inscription (1801) dedicates the monastery to "the pupils and sub-pupils of the virtuous Dhammasiddhi Sami, as shall be diligent in imparting instruction to their auditors, free from avarice and observant of the dictates of religion and justice" (Lawrie 1896: 74–76). In each case succession goes to the most deserving student—"virtuous," "not addicted to material gain," "disciplined," "learned," and "free from avarice" are the affirmed qualities of character—not the first student given the robes by the previous incumbent. The colonial period saw the succession rule that understood property as a sign of merit replaced by one that recognized only seniority.

However widespread the application of *siṣyā paramparāva*, there was considerable diversity in local practice. Historical testimony from the monks indicates great variety, and our knowledge of legal and administrative affairs in the Kandyan kingdom generally also suggests that variety was the order of the day. There were cases of one monk's controlling many monasteries, of a single monastery being controlled and enjoyed by several monks, of property passing beyond the teacher-student line, and even cases of succession controlled by lay people.[14] Thus, reformation does not invariably entail one particular mode of property holding, but it does seem a fair conjecture that experimentation with variant modes of managing property has been an attractive way during reformative times to create unity, provide materially for all monks, and establish grounds for the disciplined use of property. There was no seachange between ordinary times and reformative ones; monastic wealth remains a constant. But it seems from the historical record that a popular method to curtail the monks' abuse of wealth was to reorganize the system by putting property in the control of more monks.

Later instances support this conclusion. A good example is the case of Attudawe Dhammarakhita, the founding monk of one of the premier Amarapura *nikāya*s, a social and religious movement of Low Country lay people and monks which picked up the reformative tradition from Sinhalese kings after the British conquest. Dhammarakkhita ordained eight students, two of whom were much older than the rest and roughly his contemporaries. Dhammarakkita's will gives joint control of his monastery to his two senior students, but adds that the

> other six students can enjoy the temple land and its property, each having 1/8 share and an equal amount of power. No person can sell or gift his land without the consent of the first two monk sons. My first two students can hand over their power and rights to anyone they like before their deaths. After the death of the first two monks, according to the Buddhist system, the *nāyaka*-ship must go to the chief monk brother (*pävidi-sahōdaraya*) surviving at the time. Unity is one of the great goals, therefore you must not fight with each other over anything. You must obey your elder monk brothers, and you must kindly receive guests who come to the temple. . . .

Attudawe, Dhammarakkita
(handwritten copy
of his will owned by police sergeant
Kahakachchi, Devinuwara, Sri Lanka)

Here there is no expectation that monks will ''wander lonely as a rhinoceros,'' only the desire for unity and indifference both to the indivisibility of the office of incumbent and of property rights and to the impermeability of the line between students and outside monks of other monkly lineages. But there is the instruction that property be held in a collective way—let each of the eight students enjoy an equal share of the property—and that the office of incumbent (*nāyaka*) pass not from teacher to student, but from student to the next most senior student. Although this mode of succession goes unmentioned in the major works on Buddhist ecclesiastical law, some Low Country monks still know of it and refer to it as *vurdha paṭpattiya* (roughly, ''contrary practice'').[15]

Despite Dhammarakkhita's reference to ''the Buddhist system'' of monastic inheritance, it is not clear that there existed a clearly articulated and general ''Buddhist system'' in the Low Country during the Amarapura reformation or that *vurdha paṭipattiya* was followed by any Low Country monks beyond the Dhammarakkhita *nikāya*. In other parts of the Low Country the laity made submissions in the late nineteenth century to the colonial government, asking that it establish ways for monks to ''settle disputes according to Buddhist rules which clearly precluded the idea of individual ownership of temple properties'' (Wickremaratne 1969: 145). Although this horizontal mode of succession has no legal force now in either the Dhammarakkhita *nikāya* or Dhammarakkhita's own monastery in Devinuwara in the Southern Province, other monks of the *nikāya* have taken cases to court, arguing for the applicability of this mode of succession, and still others have left similar wills.

Here, again, wealth is not the target of reformation. Its abuse is the serious problem. The individual and exclusive ownership of monasteries and their lineal descent set up by the rule of *siṣyā paramparāva* invites the abuse of wealth by giving great power and prestige to one monk while depriving all others of both. By contrast, the rule of *vurdha paṭipattiya*, like the provision for new wealth mentioned in the Kirti Sri Rājasiṅha *katikāvata*, puts wealth in many hands—an appropriate arrangement when ''unity is one of the great goals.'' Thus, it appears that these modifications of the rules of succession have as their goal not the impoverishment of the *sangha* but the reduction of inequalities of power and privilege that invite the abuse of wealth.

Similarly, the *katikāvatas* show no interest in returning monks to poverty or the peripatetic life. On the contrary, they try to prevent monks from wandering about from monastery to monastery, practicing occupations unsuitable for the renouncer's life, and from housing lay people in monasteries.[16] Reformation consists not in a return to mendicancy, but in keeping monks in their respective monasteries. The fate of the Sri Lankan ascetic (*tāpasa*) movement of the 1950s is a case in point. Despite the charisma and extraordinary asceticism of these wandering monks, lay people and orthodox monks came to be suspicious about these monks' good behavior simply because they were on the move (Carrithers 1979: 298–304). Who knows how they act when they are elsewhere? In other contexts I have heard homeless monks referred to as *gosāva* (noise, confusion). They are people out of place.

The norm of stable monastic residence is also reflected in the naming of monks. Sinhalese monks have, at least since Kandyan times, been identified by two names, one of which indicates place of birth. Thus, Attudawe Dhammarakkita was a man born in the village of Attudawe who took the monkly name Dhammarakkhita. Monks are not obliged to remain in their natal villages, but they are expected to keep close by whatever residence they choose; a monk can shift his residence properly enough, he simply cannot always be shifting it. To do so would be to become a person of uncertain identity, without name or place. In this distinct sense the *sangha* should be "domesticated." It has been so for virtually the entirety of Sinhalese history, and it has possessed wealth in considerable amounts for almost as long. Over this same period the monastic life of practice and teaching (*grantha-dhura*) has been not only distinguished from one of isolated meditation (*vipassanā-dhura*), but also regarded as more difficult and more prestigious. The Dambadeni *katikāvata* defines the life of meditation by default: "those (monks) who are unable to master a great portion of the *grantha-dura* in the manner mentioned should be engaged in fulfilling the functions of solitude" (Ratanapala 1971: 148).

Stability in monastic residence has economic implications. A stable life in a single monastery generally brings a monk greater contact with the laity and greater opportunities for wealth, and both are encouraged. *Grantha-dhura* monks act as both teachers and exemplars. Their life is with lay people. A monk who shows promise in this life deserves promotion to higher rank and more independence from his teachers, "if [he] lives observing the *sīla* precepts, (endowed) with a great knowledge that makes him fit to become a teacher of a group and without indulging in a life of abundance and lethargy thereby leading the people who come after him into the way of wrong views'' (Ratanapala 1971: 145). Such monks have rights to property and revenues because they are not prone to abundance and lethargy. Lay possessions are not proper: ''even an ear ornament worn by one's mother should not be kept in one's possession with the idea of treasuring it'' (Ratanapala 1971: 149). But in spelling out what is not legitimate for the monkly life, the *katikāvata*s also give us indirect evidence of what is acceptable. In saying that the monastic office entitled *mahā-svami* should be filled by a ''well-disciplined *bhikkhu* endowed with virtue and wisdom, who is not attached to the gains that do not come from within (the endowments of the monastic foundation),'' the Damadeni *katikāvata* recognizes the *mahā-svami*'s proper rights to that local endowment (Ratanapala 1971: 147). A provision in the Kirti Sri Rājasiṅha *katikāvata* goes a step further in clarifying a monk's legitimate rights: ''Having spent the revenue of the villages which belong to the *vihāra* on the expenses connected at that *vihāra* itself a *bhikkhu* should enjoy (the rest of the) revenue while staying in the same *vihāra*'' (Ratanapala 1971: 170). Even though the force of the following sentence is that revenue should not be taken to another place and enjoyed, the passage obliquely suggests the legitimacy of a monk's enjoying his *vihāra*'s excess revenue and enjoying it personally, just as long as he does not move about with it. Thus, in manipulating the lines of descent between elders and their students and in encouraging stability in monastic locations, the reforming impulse has broken up individual concentrations of wealth, encouraged unity among monks by means of dispersed wealth and control, and discouraged the path of wandering asceticism.

MONKLY CHARACTER: MERIT, WEALTH, AND BEAUTY

Wealth has been a legitimate part of a Sinhalese monk's social role and it continues to be so. Local expectations and practices reveal as much. As a concluding area of investigation I want to explore the present-day Sinhalese conceptions of monkly character and physical appearance to show how wealth and merit figure in these cultural constructions of world renunciation. As always, the Lord Buddha is the preeminent model for Buddhist ideals. Most interesting for my purposes is the way he is revered for both his spiritual accomplishment and his worldly respectability and beauty. Several informants in Sri Lanka have told me, without prompting or foregrounding, that no one could find fault with the Lord Buddha. There was nothing about his lay life to bring dishonor on him. Not only was he of high caste and royal origin, he was a "great being." At birth his body bore thirty-two auspicious signs revealing his destiny—to be either a great king (*cakkavatti*) or a *buddha*. These claims serve several purposes. They express the existential grounds of the Buddha's doctrine, emphasizing that even the wealthiest and most well-to-do face the problem of suffering. But they also make possible a devotional cult revering the Buddha's person, for he is a high-status individual for whom lay people—high and low alike—can show veneration.

Buddhist monks are "sons of Buddha" and are supposed to possess similar virtues of character and appearance. The monk's social appearance is important, for his respectability ensures that his advice is worth soliciting and worth following. According to informants, the heart of this respectability is the monk's *tänpotkama* (self-control or discipline), the most important quality for a monk to cultivate, and the foundation upon which other qualities of character may be added.[17] It is also a lay person's most desired quality. Typically, self-control is associated with age, and with age, it is thought, comes selflessness and a greater interest in lay people. Accordingly, the laity prefer to deal with older monks. In the Sinhalese Buddhist perception, thirty-three is the critical age at which one's health begins to deteriorate, as do one's exuberance and selfishness. When one has mastered one's passions, this condition can be recognized by signs of calm in one's face and gestures. Monks who control monasteries these days are long past thirty-three, and they are expected to be disciplined.

The most attractive monks, ones with reputations for great virtue or learning, are said to be *pin pāṭa*. Literally, they have the "color" or "look" of merit. They have accumulated such great amounts of merit that, like mastery over the self, their virtue shows itself in their appearance. Lay people are drawn to such monks because to be *pin pāṭa* is to be *saumya* (moonlike and, hence, beautiful). Certain physical traits are associated with being *pin pāṭa*. For a man to be so, he must be heavily set, if not slightly obese, his face must be smooth and full, and his skin tone must be vital and light brown in color. In a word, he must look "healthy."

Laymen too may be *pin paṭa*. Any male, monk or layman, who has the virtues of *tänpotkama* and *karuṇāyantakama* (kindness) will be said to have *saumya* qualities. It is possible to be a handsome man without having these internal qualities (*guṇaya*), but lay people say that 75 percent of all beautiful Sinhalese men have these *saumya* qualities. To be *pin pāṭa*, and thus *saumya*, is to have the flush of success, to look like a meritorious person. Thus, wealthy merchants, politicians, and westerners in general are regarded as *pin pāṭa*. Their worldly success and beauty is thought to be matched by inward achievement. What is critical here is that no distinction is made between the look of merit as it appears in monks and as it appears in prosperous laymen. By their physical attributes (and their ideals for appearance generally) monks are linked with other well-to-do people. The opposite condition is known as *pav pāṭa* (the look of demerit). Such people can be recognized by their dull skin tone and angular features, which the Sinhalese regard as too rough (*ralu väḍiyi*). Dark skin is also associated with this lack of merit. Such people are said to be less *tänpot*, as evidenced by the fact that the town drunkard was pointed out to me as the epitome of this condition: the man was a "blackguard" in both senses of the word "black."

Thus, basic commonalities between accomplished monks and successful layman are affirmed in the Sinhalese conceptions of physical beauty.[18] The connecting link is the doctrine of *kamma*, that personal appearance reflects merit accumulated in past births which in turn influence one's fortunes in this birth. The Lord Buddha in his iconic representations is considered incomparably beautiful. Monks likewise should be beautiful. Thus, when a monk is ready to robe his first student—and thus his successor—especially if his choice is not a kinsman, he will consider two factors: the boy's horoscope and his appearance. If a monk is not handsome, householders will not be eager to associate with him.

Like the Lord Buddha's thirty-two marks, a monk's physical features stand for internal qualities. According to this reasoning, a man should be robed because he has been a monk in previous lives. A *saumya* appearance indicates his previous experience in the monkhood. Beauty makes a monk worthy of respect, a monk once told me, and monks must be respectable because even kings show them veneration. The notion that only men who have accumulated great stores of merit are robed comes into play when a young boy joins the order. On this occasion he receives gifts not only from his family and friends but also from senior monks. Ordinarily the opposite relationship applies: young initiates give gifts to their teachers. Here, however, older monks give the gifts and do so because the young initiate is thought to be a very attractive field of merit. The fact that he is being robed demonstrates his having great merit, and because he is taking on the heavy responsibility of wearing the robes, it is clear that he has violated none of the precepts that weigh upon monks. Giving gifts to him gains immense amounts of merit for older monks, because the boy has great merit, and it is unsullied.

The striking quality in these ideas is the lack of distinction among kinds of merit. The merit that made the Lord Buddha a "great being" could have been used either in the social world as a king or in renunciation as a *buddha.* The great merit that warrants a young boy's robing will also serve him in a business or political career. Their shaved heads and yellow robes not withstanding, Buddhist monks look like politicians and merchants. At least the meritorious ones do. Thus, it is thought that the prosperous merchant and the "possessionless" renunciant are, on the scale of merit, perhaps only one lifetime apart. If such monks control property and enjoy its revenues, such is not corruption but the proper consequence of their past lives and a legitimate context for their present ones. The issue is the disciplined use of property. The Sinhalese soothsayers who foretold the coming of Buddhist monks to the island saw deeper into the future than they knew: "The earth is occupied by these (*bhikkhu*s); they will be lords upon the island."

8 Buddhist Practical Moralit in a Changing Agrarian World:

A Case from Northeastern Thailand

Charles F. Keyes

Morality, as Little and Twiss (1978: 27) have said, "provides a way of responding to what we call the 'problem of cooperation' among self-interested, competing, and conflicting persons and groups." Their approach to the study of morality focuses on the patterns of reasoning different traditions employ in dealing with this problem. In my view any study of morality should also include elements of a sociology of morals, that is, an inquiry into the way in which moral "concepts are embodied or at least can be in the real social world" (MacIntyre 1981: 22). In this paper I will be concerned with the practical morality that serves to resolve problems of social cooperation within an actual social world, one found in rural, northeastern Thailand.

By speaking of a "practical morality" I mean to draw attention to the fact that as an anthropologist I will be describing the actual practices and reasoning a particular group of people employ in handling what we generally recognize as the moral problems of social interaction. This approach should be distinguished from an attempt to derive a normative ethical code from the core doctrines of a religion or from some version of reason divorced from history. Whereas the latter approach tends to ask how a set of moral concepts might orient action within a theoretical social world, my approach begins with an actual social world and seeks to identify the moral concepts that are employed and to locate the cultural and material sources of these concepts.

Within actual social worlds action is shaped by a practical morality revealed in evaluative language. The premises of such evaluative language are rooted in a world view taken to be fundamentally or absolutely true. As Alasdair MacIntyre (1981: 63) has put it, "at the foundation of moral thinking lie beliefs in statements for the truth of which no further reason can be given." In societies in which a world view has been reproduced by essentially the same cultural productions (such as ritual) over several generations, and social life follows rhythms informed by that traditional world view, the practical morality or ethos of the society becomes unquestioned common sense (cf. Geertz 1973: Chapts. 4

and 5). The givenness of such unquestioned practical morality has been undermined in many, now perhaps most, societies, by radical challenges deriving primarily from the shaking of social worlds as a consequence of their integration into a global politi[redacted]der and from the introduction of new modes of secular thought. In these transformed worlds moral action often no longer simply flows [redacted] sense; rather people confront circumstances in which they find they must make conscious ethical choices.

In this chapter I will be concerned with the way in which people in one actual society have become increasingly constrained to make ethical choices rather than simply acting in accord with a given ethos. The world view of Thai-Lao people of the northeastern region of Thailand has long been rooted in Theravāda Buddhism. The premises of this Buddhist world view have been given coherence primarily in rituals in which clergy, who trace their descent to the earliest *sangha* founded by the Buddha, play the major role. The traditional world view of Thai-Lao villagers has in recent years been reshaped as a consequence of significant cultural changes associated mainly with the increasing intrusion of the Thai state into rural life. The social world of villagers has also been significantly changed, especially since the early 1950s, through a shift in the rural economy from one based primarily on subsistence to one increasingly oriented toward national and international markets. In their transformed world villagers often find that their economic actions no longer reflect an implicit ethos. Many have come to feel a tension between the ideal of how "good Buddhists" should act and the moral significance of the actions they or others engage in. The ways in which this tension is confronted and actions are evaluated constitute a new practical morality, albeit one that is still recognizably Buddhist.

THE ECONOMIC CONTEXT OF NORTHEASTERN THAI RURAL COMMUNITIES

In exploring the transformation in Thai-Lao Buddhist villagers, I draw on researches carried out over a twenty-year period primarily in one particular village in northeastern Thailand. Ban Nǫng Tųn, located in the central northeast Thai province of Mahasarakham, is a poor village in the poorest region of Thailand.[1] As a World Bank study (1978) has shown, the rural poor in Thailand are most heavily concentrated in the northeastern region, which has a long history of underdevelopment relative to the rest of the country. In 1977 per capita income in northeastern Thailand was $112 per year, as compared to the national average of $266.

In 1976 95.7 percent of the population of the Northeast resided in rural areas, and the agricultural households of the region accounted for 40 percent of all such households in the kingdom. Ban Nǫng Tųn is typical of the rainfed agricultural communities populating this impoverished rural region.

During the past three decades Thailand has experienced one of the highest rates of economic growth of any Third World country, and the villagers of northeastern Thailand have shared to some extent in this growth. In Ban Nǫng Tųn, for example, the average household cash income in 1963 was about $150; in 1980 it had risen to $655. Even allowing for inflation, it is clear that villagers were enjoying a higher level of income. Such gains notwithstanding, the relative economic position of the Northeast vis-à-vis the rest of the country actually deteriorated over this time. Taken as a percentage of the national average, the per capita income in the Northeast dropped from 61 percent in 1968–69 to 42 percent in 1977. In other words economic growth in Thailand over the last few decades has been much more heavily concentrated in other parts of Thailand—especially Bangkok—than in the Northeast.

This economic growth has brought typical problems of social dislocation and material inequality, and these problems have been exacerbated by the ethno-regional conflicts characteristic of the northeastern region. Most of the people of northeastern Thailand are culturally and linguistically closer to the Lao of Laos than to the Central Thai of Thailand. They differ from the Lao in that they have been exposed to significant national Thai influences for several generations, particularly through the national school program. It is for this reason that I call the dominant ethnic group in the Northeast the *Thai-Lao*. The Thai-Lao themselves tend to couch their differences with the Central Thai, especially Thai officials, in regional terms, calling themselves *khon īsān*, ''people of the Northeast'' (see Keyes 1967).[2] Although the government has directed a good deal of attention to the region in the form of economic programs and military campaigns aimed at eliminating a persistent Communist insurgency, the ''northeastern problem,'' a problem that is both economic and political, very much remains.

Villagers in Ban Nǫng Tųn are conscious of their distance from the rest of the Thai, although they talk about it in different terms than those used by government policymakers and politicians. Villagers are particularly aware that their standard of living is much lower than that in urban areas. This awareness has been fueled by stories recounted by those villagers (who may constitute as much as a third to a half of the adult populations of most villages in the region) who have worked as laborers in

Bangkok. Villagers speak of themselves as being "poor" compared to those who live in Bangkok.

In spite of the unevenness of Thailand's economic development, there have been substantial economic gains in the Northeast over the last three and especially the last two decades. This growth has meant increased market demand for village produce—especially for rice and livestock and secondarily for such cash crops as kenaf and cassava—to which most, but not all, villagers have responded. This growth has also been associated with some differentiation of the rural economy; one now finds in most villages some families who run nonagricultural enterprises such as rice mills, transport firms, and shops. Together, economic growth and differentiation have created noticeable inequalities in the distribution of wealth in the villages.[3] In short, villagers in Ban Nọng Tụn, like those in similar communities throughout the northeastern region, live in a newly created situation of economic change, a situation requiring unprecedented decision making about the proper courses of economic action. Such decisions are made with reference to a world view still rooted in Buddhism but reshaped by recent cultural changes.

CULTURAL KNOWLEDGE AND THE BUDDHIST WORLD VIEW IN THAI-LAO COMMUNITIES

Northeastern Thai villages like Ban Nọng Tụn have long been guided by the order of farming conditions. There is a rhythm to the alternating seasons (wet and dry with the latter being divided into hot and cold) and the agricultural cycle that is articulated with it. There is a rhythm also in the cycle of rituals (called *hīt sipsǭng*, the "twelve customs") that punctuate the calendar. These patterns have never defined an undisturbed order, since in the past, as today, villagers experienced droughts and floods, sickness and death, and political upheaval. But such "natural" intrusions into the ordinary rhythms of life generated relatively manageable problems of meaning that Thai-Lao villagers could interpret within the patterns and themes of their traditional world view.

Central to this traditional world view and culture is the institution of the *sangha*, or monastic order. The *sangha* consists of those who leave the ordinary life of a householder and, following ordination, subject themselves to the "discipline" (*winai*, from the Pāli *vinaya*). This discipline is, in its essentials, the same for Thai-Lao monks and novices today as it was in earliest Buddhism (cf. Holt 1981). In northeastern Thailand, as in other Southeast Asian Buddhist societies, it has been a longstanding custom for most males to join the *sangha*, even if only for a limited period of time. In contrast to western monastic practices, there is no sense of failure or repudiation attached to this temporary membership. On the contrary, the practice of temporary ordination has achieved the status of a cultural ideal and has become an accepted social practice. Typically, village men enter the order shortly after the age of twenty and remain for one or two lenten periods.[4] Among the Thai-Lao in particular, this cultural ideal continues to be widely observed, with better than two-thirds of the adult male population having spent at least one lenten period as a monk or, less often, as a novice in the monastic order.[5]

Of those who continue as members of the *sangha* for life, most remain in the local village *wat*, or temple monastery. Some move to a town or urban *wat* noted as a center of learning, and a few go to live in forest hermitages. The northeastern region has a higher percentage of such hermitages than any other region in the country, and the ascetic monks who reside in them have achieved renown not only within the region but also nationally. Indeed, northeasterners have a national reputation for asceticism and disciplined piety.[6]

Inasmuch as all monks live with conscious reference to the Buddhist discipline, they can be said to have acquired some degree of tempering of the passions conducive to bad actions. Villagers prize this moral tempering, saying that a man who has been a member of the *sangha* will make a better husband and a better fellow villager. Those who become members of the *sangha* may also acquire some basic education and knowledge of a variety of religious texts. Some monks study the traditional texts that permit them to assume lay roles as congregation leaders or as practitioners of folk medicine, spirit exorcism, or securing the "vital essence" of persons. Others study the modern texts that form part of the religious studies curriculum established by the Thai national *sangha* and the Department of Ecclesiastical Affairs in the Ministry of Education. All monks memorize Pāli chants used in community rituals, and most also become familiar with vernacular texts used as sermons at rituals. Not only do most men in Thai-Lao villages learn through becoming members of the *sangha* how to act in accord with Buddhist ideals, but while serving as novices and monks they become the vehicles through which these ideals are communicated to others in their communities.

Although the Thai-Lao world view includes some elements that betray a non-Buddhist origin (e.g., notions concerning "spirits"—*phī*—and "vital essence"—*khuan*), it continues to have a fundamentally Buddhist cast. The cosmic order that villagers come to know, primarily through their participation in rituals, is one predicated ultimately on the

Buddhist "law of *kamma*" (*kot hāēng kam*). The law of *kamma* constitutes the ultimate ordering principle of existence. *Kamma* refers, on the one hand, to the force set in motion by moral actions performed in previous lives. These actions determine the place that a sentient being occupies in a hierarchy of relative well-being (*khuāmsuk*) and suffering (*khuāmthuk*). In the thought of Thai-Lao villagers, as in popular Buddhist thought elsewhere, the sentient beings distributed along this hierarchy include not only humans (*khon*) in their various statuses (female and male, royalty and commoner, and so on), but also animals (*sat*), spirits (*phī*), and deities (*thēwādā*, Pāli: *devātā*). Within the generalized constraints of the position one occupies on the moral hierarchy, one is thought to have the freedom and, indeed, the responsibility to act in morally positive ways that will yield "merit" (*bun*, Pāli: *puñña*) and to avoid morally negative modes of behaving that will yield "demerit" (*bāp*, Pāli: *pāpa*). The doctrine of *kamma* thus includes moral responsibility as well as cosmological determination. By devoting oneself to acts that "bring merit" (*ao bun*) and avoiding acts that "garner demerit" (*dai bāp*), one will ensure that in a future existence, or perhaps even in this existence, one will attain a higher place in the hierarchy. The equal importance accorded to moral responsibility and cosmic determinism in popular Buddhist notions of *kamma* belies the assertion sometimes made by proponents of change in Thailand that the religious world view of northeastern peasants is conducive to a passive fatalism. Villagers, to varying degrees, believe that previous *kamma* constrains their ability to act, but they also act under the assumption that they control their religious destiny.

Northeastern villagers also acquire from rituals, sermons, and contact with ascetic monks some understanding of the Buddhist notion of *nibbāna*—the ultimate escape from the realm of sentient existence as ordered by the law of *kamma*. *Nibbāna* is a goal, however, to which very few villagers in northeastern Thailand—indeed, few adherents of Theravāda Buddhism anywhere—consciously aspire. Still, nibbanic concerns are not absent from the Thai-Lao world view; they are given expression in the ideal of "non-attachment," which the *sangha* embodies. This ideal pervades the "precepts" (*sīn* from *sīla*) to which villagers commit themselves. At the beginning of every Buddhist ritual the laity who are present "request the precepts" (*khōsīn*) from one of the attending monks, often the senior monk. This monk, in turn, "gives the precepts" (*hai sīn*). This interchange takes place in Pāli, but unlike much of the other ritual language (which is also in Pāli), the words chanted in this ritual sequence are well understood, at least by most adults. The precepts taken by the laity on most occasions are the "five precepts" (*sīn hā*), which can be rendered into English as follows:

> I undertake the precept to abstain from taking life;
> I undertake the precept to abstain from taking what is not given;
> I undertake the precept to abstain from improper sexual acts;
> I undertake the precept to abstain from telling lies;
> I undertake the precept to abstain from imbibing or ingesting substances that cause heedlessness.

On Buddhist sabbath—literally "precept day" (*wan sīn*)—during lent, some older villagers also commit themselves to taking the "eight precepts" (*sīn pāēt*), by which is meant that they observe three additional precepts for the day. If these eight precepts were kept all the time, one would have either become a member of the *sangha* or a lay disciple who wears white robes. These additional precepts are more ascetic than the previous five and include abstention from eating after noon, from sleeping on a high bed, and from attending entertainments and adorning the body. In addition, the third precept regarding sexual relations is reconstrued to mean abstaining from any sexual relations whatsoever during the sabbath day. Those who keep the (eight) precepts (*cam sīn*) often practice some meditation as well on the sabbath day. Although keeping the precepts is said by villagers to yield merit, such action is not typically thought of as merit-making; merit-making entails, for villagers, the offering of alms to the *sangha* in the context of rituals. Keeping the precepts reflects a deeper understanding of the *dhamma*, namely, that attachment to the pleasures of life (sex, drinking, gambling, feasting, attending entertainments), not to mention giving vent to one's base passions (through anger leading to the taking of life, through greed leading to taking that which is not given, and through deceit leading to the telling of lies), will bring suffering. Villagers may not be able to emulate the non-attachment of the ascetic monk, but insofar as they do observe the precepts, they too act with reference to the nibbānic ideal.

TRANSFORMATIONS OF THE THAI-LAO WORLD VIEW

The distinctive Buddhist world view of northeastern villages and the ethos associated with it have been greatly challenged over the last four or five decades by the introduction of new cultural experiences. The government primary schools, for example, equipped with a curriculum determined by the central Thai government, communicate a rather different vision of social order than the traditional view passed on in folk rituals and culture.[7] The curriculum emphasizes the acquisition of skills using the Thai (as distinct from Lao) language and of a sense of being a citizen in a Thai state ruled by a Thai king. About the same time that compulsory primary education was being introduced, northeastern villagers participated for the first time (in 1933) in a new type of ritual, an election. Though elections have rarely had real political significance, they have had an important expressive function of communicating a new sense of identity (Phillips 1958).

In the post World War II period other sources of cultural knowledge have further attenuated the power of the traditional pattern of village life. Young men, and subsequently young women, from northeastern villages have made their way to Bangkok to work in the numerous unskilled and semiskilled jobs being created by an expanding economy.[8] Typically, these villagers spend a few months to a few years in Bangkok and then return to life in the village. In Ban Nǫng Tụn, for example, in 1963 about a third of all villagers over the age of twenty had worked for a significant period in Bangkok.[9] As the economy expanded, the role of government grew and established increasing contacts between northeastern villagers and Thai government officials (*khā rātchakān*, literally ''servants of the king''). These contacts have meant an increase in the use of standard Thai rather than Lao, thereby situating villagers in a Thai-dominated world. Furthermore, since the early 1960s radio ownership has become common throughout the Northeast and today it is a rare villager who does not listen to a radio for a few hours a day (often while working in the fields). Although some of the programming is traditional northeastern fare—songs, folk operatic performances, and the like—most villagers also listen to national news. In the late 1970s as the rural electrification program was extended throughout the region, television sets began to appear in rural communities, and by the early 1980s television was becoming a major cultural influence in Ban Nǫng Tụn as in many other northeastern villages.

These new cultural influences have not posed a serious challenge to the underlying kammic basis of the northeastern Thai world view, but they have expanded the horizon of that world view. Villagers are today well aware of belonging to a Thai social order that is distinct from the ''local'' (*phų̄nmų̄ang*) Lao order they know in the village. Since this Thai order is also Buddhist, as is apparent from the symbols associated with the monarchy, the civil service, elections, the school, and even the radio and television, villagers conceive of its elements as fitting within the same cosmic framework as they have traditionally known. At the foundation of the Thai civic order is the Buddhist monarchy, and it is from this monarchy that the order derives, for northeasterners, its legitimacy.[10]

While northeasterners have come to view themselves as belonging to a Thai social order, other cultural influences have led them also to a sense of constituting a distinctive ethnoregional part of that order. In interaction with officials, who act as *cao nāi* (literally ''masters,'' possessors of unquestioned authority over villagers), northeastern culture is implicitly, and often explicitly, denigrated. Even when the official is himself (and most officials are male) a northeasterner by origin, his conversations with villagers are typically conducted in standard Thai rather than in Lao. Of at least equal significance to these interactions with Thai officials are the experiences villagers have in Bangkok. Those who go to Bangkok literally enter another world, one that is structured in terms that are, initially at least, quite alien. A few choose to assimilate to that world, to become Thai; most, however, find common cause with others from their own region and create enclaves—at *wat*s where many of the monks are northeasterners, at restaurants where northeastern food is served, at slum dwellings where most inhabitants are also from the Northeast, and at work situations where most who are employed (usually in menial jobs) are also northeasterners. It is in this context that northeasterners often begin to speak of themselves as *khon īsān* (''northeastern people'') or *khon Lāo* (''Lao people'') in contradistinction to *khon Thai* (''Thai people''). Those who hold such ethnoregional identities take pride in their cultural heritage and point to the economically disadvantaged place that northeasterners have within the Thai economy. The recognition that northeasterners suffer more than the Thai does not imply for the Thai-Lao that they occupy a lower rung on the cosmic hierarchy. On the contrary, they are likely to assert a moral superiority by pointing to their ability to ''endure hardships'' (*ot thon*) better than other people. In this connection northeasterners may point with pride to the fact that the most renowned ascetic monks in Thailand are mainly northeasterners.

Many northeastern politicians, as distinct from centrally appointed governmental officials, have associated themselves with the cause of the *īsān* and have, whatever their ideological orientation, pushed for policies that would lead to improvements in the economic situation of people in the region. Such action on the part of politicians has made elections not only Thai national rituals, but also rituals in which ethnoregionalism is often strongly manifest. The Communist Party of Thailand has also attempted to appeal to northeastern villagers by championing the cause of the poor peasantry vis-à-vis what they call an exploitative government. But the Communist Party has never succeeded in constructing an image of the world considered legitimate by the villagers. Despite nearly twenty years of armed insurrection in the Northeast, the Party today has only a few hundred followers among northeastern villagers. In contrast, other movements, some explicitly religious in character, have gained considerable popular support and have contributed to further changes in the world view of some northeastern Thai villagers.

One such important movement since World War II goes under the name of "dhammic group" (*mū tham*). Members speak of having been "ordained in the *dhamma*" (*būat tham*), somewhat comparable to being a "born-again" Christian. Although the movement has its roots in traditional culture and more proximate sources in religious activities of the 1930s, it began to grow only in the early 1970s. By the early 1980s it had a large following among villagers throughout the central and northern part of the northeastern region. In 1980 in Ban Nọng Tụn, for example, I found 58 percent of all households to have at least one member of the movement.

Those who join the movement hope to gain access to the power of the *dhamma* (*tham*) for purposes of curing afflictions, particularly emotional afflictions, and ensuring physical well-being. To gain this power, rituals are held at which people claim to be suffused by the *dhamma* in much the same way that adherents of certain Pentecostal sects believe they are vessels filled by the Holy Ghost. The *dhamma* here takes on a meaning rather different from its traditional Buddhist association, that is, as the teachings of the Buddha, the true meaning of reality, and the way to obtain salvation. For those who are members of the dhammic cult, the *dhamma* is an immanent sacred force. Those who become suffused with the *dhamma* are said to be able to speak in foreign tongues (e.g., Chinese, English) much in the same way, once again, as Pentecostals claim the gift of tongues by the power of the Holy Ghost. To obtain the power of the *dhamma*, adherents of the cult are led in ritual practice by a "teacher" (*ācān*), a man (and insofar as I was able to discover, all are men) who has gained his position by being a disciple of another teacher. A teacher proves himself by performing apparently miraculous cures. The line of teachers is ultimately traced to the founder of the movement, a layman identified as one Cān Man.

Those who join the movement engage in weekly collective rituals and perform daily rites in their own homes, and they also commit themselves to a rather stricter moral code than is observed by most lay villagers. Dhammic cult members either give up drinking entirely or else consume very little so as to be certain of not becoming drunk; they stop killing even small animals (although they still eat meat); they avoid eating raw meat, a delicacy at traditional Thai-Lao feasts, and they refuse to gamble. Dhammic cult members are often among the strongest supporters of the local *wat*, although the movement has a strong lay-centered character, in contrast to the *sangha*-centered nature of traditional village Buddhism.

Another area of cultural change has come with the introduction of health care and medications based upon western ideas of health. Even in 1963 I found that Ban Nọng Tụn villagers tended to confront health problems with cultural practices that emphasized the importance of having one's vital essence (*khuan*) secured to the body, having the humors in balance, avoiding the malfeasance of spirits (*phī*), and "dispelling the omens of bad fortune" (*sīa khọ*). Villagers were, however, beginning to make use of western medicines, and many villagers had had some contact with western-style health-care providers. In the past twenty years, however, dramatic change has been brought about by relatively easy access to western medications (in tablet or injection form) from doctors, nurses, midwives, health-station officials, pharmacists, "injection doctors" (actually persons with little training and knowledge), and even village shopkeepers. Moreover, many villagers have had operations and nursing care in hospitals. Perhaps the most striking change, apparent in the marked decline in the birth rate, has been the widespread adoption of family planning. These changes have not led to the total abandonment of traditional beliefs, but afflictions are far less likely to be seen in terms of such beliefs and to be treated with the associated practices than they were in the 1960s.

The increasing irrelevance of religious belief for some aspects of life in Thai-Lao villages is indicative of a growing separation between religious and secular spheres of meaning. Such secularization has been associated with the acquisition by villagers of a sense of acting in a world that extends beyond their local community to at least the boundaries of Bangkok-centered Thailand. Although the cultural transformation that has taken place within Thai-Lao villages has not undermined the basic premises of the Buddhist world view, it has challenged the sheer givenness of the ethos based on these premises. No longer does social life flow naturally from an implicit practical morality. Instead, villagers today often find themselves constrained to make conscious moral choices about which of several potential courses of action they might follow.

ECONOMIC ACTION AND MORAL CHOICE

In premodern times almost every household in Thai-Lao villages engaged in the same productive activities. For about three-quarters of the year life was organized around the production of rice. Every household had sufficient land for this purpose, for if its inheritance from the previous generation was insufficient, additional land was readily available. For the remainder of the year men fished, made farm implements, and built or repaired granaries and houses while women made both cotton and silk cloth and clothing. A few village men did seek to become more wealthy than others through trade beyond their home communities in cattle and water buffaloes. Those who were successful were given a distinctive title—*hōi*—by other villagers. The limited economic differentiation in Thai-Lao villages that these traders represented may have occasionally raised some moral concern. Such concern has become far more common in the contemporary context, in which economic differentiation is much more pronounced. Within the larger national world in which they now live, villagers are strongly encouraged through various government-sponsored programs to give priority in their actions to the attainment of material ends—to work to ''develop'' (*phatthanā*) themselves and society. Villagers today often find themselves confronted with deciding whether or not their own actions or those of others deemed to lead to ''development'' entail enfringements of the Buddhist precepts that must be adhered to if ultimate rather than temporary transcendence of ''suffering'' (*dukkha*) is to be achieved.

Thai-Lao villagers in northeastern Thailand are aware that some types of economic behavior can entail the bullying or taking advantage of others, thereby violating the moral proscription of the aggressiveness that accompanies anger or greed. In Ban Nọng Tụn in 1963–64 one man was referred to as a *nakleng*, a term often translated as ''scoundrel'' or ''rogue'' but which also connotes an especially masculine quality of adventuresomeness.[11] A *nakleng* is a man who achieves his ends by inspiring fear in others. Interestingly, the successful flaunting of dominant moral values, though said to incur demerit, also serves as a sign of intrinsic power of an almost magical quality (cf. Thak Chaloemtiarana 1979: 340), a quality that is presumably a product of previous merit. Moreover, a *nakleng*, if he lives long enough, may make use of the position he attains to be a conspicuous follower of the *dhamma* (cf. Blofeld 1960: 147–60). The *nakleng*, or one who acts aggressively in pursuit of his own ends, is typically found in almost every rural community, and some, like a former headman of a commune bordering on Ban Nǫng Tųn, may acquire considerable influence within a local area.

A similarly ambivalent judgment obtains toward those who demonstrate a marked ability to generate wealth through such entrepreneurial activities as rice milling, shopkeeping, trucking, and brokering trade in agricultural and craft products. In the past villagers have tended to see the main social cleavages as being between "villagers"/"rice farmers" and "officials"/"masters." A third category has become increasingly significant for villagers, that of "traders" or "merchants." Historically, most traders were conspicuous by being ethnically distinct; most were of Chinese origin, although some were Vietnamese. Villagers called such economic middlemen *taokāē*, a word derived from Chinese but also homonymous with a Lao word meaning "negotiator of brideprice." As long as middlemen were ethnically distinct from northeasterners, their behavior was not judged according to northeastern values. But as more and more Thai-Lao have themselves become merchants and traders, this exception could no longer be maintained.

The moral status of merchants and traders is particularly ambiguous for several reasons. In contrast to governmental officials, merchants—even very wealthy merchants from large towns—do not call forth deferential behavior on the part of villagers who deal with them. On the contrary, villagers are inclined to haggle with even prominent merchants over prices. Moreover, whereas the language villagers are expected to use with governmental officials is Thai, transactions with merchants, even with those who are of Chinese descent, are much more likely to be conducted in Lao. Merchants and traders, of course, must be responsive to the concerns and interests of the villagers if they are to make deals with them, whereas officials must be sensitive only to the expectations of their superiors. Officials also derive legitimacy from a monarch who is thought to have an exalted place in the cosmic hierarchy. The position of the merchants/traders, however, is less definite: while they enjoy the benefits of greater wealth, the means used to acquire their wealth is open to moral question.

The ambivalence commonly felt toward such successful merchants can be illustrated by the case of the main entrepreneur of Ban Nǫng Tųn. Mr. K was born into a rather average farming family in a nearby village. He got his start in a new living not through the use of capital provided by his family but by working in Bangkok for about six years. After working in unskilled construction jobs, he eventually found a job in a Chinese noodle factory. He made relatively good wages at this factory, and by resisting most of the temptations of the city, he saved enough to buy a small rice mill and open a modest shop in Ban Nǫng Tụn. From this beginning in 1961 he expanded his enterprise so that by 1980 he had a much larger rice mill; a well-stocked store; a truck that he used primarily for his middleman endeavors in the rice, charcoal, and kenaf trades; a large herd (seventy to one hundred at any one time) of pigs; and 3.5 hectares of land (none of it inherited). By his own estimation, as well as in the view of almost everyone in the village, he had become by the age of forty-five the richest man in Ban Nǫng Tụn.

In 1963–64 most adult villagers had used the title of *thit* with Mr. K, thereby indicating that he had been ordained as a monk. By 1980 the most common title I heard used was the traditional one of *hōi*, although he was also called *thaokāē* and *phōkhā*, all titles indexing his achievements in trade. He was greatly admired by many in the village for his diligence (*man*; *khanjan* from Thai *khayan*) and shrewdness (*keng*; *salāt*). But others also saw him as one obsessed by seeking after wealth (*hā ngōēn*), sometimes to the detriment of others in the village. The antagonism I detected among some villagers toward Mr. K in 1980 was a consequence not only of his economic position, however, but also of his alignment with a village faction opposing the present headman and his faction.

Mr. K himself thought he acted within the framework of village morality. He pointed, in this connection, to his support of the *wat* and the local monks and to his relatively generous gifts to those who invited him to the ordinations of their sons or relatives. Even in his merit-making, however, he had begun to set himself apart from other villagers. His was the only family in the village that had ever donated the entire sum toward the construction of a building in the *wat*—in this case, an elaborate bell-tower. He probably sponsored more house-blessing rites, rites held at his own home rather than at the wat, than anyone else. In other words, although he and his family continued to participate in communal merit-making rituals, he had begun to accord greater emphasis to religious endeavors wherein the primary participants as well as sponsors were his family. Mr. K demonstrated in my presence his respect for the *sangha*, but he clearly distinguished between learned monks and those who simply performed traditional rituals. He expressed considerable admiration for those "ordained in the *dhamma*" who had committed themselves to a stricter adherence than was traditional to the Buddhist precepts, but he was also openly skeptical of the significance of the charismatic rites performed by adherents of the movement. In sum, he did not ignore the moral stances taken by his fellow villagers, but he had come to see himself as the better arbiter in most circumstances of his moral actions.

The moral questions raised among villagers about the actions of Mr. K and other merchants are illustrative of a growing ethical debate taking place within Thai-Lao villages. It is important to note that the ethical debate derived from villagers' understanding of the Buddhist precepts is carried on in a social context in which there are few punitive sanctions that can be brought against those who are deemed to be violators of a moral code. Even in those cases in which a presumed violation of moral norms has also been a violation of Thai law, the offender may still escape any consequences because he or she has the resources to buy off the police or other officials who have been made aware of the action. Short of taking the law into their own hands, an extreme rarity, villagers must rely upon social esteem and disparagement as the main methods of ensuring compliance with moral norms. In northeastern Thai villages, however, esteem and disapproval are rarely unanimous. Only the learned or ascetic permanent monk gains unequivocal respect. Universal ostracism does occur, as in the case of a monk who was known to have been carrying on affairs with a number of women. But such instances are extremely rare. Judgment of those who become *nakleng* or middlemen is usually equivocal. Disapproval of their actions on moral grounds is often offset by a respect for their control over power and wealth as well as by the necessity of interacting with them.

Although the Buddhist notion that certain types of actions generate demerit functions to constrain aggressiveness, including economic aggressiveness, the economic ethic of villagers is not rooted in this notion alone. If it were, the Buddhist-based economic ethic of northeastern Thai villagers (as well as of adherents to Buddhism more generally) might be said to inhibit, albeit weakly, economic development in the capitalistic sense. But the Buddhist values do not consist solely of prohibitions against certain types of behavior; they also include inducements to undertake certain positive acts, those that will produce merit.

Productive acts (*het ngān*), even those connected with agriculture, are not in and of themselves religiously significant since they do not result directly in the generation of merit. However, since the acts of merit-making that villagers engage in require the expenditure of wealth, productive acts are viewed as a necessary prerequisite to merit-making (cf. Spiro 1966). Thus, the way in which religious goals are attained by most northeastern villagers serves as an incentive to be economically productive; the poor person suffers not only in the here and now, but also lacks the means to alter his or her place in the moral hierarchy in the future. Some of the leaders of the dhammic cult movement have made this connection between work and merit explicit by stressing that the more "diligent" (*man*; *khanjan*) a person is and the less "lazy" (*khīkhan*) he or she is, the more wealth will be available to use in making merit. A similar stance is taken by Mr. K, the chief entrepreneur in Ban Nọng Tụn, and, I suspect, by many entrepreneurs elsewhere.

In spite of the moral ambiguities surrounding economic entrepreneurship, northeastern Thai villagers have not responded to the pressures of market forces and government incentives to "develop" by attempting to withdraw into closed moral communities; on the contrary, they have demonstrated an overwhelming willingness to take advantage of economic opportunities. They have increased production of rice through the adoption of new rice strains; they have expanded production of such other crops as kenaf and cassava, and of animals and crafts, to take advantage of new market demands; and they have, in some cases, even taken on new occupations. In nearly every village there is today at least one villager has become an entrepreneur, having built a mechanized rice mill, established a shop, or bought a truck. Northeasterners migrate in great numbers to Bangkok (or other centers) to seek temporary, or sometimes permanent, nonfarm work. Indeed, their disproportionate representation in the Bangkok work force strongly suggests that northeasterners have been more willing than villagers from other parts of the country to take on nontraditional economic roles. It would appear, then; that the tension between religious and economic values has been resolved by most villagers in a practical synthesis. I would like to go even further and maintain that, in adapting to the changing circumstances of the past few decades, many Thai-Lao villagers have drawn on their traditional world view to develop something of a Buddhist work ethic. This religiomoral stance has been accentuated by the sense most Thai-Lao have of being a distinctive and subordinate ethnoregional minority within the Thai nation-state.

THE BUDDHIST WORK ETHIC OF THAI-LAO VILLAGERS

Thai-Lao villagers are motivated, like people everywhere, to pursue goals that bring this-worldly happiness. The changed world in which such villagers now live offers them a greater number of modes of such happiness. Some, almost invariably men, choose to turn their backs on traditional village morality and to take advantage of new opportunities to indulge themselves in consuming alcohol, gambling, and purchasing sexual favors. Most, however, recognize that such indulgence brings only temporary pleasure. Many more are attracted by the possibilities of being able to buy better food, clothing, and housing than can be produced out of (dwindling) resources available in the village and to buy better health care than is available in traditional curing practices. Such possibilities provide a strong incentive for villagers to produce for the market in order to gain the incomes necessary to make such improvements in their standard of living. It is not necessary to look for a religious basis for such a motivation, as it has become simple common sense.

What is not commonsensical is the notion that, although it might be possible through hard work to achieve modest increases in this-worldly happiness for oneself and one's family, such happiness is itself impermanent. Thai-Lao villagers continue to hold the Buddhist idea that human existence in any guise is ultimately characterized by suffering (*dukkha*). This idea is not merely philosophical, for it is fundamental to the practical ways in which villagers make sense of death as well as of the lesser, but still real, pains of hard labor in the rice fields, chronic ailments for which cures cannot be found or, if they exist, cannot be afforded, and for separation from family members. The impetus to achieve ultimate transcendence of suffering, to move, in other words, toward *nibbāna*, leads villagers to turn toward ways of acting that are different from those associated with the production of wealth that can be used for this-worldly happiness.

Thai-Lao villagers share with Theravāda Buddhists everywhere the practice of making merit, primarily through the offering of alms to the *sangha*, as a major means for moving themselves along the path to salvation. In addition to merit-making, Thai-Lao villagers also accentuate the importance of being able to forego gratification in order to overcome one's base desires. The importance the Thai-Lao accord to detachment is perhaps greater than that of any other group in Thailand, save ascetic monks (and such monks, it should be recalled, are most likely to be from rural Thai-Lao backgrounds). It is the cultivation of this Buddhist ideal of detachment by those who remain in the world, still seeking improvements in their this-worldly standards of living, that has contributed to the evolution of a distinctive work ethic among the Thai-Lao.

Villagers acquire the ability to act in the world while still being detached from—or, at least, having tempered—the desires characteristic of the world through processes of spiritual discipline. These processes are different for women than for men because in Thai-Lao thought, as in Buddhist thought elsewhere in Thailand (see Keyes 1984 and 1986), women and men are believed to have different problems of attachment to the world. For women, the problem is understood primarily in terms of their relationship to children. In anticipation of the pain that will be felt when her children are separated from her through early death (a common occurrence until quite recently), through marriage and the formation of their own families, or through the renunciation of the world by sons who join the *sangha*, a Thai-Lao woman observes the postpartum rite of "lying by the fire" (*yū fai*). This rite involves an asceticlike mortification of the flesh, as for several days (longer for the first birth than for subsequent ones) a woman rests near a fire so hot it produces burns. During this period she consumes nothing but a medicinal broth that is cooked over the fire. The denial of solid food during this sequestering rite can be juxtaposed with the later woman's practice of giving food not only to her own children but to the *sangha*.

For men, the problem of attachment is understood as involving first and foremost a desire for sexual gratification and secondarily for social dominance. To gain control of these desires, a man should enter the monkhood and subject himself to the discipline (*vinaya*) of the *sangha*. Most Thai-Lao men still enter the *sangha* for a temporary period, and for the three months or longer they spend as a novice or monk they forswear all sexual activities, spurn any interest in personal possessions other than those few allowed to a member of the order, and reduce their meals to two a day, both before noon. As all women return to the world after their "lying by the fire," almost all men return to the world after having served in the *sangha*. Through these experiences many Thai-Lao become more self-conscious about their desires and gain some ability to control them even as they assume worldly roles.

Affiliation with the dhammic cult movement contributes to this ability to act in the world with detachment. "Ordained in the *dhamma*" connotes subjecting oneself to a discipline: in this case, women as well as men are ordained. Those who join the movement strongly deemphasize actions that lead to immediate pleasures. In Ban Nọng Tụn, for example, where this movement is well established, drinking was conspicuously less noticeable than in other villages in which the movement had made little progress. Members of the movement also avoid gambling and give up eating raw meat dishes, which they view as unhealthy in both a medical and a religious sense. Of particular relevance to the development of a work ethic is the fact that members of the movement also attach a positive value to industriousness and thriftiness.

The stance of this-worldly non-attachment that many Thai-Lao assume, when linked with a sense of being a disadvantaged minority, contributes to the development of a distinctive work ethic. Many villagers have gained the sense of minority status through their interactions with government officials. It is even stronger in those who have gone away to work in Bangkok. In Bangkok the wealthy and powerful are quite visible and the salience of economic activity is undisguised. For many migrants the social differences that they observe in Bangkok probably seem as fixed as the cosmic order; they enjoy what they can with the modest earnings they gain from hard labor. Having had their flings they return to the less exciting but more congenial world of the village. Other migrants, usually those who stay long enough to obtain more than the casual laboring job, make another discovery in the city. There are people, they find, whose parents started off as poor as northeastern Thai villagers and yet who have succeeded in radically improving their lot. These other people—overwhelmingly of Chinese descent—provide models for social mobility that some Thai-Lao migrants find it possible to emulate.[12]

In sum, although there are certainly reprobates, bullies, and ordinary villagers in rural northeastern Thailand who are getting along as they always have, there are also some who arrange their lives with reference to an ethic that in some ways resembles what Weber called ''inner-worldly asceticism.'' This ethic has its roots in popular Buddhist notions of forgoing that which is desired by the passions; it has been given its particular force by experiences that are more typical of northeastern Thai villagers than of others in Thailand. At the base of this ethic is the awareness that most northeasterners gain early in their lives of suffering in its existential (and Buddhist) sense as a consequence of living in the least prosperous region of Thailand. In the critical years of the late teens and early adulthood many, perhaps most, Thai-Lao villagers also learn, primarily through temporary work in Bangkok, that they are a part of a distinctive minority, discriminated against by a Thai-dominated system. They realize that it is nearly impossible for them to achieve the status of a master official (*cao nāi*). But some villagers also discover another nonagricultural status to which they can aspire—that of the merchant who through hard work and saving is able to rise economically. And here the model is provided primarily by another ethnically distinct group, merchants of Chinese descent.

To emulate the merchant model successfully requires forgoing immediate pleasures. Men learn such restraint and discipline while serving temporarily as monks, women during the postpartum rite of ''lying by the fire,'' and both men and women do so when they choose the discipline of being ordained in the *dhamma*. Although some of these factors are also found amongst other populations in Thailand, they are most pronounced among the Thai-Lao.

The practical morality of Thai-Lao villagers has its roots in a world view that is recognizably Theravāda Buddhist and as such shares the fundamental premises of the world views of Buddhists living elsewhere in Thailand as well as in other societies. While sharing these premises, the Thai-Lao have, however, evolved a distinctive ethos as a consequence of making sense of the actual world in which they live with reference to these premises. Like other Buddhists, the Thai-Lao understand that they live in a "conditioned existence" (*samsāra*) in which all experience motivated by desire leads to suffering (*dukkha*). The idea of *dukkha* seems rather more practically significant to perhaps most Thai-Lao villagers than it does to other Buddhists, especially those who live in towns, who are able much more easily to realize immediate happiness and pleasure. The Thai-Lao, constituting the poorest sector of the Thai populace, work in a harsh and unpredictable environment and, when ill, are rarely able to turn to modern health care. Their life expectancy is still among the lowest in the world. Though the Thai-Lao accept, with all other Buddhists, the truth of the doctrine of *kamma*, they have come, like most other Buddhists in Thailand who have been influenced by the same reformed Buddhist thought, to accord greater emphasis to the moral responsibility one must assume for one's present actions than to the constraints that the moral consequences of previous actions impose on one's life. In this respect Thai Buddhists generally may differ from Buddhists in such other societies as Burma. Thai-Lao villagers also share with all other Buddhists the goal of *nibbāna*, or ultimate transcendence of conditioned existence through self-awareness and non-attachment from desire. Many Thai-Lao, through their practices of "lying by the fire" for women and temporary monkhood for most men as well as, for some, through joining the dhammic cult movement, have cultivated self-awareness and non-attachment probably more than any other lay Buddhist population in Thailand. It is the cultivation of these qualities by those who continue to act within the world, a world in which they see themselves as a disprivileged ethnoregional minority, that has contributed to the distinctive work ethic that I have argued shapes the economic actions of some Thai-Lao villagers. The Thai-Lao case demonstrates quite clearly, I believe, that if we are to inquire into what moral import Buddhist or any religious doctrines may have, it is essential to situate ourselves in the context of the lives of people who are confronted with real, not hypothetical, moral issues.

9 Ethics, Wealth, and Eschatology:

Buddhist and Christian Strategies for Change

Robin W. Lovin

How one compares the religious ethics of two great religious traditions depends, of course, on how one sees each of them individually. Western observers of Theravāda Buddhism, accustomed to the pervasive concern for social relationships in the literature of Christianity and Judaism, have sometimes concluded from an examination of Theravāda texts that this form of Buddhism is a religion of insight and abstinence, a single-minded pursuit of *nibbāna* in which problems of wealth and poverty, justice, and personal relationships are matters of little importance.

Phra Rājavaramuni's essay, "Foundations of Buddhist Social Ethics" (Chap. 1 of this volume), invites us to take a different point of view. Theravāda Buddhism is, he suggests, the way of life for a whole society. The nibbanic Buddhism of the monks and the kammic practices of the laity exist not as different religious systems, but as complementary elements in a Buddhist way of life that encompasses a whole society. Buddhism and western Christianity may differ sharply in their understandings of human personality and ultimate reality, but they cannot be distinguished by saying that Christianity takes a religious interest in social relationships while Buddhism does not.

If Phra Rājavaramuni is correct, as I think he is, comparative study of the social ethics of Theravāda Buddhism and western Christianity must begin with a more holistic view of the Theravāda tradition. Although the texts of the Pāli canon focus especially on monastic life and practices, the tradition sets those institutions in a much wider social context. From these traditions and practices we can learn much about questions of wealth, political authority, and the general welfare, just as we do, for example, from the Hebrew scriptures or the Qur'an. Both Theravāda Buddhism and western Christianity recognize the importance of these social questions, and both insist that how a person responds to these issues has a significant relationship to the religion he or she professes and practices. Just as each religion has personal ideals to inspire individual progress toward salvation, each has an understanding of how persons should relate to one another in the good society. Each, too, has a strategy for dealing with the perennial fact that the world of human relationships is not as it should be. It is on this last point that we will want to compare the social ethics of Buddhist and Christian monasticism, and there we will discover some significant differences.

One must, of course, avoid the easy identification of Buddhist and Christian monasticism that led the early western writers to call the *bhikkhu*s "monks" or "priests," but there is at least a superficial parallelism between the western monk, whose vocation derives its name from the Greek *monos* (solitary) and the *bhikkhu*, who must, the Buddha says, "wander alone like the rhinoceros." In both Buddhist and Christian traditions, moreover, these solitary contemplatives came to live in monastic communities, and though they retained an ideal of renunciation and detachment from things, their communities acquired wealth and property, and they became forces to reckon with in economic and political life.

Given the lasting influence of monastic communities in both traditions, how do those who follow the monastic vocation understand their relationships to the wider society which they have renounced? What set of values regarding the world of work, family, and property is appropriate, and how shall those who have renounced these things for religious reasons understand the religious aspirations of the nonrenouncers? Here I will suggest that, despite the apparent similarities between Buddhist and Christian monasticism, an important distinction emerges, for Christian monasticism has an eschatological understanding of social evil that leads to a strategy of social *transformation*, whereas the Theravāda tradition suggests that social evils require social *purification*. The withdrawal of the Christian monks into self-sufficient communities testifies to the final insufficiency of the present world and its values, while the communities themselves anticipate the final transformation of human life by an organization that even now creates completely new ways to relate persons to one another. In this eschatological Christianity everything that belongs to the present world is deprived of its legitimacy. The Buddhist *bhikkhu*, by contrast, lives in complete dependence on the surrounding society and makes his own contribution to it by a selective legitimation of social achievements that allows the society to purify itself of those elements that are not in accord with *dhamma*. This renewal begins, perhaps, with a purification of the *sangha* (monastic order) itself. Inevitably, though, a purified *sangha* leads to a purified and prosperous society.

These quite different strategies of transformation and purification may not, of course, characterize all Christian and Buddhist social thought as clearly as they mark the normative social ethics of Buddhist and Christian monasticism. This reservation applies especially in Christianity, where monasticism is but one among many religious vocations. Nevertheless, the comparisons suggested by these two important institutions are significant in themselves and may be indicative of ways of thinking about social change that have echoes throughout their respective traditions.

Beyond these strategic differences, however, Christianity and Buddhism share the conviction that religious social norms cannot be exclusively defined in terms of the functional requirements of any one society. Each tradition seeks to guide concrete social choices through a system that nonetheless transcends the demands of the particular society to which it is applied. The monastic traditions are in each case a partial expression of this attempt. Accordingly, the focus of comparison for this essay will be the different ways that Buddhist and Christian monasticism suggest for achieving the balance between transcendence and relevance.

ULTIMATE GOALS AND SOCIAL VALUES

It has been suggested that the other-worldliness of Buddhism makes talk of a Buddhist social philosophy incongruous. Much of Phra Rājavaramuni's essay in this volume, accordingly, is devoted to refuting the western belief that, in his words, ''Buddhism is merely an ethics of the mind, and that it lacks concern for social and material welfare.'' This misconception began, no doubt, because western scholars knew Buddhist texts before they became thoroughly acquainted with Buddhist societies. The large part of the Theravāda canon given to individual liberation and questions of monastic discipline could give the impression that Buddhism is a truth for a spiritual elite without concern for social organization and with only minimal impact on the everyday life of the laity.

What made that idea plausible, however, was more than a reading of the texts without a social context. Buddhism as a religion of mental discipline and individual apprehension of fundamental truths fits all too neatly into a typology of religions that western scholarship was creating at the beginning of the twentieth century. Max Weber and Ernst Troeltsch began to distinguish Christian religious groups into types according to the inclusiveness of their membership and their tendency to form either broad territorial or tightly knit exclusive organizations. To these types of ''church'' and ''sect'' (Weber 1958a: 145) Troeltsch added a third type that seemed to fit some Christian groups of modern times, the ''mystical'' type, which relies on the believer's immediate experience of the divine and sustains only a minimal social organization (Troeltsch 1976: 745–46). For Weber, at least, these were not simply generalizations out of Christian history. They were types with considerable value for interpreting the sociology of other religions as well (Weber 1946: 267–301). Church and sect types dominate in Christian history and the Christian mystic is a minor type, but if one is convinced of the validity of the typology, there will be a strong tendency to explain the quite different religions of the East as instances in which the minor type among western religious communities is the dominant type, subordinating all forms of religious organization to its mystic quest for salvation through flight from the world. In that context Buddhism appears in *The Religions of India* as the extreme form of the mystical type, a religion of "cultivated professional monks" in which salvation is "an absolutely personal performance of the self-reliant individual . . . . The specific asocial character of all genuine mysticism is here carried to its maximum" (Weber 1958b: 213).

Thus convinced by text and typology that Buddhism is a religion of the monastic "virtuoso," whose concerns are solely with a final escape to *nibbāna*, western observers have drawn sharp distinctions between the life of the *bhikkhu*, who seeks enlightenment, and the life of the lay people, who are devoted to the mundane search for a better rebirth. When this sharp distinction is taken for granted, the notion of a specifically Buddhist social ethic seems a contradiction in terms. A true Buddhist seeks a mystical escape from mundane reality, not an ascetic reordering of it. Contemporary observers of life in Thailand, Burma, or Sri Lanka do not, of course, ignore the pervasive impact of Buddhism on the societies they study, but those who follow a Weberian analysis are inclined to treat the social aspects of Buddhism as unintended consequences of the religious search for salvation (Spiro 1982: 437).

It is precisely this sharp distinction between the value of lay life and monastic life that Phra Rājavaramuni, speaking from within the monastic vocation, calls into question. The Theravāda search for salvation is, to be sure, radically individual. No divine grace may be invoked for assistance, and though the community of the *sangha* may facilitate liberation, the achievement itself is as individual as "walking, eating, listening, and sleeping," according to Rājavaramuni. Nevertheless, this highly individualized monastic pursuit does presuppose a certain material sufficiency, and it requires a society that is secure and peaceful. He continues:

> Even with regard to individual perfection, there are many things that a good friend can do to help in the development of mental qualities, in meditation practice, and in the cultivation of wisdom by teaching, inducement, advice, and other skillful means.

> . . . In keeping with the Buddhist doctrine of dependent co-arising, individual betterment and perfection on the one hand and the social good on the other are fundamentally interrelated and interdependent.

The emphasis on the individual pursuit of enlightenment is real, then, but this does not render all questions of social organization and interpersonal relations irrelevant. One may still argue that Buddhism undermines public and political life by placing the highest goal of human life in a transmundane sphere, but that complaint can be leveled against the major religions quite generally. It would apply equally, for example, to Jacques Maritain's careful distinction between the person's eternal end, which is relationship with God, and the temporal common good, which rightly claims our attention for the building of a better human society (Maritain 1966: 56–70). Critics of this neo-Scholastic theory complain that to set anything at all above public, political life devalues it. If public life is not the most serious human endeavor, these critics say, it soon will not be taken seriously at all (cf. Arendt 1958: 22–78).

This thoroughgoing secularity condemns western and eastern religions without discrimination. One need press the case against a transcendent human destiny only slightly to make it apply to Christianity and Buddhism equally. Or, conversely, one need only note the presence of transcendent *and* immanent goals in both Christianity and Buddhism to invalidate the sharp typological distinctions between them. Both faiths have the problem of defining the appropriate relationship of a rightly seeking devotee to a rightly ordered society.

Against this indiscriminately secular view, my approach affirms that, just as the idea of a Christian society is more than the effects of Christian beliefs on society as it exists, the idea of a Buddhist society is more than the unintended consequences of Buddhist beliefs in Asian social history. Buddhist social ethics has to do with the way people organize themselves to maintain and observe the precepts that mark their lives as Buddhist. The Christian society and the Buddhist society are not identical ideals, but we cannot locate the differences between them by saying that one religion has a social ethic and the other does not.

MONASTICISM AND BUDDHIST SOCIETY

If we cannot simply say that Theravāda Buddhism lacks a social ethic, we must distinguish it from western Christianity by a more careful comparison of the views of social life that can be found in each tradition.

Here a comparative study of monasticism is helpful, for an understanding of these religious communities and their relation to the wider society suggests two quite different views of social evils and social change, views that have characteristic echoes throughout the traditions of which they are a part.

The distinction between Christian and Buddhist monks is immediately apparent in a description of the daily lives of the men (Spiro 1982: 305–10; Knowles 1969: 212–23). One notes, for example, that compared to a Christian monk who lives in the tradition of Saint Benedict's Rule a *bhikkhu* has great freedom to order his own timetable and attend to his own affairs. Outside of the ritual of the morning food round, the teaching duties of the town monks, and stipulated times for communal meetings and chants, the day is relatively unscheduled.

What is most striking, however, is that the time of the Christian monk, outside of the common meals and liturgical offices, is devoted chiefly to manual or intellectual work. Productive labor is an essential part of Christian monastic life, even in the contemplative orders. For the Buddhist *bhikku*s it is absolutely forbidden.

The fact that *bhikkhu*s may not work certainly shapes their daily existence and strongly differentiates their lives from those of Buddhist lay folk. It is apt to make their monastic life seem rather pointless to western observers who are accustomed to a pervasive connection between religion and work. Thus Melford Spiro remarks, "Boredom, no doubt, accounts for the inordinate amount of sleeping one sees in monasteries—monks are forever taking naps—as well as for the dullness and apathy frequently encountered in them. I suspect, too, that those (as we shall see, they constitute a large number) who practice alchemy, medicine, exorcism, and—in the cities—politics, do so not only for the intrinsic interest of the subject, but as an escape from the tedium of monastic living" (Spiro 1982: 330).

Spiro's observations may well reflect his experience, but they also echo his Weberian interpretation of the *bhikkhu* as a religious virtuoso (Spiro 1982: 279). Weber sees the rejection of labor as an expression of the mystic "flight from the world," as opposed to an ascetic or sectarian effort to master the environment. The results of this comparison, as we might expect, are not favorable to the mystic. "As the peasant was to the landlord, so the layman was to the Buddhist and Jainist bhikshu: ultimately mere sources of tribute. Such tribute allowed the virtuosos to live entirely for religious salvation without themselves performing profane work, which always would endanger their salvation" (Weber 1946: 289).

However well this equation of monk and landlord might serve in a reductionist economic interpretation of Buddhist societies, it completely ignores the religious dimension of the relationship between the monk and the laity. In those terms the monk is not a charge on the wealth of the lay community, but an opportunity for their spiritual welfare. As we are quick to call the *bhikkhu*s "monks," we are quick to say these "monks" get their support by "begging," but these quick translations do not quite get it right. As John Holt observes, "the *bhikkhu*s and laity did not understand making the alms round as begging; rather, making the alms round provided the laity with an opportunity to acquire merit by contributing to the welfare of the *bhikkhusangha*" (Holt 1981: 114). Maintaining a rightly ordered monastic community is thus of considerable importance not only for the *sangha* itself, but for the whole society that shares its understanding of merit. If the monk depends on the householder in a straightforward economic sense, the householder also depends on the monk for opportunities to gain merit.

The kammic concern with merit does not, however, fully explain the prohibition on labor. The different roles of monks and lay people also figure in a nibbanic ethic. Insight into reality and liberation from the suffering imposed by human illusions is a demanding achievement (Holt 1981: 83–85). It requires a discipline of compassion and harmlessness that the ordinary activities of securing food and shelter preclude. Thus the householder also depends on the monk for knowlege of *dhamma*, knowledge that is realized in monastic discipline and preserved by a pure monastic community. Without this "division of labor" there would be no relief from the immediacy of the pains and disappointments of mundane existence and no progress toward enlightenment anywhere in the society. "Thus monks," the Buddha said, "this holy life is lived in mutual dependence, for ferrying across the flood, for utter cessation of suffering" (quoted in Rājavaramuni, this volume).

So the *sangha* is, as Phra Rājavaramuni puts it, "an independent community that points toward a transcendent aspect of life. Its essential task is to maintain the *dhamma* for the society." We must be clear, however, that this is independence in the sense of freedom from ordinary occupations, not an independence that implies that either the *sangha* or the society could live without the other. Their respective roles are dictated neither by economic efficiency nor by the mystical aspirations of the monks, but by a more basic Theravāda understanding of how the *dhamma* is known and transmitted.

How is the *dhamma* to be made known and applied to an existence that is so persistently resistant to perfection? For the monks there are specific texts of discipline (*vinaya*) governing the monastic order and providing quite detailed applications of the *dhamma* to the life of the individual. Nothing quite comparable exists for the tasks and occasions of lay life, but as Phra Rājavaramuni indicates, the moral tales in the *Jātakas* (stories of previous lives of the Buddha) and the Buddha's discourses to householders and rulers do provide the practical equivalent of a *vinaya* for lay persons: they offer applications of the *dhamma* to the specific conditions of social life that now prevail.

> The *vinaya* for the monkhood has been fixed and rather closed, but that for lay society is, to a large extent, left open for temporal regulation to suit the specific time and place. The *vinaya* for the community of monks has been laid down by the Buddha. The *vinaya* for the laity is left open for able and righteous people like enlightened monarchs to formulate based on the general ideas and principles enunciated by the Buddha. (Rājavaramuni, this volume)

The complex relationships between the monks who maintain the *dhamma* and the wider society that also seeks to live by it are well illustrated in the role of the *cakkavatti*, the ideal Buddhist king who orders society by the *dhamma*. The king is a patron of the monks, but he is not one of them, and though he is respectful toward them, he is not subordinate to them. Society is ordered by the king's commands, but a wise king attends carefully to the words of the monks. Under the best circumstances the voice of the monk may symbolically become the voice of the king, for some kings (as an act of piety) have allowed a monk to deliver the sermon for the ordination ceremony while seated on the royal throne (Tambiah 1976: 159–78). Ideally, the king plays a mediating role between the perfect transcendence of the *dhamma* and the rough and ready actualization of *dhamma* in mundane society. Some measure of independence from the *sangha* is necessary for the king and some distance between the *sangha* and the day-to-day ruling of society is required if the *dhamma*'s purity and its relevance are to be maintained. In a formal sense, then, the application of *dhamma* to society is the business of the king, not the monks. But when an actual Buddhist ruler wants to know how to approximate the ideal of the *cakkavatti*, he must rely on the monks for guidance.

The monks' knowledge of *dhamma* remains socially important even when the monks in general have become heretical or corrupt. Then the king must take the initiative to institute reforms and purify the *sangha*, but even in this extremity he can hardly proceed without some uncorrupted guidance from one who lives within the monastic discipline.

> The *Mahavaṃsa* account of this purification is explicit about the wrong and the right procedures for political authority to adopt vis-à-vis the *sangha* in achieving the objective. At first the king sent a minister, commanding him, ''Go, settle this matter and let the *uposatha* festival be carried out by the community of *bhikkhus* in my *arama*.'' This ''fool'' went thither, and upon the *bhikkhus*' refusal to hold the festival with those whom they considered heretics, the minister struck off the head of several *theras*. The king himself was held guilty by some monks of this crime of violence, but he was exonerated and later saw his way to the conduct of purification in the appropriate manner. This correct manner consisted in the king's *requesting* the great *thera* Moggaliputta, who had sought solitary retreat in the face of the corruption of the *bhikkhus*, to help him restore the religion by saying ''be our helper, venerable sir, to befriend religion.'' (Tambiah 1976: 167)

So the result in practice is that the king commands, but he depends on the monks to know what he ought to command.

The monks' fundamental task of preserving and teaching *dhamma*, for which they must be released from everyday work, provides the necessary foundation for their providing guidance to the laity. The judgment of what, precisely, will count as a correct application of *dhamma* to the requirements of the time cannot, of course, be settled simply by asking the lay technical expert what will work. In a world in which things are not what they seem, only a comprehension of the *dhamma* allows one to distinguish true success from appearances. Material prosperity is valued, both in itself and as a condition that allows untroubled contemplation, but wealth is never endorsed unconditionally.

> What is blamed as evil in connection with wealth is to earn it in a dishonest or unlawful way. Worthy of blame also is the one who, having earned wealth, becomes enslaved through clinging and attachment to it and incurs suffering because of it. No less evil and blameworthy than the unlawful earning of wealth is to accumulate riches and, out of stinginess, not to spend them for the benefit and well-being of oneself, one's dependents, and other people. Again, it is also evil if one squanders wealth foolishly or indulgently or

uses it to cause suffering to other people. (Rājavaramuni, this volume).

It is these dhammic constraints on what might otherwise seem a purely technical activity, the creation and use of wealth, that mark a society as a Buddhist society. It is the monk, as teacher of *dhamma*, who draws the line between successful activity that is also righteous and activity that, because it is unrighteous, can give no more than the appearance of success. The monk provides guidance for the householder, and the monks and the king together periodically purify the society in ways that ensure that its success is true success and its prosperity, true prosperity.

We are now in a position to understand Phra Rājavaramuni's description of the *sangha* as "an independent community that points toward a transcendent aspect of life" and whose "essential task is to maintain the *dhamma* for the society." The *sangha*'s independence is not the indifference of religious adepts to ordinary human preoccupations and the material requirements of society. Indeed, the *sangha*'s dependence on the material prosperity and good order of the wider society is total. The independence of the *sangha* is not based on a renunciation of the achievements of the society. It is, like all liberations in Theravāda Buddhism, the result of disciplined insight. The monk renounces possessions and family in order to be free of the particular interests that tie most persons' thinking to specific, immediate needs and goals and teach them to evaluate their actions strictly in terms of mundane results (Rājavaramuni, this volume). This practical wisdom is not rejected, but it must be understood in relation to the transcendent standard of the *dhamma*, which is the fundamental law of individual development and perfection (Rājavaramuni, this volume). The monk lives in transcendence of the society insofar as he is able to judge it by a standard that is itself independent of the functional requirements of any particular society. He guides the actions of kings and householders, not only in specialized acts that gain them merit and so advance their kammic goals, but in the wider observance of *dhamma* that makes them Buddhists and marks their social institutions as legitimate.

CHRISTIAN MONASTICISM

Christian monasticism as represented by Benedictine monks expresses a quite different relationship between religious insight and social order. Although monasticism is not the only institutional expression of Christian social thought, its persistence from an early point in

Christian history calls our attention to an important set of ideas about society and social change which distinguish Christianity from Theravāda Buddhism.

True monks in the western church live according to some version of the Rule of Saint Benedict (ca. 480–547) and must be distinguished from secular clergy and from Franciscans, Dominicans, Jesuits, and members of other orders that exist to perform specific tasks in the ministry of the church. Benedict's rule called for five or six hours of work a day, and the work intended was primarily in field, garden, and workshop in order to support a self-sufficient community. Hard manual labor was the original norm, and some measure of it is demanded even of those whose talents and training place them for the most part in more intellectual occupations. The monk acknowledges his unity with the rest of humanity by earning his living with his hands (Bouyer 1955: 160–67).

Paradoxically, this expression of solidarity actually attenuates the everyday ties between the monastery and society. Monastic literature contains many references to the cosmological significance of the monks' prayers, which sustain a distracted world that is heedless of God, but there is little suggestion that this order-maintaining activity should take the form of directly prescribing to secular authorities the appropriate pattern for a Christian society. Of course, monastic clergy have sometimes played important roles in politics and cultural life, but reformers of monastic life have consistently sought to eliminate these exceptions. Among contemporary monastic writers, Thomas Merton, for example, stresses that even pastoral and teaching tasks usually associated with secular clergy and nonmonastic orders are inappropriate for monks (Merton 1949: xxxi–xxxvii).

While monastic work reduces the monk's dependence on any specific lay community, it has a role as a symbol of the human condition, and the monk who sets himself to work reminds himself of his share in that humanity. Labor, we are told, is a consequence of sin, and the monk who puts his hand to the daily tasks is constantly reminded that the world in which he lives is fallen (Genesis 3:17–19). The monastery is not a community in which human labor is brought to perfection; it is an opening on a better world, a *paradisus claustralis*, in which the insufficiency of all that is possible within the limits of the present reality becomes apparent (Merton 1949). Monastic work is thus an expression of solidarity with the world and at the same time a judgment upon it. It is the paradoxical sign of a complex eschatology that has found a place in Christianity from the very beginning.

In the face of pressures on a Jewish sect to reject violently the prevailing hellenistic culture, early Christianity adopted an apocalyptic stance that left the world intact but proclaimed its imminent passing away. With the passage of time this eschatological Christianity found expression in the heroic asceticism of the desert saints and later in the organized ascetic life of the monastic communities (Troeltsch 1976: 58–64). Particular questions of value were not argued, but all of the values of the present world were denied any ultimate meaning.

The denial of ultimate importance to worldly affairs made Christianity especially adaptable to changing cultural settings. As Troeltsch argues in one of his last essays, "The Social Philosophy of Christianity," Christianity survived and grew because it was able to make the transition from Roman-occupied Palestine to the hellenized Empire and did so by adopting a Stoic social philosophy from its gentile neighbors.[1] We may expect that pattern to be repeated, Troeltsch explains, because the eschatological position, which rejects any religious appreciation of social achievements, can sustain itself as a widely held view only for short periods of social crisis. When that pressure subsides, Christianity soon adopts some way of understanding society for its own purposes. However, just because this eschatological orientation is an original feature of and a permanent possibility in Christianity, Christianity has no *social theology*, "no social theory springing directly from its religious idea, either directly as a dogma or indirectly as a logical consequence" (Troeltsch 1922). The necessary social philosophy is acquired only by borrowing from the surrounding culture, a process that began with the Christian adoption of Stoic ideas, which became the basis for the natural-law theory of society.

Taken strictly as a historical description, Troeltsch's claim that eschatological Christianity is the original form of the faith is perhaps too broad a generalization. In the early Christian communities there were no doubt alongside the eschatological believers those who integrated their faith in Jesus as messiah with their daily practice of Judaism or understood this liberator-savior to free them precisely for better observance of those hellenistic virtues they already knew. The eschatological form of Christianity does not have an absolute historical priority, but what Troeltsch correctly saw is that it remains a permanent possibility in Christian faith. And the presence of this eschatological impulse in Christianity secures for that faith an independence from social forms that is similarly lasting.

There are, of course, severe limits on our ability to generalize from observations on Christian monasticism to the tradition as a whole. The connection between the monastic community and the teaching of Jesus is neither so direct nor so exclusive as that between the *sangha* and the teachings of the Buddha, and in the traditional Christian understanding it is the bishops in their churches rather than the monastic brotherhood who are the direct successors to Jesus and his disciples.[2] Serious tensions are at work here in the Christian tradition, and as a result, monastic literature directs much of its criticism against the more humanistic and pastoral forms of church life which continually threaten the rigor of monastic discipline. But what the monastic tradition powerfully represents is the survival of the early Christians' refusal to compromise their understanding of Jesus' way with any of the requirements of the world. And although monasticism is by all statistical measures a very small part of the modern life of the western church, its eschatological consciousness and literal faithfulness to certain Christian virtues occupy an influential place in the Christian tradition which changes the tradition as a whole, even in its most secular, world-affirming forms.

For our purposes the most important expression of this eschatological consciousness is Christian monasticism's distinctive rejection of worldly success. From the point of view of its practitioners, only the radical monastic pattern of renunciation can escape the world's distortion of every search for truth. ''That is why the only humanism that can succeed must be an eschatological humanism: not one which capitalizes dead treasures around a heart fossilized by sclerosis, but one which sacrifices the dearest affections to find them again, one hundredfold, after death'' (Bouyer 1955: 209). Like Saint Paul, the modern monk strives to say of all the sources of worldly pride, status, and security, ''I reckon them as garbage that I may gain Christ'' (Philippians 3:8).

It is a point of common sense, and one much noted in the literature of monastic spirituality, that one cannot renounce something unless one finds it somehow good. We can avoid pain, sickness, hunger, but we renounce comfort, wealth, family, and career. By bearing this in mind the Christian monk avoids a sour misanthropy, but the dominant theme remains a radical, eschatological denial of all ordinary values. There is a peace and happiness in the monastic life, but it is a happiness that reproaches the ordinary sources of satisfaction. ''It condemns the spririt by which the world lives. It accuses the rich men of their injustice and the Communists of their unhuman and complacent hatreds and the humanists of their insufficiency. It denies everything that the world stands for'' (Merton 1949: 333).

Such passages could be multiplied indefinitely from the monastic literature of the twentieth century, without touching on the more violent renunciations of earlier times. This deep suspicion of wealth, leisure, and human companionship, combined with the material independence secured by monastic labor, precludes the positive assessment of prosperity and order as the infrastructure for the contemplative life which we find in Phra Rājavaramuni's account of Buddhist monasticism in contemporary Thailand. Eschatological Christianity envisions a radical transformation of the social order, not the right acquisition and use of its resources.

PURIFICATION AND TRANSFORMATION

Our first question in this essay was whether there can be a Buddhist social ethic. To some western observers the sharp contrast between an asceticism that disciplines and orders the conditions of life and a mysticism that sees unreality in all apparently solid human facts suggests that Buddhism cannot concern itself seriously with the problems of society. From that viewpoint the economic and political activism of Buddhist monks in contemporary Thailand appears to be an Asian manifestation of the secularization of religious life already familiar in the West, and Phra Rājavaramuni's discussion of practical advice for modern Buddhist lay life must seem an odd extension of the mystical aims of the monastic texts.

There is a sense in which this line of Weberian analysis is perfectly correct, for the limited value Buddhism assigns to all social achievements is apparent even in Phra Rājavaramuni's positive view of society, wealth, and human goods. The Theravāda quest for liberation is a solitary one, however much it may need human community as an infrastructure for its efforts. The *bhikkhu*'s separation from ordinary familial and economic relationships expresses a determination to do for himself what no one else can do for him and to hold that activity higher than all the other goods that can be achieved by human cooperation.

Likewise, there is no Buddhist social ethic, if one means a single, normative form of society that all Buddhists (or even all Theravādans) recognize as applicable in all ages and from which one may deviate only as a matter of dire necessity. Phra Rājavaramuni notes that the *vinaya* for lay folk, though no less important than that for monks, is not so rigidly fixed. A good deal of it must be left to the "able and righteous people of the time." What they prescribe must always be measured against the universal *dhamma*, rather than merely against practical standards of success, but the range of ideas and systems that can be encompassed by a Buddhist social order remains very wide. As Stanley Tambiah observes, "in the Buddhist polities new content can be poured into the sociopolitical molds because they are like hollow vessels that have in the past and could in the future hold varying contents" (Tambiah 1976: 431).

In these quite straightforward ways one could accurately say that Theravāda Buddhism has no social ethics. The problem with this sort of approach to comparative studies is that by these criteria Christianity has none either. The Christian insistence that "a single human soul is worth more than the whole universe of material goods" (Maritain 1966: 61) puts a similar halt to any claims about the ultimate value of social achievements, and the flexible response of Christian faith to changing political and social conditions—what Troeltsch traces to the absence of a social theology—parallels the diversity that has characterized Buddhist polities in the lands of South Asia.

Both traditions can be made to appear irrelevant in the face of a radically secular account of human hopes and achievements, but this only sets both of them in opposition to a third force—"modernity," perhaps. It does not help us to appreciate the similarities between Buddhist and Christian monasticism or to understand the very real differences that have long been observed between them. In place of the Weberian typology of ascetics and mystics and against a onesidedly secular orientation, we need a more complicated model that acknowledges that each tradition places a distance between its religious ideals and any social achievements and then goes on to consider the quite different strategies of social change which emerge when the traditions do turn their attention to problems of social order.

Both western Christianity and Theravāda Buddhism give a limited but significant place to social relationships in the realm of spiritual achievements. If the goal of religious life always transcends the individual's social role, it is nonetheless true that right relationships to others are an important preparation for a more complete relationship to God or a more efficacious pursuit of merit or enlightenment. And in both traditions this insistence on a human destiny that transcends any possible social achievement provides the basis for a flexible social ethic that takes social relationships seriously but does not make the creation of any particular social order the first goal of religious life. The adaptation to circumstances, not only in institutional arrangements but in the social thought of the traditions themselves, helps to explain why each has become a widespread and enduring religion.

Yet it is also apparent that the reasons for this adaptability differ markedly between the Christian and the Buddhist cases. In Christianity the distance between religous goals and social achievements is supplied by an eschatological tradition that insists that a total transformation of the existing order must precede the appearance of the Kingdom of God. In Theravāda Buddhism, by contrast, the formal independence of the *cakkavatti* king, having authority over both the *sangha* and the laity and responsibility for both spiritual and material welfare, creates a mediating force between timeless ideals and mundane choices. This institutional arrangement, together with the absence of a canonical set of rules for lay life, is self-consciously designed to allow the tradition to adapt its lessons to the abilities of its audience.

Reflective social thinkers in both traditions will likely dwell on the distance between the religious norms for social relationships and the existing social reality, but the ways they address that problem may differ dramatically. We may summarize these different approaches to social change, as we suggested at the outset, by calling the Buddhist approach a strategy of *purification* and calling the Christian approach a strategy of *transformation.*

The monastic role in the Theravāda strategy of purification is carefully structured, in relationship both to the ruler and to the wider society. The myths of cosmic devolution which Buddhism shares with other Indian traditions do not lend themselves to an optimistic or progressive view of human life. Decline from a golden age of harmony and abundance is pervasive, and where the cosmogony of world cycles or successive stages of decline is stressed, selfishness and poverty may seem to be inevitable. This is not, however, a counsel of moral despair. There may be no hope of halting the decline, but it can be temporarily arrested. No human action can bring back the golden age, but there is a religious obligation of compassion to ameliorate the evils of the age in which we now live (Reynolds 1985). Individual achievements in this effort may be important, and the scope for improvement of life by a rightly guided ruler is great indeed.

Buddhism's strategy of purification envisions improvement and decline as gradual developments involving methods and processes continuous with the present order. Within the kammic framework, for example, wealth and power are the predictable results of attentiveness to one's duties as a householder or as a ruler. These achievements in turn provide favorable conditions for still greater progress against selfishness. The Theravāda tradition thus lacks eschatological Christianity's inherent suspicion of wealth and power and its apocalyptic vision of discontinuous moments of divine intervention.[3] Although there are definite stages in the Buddhist path of spiritual development, each step up to *nibbāna* is connected to every other by a chain of merit-making and a web of rebirths. Each advance is dependent upon the favorable conditions of the previous moment.

Given this religious preference for piecemeal reform, Theravāda Buddhist social philosophy envisions a complex relationship between the laity, the householders and the leaders who know how to get things done in the mundane sphere of existence, and the *bhikkhus*, who, by their knowledge of the *dhamma*, are able to place these accomplishments into a more ultimate perspective. Monastic poverty is not an exercise in self-sufficiency; it is the creation of a field of merit in which prosperous lay persons may enhance the kammic basis of that prosperity by supporting those who have vowed not to support themselves. In return, the *sangha* maintains the *dhamma* for society. That is, the *sangha* studies and teaches the basis on which prosperity and apparent success can be truly evaluated.

The same relationship prevails on a larger scale between the *sangha* and the king in a traditional Theravāda polity. Royal patronage earns merit for the ruler and legitimates his power and prosperity in the eyes of his Buddhist subjects, but the monks may stubbornly refuse to accept this patronage or lend this legitimacy unless the ruler also attends to their advice on the right ordering of matters that pertain to the *dhamma*. The *sangha*'s strategy for change in a traditional Theravāda polity is, thus, a demand for purification. They do not envision the destruction of existing authorities, but they selectively seek to enlist their power in rooting out the elements that aggravate the inevitable sufferings of this age and threaten that observance of *dhamma* which is possible in the present human condition.

The Christian strategy is one of *transformation*. Eschatological Christianity begins by depriving everything of legitimacy. The apocalyptic vision looks for the cataclysmic destruction of the present order and divine inauguration of a new level of existence. As the present world can make no claims on the faithful, the Christian has the option of living an eschatological vision in the face of present reality. This may occur in several ways. The withdrawal of the monks and the self-contained communities of sectarian Protestantism testify to the final insufficiency of the present world and its values. The activism of a Christian Marxist, or even a radical application of natural law, anticipates the final transformation of human life in social changes that even now aim to create completely new ways to relate persons to one another in society.

It is true that the strategy of purification also has some echoes in Christianity. Old Testament stories of the purification of temple worship by several of the Davidic kings have provided canonical sources for

Christians who have wanted to interpret their social action in this way (II Chronicles 29–32, 34–35). Still, the strategy of transformation is more clearly the norm for Christian reforms, and even when Christians speak of purification of church and society, they tend to mean a rigorous observance of religious norms in anticipation of some new era of grace, rather than a restoration of past order or the slowing of a long-term process of decline. The Puritan movement in seventeenth-century England, perhaps Christianity's most important "purification," certainly did not lack a hope for eschatological transformation. The strategy of transformation, with its delegitimation of existing authority and an undercurrent of eschatological fervor, is more suited to mass movements than the centralized investigations and authoritarian reforms of the purification strategy. Where political leaders are responsive to this eschatological Christianity, they tend to invite their followers to enter new worlds, rather than to participate in the restoration of the old (Berman 1983: 25–28).

CONCLUSION

Christian monks and *bhikkhus*, though they may feel themselves spiritually united in their coenobitic ways of life, have had quite different ways of relating themselves to the wider society and its religious aspirations. The Theravāda strategy of purification and the eschatological Christian emphasis on transformation have, in turn, profoundly affected the religious social ethics of the larger traditions in which these monastic vocations are set. If the world-transforming energies of ascetic Christianity have no precise parallel in the history of Theravāda Buddhism, that should not lead us to conclude that the Theravādans are "mystics" without a social ethic. It should alert us to the fact that their concerns in social ethics will be quite different from those of western Christianity. They will be less suspicious of established wealth and power, more selective and less sweeping in what they legitimate and what they condemn. Though they will never simply identify material prosperity with right observance of *dhamma*, they will be less embarrassed than many of their Christian counterparts to claim that right observance, on a wide scale, leads to prosperity. Which of these strategies better suits a tradition to survive in the modern world or which better protects a tradition's religious goals from the corrosive demands of modernity remains to be seen.

On that note it is well to remember that though we have stressed the differences in strategy between Buddhist and Christian monasticism we have also noted an important similarity in their goals. Phra Rājavaramuni's succinct characterization of the *sangha* could equally well stand as an account of eschatological Christianity: ''It is the independent community that points toward a transcendent aspect of life. Its essential task is to maintain the *dhamma* for the society.'' That is not to say that the *dhamma* and the Good News of the Kingdom of God are the same thing, but each has inspired in its hearers a continuous concern for the moral state of the whole society, and each message has created a community that is neither completely mystical nor completely materialistic. Each community understands itself as having a distinct responsibility toward the wider society, yet each insists that the truth it has heard transcends the truths that happen to work in the present social setting.

Part V.

BUDDHISM AND BEYOND

The Universality of the Problem of Distributive Justice

Introduction

The final section of this volume offers theoretical reflections on the universality of the problem of distributive justice in human society. These essays examine the distinctive and the universal elements within Buddhist attempts to define and address the problems of wealth, poverty, and the use of political power for social well-being.

In Chapter 10 Ronald M. Green sets out a general framework for moral reasoning about wealth and traces the embodiment of such reasoning in several central Buddhist texts. This procedure, he claims, helps illuminate the paradoxes and parallels often found in religious ethics. In his view Buddhism displays basic acceptance of the fundamental characteristics of morality as applied to economic matters: a presupposition in favor of equal distribution of wealth, a qualified justification of inequalities of wealth on the basis of their contribution to social well-being, and a central role for public consent in establishing the prerogatives of kingship. Thus Green argues that Buddhism possesses a perspective on justice and social order remarkably similar to recently developed views in the West.

By contrast, in Chapter 11 John P. Reeder analyzes the underlying components of the West's reasoning about matters of justice and finds western theories of morality and justice to be extraordinarily complex structures based on a number of theses that have been considered individualistic. Although these theses are not universally shared (and here Reeder parts company with Green) in Asia, or even in the West, Reeder argues that they are sturdier and more widespread than has often been recognized. In Reeder's view Buddhism is better seen as embodying both hierarchical and egalitarian impulses in religious and social life. However one regards these theses from a normative point of view, he concludes, they cannot be assumed for descriptive work. By making these assumptions explicit, however, one is better prepared to observe fundamental differences between traditions in handling matters of social cooperation.

The connection between equality and political legitimacy is a central concern in both essays. Recent western philosophical reflections on wealth and poverty have focused not so much on the place of wealth in individual fulfillment as on the issues of social justice and the proper ordering of society. The problem of achieving a morally justified distribution of goods within a cooperative society—that is, the problem of distributive justice—has itself been only the most tangible expression of the broader concern of achieving a "well-ordered society"—a society that would morally deserve the allegiance of its citizens. Instead of asking, "What is the place of prosperity in a life worth living?" or even, "How much of the communal pie does such and such a person deserve?" philosophers have concerned themselves with the question, "To what kind of society could all rationally consent?" and, "How shall we derive principles of social order that all should freely accept?"

Naturally, the intellectual task of justifying social power arises primarily when old forms of legitimation are felt to be insufficient. It is when one's society appears fragmented and longstanding loyalties to the state become problematic that new theories of legitimation are required. Accordingly, the question of political legitimacy reemerged in the West in the face of the pluralistic legacy of the Protestant Reformation and the secularizing legacy of the Enlightenment.[1] It is, of course, possible to imagine the contrasting situation. If there exists a communally accepted vision of the good life and the well-ordered society that fosters it, and if the current regime sufficiently approximates that vision, no problem of legitimation arises. Religious unity generally entails agreement on the aim of existence or the nature of the good life and often includes a widely shared understanding of how society can best foster the achievement of such a life. Under such circumstances, the task of the ascendant regime is relatively straightforward, and the appearance of piety can provide potent religious legitimation for state power.

From this vantage point we can identify two divergent conceptions of equality within society. In a pluralistic society equality of consideration (of the individuals within that society) may mean a social policy of neutrality toward any particular conception of the good life. To treat one's citizens equally under such conditions of religious and philosophical diversity, we might say, means to let each choose his or her own vision of the proper end and meaning of life. Society's task is to provide an equal opportunity (i.e., an equal amount of the basic necessities for life and the pursuit of one's goals) for each individual to pursue his or her own ends.[2] By contrast, in a unitary society equality is understood as the equal opportunity to pursue the unanimously acclaimed purpose of life. Here the well-ordered society is anything but neutral; its virtue lies in the extent to which it encourages the life its citizens acknowledge as virtuous.

John Reeder's essay devotes close attention to the work of the philosopher John Rawls, whose theory of justice is explicitly fashioned to take account of the diversity of a pluralistic society. In particular, Reeder examines Rawls's theory of the good life, most specifically Rawls's "nonessentialist" theory of the good, which attempts to preserve neutrality toward particular conceptions of the good life. Reeder's purpose is to see if such neutrality is really possible and to consider the sort of comparison that can be made with a religiously guided ordering of society such as we find in Buddhist societies.

The neutralist approach is not necessarily rooted in an antagonistic attitude toward religion; it is not the same as saying that there is no such thing as a proper aim of existence. Rather, theories of justice based on the neutralist approach purposefully attempt to avoid making any claims whatsoever concerning the point of life. In the face of religious and political diversity, these theories conclude, it is not the place of society to impose some vision of the meaning of life on its citizens. Instead, society must find a way to order itself, must find a way of distributing the burdens and benefits of cooperation which all can agree to while living without a shared vision of the purpose of life.

Reeder's essay examines in detail a number of objections that have been raised about the neutralist approach and its attempt to unite pluralistic society by means of universal reason. The charge has been raised that the West's notion of reason is one more part of its "atomistic" model of the self, laden with the liberal impulse of egalitarian individualism. Why, after all, should we assume, in the face of religious pluralism, that the well-ordered society is the one to which all will consent? Why are the private and possibly antisocial interests of each individual to be taken with equal seriousness? Although Reeder defends the West's egalitarian conception of reason against certain sociological objections, he does conclude that it is not universally shared and that the question of assuming an egalitarian starting point in thinking about justice is still open.

By contrast, Ronald Green's essay defends the universality of Rawls's approach. As Green puts the case, "morality" is the method of social ordering which "adjudicates social disputes with reference to a set of principles of conduct that are freely accepted by members of the social group." This root idea, that morality involves the rational resolution of the problems of social cooperation by "free assent" to principles, is reflected in the way people talk when they wish to demonstrate the justness of an existing social order. Basic as it sounds, this conception of morality has, according to Green, certain crucial implications for economic distribution, most especially in making the principle of equality the fundamental impulse of a moral ordering of wealth. Further, Green argues that Theravāda Buddhism shows ''basic acceptance'' of ''morality'' as the proper way to order society and of equality as the fundamental principle for handling material wealth: Theravāda's prohibitions against hoarding, greed, and pride indicate a rejection of material accumulations based on power or special virtue; its exhortations to the prosperous about generosity attempt to qualify the inevitable inequalities in society; its ideals of kingship suggest a principle of consent of the governed.

Thus, Green believes that the universal logic of moral reasoning can bridge people's diverse conceptions of the ends of life and provide a common conception of the proper distribution of social goods. The comparative task, for one coming from such an approach, is to identify the ways that particular religious traditions express, in their own cultural matrix, the ''basic logic'' of moral reflection.

Naturally, one may question Green's claims for Rawls's work; Reeder's analysis of the theory's underpinnings reveals that these are complicated and still-disputed matters, even in the West. Similarly, Green's assessment of the Theravāda tradition is open to scrutiny; Reeder acknowledges various egalitarian impulses in the tradition but is skeptical about their depth and correspondence with western assumptions. Green himself speaks of several unresolved matters in establishing conformity between the tradition and his ideal structure and calls for additional historical study now focused by these issues. We will need to know more about what constitutes the tradition's ''acceptance'' of the ''moral'' approach before we can make a definitive judgment about Green's method. In particular, we may want to ask how far Buddhists themselves would accept Green's reading of their texts. Even if one is not convinced of the universality of western notions of morality, it is certainly illuminating to trace the continuities and discontinuities between East and West along the lines suggested by Reeder. At any rate, Green's advocacy and Reeder's skepticism nicely frame the questions confronting readers of the volume as a whole, as they try to place the Theravāda tradition's reflections on wealth and social order into a broader, comparative perspective.

10 Buddhist Economic Ethics:

A Theoretical Approach

Ronald M. Green

Are there any universal moral principles governing the distribution of scarce economic resources? Where distributive justice is concerned, can we speak of moral rules that transcend cultures and that evidence themselves in the teachings of diverse religious and ethical traditions? In the remarks that follow, I want to defend the view that some universal moral values do exist in the area of economic distribution, and I want to suggest that Buddhism, along with a variety of other religious traditions, displays basic acceptance of these values in its teachings about economic life.

The approach I take in defending these claims is somewhat unique in the field of comparative religious ethics. Much existing work in this area, including many of the essays in this volume, begins with the task of description: with an identification and presentation of the relevant moral teachings of a religious tradition. Comparison begins only after the most painstaking descriptive preliminaries are accomplished and the teachings of the tradition have been represented with fidelity. As an alternative, some efforts have been made initially to develop more formal categories of moral analysis, but as in the work of Little and Twiss (1978), these categories are elaborated primarily as an aid to the process of description. Various formal patterns of reasoning and justification are identified in this approach. It is asked whether these patterns can help us order and arrange different traditions, but no effort is made in this essentially taxonomic enterprise to claim that *specific* normative principles or methods of reasoning underlie (or must underlie) the diversity of religious-ethical teaching.

The approach I take here is quite different. Proceeding in a diametrically opposed direction, I eschew the descriptive task at the outset and begin instead with an independent analysis of the logic of moral discourse, in this case the logic of moral reasoning about basic distributive questions. My presumption is that all human beings, as rational creatures, face common problems in the organization of their social relationships and that these common problems, when approached rationally and morally, admit of reasonably common solutions. To some extent, these common solutions can be independently developed through a process of abstracted moral reasoning, and in turn, they may constitute a guide for subsequent descriptive inquiry. Employed heuristically, they can help us identify and highlight important elements within a particular religious ethic.

Quite obviously, the peril of this approach is that it may lead to the imposition of alien concepts on a tradition. It also risks distorting a tradition or fostering the neglect of important indigenous elements as efforts are made to fit the tradition into a preconceived mold. However, if this approach is used with sensitivity to the actual teachings and practice of historical traditions, it can greatly facilitate comparative analysis. It can help penetrate the thicket of diverse elements in a tradition and can aid in the identification of those key elements that shape moral and religious reflection. By focusing on these central elements, this approach can also help explain the development of a tradition. Finally, it can highlight diversity by pointing to the ways in which a tradition has adapted and shaped the underlying universal dynamics of moral reasoning to its own purposes and conditions. In the end, descriptive adequacy is no less the aim of this approach than others, but by seeking first to comprehend what I like to think of as the ''deep structure'' of the moral reasoning process, we hope to be in a better position to understand the complex surface contours of a religious-ethical tradition.[1]

Against this background let me outline how I shall be employing this method below. First, I propose to explore the ''logic'' of moral reasoning on economic and distributive questions. In conjunction with this approach I shall try to identify a basic set of considerations and principles that I believe follow from the effort to regulate morally the control of scarce economic resources in a cooperative situation. Finally, I hope to demonstrate that these principles and their underlying rationale help illuminate economic teachings within Buddhism. My focus here will be on Buddhism, but I shall occasionally make forays into other traditions in which we find these principles and their deeper logic at work.

To speak of the ''deep structure'' of moral reasoning about economic questions would appear foolhardy, not to say irresponsible, in view of the enormous diversity of beliefs about just economic distribution which exists even in our own western cultural area. With socialist and libertarian views both vying for acceptance in public policy, how can one hope to find underlying agreement on moral principles in widely different societies? Although the challenge is substantial, recent work in moral theory has argued there may be a basic and common way of reasoning about these matters, one that eventuates in the identification of some broad common principles governing economic life. Indeed, it is the claim of one of the leading contemporary proponents of this view, the philosopher John Rawls, to whose work I am greatly indebted, that much of our own western disagreement about the moral validity of differing economic precepts can be explained and ordered by resort to this more basic mode of moral analysis (Rawls 1971: Sec. 47).

At the heart of this view is an understanding of the nature of moral discourse and moral justification. Morality, it is argued, represents fundamentally the effort to arrive at a reasoned, noncoercive settlement of social disputes. To some extent all societies experience conflict when individuals or groups seek to assert their interests over those of other members of the society. In regulating and ordering these conflicts, however, two major methods of settlement present themselves. One method, open to human as well as nonhuman societies, is coercion. It allows force to create ordering as centers or coalitions of power determine whose interest shall be respected and pursued. The alternative method of social ordering, morality, is uniquely open to rational creatures like ourselves. It adjudicates social disputes with reference to a set of principles of conduct that are freely accepted by members of the social group. Its characteristic discourse of normative words ("right" and "wrong," "good" and "bad," "just" and "unjust") makes appeal to these principles, and these principles are presumed to influence behavior because they are thought in some way to be adopted by all responsible members of the society.

This conception of morality is obviously very basic. It is also seemingly neutral in terms of the question of whether there is only one or a plurality of moral systems. It does not stretch this common-sense understanding of the term morality, for example, if, when speaking of a "Roman morality" or a "Hebrew morality," one means the principles of conduct widely accepted within each of these respective societies. Nevertheless, the root idea that morality involves free assent to principles has powerful implications. It points to a method of moral justification that guides any moral reasoning process to some very common conclusions. This explains why, despite the diversity of moral systems, whenever moral justification is taken seriously certain universally prevalent principles tend to emerge as favored solutions for adjudicating social disputes.

THE BASEPOINT OF EQUALITY

We can understand this better if we try to apply this basic view of morality to the matter of economic distribution. In its very conception, we have just seen, morality involves an appeal to freely shared principles of conduct. This means that implicit in the understanding of morality is the idea of uncoerced assent to, or free acceptance of, the basic rules governing social interaction. Such a conception is only an ideal, of course. No human community ever gathers to determine what its basic moral principles should be, and there is probably a great deal of disguised coercion or manipulation behind the alleged ''assent'' to any existing moral code. But this is the ideal in mind whenever the effort is made to *justify* conduct or to demonstrate the justness of an existing social order. At such moments justification involves the claim that the relevant patterns of conduct and the basic principles underlying them are of the sort that *could be* accepted by all members of the social group. It is this idea of implicit consent that makes such conduct or principles *moral* and not merely the preferred social rules of powerful constituencies.

If consent by all members of a society to the principles governing their conduct is, in fact, the basic assumption in all moral discourse and all efforts at moral justification, it is worth asking what general implications this understanding has for the matter of economic distribution. Before looking at any specific principles of justice espoused by particular communities, in other words, we can ask whether this basic rèquirement of common consent imposes any overall constraint on reasoning in this area and whether it predictably shapes the outcome of basic human reflection about justice.

One way of examining this matter is to ask what principles of economic distribution would be selected by a society whose members had been reduced to the barest and most rudimentary situation of moral choice. Imagine, if you will, a society whose members do not yet have any views about just economic distribution. They have not yet developed any morally laden notions of ''desert'' or of ''rightful possession.'' They know only that a stock of vital resources must be distributed among themselves. Since a distributive problem is assumed to exist here, we can further suppose that these resources are at least sufficient for everybody but not superabundant and that every individual has very good reason to want as large a share as he/she can reasonably secure. In view of this choice situation, what principles will the members of this society select to govern the distribution of these relatively scarce vital goods?

I might add here parenthetically that the exclusion of strong notions of ''desert'' or ''entitlement'' and the restriction of all our hypothetical negotiators to the barest nonmoral information is not arbitrary. The fact is that human beings sharply disagree about what constitutes moral entitlement to material rewards. Nor is it clear that many of the qualities often held ''worthy'' of material reward, such as endurance or intelligence, really are *morally* estimable, as opposed to being the fortunate happenstance of birth. By excluding these ideas from the very outset, by deriving the choice of principles from rational choice in the most elementary circumstances of conflict, we aim to establish whatever principles emerge on the surest and most uncontested foundation.[2]

To continue this analysis, we can further imagine various alternative principles of distribution that might be proposed in this context. If the goods at issue are in no one's possession, someone might propose a rule of ''catch as catch can,'' allowing anyone able to do so to appropriate as many goods as he or she can. It takes very little reflection, however, to see that it would not be reasonable for all the members of this hypothetical situation freely to consent to this rule of choice, since its adoption will produce a pell-mell race for acquisition and may thrust some who lag in this race into destitution. If these resources were already under someone's control, we might further imagine the proposal being made that existing ''owners'' be allowed to retain these goods for their personal use. This proposal might avoid the mad race for acquisition, but such a ''right of possession'' amounts, where the ''losers'' or prospective ''losers'' are concerned, to the same thing as the unacceptable rule of ''catch as catch can.''

It is not hard to see, I think, that the only principle likely to receive the assent of all in this situation is something like a rule of equal distribution. True, some individuals would wish to receive a larger share than others, but it is unreasonable to believe that those others would freely accept such a distribution. Similarly, if some individuals have already happened to come into possession of goods, it is understandable that they would initially resist any effort at redistribution. But their intransigence will promptly lead to a stalemate in moral deliberation and to the breakdown of efforts to arrive at a moral (or noncoercive) adjudication of this distributive problem. Any individual not in possession of sufficient goods and facing serious hardship would find it unreasonable to relinquish his claim to them. Such individuals would presumably rather abandon the whole effort at moral resolution and choose to resort to force in order to acquire what they need to survive. If ''owners'' choose to preserve the option of moral settlement, therefore, the best they can do for themselves is something like a rule of equal distribution.

What this reasoning suggests is that a rule of equal distribution of scarce vital resources is not just one moral principle among others. Rather, it is the fundamental rule of choice in the most rudimentary situation of distributive conflict. It is the rule that imposes itself with powerful logic as long as almost nothing else but the basic circumstances of choice are assumed and as long as the requirement of free consent by all (the ''moral'' requirement) is taken seriously. We can say, then, that equal distribution represents the ''basepoint'' for thinking about matters of just distribution of scarce vital resources. That such goods will be distributed equally and without prejudice among members of a social group is the beginning moral presumption. Equality of possession or equal access to goods needs no justification because it follows directly from the requirement of free consent by all, whereas departures from equality require justification. Whenever it is proposed that goods be distributed unequally, in other words, some further and persuasive reasons must be given for going beyond the equilibrium point of equal distribution.

BEYOND EQUALITY

To this point we have been examining only the most rudimentary situation of moral choice: the distribution of a stock of vital goods among competing claimants with no further factual or moral beliefs assumed or introduced. Equality of distribution is not only the first presumption arising out of such circumstances, it is also probably the appropriate rule for those real-life circumstances of choice that approximate this hypothetical situation (e.g., the distribution of public foodstuffs in time of famine, or the distribution of newly discovered resources of land or water). But now we must add some further factual considerations relevant to most human societies, considerations that make our choice situation more complex. Our initial assumption, remember, was that a stock of independently existing resources was to be distributed. But this is clearly not the way goods exist in most societies. Rather, the stock of resources does not unusually exist apart from human endeavor but is created and recreated through the application of human effort, initiative and energy. Because this is so, the stock of vital resources is not fixed but is inevitably affected by the moral principles developed in our initial circumstances of choice.

With this qualification in mind, it is easy to imagine a problem generated by our initial solution of equal distribution. Since resources do not just exist *out there* independently of human effort, a decision to redistribute goods equally on an ongoing basis can adversely affect productivity, reducing the amount of goods available for redistribution. Why, after all, should some individuals strive energetically to contribute to the common stock if the efforts they make do not advantage them in any way more than those who strive far less? It is true that the situation of uncoerced liberty which moral agreement makes possible is attractive to such producers, as it is to everyone, but presumably it is not so attractive as to induce them to generate prodigious supplies of goods for the common stock. Rather, it is probably rational for them to generate as few resources as are needed for bare survival, consistent with the redistributive scheme. They might even consider becoming ''free riders'' supported by others' exertions.[3]

Basic moral reasoning about distributive questions, therefore, reveals a dilemma. On the one hand, the logic of equality is clear. Indeed, this logic always remains in force, even when the facts of human initiative are taken into account, since it is unreasonable for less able (or less willing) producers totally to relinquish their claims to a share merely because others have produced and are in possession of the contested goods. Furthermore, rational individuals have substantial reason to fear the proliferating and enduring inequalities to which unregulated private possession might lead. However, it is also very clear that, in the absence of an extraordinary degree of fellow feeling on the part of human beings, some bid to the principle of possession, with its corresponding inequalities, is needed if the stock of resources is not to be diminished as individuals refuse to produce for the common good.

The principles of equality and unequal possession are thus in substantial tension with one another within the logic of distributive reasoning. Each principle represents a real and valid concern of equally situated moral personalities, and each reflects certain real circumstances of distribution of scarce resources. In view of this we might suppose that neither principle will be relinquished in any resulting moral settlement. Instead, each principle will be insisted upon, but each will be allowed, whenever possible, to temper the other. Private property and inequalities may be allowed, but they will be hemmed in by moral qualifications and restraints. Nonproductive acquisition or possession (gain through chicanery and ostentatious personal consumption) will be brought under sharp criticism. Active sharing and generosity will be encouraged, especially when the survival of society's poorest members is at stake. Throughout, the underlying basepoint of equality will exert its pressure by generating a public sense of uneasiness over economic inequalities not clearly related to the common good.

Against this background of abstract and formal reasoning we might now make some more specific anticipatory claims or predictions about the basic structure of traditional moral and religious attitudes toward economic life and just economic distribution. Traditional societies, it will be noted, closely approximate both of the circumstances presumed in this preliminary reasoning: they exist near the survival level with stocks of scarce vital resources. Some of these resources are nonproduced, but the bulk are the direct outcome of human labor and initiative. If what I have been saying is correct, we can expect that the moral and religious systems of these societies will largely validate the right of property and inequality of possession. However, they will look with special favor on that property whose possession substantially contributes to the commonweal, and they will be deeply suspicious of property or acquisition that makes no productive contribution or whose possession is actually counterproductive. At the same time, in a bid to the equality principle and in the effort to develop the moral limits of this right of possession, these societies will characteristically encourage generosity, sharing, and liberality. Individuals will be permitted affluence and may even be praised for it, but only when this affluence is regarded by them not as an uncontested right but as an opportunity for the generous bestowal of goods on others. This model of qualified possession most closely approximates the interests of *all* parties in our initial circumstances of choice.

In the preceding remarks, I have tried to outline and to justify an "ideal-normative" structure for economic life—a series of considerations that can be expected to underlie any reasonable, moral economic order. On the supposition that these considerations have applicability across cultural lines, I want now to turn to Buddhism in the effort to see whether this "deep structure" helps us better understand Buddhist teaching about poverty and wealth. Unfortunately, measuring Buddhist teaching against this ideal-normative structure is no easy task. For one thing, there is a wide variety of texts and teachings related to economic life and not all of them are entirely consistent with one another. At best, one can hope, without unfair selectivity or prejudice, to identify some key text or texts that yield a basic and widely shared set of attitudes about poverty and wealth. My own choice for one such text is the Aggañña Suttānta, the so-called "Buddhist Book of Genesis." I shall try to explain and justify this selection shortly.

Another serious problem is presented by the view, often held by western scholars, most notably Max Weber, that because of its fundamental teachings Buddhism cannot have an economic or social ethic in any recognizable sense. At least three reasons are commonly advanced to support this claim. First, it is argued that the doctrine of not-self (*anatta*) must fundamentally undermine moral concern for the welfare of one's neighbor or one's community. As Max Weber (1958: 213) put it, any kind of social ethic predicated upon the value of individual persons "must be as remote as possible from a salvation doctrine which, in any value emphasis upon the 'soul,' could discern only the grand and pernicious basic illusion." Second, it is claimed that Buddhism's central emphasis on the transmundane goal of *nirvāṇa*, on monastic withdrawal from the world, and on individual self-extrication from *saṃsāra* can produce at best only an attenuated social ethic. Thus Weber, again, regarded Buddhism's entire lay ethic as an afterthought, an "insufficiency ethic of the weak" and an ethic altogether lacking in normative specificity with regard to economic life (Weber 1958: 215). Third, and finally, it is sometimes claimed that the *karma* doctrine itself erodes any possible critical perspective on an existing economic order. Since every individual's material circumstances—whether he be rich or poor—can be traced to his prior moral conduct, all social and economic status becomes "deserved" and immune to criticism. Related to this is the observation that, in Buddhist lay morality, karmic aspirations frequently focus on the hope of improved material conditions and wealth (Weber 1958: 218f.).

None of these alleged difficulties, I think, need dissuade us from looking for a Buddhist social and economic ethic. At least since Weber posed the challenge, commentators have observed that Buddhism has developed an important body of social-ethical teaching. Indeed, these commentators have sometimes traced this teaching to the very doctrinal positions that Weber and others believed to undermine the possibility of a Buddhist economic ethic. For example, it has been repeatedly observed that the doctrine of not-self has not usually been interpreted by Buddhists in such a way as to erode moral regard for the neighbor. Rather it has been used to encourage "selfless" compassion for others. In the economic domain it is asserted that this teaching is meant to counter the sense of "mineness" that stimulates greed and the lust for material acquisition (Sarkisyanz 1965: 40). The second claim, that Buddhist ethics focuses principally on the monastic community with lay conduct an afterthought, has likewise been brought under sharp criticism. Tambiah (1976: Chaps. 1–5), Sarkisyanz (1965: Chaps. 6, 7), and others have stressed that Buddhist social ethics are badly misunderstood if the ethics for the monastic community is severed from the rich body of teaching regarding the ideal political order and the duties of the Buddhist righteous ruler, the *cakkavatta*. The fact that the Buddha himself was predicted to become either a great world renouncer or a great world ruler suggests to these writers that the idea of individual spiritual salvation *and* the hope for political and economic reform may have been part of the earliest Buddhist vision. For those who interpret Buddhist ethics in this way, the monastic community ideally serves as the conscience for political and economic society, while that society provides the moral and the material context for all of its members' eventual world renunciation and attainment of *nirvāṇa* (Sarkisyanz 1965: 14).

Also very questionable is the claim that Buddhism's teaching of *karma* implies acceptance of any economic status quo. This claim derives from a confusion of the question of how the law of *karma* operates with the question of how individuals should respond to the operation of that law. One may well believe one's wealth (or political power) is the result of one's prior deeds and yet also (consistently) affirm that in some cases this (deserved) wealth or power is being or can be abused. Belief in *karma*, therefore, in no way undercuts the possibility of specific normative regulations for the conduct of economic life, nor does it rule out a critique of existing economic arrangements in the light of an ideal moral vision of the economic order. Indeed, we find both of these in Buddhist teaching: specific moral rules for the employment of wealth and a moral vision of an ideal economic order which further implies a critique of existing society. I might add that on close inspection both these specific rules and the more basic moral vision display substantial conformity to the ideal normative structure I outlined at the beginning. Let us look at this in some detail.

DĀNA AND SOCIAL JUSTICE

We need not dwell very long on Buddhism's specific norms for economic life since they are so well treated in several of the other essays in this volume. These norms permit the possession of private property on the part of the laity, but they strongly encourage an attitude of "non-attachment" to one's possessions and they place a premium on religious giving (*dāna*). The toleration of private property should not surprise us here since we know that rational persons have reason to regard this as an efficient means of stimulating economic effort and of allocating its product. At the same time, we should also not be surprised to see a great deal of stress on the need for generosity and the sharing of one's material goods. Our previous abstract discussion suggested that when it comes to the moral distribution of wealth it is not the poor (or those who anticipate being poor) who must be persuaded of its value since any such distribution must certainly help them. Rather it is the prosperous—or those who within the constraints of the moral-choice situation anticipate prosperity—who must be persuaded that it is in everyone's interests not to allow unregulated accumulation, possession, or consumption. These people must be made to see that the absence of regulation imperils the prospect for a total moral settlement of social disputes and threatens to drive society to continual strife and disharmony. What is rational under deliberative conditions of moral choice, however, is not always rational in the real circumstances of social life. Prosperous individuals are always tempted to abandon the "social contract" as it bears on wealth and to opt for a social adjudication based on power. This is why lively traditions of moral teaching, especially religious-ethical traditions, often address their most strenuous pedagogical efforts to the wealthy. This may take the form of encouragements to fellow-feeling with the less advantaged or it may emphasize the spiritual dangers of wealth. Or it may involve some combination of these two approaches. In Buddhism the emphasis appears to be on the spiritual dangers to the self posed by excessive attachment to material goods. Nevertheless, this singular emphasis on self-regarding religious reasons for being generous (as opposed to the Jewish or Christian emphasis on compassion for the less fortunate neighbor) should not obscure the fact that the net objective is the same: leading the powerful and prosperous, quite against the natural course of human psychology, to place some distance between themselves and their possessions and to be willing to share their wealth.

It may be objected here that despite the similarity to other notions of economic ethics Buddhist generosity is really very different from the ideas of economic sharing and social justice we have been discussing. Buddhist giving, *dāna*, is essentially religious in nature and in purpose. Not only is the motive behind giving self-regarding and religious, its object is purely religious: the aim is to support not the weak and needy but the community of religious virtuosi. *Dāna*'s primarily religious quality is epitomized in the teaching that the worth of giving is a function of the spiritual advancement of the recipient, not his economic need and that the *sangha* (community of monks), not the poor, is the primary "field of merit" for charitable giving (Narada 1972: 270; Cone and Gombrich 1977: xxv).

Obviously, this is a serious objection. It may suggest a fundamental problem for a view that would try to assimilate Buddhist economic teachings to a rational normative structure based on allegedly western notions of individualism and the value of material life. The claim that this moral perspective is a merely "western" neglects the logic of moral justification I have described, which is held to be applicable to any conceivable social group in which the circumstances of conflict exist and the need for rational adjudication is present. Nevertheless, gross disparities between ideal rational analysis and the teachings of a specific cultural tradition should not be ignored and may force a rethinking of the complexity of moral reasoning in context. Be this as it may, I am not sure that such rethinking is needed in this instance because it is by no means clear that the distinction between "religious" and "ethical" giving suggested by Buddhist *dāna* is a valid one. In fact, this whole matter raises complex social and historical questions whose resolution is well beyond the scope of this discussion. It might be asked, for example, to what extent the *sangha* has served historically as a center not just for spiritual advancement but for economic distribution, by providing livelihood, education, and opportunity to individuals from the lowest social classes. If this has been a major feature of life in Buddhist societies, then purely religious giving would have important redistributive implications. Again, to what extent has the *sangha* served as the welfare institution of last resort—stepping in to aid orphans, widows, the infirm, or the destitute when that other basic social-welfare institution of agrarian societies, the extended family, proved unable to meet pressing need?[4] Finally, to what extent has support of the *sangha*, by promoting adherence to *dhamma*, maintained the very stability and prosperity of society, whether through the immediate moral effects of such adherence or through the pervasive cosmogonic consequences often attributed by Buddhists to proper observance of the teaching? Questions like these must be answered more thoroughly before we conclude that the primarily religious motivation and objective of *dāna* renders it wholly different from the forms of redistribution found in many other societies.

Buddhism's specific moral rules for economic life can thus be said to leave unresolved the question of the tradition's conformity to our ideal normative structure. Some intriguing correspondences—especially the strenuous encouragements to self-detachment from wealth—are offset by apparent differences that require further investigation and research. However, when we turn to what I earlier called Buddhism's "vision" of an ideal social order (with its implicit criticism of existing social conditions), fewer questions are left unanswered. In fact, when imagination is allowed free rein, as it is in the cosmogonic speculation of a text like the Aggañña Suttānta, the parallels to other traditions' understanding of the economic life are both specific and striking. Moreover, Buddhist thinking in this case tends to move uniformly in the direction suggested by our ideal normative structure.

THE AGGAÑÑA SUTTĀNTA

Perhaps the best way of developing this Buddhist vision of the economic order is to present a synopsis of the process of world evolution outlined in the Aggañña Suttānta. Following a series of prefatory remarks criticizing the existing caste order, the text turns to cosmogony and picks up the narrative at the end of a previous world cycle:

> When, after a very long period, the world cycle passed away, beings were mostly reborn in the world of radiance, where, made of mind, they dwelled "feeding on rapture, self-luminous, traversing the air, continuing in glory" (Rhys Davids 1921: IV, 82). After a long time, the world begins to reevolve. Beings who had deceased from the world of radiance usually were reborn as humans, albeit self-luminous humans, traversing the air, made of mind, without sexual differentiation, feeding on rapture.
>
> The world was then watery and dark, neither sun nor moon nor stars having yet come into being. In time, just as a scum forms over the surface of boiled milky rice, the earth appeared over the waters. It was endowed with the color of pure butter and the flavor of honey. Spurred on by a "greedy disposition," one of the human beings tasted the savory earth with his finger. Others followed him and, "suffused with the savour, . . . a craving entered into them" (Rhys Davids 1921: IV, 82). They began then to break off large lumps of this food. As a result, they became permeated with the earth material, their luminance faded away, and the sun, moon and stars appeared to replace the beings' vanished light.
>
> For a long time these beings continued to eat the savory earth. Their bodies thus became more solid, and differences in comeliness became manifest. Some beings were well-favored, some were ill-favored. Those who were well-favored gloated pridefully over their state and "despised" those who were less favored (Rhys Davids 1921: IV, 84). This vanity and conceit caused the savory earth to disappear.
>
> A new form of nourishment now appeared in the form of mushroomlike growths with the color of butter and the flavor of honey. But these caused the bodies of the human beings to become even more solid and more differentiated from one another. Once again, this occasioned pride on the part of the better-favored, and the growths ceased, to be replaced by sweet-tasting, creeping plants.

Like the foods before them, the plants increased the humans' bodily solidity, and differences in physical appearance among individuals became even more manifest. Pride also increased and the plants vanished, giving way to a fragrant, huskless rice. This was so abundant that when gathered in the evening for supper, a new crop was ready to be harvested the next morning for breakfast. Eating this rice, however, accentuated human solidity and differentiation. As a result, the distinction between males and females appeared, sexual lust arose and with it immoral conduct. To conceal their immoral behavior, beings constructed huts.

At this time some being "of a lazy disposition" asked "Why do I wear myself out fetching rice for supper in the evening, and in the morning for breakfast? What if I were to fetch enough rice for supper and breakfast together?" (Rhys Davids 1921: IV, 86). He acted on this idea and others followed his example, storing up rice for four and then eight days. As a result, powder and husks enveloped the grain and the reaped and cut stems of the plants did not grow again. "The rice stubble stood in clumps" (Rhys Davids 1921: IV, 86).

Lamenting their condition and the degenerated state to which "evil and immoral customs" had led them, the beings now resolved to divide off the rice fields and set boundaries thereto. But then one being "of greedy disposition," while watching over his own plot, stole another's plot and made use of it. The others seized and remonstrated with him, but he persisted in his conduct until the others were forced to strike him with their hands, with clods, or with sticks. Thus "did stealing appear, and censure and lying and punishment" (Rhys Davids 1921: IV, 87).

Gathering together to bewail these things, the community resolved to select one among them to censure what should rightly be censured. They chose the most attractive and most capable of their number for this task and agreed to give him a proportion of their rice in payment for his services. This king "chosen by the whole people" was given the name Mahā Sammata, the great elect (Rhys Davids 1921: IV, 88).

With the selection of this royal person there emerged the social circle of nobles. The origin of the members of this group was identical to that of other human beings, but like the king they were appointed to political service. In time a second group, the Brahmin

> renouncers, also emerged, consisting of those individuals who had forsaken the world of evil deeds for forest meditation.
>
> Eventually, some among these proved incapable of meditation and settled in the outskirts of villages where they made books. "At that time they were looked upon as the lowest; now they are thought the best" (Rhys Davids 1921: IV, 90). Eventually, the two remaining groups of the caste order emerged: the Vessas, who adopted the married state and set on foot various trades, and the Suddas, a hunter caste. No group emerged from physically distinct types: all shared a common human nature.

Having depicted the full evolution of the world order as we know it, the Suttānta describes a final important historical event:

> Some Khattiya, "misprizing his own norm," went forth into the homeless life resolved to become a recluse. He was followed by like-minded Brahmins, Vessas, and Suddas. Whoever among these has destroyed "the intoxicants," has "laid down the burden," and who, "through knowledge made perfect is free," is declared chief among their number (Rhys Davids 1921: IV, 93).

Obviously, one must be careful in reading or interpreting a myth like this. To a large extent it is a whimsical, imaginative effort, with humorous and ironical dimensions. Part of its aim is certainly to poke fun at brahmanical pretensions and at the brahmanical account of the creation of the world and the social order (Tambiah 1976: 9). Nevertheless, the fact that a text is imaginative and humorous does not mean that it cannot also convey important beliefs. Because many of the themes in this myth are reflected in more orthodox Buddhist teachings, there is good reason to consider it a serious statement about human nature and human destiny. Regarded as such, it displays some remarkable parallels to elements of the ideal normative structure we outlined earlier.

One major parallel is the perspective offered on unregulated material acquisition and possession. In full conformity to major Buddhist teachings the Suttānta presents a sharp criticism of human beings' lust for sense pleasures and material satisfactions. Appetite and the desire for acquisition are viewed as driving forces in what is essentially a degenerative process of world evolution. Beings that begin as luminous spiritual entities whose most basic needs seem to be automatically satisfied are here presented as greedily ingesting base material, with the result that their very natures become corrupted and coarse. Greed and hunger produce even more greed and hunger. This process continues remorselessly until it corrupts almost every dimension of human existence: material lust gives rise to sexual lust, nature becomes debased as her uncultivated bounty gives way to sterility, and the human contest over now-scarce resources produces theft, violence, and a harshly punitive political order.

The parallels here to the western biblical account of man's prehistory are obvious, as are the contrasts. No God enters to punish human wrong-doing, and the cardinal sin is not pride or the desire to become God. Nevertheless, where material desires are concerned, the lesson of both texts is the same: human greed is its own undoing. Nature is viewed as having been constituted to provide enough for man's modest needs, but when individuals quest for more than their proper share, they invariably end up with less. Disordered self-assertion diminishes nature's abundance, corrupts the human body, promotes strife and violence between men, and makes necessary a coercive and hierarchical political order.

In this connection it is worth noting that the passage in the Aggañña Suttãnta dealing with rice's loss of fecundity after an episode of hoarding has a striking parallel in Exodus 16. In the biblical text we read of God's bestowal of manna on the wandering Hebrews. Each family is provided daily with what it can eat and no more. Despite an explicit prohibition against saving up the foodstuff, some individuals gather more than their share. They promptly find that the excess has been infested with maggots, and those who violate God's prohibition against gathering on the sabbath are unable to find any food at all. The specific religious dimensions of the Hebrew and the Buddhist text clearly differ. The Israelites' behavior is another instance of their lack of faith in God and their disobedience of the divine command. But on a moral and economic plane the lessons of the two passages are very similar: selfish hoarding is viewed as counterproductive; those who try to buttress their positions by acquisitiveness or those who are greedy and lazy end by undermining their own positions and possibly jeopardizing the welfare of the whole community.

Textual parallels like these are important data for the enterprise of comparative religious ethics. The challenge is to understand why they exist in widely different traditions. My own view is that, in this instance at least, these correspondences are not accidental. They grow out of some very basic considerations found in our ideal normative "deep structure" of economic ethics. In the course of our earlier analysis we saw that unfettered individual acquisitiveness—of which hoarding is symbolic—runs directly counter to the sense of cooperativeness needed for harmonious economic life. We saw that this "catch as catch can" and "go it alone" mentality is the chief obstacle to developing a moral point of view for economic life, and it is the real obstacle to the maintenance of any existing order of economic justice. To the extent that selfish individuals opt out of a cooperative order, they make violence and power the governing rule of life and they thereby undermine the very basis of their own and others' prosperity. Our two texts make this point on a mythic level, I believe, and their parallelism is explained by reference to this deeper moral logic.

A second major parallel between the Aggañña Suttānta and our ideal normative structure is what I would call an emphasis on the essential equality and autonomy of persons. The issue of equality is very much to the fore in the Suttānta's treatment of brahmanical ideas of creation and society. We read repeatedly that the various social orders of the caste system do not reflect any indwelling (or ontological) differences among human beings, nor do they stem from a divinely effected act of creation as claimed in the Vedic cosmogonic myth, Purusha-Sukta (*Rig Veda* 10:90). Rather, whatever caste or class groups exist reflect functional specialization. These groups also do not possess enduring moral significance. The ultimate worth of an individual is a result not of his caste position, but of his moral integrity. It follows from this that religious salvation is open to members of every caste group.

This relatively egalitarian spirit is also evidenced in the Suttānta's sardonic criticism of human pride. We learn that differences in "comeliness" are one of the unfortunate results of the process whereby human beings become coarser and more differentiated. In their stupidity and ignorance, however, the more comely individuals do not look at things in this way: they regard their lesser disadvantage as a fully merited occasion for disdaining their "inferiors." This foolishness and pride, of course, only accelerate the degenerative process. Compare this perspective with elements of our earlier independent moral analysis. We saw that a rational moral perspective does not begin with intuitive notions of "worth" or "merit" as a basis for allocations of social resources, opportunity, or power. This is partly because notions of "worth" are so various, but more importantly, it is because rational persons must realize that many of the qualities often deemed "meritorious," such as physical attractiveness or prowess, intelligence or endurance, are often the result of one's birth or home environment and are thus essentially "nonmoral." Rational persons may come to reward these qualities, but they do so because they regard them as socially useful assets (and on condition that they be employed for social benefit), not because they attribute intrinsic moral worth to these qualities or to their possessors. In view of this attitude it is clear that prideful assertions of one's own worth and the insistence on favor and reward run directly counter to the spirit required for cooperation with a morally structured social life. Such attitudes do not withstand objective rational assessment, and in practice they make the moral settlement of disputes extremely difficult. Quite expectedly, therefore, religious-ethical traditions try to combat attitudes of this sort. In western religious traditions these morally pernicious attitudes are handled by the constant criticism leveled against pride and by the insistence that one's natural assets are, at best, "blessings" bestowed by God for use on others' behalf. In this Buddhist text the tone is gentler but the point is similar: one should not view one's advantages, however obtained, as an occasion for arrogance or pride, and those who succumb to pride are usually the least entitled to do so.

Following from this stress on the relative moral equality of all persons is the notion of autonomy, or the principle of respect for persons. Because all persons are morally equal, all should have a say in the establishment of the principles or institutions that govern their society. This idea, of course, underlies the whole rational perspective we developed earlier. Its ideal of unanimous consent to principles reflects the belief that to establish a harmonious social order, a moral communal life, one must respect the autonomy of every possible rational participant. In the Aggañña Suttānta we have an important expression of these ideas in the understanding that kingship in its ideal sense is an institution created by consensus. Selected only for his relative integrity, the Mahā Sammata, one of the people, is "chosen by the whole people." Clearly, this occurrence is favorably regarded by the author(s) of the text. Kingship is not an example of further decline but represents a first major effort to halt the process of degeneration. With it a "corrective power" is added to the cosmogonic process, a power "making for the best and economizing the worst" (Paul Mus in Tambiah 1976: 39). In this respect the Suttānta supports the claim of those who see righteous kingship as an important part of the Buddhist social vision. More significant for our purposes, however, is the fact that this vital institution and specific holders of royal office are thought, at least in principle, to derive their power from the unanimous consent of the ruled. The fact that the idealized *cakkavatti* and the *bodhisatta* (during his service as a ruler) were also thought to derive their authority from the uncoerced assent of their subjects[5] indicates how complete the correspondence is at this point between Buddhist social ethics and the ideal normative structure we developed earlier.

A final major correspondence relates to the Suttānta's vision of an ideal order beyond the sphere of private possession and property. In developing a rational normative ideal, I tried to indicate that equal access to necessary goods is the basepoint for reasoned reflection on economic life. Private property and inequalities in possession are admitted only as a concession to the brute facts of human life: as a counter to individual sloth, to greed, and to people's lack of fellow-feeling. Even when private possession and inequality are allowed, however, rational persons have good reason to be anxious about the risks to equality which this departure allows. They fear the unchecked and uncheckable differences in wealth to which property can lead—hence the stress on liberality and the redistribution of wealth. In the western religious traditions all these ideas receive repeated expression in various ways. Underlying these traditions is an insistence on social justice and on private charity. They also help explain the motif—perhaps most salient in the Christian tradition—of a primitive state "before the fall" marked by common possession and sharing, a state to be recreated in the eschaton when private property vanishes again and a communism of love takes its place.[6]

Despite the different point of departure, sentiments very similar to these are found in the Aggañña Suttānta. It is true that we find no ringing criticism of private property: though clearly not viewed as favorably as the institution of kingship, property is a useful 'historical' countermeasure to the anarchic appropriation of material goods. Nevertheless, within this acceptance of private property a subtle criticism can be detected: private possession is not a part of the happy original order of things; it is introduced not just as a remedy for greed, but as a consequence of greed, and its introduction produces new evils of violence and punishment. More importantly, the Suttānta's "eschatological" vision, if it can be called that, is one in which private property is transcended. In the most decisive response to the evolutionary process of degeneration the "company of recluses" comes into being. Like the brahmin renouncers before them, these recluses abandon the struggle for material gain; they subsist only on the modest daily offerings of the householders. Unlike the brahmin renouncers, however, this company draws its members from all castes and classes. Freed now of all sins—of pride and of greed—its members are able to push on to final liberation from the degenerative process of becoming. According to this vision, therefore, the Buddhist monastic community reconstitutes the primordial state before material greed has corrupted and debased human nature. So established, it serves as a fitting staging point for final liberation from rebirth.[7]

The Aggañña Suttānta is very much a Buddhist text. It focuses upon ignorance, craving, and greed as the moving forces behind human suffering and wickedness. Human emancipation requires that these forces be checked at both the social and the personal level. Supporting those who claim that righteous kingship is central to the social aspect of the Buddhist vision, the Suttānta spares monarchy the criticisms leveled against almost all other social institutions. Kingship is exceeded in esteem by only one other institution: the company of recluses. In this double emphasis we see the outlines of a full Buddhist theory of society.

Most important for our purpose, however, is the fact that this social vision resonates with many of the basic concerns and normative preferences associated with our previous rational analysis of a justly ordered economic life. Thus it seems that this rational analysis is not merely culture-bound, as some would contend, but has wide applicability to basic problems of social and economic life wherever they appear. Indeed, the fact that one can locate explicit parallels in the relevant texts of widely different traditions—witness the similar criticisms of hoarding we encountered—gives some evidence of the existence of a ''deep structure'' of moral reasoning beneath a surface of apparent diversity. If I have not entirely demonstrated this point here, I hope at least to have suggested that it is not irresponsible to contend that moral reasoning is a broadly human phenomenon and that the techniques and insights of rational moral philosophy may assist our understanding of different religious and cultural traditions. I also hope to have shed light on some important features of Buddhist social and economic teaching.

11 Individualism, Communitarianism, and Theories of Justice

John P. Reeder, Jr.

The allocation of income and wealth is one of the primary subjects of theories of distributive justice in contemporary Western moral theory. Fierce debates rage. Should resources be distributed in the direction of equality? Should a social minimum be provided? Or is any distribution right, however unequal or burdensome, provided that it results from just procedures by which persons acquire or transfer assets? Is the key to economic justice the ownership of the means of production? Rawlsians do battle with Nozickians; Marxists and feminists say a plague on both your houses.

Despite the appearance of wide disagreement, however, some interpreters claim that modern Western theories of justice are members of a genus; Rawls, Nozick, and even Marx, Louis Dumont would claim, are peas in a pod (1977; cf. Gould 1978). Their similarity lies in their individualism, their theory of the self. This individualism, in turn, derives from a model of the person in a capitalist society, or more specifically, from the model of the person in the economic theory that emerges from that society.[1] David Gauthier (1979: 547) sums up the theses about the self which form the background of modern theory:

> The problematic of modern moral theory is set by three dogmas which philosophy receives from economics. The first is that value is utility—a measure of subjective, individual preference. The second is that rationality is maximization: the rational individual "will maximize the extent to which his objective is achieved." The third is that interests are non-tuistic: interacting persons do not take "an interest in one another's interests." Modern moral theory determines the possibility of morality in relation to these dogmas.

By rejecting one or more of these dogmas or by embracing them all, as Gauthier believes Hobbes did, modern theorists have tried to erect a moral and political framework for *homo economicus*. A picture of the self sets the problematic even when aspects of it are modified in order to build a moral framework. As Dumont would say, the problem of modern ideology is to legitimate, to justify each individual in the free and equal pursuit of self-interest.

I propose to raise three sorts of issues in relation to each of Gauthier's dogmas: What are the historical roots of Western theories? What are some major objections to current theories such as Rawls's? And what light if any do such theories shed on non-Western traditions such as Theravāda Buddhism? First, although I cannot speak as a historian, I want to suggest that modern theories of distributive justice do indeed reflect strands of Western thought, but that the situation is more complex than Gauthier and Dumont picture it; the three assumptions are perhaps not just the product of economic theory or capitalism, but seem to reflect older and deeper currents of western culture. Second, I want to assess some of the objections to individualism often brought against Rawls and others. And third, I want to discuss whether Gauthier's dogmas and another key idea, the notion of acceptance by any agent, are shared by other cultures. The fact that theories are rooted in particular cultural assumptions does not in itself settle the issue of their validity. But the question here is to what extent Western points of view overlap with the approach to distributive issues in a variety of cultures, particularly the strands of Theravāda Buddhism investigated in this volume.

THEORY OF THE GOOD

Gauthier's first dogma, which he says is bequeathed from economics to philosophy, is that the measure of value is utility, based on subjective preference. But modern economics, I should think, takes its theory of value from strands of modern culture; the economic theory of value (it has a history of its own, of course) is the technical adaptation of broader and deeper ideas about the nature of human good which may antedate modern capitalism. According to Alasdair MacIntyre, for example, the loss of confidence in an Aristotelian theory of the good occurred earlier and for different reasons (1984a).

I leave to historians the task of tracing its growth and development, but here is a rough approximation of the "subjective preference" view of the good (cf. MacIntyre 1988: 336ff.).[2] It is not the case that human good consists essentially in certain states (the actualization of characteristic potentialities or whatever). To ascribe goodness or value to a particular state or object is to appraise it in light of the desires and aims of the agent; the purposes of human beings are not reducible to those which are "essential" and those which are not; the aims and hence the good of human beings is multifarious.[3] Since there is no "essential" or "true" human good, there is no one end or good (or set of goods) to which all others necessarily contribute. Our judgments of value are not necessarily arbitrary, however. We share a good number of physical and psychological needs and desires. Against this background most people value survival, health, and other basic goods. In addition, it seems to be the case that people in many cultures value the products of social cooperation which enable them to satisfy basic needs and desires. But it is not necessary that one find even survival good. Individuals have the capacity to differ in their desires and hence their purposes; we have the ability to form widely divergent ''plans of life.''

Let us consider two important objections to this theory of human good. First, to claim that there is no essential good is in fact to assume one, namely, the value of being free to choose a variety of ends. Robert Johann (1979) quotes John Rawls's well-known statements in order to refute them: ''it seems indisputable, then, that there is no dominant end the pursuit of which accords with our considered judgments of value'' (1971: 558); ''to subordinate all our aims to one end . . . strikes us as irrational, or more likely as mad'' (1971: 554); ''human good is heterogeneous because the aims of the self are heterogeneous'' (1971: 554). Johann argues that the notion of a ''final end,'' one to which all others are subordinate, should be considered not as some external ''state of affairs'' (1979: 15), but as an end ''to which the subject self is ordered by its very nature . . . antecedent to its particular intentions.'' The self does not choose this end; it is constitutive of the choosing self (1979: 17). Even Rawls has to claim that the self would go contrary to its nature, disfigure itself, if it chose some inclination as a dominant end; in other words, the freedom of the self is its final end or good, according to Rawls (Johann 1979: 11).

Second, to appraise the worth of a plan of life one must assume a substantive criterion. Johann argues that Rawls's notion of self-respect—the worth of a plan of life—makes sense only if there is an ''original interest underlying all the subject's actions in the light of which they can be appraised'' (1979: 20). Michael Sandel also states this sort of objection. For Rawls, to choose a plan of life is only to take into account ''the contingent wants and desires and preferences of the self, but not the self itself'' (Sandel 1982: 159). Reflection is limited to asking what I want and how intensely I want it; even second-order desires (my desires about my desires) are merely further facts about my preferences. Rawls cannot appeal to the ''intrinsic worth of a desire or its essential connection with the identity of the agent . . .'' (163–64). According to Sandel (1982: 165), however,

> If my fundamental values and final ends are to enable me, as surely they must, to evaluate and regulate my immediate wants and desires, these values and ends must have a sanction independent of the mere fact that I happen to hold them with a certain intensity. But if my conception of the good is simply the product of my immediate wants and desires, it would be governed by the same contingencies.

For Rawls, says Sandel, the self does not provide the needed standard of intrinsic value.[4]

How would defenders of the preference theory reply? To the first objection that the theory in fact assumes a final end, the freedom of the self to choose a set of ends, the Rawls of *A Theory of Justice* (1971) would reply to Johann along the following lines: I only denied what you yourself denied, namely, that there is a constitutive end among the various inclinations of the self, for example, ''the exercise of political power, or the achievement of social acclaim, or maximizing one's material possessions'' (1971: 553). I do affirm that the self is free to choose its ends, but I see no reason to speak of this as its final end, somehow constitutive of itself. That the self is free to adopt ends is not a fact about the ends of the agent; it is a thesis about the relation of the self to its ends.

Furthermore, Rawls might continue, I do not, despite some of my own statements, want to deny to individuals the possibility of choosing some dominant end or ends (as opposed to a heterogeneous set). My crucial point is that individuals are free to choose the good; they are free to choose a dominant end or not. Human beings therefore posit the ends or goods they seek. What the objector must do, Rawls would insist, is to show why one should accept any other view of the self and its ends.

Would the objection that self-respect requires a standard of worth show the inadequacy of the preference theory? The Rawlsian defender can say that one can appraise one's plan of life by using the principles of prudential reasoning (how effectively can I realize my goals); the defender could also argue, as R. B. Brandt does (1979: Chap. 6), that one should analyze one's desires therapeutically (how well do I know myself, are my goals influenced by unconscious motivations). Worth can be appraised by means of these procedures, whereas Johann thinks it requires some ''original interest.'' Sandel's similar claim that one must have a standard of intrinsic worth seems merely stipulative outside of a theory that shows there to be such a thing. The Rawls of 1971 did not believe that we discover ends which furnish a standard of intrinsic value by which we could judge our more immediate desires and aims. On the preference theory, the worth of a plan of life can be appraised only in light of the desires and aims of agents; one can appeal to "second-order" desires—desires about desires—but one cannot get outside of the nexus of desire, purpose, and value in order to find a transcendent standard.

So far, then, the preference theory is intact. It may have a relatively circumscribed historical location, but it seems to stand up at least to the objections considered above. What would it take to unseat the preference theory? It would take an entirely different theory of the self and its relation to its ends. Sandel, for example, would have to present a theory showing that there are indeed constitutive ends of the self, ends that the self does not choose but discovers. For example, he might argue for a constitutive communal good such as MacIntyre wants to retrieve from Aristotle:

> For what education in the virtues teaches me is that my good as a man is one and the same as the good of those others with whom I am bound up in the human community. There is no way of pursuing my good which is necessarily antagonistic to you pursuing yours because *the* good is neither mine peculiarly nor yours peculiarly—goods are not private property. Hence Aristotle's definition of friendship, the fundamental form of human relationship, is in terms of shared goods. (1984a: 229; cf.190–91, 195, 219–20, 232, 250–51)

Such a theory would find in the preference conception of human good a reflection of a distorted view of freedom, a view that, if not the product of industrial capitalism, finds in that political economy its most familiar modern expression. When older theories of essential good fail (MacIntyre 1984a: Chaps. 13, 14), the individual is left to choose its ends, to constitute itself. MacIntyre wants to anchor social justice in the good of community rather than to begin with a "liberal" preference theory of the good according to which the self is "free" to select any plan of the good. And Sandel also seems at times to want to displace the preference view with the theory that a communal good (of some sort) is a constitutive end of the person (Sandel 1982: 161ff.)[5] (but see ahead for alternative interpretations of Sandel). MacIntyre (1988: 88–89, 130, 267, 125) in any case clearly argues (*a*) that there is something good for persons qua persons (the "good for man"); that is, some goods are "essential" to persons because of (warranted by) what persons are. And furthermore, (*b*) one of the goods essential to persons is a communal good (of which justice is a part) that will function as the bond of social union (cf. various notions of communitarianism discussed in Rosenblum 1987: Chap. 7). Conceptions of the good change, but we should structure society on the basis of some vision of a communal good (cf. Taylor 1985).

However this debate is resolved, it is at least clear that in other cultures, indeed in strands of Western culture, there is a different assumption about human good than Rawls's (see Galston 1980: 56, 113–15; Barry 1974: 59–65): whatever their empirical desires, human beings do not choose their fundamental good; human good consists essentially in certain states that human beings discover (see Sandel 1982: 15–24, 116–17, 152–54). For example, a thinker in the Thomist tradition such as Johann would not define the problem of justice as a Rawlsian does. The Rawlsian begins with the view that the self is free to choose its ends; individuals can be assumed to agree only about the so-called primary goods, goods instrumental to any set of aims the self may adopt (1971: 90ff.).[6] The Thomist, in contrast, postulates a constitutive human good that includes virtues such as justice. Strands of Theravāda tradition can be interpreted as a complex ethic of virtues in which there is a hierarchy of goods and in which justice assigns various benefits and burdens according to merit measured by contribution to the common good (cf. MacIntyre 1984a, 1988). Thus, we can say that it will not do for descriptive ethics to assume a preference theory of human good. The jury is still out in the normative debate, but if we are trying to investigate how various cultural traditions address issues of distribution, it will not do at the outset to assume a preference, or by the same token, an essentialist starting point.

MOTIVATION AND ASSOCIATION

Gauthier's third dogma is that individuals do not take an interest in each other's interests, or at least they cannot be supposed to for the purposes of moral theory. This assumption should be discussed now, for it forms, along with the theory of the good, a crucial part of the view of the human problem for which "reason" (Gauthier's second dogma) has to devise a solution. Dumont would see nontuism as a crucial part of atomistic individualism (cf. Wolgast 1980: 138–39): persons are conceived as asocial entities; each intends primarily his or her own private good and relates to others in society only insofar as it furthers self-interest; the economic model is projected onto social relations generally (cf. Ruth Smith 1985).

Now the first question is whether this so-called atomism derives from capitalistic social structures and economic thought. It seems to me much more likely, as in the case of theory of value, that the model of self-interested individuals is a more general pattern of thought of which *homo economicus* is merely one development.

Gauthier's dogma is often presented, for example, as part of a picture of the human condition which explains why human beings need notions of justice. Supplanting (but perhaps indebted to) a theological picture of fallen humanity, Hume describes the moderate scarcity human beings face most of the time and characterizes their motivation as "limited generosity": from Adam's toil to moderate scarcity, from fallen self-love to the predominance of self-interest. We do not experience, at least to any great extent, "*abundance* of all *external* conveniences" to satisfy our desires, nor do we experience in our fellow human beings "an extensive benevolence" such that everyone "feels no more concern for his own interest than for that of his fellows" (1957: 15, 17; cf. 14–23). Thus the dynamics of scarcity and self-love formerly diagnosed and prescribed for under a sacred canopy are now interpreted empirically in hypotheses about self and society. Capitalism and social theories associated with it may have given a predominant place to self-interest, but the roots of this emphasis may be deeper in Western culture.[7] Moreover, the self-love assumption has also been traced to patriarchal socialization that identifies nurturance, caring, or benevolence as "feminine" traits and relegates women to the "private" as opposed to the "public" sphere of life with which a theory of justice is concerned; self-love is the "sin" emphasized by and characteristic of patriarchal males.[8]

Whatever the merits of these historical suggestions, Rawls, for example, stands in the Humean tradition. The problem of justice is the distribution of the benefits and burdens of cooperation. Persons who cooperate have an identity of interests since they can have a better life together than alone, but they have conflicts of interest as well, for "they each prefer a larger to a lesser share" (1971: 126–27). The cooperative situation and the need for justice rest on two sorts of facts which constitute the "circumstances of justice." There are the "objective" circumstances: moderate scarcity, geographical coexistence, the rough physical and mental similarity of human beings, and their vulnerability; there are also the "subjective" circumstances: similar basic needs and desires but diverse ends or plans of life, which lead to conflicting demands on natural and social resources. We cannot rely on "ties of natural sentiment" or benevolence (1971: 129); we need principles of justice to resolve conflicts of interest.[9]

The objection to Rawls's depiction of the problem of justice I want to focus on is that it unnecessarily accepts selfishness, a dominant orientation to self-regard, as the characterizing feature of human nature. The human propensity to self-interest, now given play in capitalism, becomes the central motivation in human relations; Rawls's contractors are rational in the sense that they desire and bargain for as big a share of the primary goods as they can get. (The primary goods are instrumental to the achievement of any full conception of the good or plan of life; they include liberties and powers, opportunities, income and wealth, and the social bases of self-respect; see 1971: 165–66; 1975a: 97; 1975b: 536.)

How would a Rawlsian reply? The canonical answer is that not taking an interest in others' interests does not mean selfishness in a society structured by the principles of justice. What one assumes is that the interests, the desires and aims of an actual self, may be either self-regarding or other-regarding (1971: 129; cf. Sandel 1982 and Werpehowski 1982). As Gauthier puts it, "it is not interests in the self, that take oneself as object, but interests of the self, held by oneself as subject, that provide the basis for rational choice and action" (1986: 7). My *actual* plan of life may include procuring goods for others or it may not; all that we assume about the circumstances of justice is that each agent prefers as large a share of the primary or instrumental goods as possible in order to advance a plan of life that may very well include "altruistic" as well as self-regarding aims among the "interests of a self." Although some plans of life may be other-regarding, concern for others, however, cannot be assumed as part of the circumstances of justice (1971: 129). Rawls, like Hume, makes an assumption about the limited extent of benevolence, but he explains it in terms of his theory of the good. We cannot assume "extensive ties of natural sentiment" or benevolence in the circumstances of justice, for such relations are part of particular plans of the good, and as matters of preference, plans of the good can be expected to vary widely. What can be assumed as characteristic of all agents is that they want a larger rather than a lesser share of the primary goods in order to advance their life plans, whatever they may be (1971: 93).

Thus Rawls would respond that nontuism rests on the diversity of human ends and plans of life, a diversity extending not only to what is good, but to who gets it. But the model of the rational acquisitor shapes Rawls's model at a deep level. The primary goods are socially produced but appropriated as private goods, possessed separately and divisibly by individual selves. This root assumption, which in Rawls's case rests on his theory of human good, is the basis of his view of justice, in contrast to the sort of assumption MacIntyre would make, namely, that there is a good of community that is not privately possessed. MacIntyre (1984a, 1988) therefore would not accept the Hume-Rawls notion of the "circumstances of justice." For MacIntyre the neo-Aristotelian, justice pertains to the distribution of burdens and benefits within a community based on a shared vision of a nonprivate "good for man." For Rawls, agents may happen to be benevolent or value forms of community, but this cannot be assumed ab initio. "Justice" is what one devises when one cannot assume benevolence or an Aristotelian communal good as starting points (see Gutman 1985: 312n.18; Rawls, 1988).

What one assumes, therefore, in the original position (the initial set of assumptions on the basis of which principles of justice are derived) is that the contracting agents desire more of the primary goods rather than less; benevolence and interpersonal values may evolve but only as part of the plans of life fashioned by individuals on the basis of their privately possessed shares of the primary goods. Despite Rawls's provision for benevolence and comprehensive goods of community, they occupy a secondary place as possible developments based on the bedrock of rational agreement.[10] The only communal good Rawls requires is that of individuals who *come to* value their association based on the principles of justice as a final end or intrinsic good. In a number of senses we are social by nature—*prior* to adopting principles of justice—and we can hope for more as well:

> Now the sociability of human beings must not be understood in a trivial fashion. It does not merely imply that society is necessary for human life, or that by living in a community men acquire needs and interests that prompt them to work together for mutual advantage. . . . Nor is it expressed by the truism that social life is a condition for our developing the ability to speak and think. . . . No doubt even the concepts that we use to describe our plans and situation, and even to give voice to our personal wants and purposes, often presuppose a social setting as well as a system of belief and thought that is the outcome of the collective efforts of long tradition. These facts are certainly not trivial; but to use them to characterize our ties to one another is to give a trivial interpretation of human social ability. For all of these things are equally true of persons who view their relations purely instrumentally. (1971: 522)

Thus Rawls expects something more than a private society of atomistic individuals united only "instrumentally" in mutual self-interest.[11] But as Proudfoot (1974), Werpehowski (1982), and Sandel (1982) have pointed out, social justice consists of the agreements and ends of the rational contractors.[12]

Moreover, although Rawls (1975b: 544, 550) is correct that the "moral persons" of his society would not necessarily be entirely consumed by acquisitive self-regard—they would, he assumes, pursue "communal" as well as "individualistic" ends—most of the members of a society built on the principles of justice would retain the desire characteristic of the original position for as large a share of primary goods as possible. While "wealth" as a primary good signifies only legal command over the means of satisfying needs and desires (1975b: 540), I am not convinced as Rawls is that if people can rely on just institutions they will be less anxious about their private possessions (1975b). On Rawls's own theory of the instrumental character of primary goods the greater a share one has the greater freedom one will have to decide upon, revise, and pursue one's ends (1975b: 553; cf. 1982: 173). Thus in actual life insofar as one has a "highest-order" interest in this freedom, one will want to get as large a share of primary goods as possible compatible with the principles of justice.[13] Even if income and wealth have a declining marginal utility for the very rich, the vast majority of Rawls's commonwealth would still want more.

Thus the rational self-interest of the parties in the original position is not "artificial" since it reflects the need everyone has for primary goods; nor is the "egoistic" objection removed by saying that one has begun with a notion of a "moral person" with highest-order interests in living justly and devising ends (1980: 527, 531). The rational acquisitor is modeled in the original position *and* in society; it is embodied in the "person" Rawls assumes in both. Just as the rational agent of the original position is restrained by the veil of ignorance and other conditions, so actual acquisitors are restrained in society by the principles of justice (cf. 1980: 533).

The debate in regard to Rawls's assumptions will focus on the starring role he gives to the pursuit of primary goods and the supporting role he gives to benevolence and the good of community. If, as I said above, the motivational assumption rests on his theory of the good, his position does not rely on empirical observations about the relative weakness of benevolence.[14] Because benevolence and the good of the community are merely a part of some life plans, and because all plans need primary goods, persons desire more rather than less of these goods; we need an alternative normative structure to resolve the resulting conflicts of interest.

But what of the descriptive question? Is it assumed in Theravāda Buddhism that the circumstances of justice obtain (not necessarily by that name, of course)? Is it assumed that there are facts about resources on which the need for social cooperation rests (the objective circumstances)? Is it assumed that to have norms for the distribution of benefits and burdens, we cannot rely on benevolence or on the good of community (the subjective circumstances)?

I am not going to try to offer historically informed answers to these questions, but some speculation may be in order. I see no reason not to think that something like Rawls's notion of the objective circumstances (moderate scarcity, the need for a system of cooperation) is presupposed in Theravāda tradition as in other cultures. But regarding Rawls's assumption that we cannot rely on benevolence or a nonprivate good of community, it certainly seems clear that Theravāda sources do not share the theory of the good that lies behind Rawls's view (given the diversity of ends, we cannot assume other-regarding plans of life; we can only assume a desire for as large a share of the primary goods as possible).

Compassion and benevolence, for example, do not appear as mere options but seem to be part of what should and can be assumed about social existence. In *The Book of Gradual Sayings* (Vol. I, Chap. 6) the king, no less than an enlightened *arhant*, is motivated by a concern for the well-being of all[15]:

> Monks, these two persons born into the world are born to the profit and happiness of many, to the profit, happiness and welfare of many folk. What two?
>
> A Tathagata, an Arahant who is a Fully Enlightened one, and a world-ruling monarch. These are the two so born. (Woodward 1932–36: 19)

Stanley Tambiah (1976: 58) writes that the rock edicts of King Aśoka "are an outcome of the Buddhist stress on *metta* (loving kindness), *mudita* (sympathetic joy), *karuna* (compassion), charity and donorship (*dana*), and so on, as the supreme virtues of conduct of all beings (including the seeker of nirvana who engages in detached action without interest in the fruits of action)."

Moreover, as I noted earlier, it may be the case that strands of Theravāda tradition assume a MacIntyre-like relational good as the basic bond of society. If such a good of community were assumed, it could include the good of benevolent relations and the virtues which express them; such relations would be valued, in MacIntyre's terminology, as part of the "good for man." Furthermore, justice could be part of the good as well, assigning benefits on the basis of merit measured according to contribution. A number of authors in this volume argue that Theravāda Buddhism assumes a principle of distributive justice through the doctrine of *karma*.[16] Moreover, there is the suggestion that the hierarchical and unequal distribution of positions of wealth and power are understood as morally justified, independent of individual assignments based on past lives (Green, Chap. 10, this volume); perhaps it is believed that in this eon or cycle of existence the structures of society (king-subjects, various roles and their duties) are necessary. Even the ''giving'' (*dana*) that obtains between monks and laity as an expression of benevolence and non-attachment is accompanied by the notion of reciprocity. According to Phra Rājavaramuni, the monks' ''task'' is to work ''for the good of people both as an act of compassion and as that of reciprocity'' (Chap. 1, this volume). Now we need not take reciprocity to mean justice in Hume's sense—a convention based on mutual self-interest—to interpret it as a matter of fairness or justice in exchanges. The ''helpful interdependence'' of monk and laity, then, is apparently structured in terms both of justice and benevolence.

On this interpretation, Theravāda tradition would overlap with Rawls's view of the objective circumstances. But what is not shared is the preference theory of the good which underlies Rawls's version of the subjective circumstances and relegates benevolence and the good of community to the periphery of the distributional system. The problem of justice may not begin with conflicts of self-interest, but it may proceed on the assumption of a commonly desired good of community. Given the place of compassion and benevolence in the worldview, moreover, *dana*, *metta*, and related notions have a greater role in the overall pattern of distribution and redistribution than the Rawlsian envisages. That benevolence grows weaker as it extends from self, to family and friends, and then to strangers is one of the facts which makes justice necessary, according to Hume. In some Buddhist traditions, I gather, it is believed that humans can extend an equally intense benevolence out in widening circles, even to enemies.

REASON AND ITS EMPLOYMENT

In sum, some contemporary theories of justice assume that there are no essential human goods and that human beings are predominantly oriented toward their own goal-directed autonomy and therefore toward a greater rather than lesser share of social goods. These propositions could be true or at least they could be believed to be true (see Sandel 1982), but they have not been universally assumed. As I have noted, strands of Theravāda Buddhism do seem to hold that norms of justice are and must be part of social existence (at least in the realm of *samsara*). But the conception of justice and the role of compassion and benevolence are different because of different assumptions about the good and about motivation.

But what of Gauthier's other dogma, that reason is maximizing? This, too, seems part of the "atomistic" model of the self who chooses ends, wants the primary goods in order to pursue a life plan, and hence uses means-ends, maximizing reasoning. But it is also the case that for many contemporary thinkers in the Kantian tradition reason is not only maximizing, but is employed from an egalitarian point of view. Solutions to the problem of justice begin from this point of view. For R. M. Hare (1981), moral thought and discourse require that moral principles be universalizable, that is, in his view, acceptable to anyone whatever his or her circumstances or values; for Alan Gewirth (1978), the principle of consistency requires that I acknowledge the rights I, as any agent, demand of others; for Rawls, the rational contractors are willing to go behind a veil of ignorance where they will think of themselves as stripped of natural and social characteristics (including their values), as anyone rather than someone, and thus reason employed from this perspective (in the original position) will select principles of justice which will not favor anyone's particular place in the natural or social lottery or conception of the good (cf. Dworkin 1978), but will maximize everyone's prospects.

Is the notion of choosing principles acceptable to anyone (regardless of their circumstances and values) merely an expression of the model of *any* rational economic agent? Again, it seems to me that the notions of maximizing reason and the standpoint of any individual have deeper antecedents in Western culture. The notion of instrumental, goal-achieving rationality certainly predates industrial capitalism, and it seems that the idea of principles acceptable to anyone has resonances in strands of Judaic and Christian tradition (the Golden Rule, love of neighbor) as well as in Enlightenment notions of universal reason. These traditions then become the moral vehicle for modern conceptions of economic and political order, and insofar as males are socialized for this order, a notion of justice rooted in universal acceptability becomes characteristic of male sensibility (Gilligan 1982, 1986).

The question of historical explanation aside, however, what are the chief objections to the egalitarian starting point? Carol Gilligan would insist that it not furnish the sole starting point of morality, but should it be retained at all? The neo-Kantian requires us to adopt the perspective of anyone, but does this violate what Dumont calls the sociological apperception? Is it a fatal failure to understand the social nature of human existence (1970: 4–11)?[17] Maximizing reason is constrained, but is the constraint itself merely another manifestation of an atomizing failure to appreciate constitutive sociality?[18]

Steven Lukes does not think that the acceptable-to-anyone constraint has to violate the sociological apperception, for it is not necessary to engage in a fatal process of abstraction from historical and social particularity.[19] One does not have to see individuals as possessed of some context-free set of tendencies or characteristics; one sees them rather as having common capacities which are socially shaped, for example, the capacity to have desires and intentions, make choices, develop themselves. ''Abstract individualism'' gives persons presocial, context-free features; Lukes sees them in social roles and positions but not as equivalent to these facets of their social identity (1973: 146–47). Thus to realize that individuals are not presocial, that in important respects human consciousness and identity are socially constituted, does not preclude the identification of common capacities as part of a normative moral outlook; in this sense we can think of ourselves as anyone.

Thus Rawls would not fall prey to the sociological objection because he, too, as we have seen, assumes familiar notions of the social character of knowledge and personal identity (1971: 522).[20] In the eyes of Sandel, indeed, the problem with Rawls is not ''sociological'' but ''metaphysical.''[21] But what metaphysical mistake is Rawls guilty of? MacIntyre would say that Rawls assumes a self that does not quest for or discover the ''good for man.'' If this were Sandel's critique, it would be aimed correctly. Those who do not share Rawls's theory of the self would not enter upon the Rawlsian project, for the preference metaphysic is a crucial assumption in the original position. To enter the original position is, of course, not only to hold certain metaphysical and factual beliefs, but to adopt a moral point of view (see Gutman 1985). The moral assumption of the original position (the veil of ignorance) is that I take a stance that disregards my actual ends as much as my natural and social inheritance.[22] From the fact that as a self I am free to choose the ends I prefer, it does not follow that I *should* disregard my actual plan of life, my conception of the good, in deciding which principles of justice to adopt: to disregard it is a moral position.[23] But since I believe that the ends we decide upon are contingent matters of preference, subject to natural and cultural conditioning, I choose morally to exclude them just as I choose to disregard the natural and social lottery (cf. Dworkin 1974 and Nagel 1973: 227–29); in so doing I give expression to the deep moral belief that the principles of justice should not reflect the happenstance of birth and social condition. Thus, on the assumption that ends are contingent like other features of the natural and social lottery, Rawls morally excludes them behind the veil of ignorance. His "metaphysical" assumption—which critics regard as a mistake—is a crucial premise in his moral reasoning (cf. Rorty 1988). Rawls, says the critic, mistakenly puts our ends into the category of happenstance along with other features of the natural and social lottery; this is a metaphysical mistake, because there are ends which we discover to be constitutive of human nature as such. If, as MacIntyre says, we believe there is a "good for man," then we will understand our conception of the good not as a contingent product of choice or preference, but as a reflection of our view of our essential nature; thus, the critic continues, we would derive our view of justice directly from the good, or at the very least we would take our view of the good with us behind the veil of ignorance as we rationally work out principles of justice maximally conducive to the interests of everyone. In any case, to adopt the perspective of anyone regardless of their conception of the good is to incorporate a fundamental metaphysical mistake about the relation of the self to its ends. Rawls may say, as he apparently does in some later essays, that to join his project one does not have to hold the preference theory, one merely has to bracket one's actual theory of the good; the suggestion is that even a MacIntyre would find a compelling reason in a pluralistic society to go behind the veil of ignorance. But the MacIntyrean would reply as follows: those whose conception of the good is based on convictions about the nature of persons (the "good for man") will not have any such reason to bracket that conception; to bracket one's theory of the good is tantamount to abandoning one's most fundamental view of oneself.[24]

Thus the Rawls of 1971 makes a metaphysical assumption about the nature of persons and their ends and on the basis of that assumption takes a moral point of view about conceptions of the good held by particular persons. And the later Rawls also asks those like MacIntyre who believe there is a "good for man" to do what they can say they cannot do, namely, give up their basic view of themselves. It is important to note, however, that the Rawlsian does not ask the contractors to make another sort of metaphysical assumption, namely, that ends are not part of *personal* identity, a thesis some critics adduce as the fatal flaw in the notion of choosing principles of justice acceptable to anyone regardless of their circumstances or values. The Rawlsian can admit that although selves are free to choose ends, the personal identity of *particular* individuals is constituted in part by the history of their choices; the point for the Rawlsian is that one takes a moral view about one's history (cf. MacIntyre 1988: 133).[25] Sandel (1982) sometimes seems to say that going behind the veil of ignorance amounts to denying that ends are constitutive of personal identity (whatever accounts for our sense of continuity through time; our sense of our identity as particular persons, in contrast to our beliefs about the nature of persons as such). But Rawls has always said that identity may well incorporate facets of natural and social circumstances as well as values and character; the original position, in particular the veil of ignorance, represents a moral viewpoint which is also part of one's identity, one's narrative, if you will (cf. MacIntyre 1988, on liberalism as a tradition).[26] What Rawls will deny is another thesis Sandel also argues: my ends or ''allegiances'' within and to particular communities, which in part define my personal identity, should not be *morally* outweighed by any requirements of justice owed to ''human beings as such'' (1984: 90; cf. 1982: 179. Cf. Barry 1984 and Narveson 1987). My allegiances, Sandel seems to be saying, weigh morally with me; to subordinate my ends morally is to empty or shrink my moral sense of my self in a way I am not prepared to accept. Sandel and the Rawlsian simply part company here; the Rawlsian's deepest moral conviction is that particular allegiances should be regulated by principles of justice adopted from a perspective which disregards the self's actual ends.

The critic, then, correctly sees a gulf between the Rawlsian and any morality which asserts, with MacIntyre, and perhaps with Sandel, that there is a ''good for man.'' Although the Rawlsian can admit that personal identity is constituted partly by one's ends (and particular moral relations), justice must be derived by reasoning about what is acceptable to anyone regardless of their particular conception of the good, and justice must always be overriding. Dumont's descriptive point in any case seems valid: there are cultures in which Rawls's ''as any one'' starting point is not assumed.[27] What of Theravāda Buddhism in particular? Evidence would have to be forthcoming that the notion of principles acceptable-to-anyone (regardless of circumstances and values) lies behind the norms of justice structuring familial, economic, and political relationships. That there are justified inequalities (e.g., king-subjects) does not prove that the starting point is not the same, for Rawls also justifies inequalities. In other words, that one finds principles of justice in Buddhist cultures different from Rawls's could be explained as the result of different choices from the same starting point; traditional Buddhist cultures would legitimate different inequalities than Rawls would, perhaps in light of different beliefs about self and society. But the question is whether Buddhist assumptions about social justice rest on anything like the Rawlsian veil of ignorance and the original position model, even implicitly.[28] In regard to salvation, several essays in this volume suggest a notion of equal access to the salvific goal (at least for individuals in a certain existence and at a certain level of moral readiness), and norms of equality also seem to operate in the *sangha* and in visions of an ideal future society (see Reynolds, Chap. 2). But that we find substantive notions of equality as well as justified inequalities would still not indicate that Rawls's acceptable-to-anyone model underlies convictions about justice. To accept is not necessarily to accept as maximally conducive to the interests of anyone; one could accept a system of justice for other reasons. If a MacIntyre-like conception of a communal good is assumed in Theravāda tradition, perhaps the distribution of burdens and benefits is justified not because it is acceptable to anyone no matter what their conceptions of the good or place in the natural or social lottery but because it reflects the structure of the good at all levels, including, but not limited to, the human.

Nonetheless, is there not an important affinity between the Rawlsian moral point of view (acceptable to anyone) and the view Steven Collins (1982: 193–4) says is a corollary of *anatta*, namely, the loss of attachment to a particular "I" and an affirmation of the good of all? Could it be that the Buddhist reasons from the acceptable-to-anyone point of view, but assumes a "thick" conception of the goods constitutive of human nature? One arrives at principles of justice by thinking of what anyone needs, given what everyone's true good is. This would be different than a MacIntyre-like morality, because for MacIntyre justice is inherent in the good as one valued relation among others; the virtue of justice is both instrumental to and ingredient in the good. The suggestion is rather that the Buddhist might think like a modified Rawlsian: even if one assumes a "thick" conception of the good (as opposed to a "thin" conception of primary goods), one must still derive principles of justice by thinking about what is maximally conducive to the true good of each individual. My provisional view is that the traditions may overlap normatively but that the underpinnings are different (cf. Green, Chap. 10, this volume). For Rawls, the point of the acceptable-to-anyone view is to secure the moral separateness of persons. Acceptable to anyone is an abstraction but one made by the self for the sake of a system that protects and promotes the basic well-being of each self. Furthermore, the abstraction reflects the deep conviction that the natural and social lottery should be morally disregarded. For the Buddhist, the loss of attachment does not protect and promote each self, nor does it spring from a sense of the *moral* unacceptability of the natural and social lottery (indeed, *karma* legitimates inherited capacities and positions). Rather the *anatta* metaphysic, which helps one transcend *karma*, seems to replace the ordinary world of bounded selves with a new way of conceiving sentient existence. As part of this new way of seeing, I will no longer desire the good of my self or any self but rather the good of sentient existence as a whole, without discriminating between particular beings. I remarked earlier that justice in Buddhist traditions might be regarded as part of the good in a MacIntyre-like ethic of virtue. The role of *anatta* may be to ground a virtue of ''love'' which would fulfill but also transcend the ordinary compassion and benevolence experienced by karmic selves. As Steven Kemper says in this volume,

> Where Hobbes sees society being held together and materially improved by honest self-interest, Buddhism sees society being held together and materially improved by the charity that follows upon the recognition of the non-reality of the self and its interests.

While the compassion and benevolence which operates in *samsara* may not be directly grounded in *anatta*, but in the ability of one self to appreciate and desire to relieve the suffering of another, nonetheless ordinary compassion and benevolence are perhaps transmuted and fulfilled in non-discriminating love (see Aronson 1980 and Swearer, forthcoming).

CONCLUSION

I have suggested that certain assumptions in modern theories of justice do not simply mirror economic theory or capitalism. I have also tried to assess some ''communitarian'' objections to the individualism of contemporary theory. My conclusion is that Rawls, for example, can successfully rebut a number of objections brought against his theory of the good, his doctrine of the subjective circumstances, and his notion of choice from behind the veil of ignorance. But I also point out that it is in his theory of the good, the related notion of a self-regarding desire for primary goods, and the idea of principles acceptable to all no matter what their theory of the good that his theory is vulnerable. Finally, I have suggested that as far as I can tell there may be overlaps between, say, Rawls's views and Theravāda Buddhism, but that there are divergences as well in assumptions about human good, the circumstances of justice, and the reasoning behind structures of inequality and equality.[29]

Abbreviations

1. FOUNDATIONS OF BUDDHIST SOCIAL ETHICS

A	Anguttara Nikāya
D	Dīgha Nikāya
Dh	Dhammapāda
DhA	Commentary on the Dhammapada
It	Itivuttaka
Kh	Khuddakapaṭha
J	Jātaka
JA	Jātaka Commentary
M	Majjhima Nikāya
Nd^2	Cullaniddesa
S	Saṇyutta Nikāya
Sn	Sutta Nipāta
SnA	Sutta Nipāta Commentary
Vin	Vinaya Piṭaka
Vism	Visuddhimagga

6. EXEMPLARY DONORS OF THE PĀLI TRADITION

Primary Source Texts

From the Vinayapiṭaka:

Cv	Cullavagga
Mv	Mahāvagga
Sv	Suttavibhanga

From the Long Nikāyas:

M	Majjhima-Nikāya
A	Anguttara-Nikāya
S	Saṇyutta-Nikāya

From Kuddaka-nikāya and/or its commentaries:

J	Jātaka legends and commentary (Ja)
Dh	Dhammapada

Th Theragāthā stanzas and commentary (Tha)
Vv Vimānavatthu

Pāli Text Translations Cited in the Manuscript

From the Vinaya:

BD *The Book of the Discipline* (Vinaya-Piṭaka). Trans. I. B. Horner. In 5 vols.: Sacred Books of the Buddhists, 10, 11, 13, 14, 20 (London: Luzac, 1948–63).

From the Long Nikāyas:

GS *Book of the Gradual Sayings* (Anguttara-Nikāya) or *More-Numbered Suttas.* Trans. F. L. Woodward and E. M. Hare. In 5 vols.: Pāli Text Society Translation Series, 22, 24–27 (London: Luzac, 1960–65).

KS *Book of the Kindred Sayings* (Saṇyutta-Nikāya) or *Grouped Suttas.* Trans. C. A. F. Rhys Davids and F. L. Woodward. In 5 vols.: Pāli Text Society Translation Series 7, 10, 13, 14, 16 (London: Luzac, 1950–56).

MLS *The Collection of the Middle Length Sayings* (Majjhima-Nikāya). Trans. I. B. Horner. 3 vols.: Pāli Text Society Translation Series 19–21 (London: Luzac, 1954–59).

From Kuddaka-nikāya and/or its commentaries:

BL *Buddhist Legends Translated from the Original Pāli Text of the Dhammapada Commentary.* Trans. Eugene Watson Burlingame. In 3 parts: Harvard Oriental Series 28–30 (London: Luzac, 1969).

J *The Jātaka, or Stories of the Buddha's Former Births.* Ed. E. B. Cowell; various translators. 6 vols. in 3 bindings (London: Luzac, 1957–69).

PB *Psalms of the Brethren* (Theragātha and Theragāthāṭṭhakathā). Translated by C. A. F. Rhys Davids. Pāli Text Society Translation Series 4 (London: Luzac, 1913).

SM *Vimānavatthu: Stories of the Mansions.* Trans. I. B. Horner. *The Minor Anthologies of the Pāli Canon, Part IV.* Sacred Books of the Buddhists, Vol. 30 (London: Routledge and Kegan Paul, 1974).

SD *Petavatthu: Stories of the Departed.* Trans. H. S. Gehman. *The Minor Anthologies of the Pāli Canon, Part IV.* Sacred Books of the Buddhists, Vol. 30 (London: Routledge and Kegan Paul, 1974).

Notes

INTRODUCTION

1. A comparative point: Christianity would like to be able to make this claim, that virtue and prosperity are compatible in the world, but feels compelled by its vision of reality (i.e., its belief in the power of sin in history) to qualify it. By talking of life fulfillment in nonprudential terms, or in terms of reward in an afterlife, or by pinning their hopes on an eschatological transformation of history, most Christians forgo the claim that virtue leads inevitably to worldly success.

2. In Jesus' parables of the Kingdom of God (Mt 13:44ff.) Christianity's religious goal is presented as infinitely valuable, to the disregard of all other values; in Jesus' rebuke to the rich young ruler (Mk 10:17 and parallels) attachment to one's wealth is identified as a primary obstacle to spiritual fulfillment; in the story of the widow's offering (Mk 12:41ff. and parallels) the heedlessness with which she gives and the sincerity of her gift are identified as the marks of virtue. Like comparable observations in Buddhism, these passages in Christianity also raise in vivid form the paradox common in religious language of identifying self-fulfillment with self-negation—these apparently self-sacrificing actions are offered by the tradition as the wisest (i.e., most prudent) behavior, given the way things really are.

3. On this matter Jesus taught that "he who loves father or mother more than me is not worthy of me; and he who loves son or daughter more than me is not worthy of me" (Mt 10:37). In a similar fashion with Buddhist imagery Kemper uses the case of a monk who cherishes an ear ornament worn by his mother as an example of unacceptable worldly attachment. It is not the amount of wealth but the orientation one holds toward it that is important. Family ties, with their plausible appeal to moral responsibility, are singled out as a significant threat to religious devotion.

4. A more detailed exposition of Little's approach and its application to Theravāda Buddhism can be found in Little and Twiss (1978). Obviously a number of very basic matters are at stake in how religion and morality are defined in establishing a method for comparative religious ethics. Specific attention is given to this and other methodological matters in the essay by Sizemore in this volume (Chap. 4).

5. A suggestive comparative point here is that the Christian tradition has cherished a different slogan, namely, that all men are to be as brothers.

6. Clifford Geertz's *Islam Observed* (1968), a masterful elucidation of both the flexibility and rigidity of Islamic social philosophy, clarifies and qualifies this generalization.

7. The extraordinary giving festivals described by Strong, for example, suggest that social advances still come by the ordinary methods (vigorously applied on special occasions). Lovin contrasts this perspective with the expectations of eschatological Christianity, which envisions a radical break in history to transform rather than purify social reality. It should also be noted that the Christian tradition possesses a variety of religious vocations and institutions in its attempt to incorporate its transcendent values into the mundane sphere of existence. By contrast, in Theravāda Buddhism the monastic order must serve as both church and monastery, and hence the tradition works to define the *sangha* with enough flexibility to handle a variety of tasks.

8. The role of religious symbols in integrating a culture's world view and ethos has been championed by anthropologist Clifford Geertz (1973). The classic sources for this sort of analysis are Ernst Troeltsch and Max Weber, whose method Lovin follows even as he is critical of some of their conclusions.

9. Like the Christian belief in a thoroughgoing providence, the Buddhist doctrine of *kamma* seems to require complete faith in in its inevitability, regardless of how circuitous is the path by which people reach their destinies. Consequently, in analogous ways both traditions are typically restrained in interpreting the exact meaning of any particular event. Again, how human choice and individual responsibility are to be preserved in the face of a belief in divine providence or *kamma* is a problem for Buddhist as well as Christian moral psychology, although Christians have an extra difficulty because they wish to affirm that God is merciful as well as just.

10. This conclusion is formally similar to the western view that supporting educational institutions is the best investment in the future. What these views require is a certain belief in the value of education and faith in certain vehicles for cultivating wisdom. One result of this faith in the social value of supporting the *sangha* is, as Ronald Green emphasizes in Chapter 10, that the distinction between religious and ethical giving is not valid in the case of *dāna*—that religious motivations and the social rationale for support of the *sangha* have been fully integrated.

11. One may also conclude that part of the difference has to do with the fact that Keyes's study follows an ethnic minority in Thailand, who would quite naturally have heroes who oppose the existing state of affairs, whereas Kemper is looking at the dominant cultural groups in Sinhalese Buddhist society.

12. Falk's stories about the petty donors who give to free their deceased parents from their deserved tortures are reminiscent of the medieval Christian practice of buying indulgences from the Church to free one's parents from the sufferings of purgatory.

13. As Reeder's essay shows, the various assumptions or dogmas that are a part of the theory recommended by Green are not a matter of consensus even in

the West. Certainly there are various theories of justice and social order that do not share them, and much of the recent recovery of virtue theory in the West has been very critical of these developments in western thought. In particular, we should not expect many religious traditions to embrace the position of state neutrality toward all religious belief; to make this an essential feature in defining morality is certainly problematic for a descriptive approach in cross-cultural studies.

1. FOUNDATIONS OF BUDDHIST SOCIAL ETHICS

1. See the two kinds of extremes, the ten kinds of lay people or enjoyers of sense-pleasure, and the three kinds of ascetics in the *Rāsiya Sutta* S.IV.330ff. Buddhist thought is characterized by several polarities that are often similarly misunderstood: for example, the mundane (*lokiya*) and the transmundane (*lokuttara*), the laity (*gahaṭṭha*) and the monks (*pabbajita*). Some might think of these so-called polarities as conflicting or incompatible, but in reality they are complementary parts making a complete whole. Some are natural necessities, and others are human designs intended to maintain consistency with the natural ones.

2. This is the meeting for a fortnightly recitation of the *pātimokkha* that is prescribed by a disciplinary rule: "I allow you, monks, to assemble together on the fourteenth, fifteenth and eighth days of the half-month." And "I allow you, monks, having assembled together . . . to speak the *dhamma*." And "I allow you, monks, to recite a *pātimokkha*" (Vin.I.102). For some extraordinary cases see Vism.608f.

3. For example, S.V.2–30; A.I.14–18; It.10. (The matter will be discussed more fully at a later point.)

4. Cf. the Nāthakaraṇadhamma (D.III.266, 290; A.V.23).

5. According to the commentary on the *Dhammapada*, hundreds of people lived on the leftovers from the monks in the monastery in the Jeta's Grove where the Buddha most often stayed.

6. Two points should be noted here. First, this Thai traditional twelvefold set of the *Cakkavattivatta* is a later version found in the Commentary on the *Dīghanikāya* (D.A.III.46). Items 1 to 10 are simply reenumerations of the original teaching in the *Cakkavatti-Sutta* (see D.III.61), and items 11 and 12 are accretions based on other parts of the teaching in the same *Sutta*. Second, the original emphasis in the *Sutta* on the righteousness of the ruler seems to be slighted here. In the original version of the *Sutta* the ruler as *dhammādhipateyya* (one who holds the *dhamma* supreme or one relying on the supremacy of righteousness) is of great importance.

7. S.I.76; discussion of this set of virtues can be found in the *Kūṭadanta-Sutta* (D.I.135). It is explained in some commentaries (S.A.I.145; SnA.321).

8. D.III.152, 232; A.II.32, 248; A.IV.218, 363.

9. E.g., A.II.204; cf. the *Cūḷakammavibhaṅga Sutta* in M.III.

10. The personal name of this millionaire was Sudatta. He received his honorary name (Anāthapiṇḍika), which means "the provider of food to the desti-

tute,'' through his acts of charity. See also the essay in this volume by Nancy Falk (Chap. 6) on Anāthapiṇḍika and other exemplary givers in the Pāli tradition. The Commentary on the *Dhammapada* and that on the *Jātaka* contain several stories on the taming of stingy millionaires.

11. S.IV.331; A.V.176. The distinction between the mundane and the transmundane is made here on the basis of the Buddhist principles of the Noble Disciples.

12. A large number of teachings and sayings stressing the importance of association and environment can be found scattered in the Pāli canon. Many stories illustrating the same prescription can be found in the *Jātaka*.

13. Nd^2 26. In older texts of the Pāli canon only the first two of these three goals are usually mentioned, the third being included in the second one, e.g., S.I.82, 87; A.III.49; It.17; and the *Brahmāyusutta* in M.II.

14. Nd^2 26; A.I.158, 216; A.III.63; A.IV.134.

15. The difference between the two sets is that the first four are mental qualities to be developed in the mind as part of individual perfection. Hence they belong to the category of *samādhi* or *adhicitta-sikkhā* (the training in the development of mental qualities). (The *Visuddhimagga* devotes twenty-six pages to the development of these four mental qualities [pp. 244–70], but there seems to be no traditional text dealing with the four counterpart virtues of social action.) They are virtues or qualities of the mind or character, not of outward or social action. We can act out of *mettā*, but we cannot perform or do *mettā*. The second four virtues, by contrast, are acts intended for outward or social expression. They belong to the category of *sīla*, or morality. The interrelationship or interdependence between the two sets is that the virtues for social action can be sincere, genuine, pure, resolute, and lasting only when they are based on the firm foundation of the four mental virtues. Loving-kindness, compassion, and sympathetic joy may lead to charity, kindly speech, and acts of service on various appropriate occasions, and equanimity (or neutrality) is essential for equality and impartiality.

2. ETHICS AND WEALTH IN THERAVĀDA BUDDHISM

1. For such a discussion see the introduction entitled ''In the Beginning'' in Lovin and Reynolds (1985).

2. For a fuller statement and defense of these three presuppositions, see my articles, ''Four Modes of Theravāda Action'' (Reynolds 1979) and ''Multiple Cosmogonies and Ethics: The Case of Theravāda Buddhism'' (in Lovin and Reynolds 1985).

3. In this chapter *renunciation* refers to the particular expression of non-attachment that involves renouncing the household life in favor of the life of the hermit or wandering mendicant. *Non-attachment* refers to the attitude of non-craving or non-grasping that may be expressed in other forms of Buddhist life as well.

4. For a fuller discussion of the conception and practice of this system of exchange, see Reynolds and Clifford (1980).

5. This story appears in a text known as the Phra Malai Sutta. See *Dika Malai Deva Sut* (Bangkok, 1971).

6. This point should be qualified by the recognition that in some strands of the tradition kings do have the soteriological advantage since it is held that they, unlike ordinary Theravāda lay people, are practicing the *bodhisattva* path, which leads to the attainment of the extraordinary goal of Buddhahood.

7. For a discussion of certain aspects of monastic wealth and reform in Sri Lanka see the essay in this volume by Steven Kemper.

8. On this point, see especially Swearer (1978).

9. For a fuller discussion of these figures and a more extended treatement of the nature of religious giving, see the essays in this volume by Strong and Falk.

10. Some of these movements and their associated philosophies are discussed in Macy (1983).

3. ETHICAL ANALYSIS AND WEALTH IN THERAVĀDA BUDDHISM

1. I concede that this choice of words is rather presumptuous, as though only students of ethics were capable of making "ethical translations." I simply could not think of a more felicitous term.

2. I am assuming here that Reynolds's unified characterization of the entire Theravāda tradition is correct in respect to the subject of wealth and poverty, together with his other comments about the *dhamma* and so on. In the discussion of the fourth point, below, I raise some questions about the need of the "holist" like Reynolds to spend a bit more time substantiating his generalizations by means of careful textual and historical analysis. Naturally, if Reynolds's discussion turns out to be oversimplified, then to that extent my "translation" is similarly oversimplified.

3. See Little and Twiss (1978: 239–41). Though we suggest three possible patterns of validation, it seems increasingly clear that the extrapersonal teleological one provides, all things considered, the most satisfactory description. This is Aronson's view, though his suggestion of a "hybrid" validating pattern (egocentric/altruistic) retains some of the tension that may continue to lie beneath the surface of the tradition (see Aronson's excellent study, 1980: 91ff.) In our terms that tension is between the two types of "transpersonal teleology": "qualified intrapersonal" and "qualified extrapersonal." All this needs the most careful ethical scrutiny.

4. See Little and Twiss (1978: 213–15). This point has also been conceded in response to other criticism; see Little 1982.

5. Mention should also be made here of the doctrine of the suitable recipient. A discussion of this doctrine is indirectly taken up in Little and Twiss (1978: 227–29); it is more fully examined in Gombrich (1971: 248–51). Accordingly, the *sangha* is described as " 'the best field of merit in the world,' which is to say that a good deed done towards the Sangha (especially a gift given to it) will bear more fruit for the doer than if bestowed elsewhere" (Gombrich 1971: 248).

6. Reynolds exemplifies this method most explicitly in Reynolds 1980. Although the results are interesting, one is again struck by the lack of careful documentation upon which to base the broad generalizations.

4. COMPARATIVE RELIGIOUS ETHICS AS A FIELD

1. These designations are crude and somewhat misleading but have been commonly employed, particularly in the debate in comparative religious ethics. On one side have been the "ethicists"—scholars trained in Western philosophical ethics, with interests in philosophy of religion and social-scientific theories of religion. They have approached comparative work with terminology drawn from these fields of expertise. David Little and S.B. Twiss's *Comparative Religious Ethics* (Little and Twiss 1978) and Ronald M. Green's *Religious Reason* are notable recent expressions of this approach. John P. Reeder's 1978 essay was in many ways programmatic as a systematic statement of the ethicists' conception of the field of religious ethics (Reeder 1978). The "historians," or, sometimes, the "comparativists," have typically been specialists in some particular non-Western religious tradition; many have had considerable previous experience in comparative studies. They have been more historically and sociologically minded. The work of W. C. Smith and Robert Bellah has helped inspire this group, and in Christian ethics, Stanley Hauerwas's work on narrative and virtue has been a normative expression of this sort of approach. Without anticipating too much of the argument to come one can say that it would be better to think of both groups as ethicists, as doing ethics, one from the vantage point of modern moral philosophy, the other from the standpoint of historical studies in religion. In the context of the broader questions about the field of religious studies generally, these different origins lead to correspondingly different approaches to evaluating the truth claims of religious traditions.

2. Although we differ somewhat on the final significance of these matters, I am indebted to David Wills of Amherst College for comments suggesting this approach to the debate.

3. Cf. the extraordinary depth and precision Little and Twiss give to their definitions of moral and religious "action-guides" in their volume *Comparative Religious Ethics* (1978: Chap. 1–5). Clear definitions of religion and morality are crucial to Little's method because in his epistemological stance they are separable employments of human mentality. By contrast, breadth of source material and attention to religious affections are crucial to Reynolds's method because in his epistemological orientation religious vision and moral sensibility are inseparable.

4. Jeffrey Stout's *Flight From Authority* (1981) is a particularly powerful contemporary statement of this point of view.

5. Cf. H. Saddhatissa (1970) and his interpretation of Buddhism as "mind-culture."

6. There are times when Christians, like Buddhists, speak as if the justification for an action was the actor's future reward in heaven or some other

form of prudential benefit. But taken in context these utterances seem to be more examples of religious appropriation of everyday language than genuine evidence of an egoistic theory of the good life.

7. This is precisely the method implicit in James M. Gustafson's four "base points" in moral discourse as applied to Christian ethics. Gustafson (1965) traces the theological underpinning that influences various forms of ethical reasoning in different Christian ethicists. His approach is closely related to that of Troeltsch's classic, *The Social Teaching of the Christian Churches* ([1911] 1976).

8. Little is particularly enamored of Weber's analysis of the form of rationality that emerged in the modern West. On this topic see his article on Weber's contributions to the study of religious ethics (Little 1974). He is less attentive to the significance Weber attributed to the social shaping power of soteriological doctrines, but his interest in the contrast between the Puritan work ethic and Buddhist attitudes toward wealth finally helps draw in this other side of Weber.

5. RICH MAN, POOR MAN, *BHIKKHU*, KING

1. Except when indicated all Buddhist terms and names are given in their Pāli form (even when Sanskrit sources are being discussed). The ten good deeds are giving, keeping morality, meditating, transferring merit, rejoicing in another's merit, giving service, showing respect, preaching, listening to preaching, and right beliefs. See also Cone and Gombrich 1977: xxv.

2. For a much fuller discussion of Anāthapiṇḍika as a model of *dāna*, see Nancy Falk's "Exemplary Donors of the Pāli Tradition," Chapter 6 of this volume.

3. Occasionally, as we shall see below, *pañcavārṣika*s were said to be sponsored by rich merchants. See also Feer 1891: 288; cf. Vaidya 1958: 191.

4. Actually, in the Pāli tradition Aśoka builds eighty-four thousand monasteries (*vihāra*s).

5. Paul Mus (1935: 12) has argued that in India there is a mystical equivalence between one's son and one's self that should be taken quite literally. Thus, we should see Aśoka's action not just as a commitment of Mahinda to the monastic order, but also as a commitment of himself. See also Strong 1983: 82.

6. There were, of course, less dramatic but equally symbolic ways in which a king could give himself and his sovereignty to the *sangha*, and Theravāda monarchs did not hesitate to adopt them. Several Sri Lankan kings, for example, are said to have made symbolic gifts of alms to the *sangha* equal to their body weights or some multiple thereof (Geiger 1973: I:160, 216; II:2). And Duṭṭhagāmaṇi, the Sinhalese monarch who perhaps most closely resembles Aśoka, is reported to have given to the relics of the Buddha all of the jewels, ornaments, and other regalia on his person and to have made his ministers, dancing girls, and even the local deities do the same (Geiger 1960: 218; cf. Geiger 1958: 255). All of these monarchs then, like Aśoka, return anew to their sovereignty.

7. For a study of somewhat different ritual transformations of the milieu in which *dāna* takes place, see Strong 1979.

8. Interestingly, at the center of this area was a pillar used by Aśoka for one of his inscriptions. See Irwin 1983.

9. For a recent critique of this position, see Aronson 1979.

10. These "earnest wishes" for being reborn at the time and place of the Buddha Metteyya often express quite clearly the link between *deva*hood and *nibbāna*. See, for example, a Sinhalese wish recorded by Gombrich 1971: 337, in which the donor expresses his desire to be:

> reborn in the excellent capital city, *fit for the gods* [*deva*s], called Ketumati, and see the *holy king Buddha* Maitrī, the Good Friend of infinite glory, and offer to a hundred thousand holy *arhats*, including Him, the four requisites of robe, etc., and hear the preaching of the Four Noble Truths . . . which would be preached by the *holy king Buddha*, . . . and so attain eternal, auspicious, supreme, beautiful, tranquil, happy, exquisite, superior, final, immortal, great Nirvana! [Emphasis added]

In the context of reflections about *dāna*, *nibbāna* is often conceived of as being achieved by virtue of rebirth at the time and place of the Buddha Metteyya; in this perspective, enlightenment results not so much from one's own meditative efforts as from the gift of *dhamma* one receives from Metteyya by virtue of one's own merit-making. At the same time, being reborn at the time and place of Metteyya is seen as equivalent to achieving *deva*hood.

11. Consider, for example, the following earnest wish cited by Melford Spiro (1970: 79):

> Before I reach Nirvana by virtue of this great work of merit I have done, may I prosper as a man, be more royally happy than all other men. Or as a spirit [deity] may I be full of colour, dazzling brightness and victorious beauty, more than any other spirit. More especially, I would have a long life, freedom from disease, a lovely complexion, a pleasant voice, and a beautiful figure. I would be the loved and honoured darling of every man and spirit. Gold, silver, rubies, corals, pearls and other lifeless treasure, elephants, horses and other living treasure—may I have lots of them. By virtue of my power and glory I would be triumphant with pomp and retinue, with fame and splendour. . . .

6. EXEMPLARY DONORS OF THE PĀLI TRADITION

1. See, for example, G. P. Malalasekera's descriptions of recitations from the *Jātaka*s and Dhammapada commentary in his native Śrī Lankā (Malalasekera 1928: 51, 119).

2. For a brief summary of this process, see note 8 below. A more extended reconstruction may be found in Malalasekera 1928: 13 – 129; and Geiger 1956: 9 – 38.

3. For the concept and evaluation of the gift of *dhamma*, see Strong 1977.

4. For an engaging translation illustrated by photographs of temple paintings from Śrī Lankā, see Cone and Gombrich 1977.

5. Aggaṃ dāyakānam (*m.*), aggaṃ dāyikānam (*f.*). The two designations are found in the "list of firsts" in Anguttara-Nikāya's "Book of Ones" (A 1.14.6–7); unfortunately, the Pāli Text Society translation offers different renditions for these two equivalent male and female terms: Anāthapiṇḍika is called "first among almsgivers," but Visākhā becomes, for unknown reasons, "first among those who minister to the order"—an accurate description but a misleading translation (cf. *GS* 1, 23–4).

6. See Dutt (1962: 61–65) for a description of findings at the Jetavana (Sāvatthi), at Jīvaka's "mango grove" monastery (Rājagaha), and the "park" of Ghosita at Kosambī.

7. This economic expansion was fed, in no small measure, by the opening of new trade routes to the west. Sāvatthi was located astride a major overland route extending from the eastern seaport of Tāmraliptī through the northern Ganges valley to the Punjab and on through passes of the Hindu Kush to Persia. It has often been noted that the expansion of Buddhism followed these trade routes, and monastic settlements were often funded by wealthy merchants. Cf. the discussion of the role of traders' wealth in construction of the western cave monasteries in Dutt 1962: 138–61.

8. To infuse some sense of passing time into this study, I have adopted the device of separating the canonical legends from those of the commentaries. The materials of the Pāli canon, to be discussed in my first two sections, were "frozen" into writing in the first century B.C.E., when the Śrī Lankān Buddhist community decided to record them. (They had actually been fixed in form in India many years earlier, the monks and nuns having passed them on by rote memorization.) A tradition of commentary had been established even while canonical works were still strictly oral, but commentaries were allowed to remain freer in form, and we may presume that they continued to develop until they, too, were written down over the course of many centuries. The two well-known commentaries from which my third section draws its examples were collated and translated into Pāli, also in Śrī Lankā, during the fifth century C.E.

9. "*Seṭṭhi*" literally means "chief" or "best." It has sometimes been translated "treasurer" because of the *seṭṭhi*'s frequent association with kings, and sometimes "banker" because of references to loans such as that in the story of Anāthapiṇḍika's "house fairy." It most probably designates a leader of the merchant community who has gathered enough of a personal fortune to finance the enterprises of others—that is, a merchant-patron with dependent clients.

10. Abbreviated references for quotations from the canonical texts and the most readily available English translations will be supplied in the text. A key to the abbreviations precedes the chapter notes to this volume. The principal canonical accounts of Anāthapiṇḍika are found in four sources: the Cullavagga of the Vinayapiṭaka, Majjhima-Nikāya, Anguttara-Nikāya, and Saṇyutta-Nikaya.

11. I have glossed over far too quickly this extemely fascinating story, which offers a vivid portrayal of psychological agitation. Anāthapiṇḍika hallucinates, or perhaps dreams, that light has come, and he rushes out of the house to see the Buddha. But the light vanishes, and he finds himself in a lonely and dark place, surrounded by inhuman creatures. Frightened, he wants to go back, but he hears Sakka, king of the gods, calling to him to advance, stating that elephants and horses and maidens with jewels in their ears are "not worth the 16th fraction of a single stride." The merchant's alternating elation and terror, together with the words spoken by Sakka, suggest that the prospect of meeting an Enlightened Being to whom he would offer virtually all his possessions was perhaps not as unambiguously comforting as the rest of the story seems to indicate (Cv 6.4.2–3; *BD* 5, 218–19; see also S 10.8; *KS* 1, 211–13).

12. I have simplified the story. According to the Cullavagga account, Jeta asserts that he will not sell, not even for one hundred thousand coins. But he has made a mistake in thus naming a price, for the clever merchant then succeeds in holding him to it. In a second account, which was still circulating orally at the time of the Chinese Pilgrim Hsüan Tsang, Jeta stipulates as price enough coins to cover the ground of the grove; cf. Beal 1884: II, 4–5. The "ground-covering" incident was popular in Buddhist art from very early times; see, for example, the plate from the Bhārhut *stūpa* duplicated by Foucher 1963: 19. The Cullavagga account has apparently tried to reconcile two versions of the story.

13. *Complex* is the appropriate term, for the text speaks of dwelling places, cells, porches, attendance halls, fire halls, halls for what is allowable, privies, places for pacing up and down, halls in the places for pacing up and down, wells, halls at the wells, bathrooms, halls in the bathrooms, lotus ponds, and sheds (Cv 6.4.10; *BD* 5, 223).

14. As the Buddha's discourses (*sutta*s) were collected and transmitted, it became standard practice to identify the locale and recipient of each as part of the process of verification. The frequency of discourses located at Jetavana seems to indicate that the Buddha spent a great deal of time there. According to the commentaries, he did, in fact, spend nineteen rainy-season retreats at Jetavana—and an additional six at Visākhā's Pubbārama, or "Eastern Park," for a total of twenty-five rainy seasons at Sāvatthi (Dh 1.1; *BL* 1, 147). If this is accurate, it helps us to understand the pronounced prominence of the Sāvatthi donors. They simply had more access to the Buddha than donors of other locations, for they were, in effect, funding his headquarters during a substantial portion of his lifetime. The fact that monastic complexes were commonly called by the names of their initial donors further enhanced the reputation of Anāthapiṇḍika (or any other donor); for each time the Jetavana was identified as the site of a discourse, his name was also recited and, hence, remembered.

15. The model offered in these Pāli stories also differs from contemporary practice in Theravāda countries as described, for example, by Gombrich 1971: 217–26; here the resolution is called *prārthanā* (Pāli *patthāna*, "earnest wish") rather than *pranidhāna* (Pāli *paṇidhi*). Of course, the Buddha, the ultimate model,

makes a *paṇidhi* in taking his vow to become a Buddha. According to Gombrich, the term *paṇidhi* has come to mean exclusively this vow to become a Buddha in Śrī Lankā; hence the substitution of *prārthanā* for other forms of resolution (Gombrich 1971: 221–22).

16. Apart from some references in Anguttara-Nikāya, most Visākhā materials are found in the Vinaya. They are located in all three divisions—not only in Cullavagga, but also Mahāvagga and Suttavibhanga. According to the commentaries, Visākhā's matronymic title was derived, not from her biological son Migāra, but from her father-in-law Migāra, who became "son" to her when she accomplished his conversion to Buddhism. See below for the conversion story. Visākhā's other son, Migajāla, has a six-stanza "victory psalm" in the Theragāthā. The commentary establishes the relationship; see Th 417–22 and ThA 6.8; *PB* 216–17. Migajāla receives two discourses of Sanyuttanikāya (S 35–38.63–64; *KS* 4, 16–19), but the account specifies no relationship between the monk and Visākhā—as of course would be appropriate for one who has broken worldly ties.

17. The other, on the importance of keeping Observance Day, is repeated a number of times with a number of different recipients. For Visākhā's version, see A 8.43; *GS* 4, 174.

18. The schismatics would have been a problem for lay persons because the latter were expected to provide all monks and nuns with food and shelter.

19. This structure may have been a loan, rather than a gift; Dutt has noted its ambiguous status (1962: 95–96). The later commentators clearly understood it to be a gift (see below). The translation "storied palace" is most likely an exaggeration; the term *pāsāda* merely means a "multistoried structure."

20. I am speaking particularly of the Ganges valley region of northern India; the status of women varied significantly both on the Indian subcontinent itself and between India and ancient Śrī Lankā.

21. As specified by the gender of the pronoun.

22. I was unable to gain access to texts of the Dhammapadāṭṭhakathā or the (later cited) Vimanavatthaṭṭhakathā when compiling this chapter; hence I have had to rely exclusively on the translations for citations. In these cases "book" and "division" numbers cited in the text are those cited by the translators.

23. Like the *Dhammapada* and the "canonical" section of the *Jātaka*s, the Vimānvatthu and Petavatthu proper consist of verses called *gāthā*s; like the *Dhammapada* and *Jātaka gāthā*s, these verses are included in the segment of the canon known as the Khuddaka (little)-nikāya. The Vimānavatthu and Petavatthu *gāthā*s, however, are far more elaborate than their *Jātaka* or *Dhammapada* counterparts, and they are generally considered to be later in origin than either the preceding, the Vinaya, or the other four Nikāyas. They, too, have come to us with commentaries, both attributed to the *thera* Dhammapāla, a near-successor of Buddhaghosa.

24. For a description of the Buddhist cosmology, see Law 1925: 1–35.

25. The phrase that I have translated below as "put thoughts on" is in Pāli *cittam paṇidhāya*; it is significant, I think, that she uses the traditional language of "resolve" here: *paṇidhāya* is the gerundive form of *paṇidhi*, the Pāli equivalent of *praṇidhāna*; see note 15.

26. The closest historical precedent that I know of lies in the Hindu offerings to the *pitṛ*s, the ancestral dead. But one should also consider the reference to ancestral offerings in the discourses on giving offered to Anāthapiṇḍika. The issue is confused here, because the same Pāli term, *peta*, designates both ancestors in general (Sanskrit *pitṛ*) and the "hungry ghosts" (Sanskrit *preta*); thus an offering to the ancestors readily becomes an offering *for* the *preta*s. See Gombrich 1971: 226 – 40 for an excellent analysis of this problem.

27. For examples, see Schopen 1984, 113 – 18.

7. WEALTH AND REFORMATION IN SINHALESE BUDDHIST MONASTICISM

1. Compare the observation of Paul Levy: "it has not been sufficiently emphasized that Buddhism is solidly based on a rigid system of gifts and exchanges" (Levy 1951: 108).

2. The view that the renunciation of the poor man lacks the religious impact of that of the rich man is not limited to Buddhism alone: "only the rich man, by abandoning his goods for the sake of his faith, can offer altogether convincing proof that he is indeed voluntarily poor" (George and George 1966: 399). Until the twentieth century the Roman Catholic sainthood was dominated—by some 1,939 of 2,489 individuals—by "aristocratic" saints.

3. See Bardwell Smith 1970: 96 – 106 and the essay in this volume by John Strong (Chap. 5).

4. Though *vihāras* are not reclaimed, monks can be expelled from the order, and other monks can be installed in their former monasteries. Such monasteries continue to be *sanghika* (vested in the monkhood) property.

5. According to Weber's account, the religion that began as a "technology of wandering mendicants" was transformed by King Aśoka into a popular religion. The transformation was a political one, serving Aśoka's need to "domesticate" the masses. In the process a religion concerned with the ultimate realization of a few religious virtuosos became a mass religion fixed not on *nibbāna*, but on rebirth in a better condition. In the first centuries after the Buddha's life the monastic order became "domesticated" and the monks settled in monasteries. Kings and laity began to give them land—both to earn merit for themselves and to guarantee the continuity of the religion. Thus the monks became, to follow Weber's characterization, "monastic landlords" (Weber 1958: 204 – 30; for a critique of Weber, see S. J. Tambiah 1976). In the present context, the problem with Weber's analysis is that it inclines us toward the idea that wealth as such is an impediment to good monkly behavior. Sinhalese history is then seen as the story of the gradual domestication and corruption of an ideal Buddhism. As a point of

fact, however, Aśoka's transformation was an accomplished fact by the time Buddhism reached Śrī Lankā.

6. The continuity between the two moral courses is seen at both ends of the continuum. Monks follow the fundamental Buddhist precepts—the *pan sīla*—which are required of the laity, and the laity on frequent occasions temporarily assume additional rules—*aṭa sīla*—which would otherwise define them as monks.

7. An interesting complementary account from the *Vaṃsatthappakāsinī* shows the Buddha himself taking physical possession of the island. In wresting Śrī Lankā from its original nonhuman inhabitants (the *yakkha*s), the Buddha appears to the *yakkha*s and asks for a place to sit. They offer him the entire island. Then, seated on a leather rug, the Buddha causes the rug and his own body to expand to the same dimensions as the island, thus driving off the *yakkha*s (see Malalasekera 1935: I, 79).

8. The rule of *dhamma* over the island naturally tends to imply rule by the monks, a situation that of course creates a delicate relationship between the king and the monastic leadership. The ambiguities of the relationship have not been overlooked: when Mahinda's group first entered Anuradhapura, raised seats were prepared for them. The royal soothsayers saw these seats and prophesied: "the earth is occupied by these *bhikkhu*s; they will be lords upon the island" (*Mhv.* 14.53–54). On the other hand, it is the king who is responsible for reforming the *sangha.*

9. There is also evidence that the *nikāya*s (the monastic groups that comprise the *sangha*, usually translated "sects") in the early medieval period should be regarded not as doctrinal groups holding to a common doctrine, but corporate landholding units supporting monks holding various views. See Gunawardana 1979: passim.

10. Geiger lists only nine reformation periods, leaving out Silameghavanna, Parakkamabahu I, Parakkamabahu II, and Rajadi Rajasinha (Geiger 1960: 205). I do not claim absolute accuracy for these dates and the ones in the table below, some of which are estimates. Geiger dates these reformations by century, but I think that a less rough date is helpful to show the spacing of the reformative movements; however the reader should be warned about their lack of precision.

Sinhalese Buddhist Reformations until British Conquest

	Sinhalese King/ Monk	Date	Account in Sacred Histories
1.	Moggallana I	496	"By a regulative act he purified the good doctrine, the Order of the Victor" *Cv.* I 39.57.
2.	Kamaradhatusena	513	"In a vihara built by his father, he had repairs carried out, he had a revision made

		of the sacred texts and he reformed the Order'' *Cv*. I. 41 – 2.
3. Moggallana III	611	''By a regulative act he reformed the Order of the Perfected One'' *Cv*. I 44.46.
4. Silameghavanna/ Bodhi	617	''When the Monarch had thus gained the victory . . . a bhikkhu named Bodhi . . . begged him to proclaim a regulative act. The king had the regulative act carried out . . . Then all the undisciplined bhikkhus who had been expelled . . . murdered Bodhi . . . and annulled the act. When the King heard that, he . . . made them, their hands cut off and in fetters, guardians of the bathing tanks; another hundred bhikkhus he expelled to Jambudipa'' *Cv*. I 44.74 – 79.
5. Aggabodhi VII	766	''By legal acts he carefully reformed the Order of the Conqueror'' *Cv*. I 48.71.
6. Sena II	833	''By a regulative act he . . . reformed the three fraternities'' *Cv*. I 51.64.
7. Kassapa IV	896	''. . . the King had expelled those bhikkhus in the three fraternities whose discipline was bad'' *Cv*. I 52.10.
8. Kassapa V	913	''He reformed the whole Order of the Master by a regulative act'' *Cv*. I 52.44.
9. Parakkamabahu I	1156	''. . . he cured like a clever, expert physician who distinguishes between curable and incurable disease those which were curable and set aside those which were incurable by the method prescribed by the rules of the Order . . . And he made the Order as uniform as milk and water'' *Cv*. II 73.1 – 22. Also see 78.18. He issued the Maha Parakkamabahu *katikāvata*.
10. Parakkamabahu II/ Mahasvami Medhamkara	1266 – 7	''All the corrupt bhikkhus he sought out rigorously, (and) dismissed them from the Order (He) . . . caused to be brought . . . many respected Cola bhikkhus who had moral discipline . . . and so established harmony between the two Orders''

		(Mahayana and Theravada) *Cv.* II 84.7–10. He issued the Dambadeni *katikāvata.*
11. Bhuvanekabahu	1372	"... he gathered the bhikkhus together, ascertained those who lived immoral lives and had them cast forth from the Order, but he showed favour to the conscientious, obtained for them precedence and so made the Order of the Victor shine" *Cv.* II 91.10.
12. Kirti Sri Rajasinha/ Valivita Saranamkara	1753–4	"As the King was minded to further the Order ... he strengthened the influence of the high principled and in many ways gave the Order support" *Cv.* II 100.53–4. He issued two *katikāvatas* which bear his name.
13. Rajadi Rajsinha/ Moratota Dhammakkhanda	1782–98	The *Cūlavamsa* is silent on the reformation marked by the proclaiming of the Rajadi Rajasinha *katikāvata*, saying only that he "... continued that furtherance of the laity and the Order which his brother [Kirti Sri Rajasinha] had carried out" *Cv.* II 101.3.

11. Three notable examples are Kuncanaga (187–189), Dathopatissa I (639–650), and Vikramabahu (1116–1137).

12. It is not clear, historically or etymologically, whether this rule requires control by a single student or permits joint control. Thus the ambiguous wording of this sentence is intentional.

13. I believe that this *katikāvata* was intended for the Nittawela *vihāra* in Mawilamada, north of Kandy in Yatinuwara. See Lawrie 1896: II, 560–61.

14. Consider this testimony in 1893 by Mahawellatenne in a dispute over control of a monastery in Balangoda: "This is one of the temples built by and endowed by my ancestor Mahawellatenne *adigar* (chief governor). ... I deny that the petitioner [a resident monk] has any right whatever to the *vihāra* or the endowment, as we have not given the temple over to any priest whatever, for we always placed any priest we like to look after the *vihāra* just as at the *Dharmasalawe* at Ratanapura or the *Dharmasalawe* at Pelmadulla" (Ceylon National Archives 45/2956, 30 March 1893).

15. Woodhouse (1917–18), H. W. Tambiah (1962), and Dissanayaka and Soysa (1963) all say nothing of it. I have heard Low Country monks refer to this mode of succession as *sivuru paramparāva*, which is apt—since succession passes according to order of robing (*sivuru*)—but wrong.

16. See the Maha Parakkamabahu *katikāvata*, verses 9–11, 14, repeated and extended in Dambadeni *katikāvata*, verses 40–43, 47, and 70, Kirti Śrī Rajasinha *Katikāvata* I, 35–38, 42, 65, 68, and Kirti Śrī Rajasinha *Katikāvata* II, verses 18–19, and Rajadi Rajasinha *Katikāvata*, verse 7, in Ratanapala 1971.

17. Gombrich refers to this same quality in people who are praised for being *sānta dānta* (having quiet self-control) (Gombrich 1971: 266).

18. This notion resonates with the ancient view (*upanissaya*), whereby qualities, aptitudes, and marks of an individual show that he is destined to be an *arhant*. See *Mhv*. 5. 43–46, 126, 182, 195.

8. BUDDHIST PRACTICAL MORALITY IN A CHANGING AGRARIAN WORLD

1. In 1963 and 1964, with the assistance of my wife, I spent eighteen months working in Ban Nọng Tụn and traveling about much of the northeastern region. On subsequent trips to Thailand, and especially in 1972, 1980, and 1983, I returned to Ban Nọng Tụn and the Northeast to observe the changes and continuities in rural life. I am grateful to the Foreign Area Fellowship Program for support of my original research, to the Ford Foundation Southeast Asia Fellowship Program for support of my research in 1972, and to the U.S. Agency for International Development for support of my research in 1980. I am also grateful to the University of Washington and the Guggenheim Foundation for support during the period when I prepared the final version of this paper.

I wish to thank Jack Hawley, Frank Reynolds, Louis Gebaude, E. Valentine Daniel, and Donald Swearer for their criticisms and suggestions. For the purposes of publication the present form of this essay is a considerably revised and condensed version of the original.

2. Words in Lao and Thai, the languages spoken in northeastern Thailand, have been transliterated with indication of vowel length but without indication of tone. Both Lao and Thai systems follow the modified Library of Congress/Cornell systems. Transliterations of Pāli terms follow the Pāli Text Society form.

3. Such differentiation was not absent in traditional villages, but it was not as marked as it has become since the villagers began to orient themselves toward the market economy. In 1963 older villagers in Ban Nọng Tụn told me that there had been few rich villagers, just as there had been few poor villagers, in the communities they remembered as children. By 1963, however, 22 households out of 120 had a minimal annual cash income ($20 or less), while three households had incomes of over $600 (Keyes 1966: 252). This tendency has continued, although there has been a skewing of income levels upward. By 1980 only 4 households out of 129 had a minimal cash income ($50 or less), 26 had incomes of less than $250, and at the other end of the spectrum, 3 households had incomes exceeding ten times that amount, that is, over $2,500.

4. Buddhist lent lasts for three lunar months and always falls during the rainy season. Throughout Buddhist Southeast Asia, time spent in the *sangha* is

calculated in terms of the number of lents that one has been a monk or a novice. A man who had spent one lent in the order would have been a member of the *sangha* for at least three months; a man who had spent two lents could have been a member for as little as fifteen months or as long as two years.

5. In 1963 in Ban Nọng Tụn, for example, 60.3 percent of all men twenty-one years of age and older had been monks (the figure includes some who had also been novices) and an additional 9.6 percent had been novices only. In a 1980 restudy I found no significant changes in this level of observance.

6. See Burns 1971; *Nangsụ̄ phāp chīwaprawat lae pathipatthā khōng phra ācān Fan Ācārō* 1978; Placzek 1979; Keyes 1981; Tambiah 1984. Even these ascetic monks do not withdraw totally from society; forest hermitages become centers for instruction in the *dhamma* and the practice of meditation by lay people as well as monks.

7. In another work (Keyes in press) I discuss the way in which the traditional Thai-Lao world view was altered following the introduction of compulsory education.

8. Although not all temporary migration has been to Bangkok, the experience there has been of greatest cultural significance.

9. In 1980 this percentage was relatively unchanged. In other villages in the region the percentage would be even higher; in few villages would it be lower.

10. I have discussed the Buddhist monarchical roots of the Thai civic order at length in *Thailand: Buddhist Kingdom as Modern Nation-State* (Keyes 1987), especially in Chapter 7.

11. The Īsān-Thai dictionary (*Phācananukrom phāk īsān-phāk klāng* 1972: 355) defines *leng* as "doing what one wishes" and gives as an example a woman who becomes a prostitute. It would seem that the prostitute is for women what the *nakleng* is for men. For a further discussion of *nakleng* as a model for one type of maleness, see Keyes 1986.

12. The experiences of the northeasterners in many ways parallel those of the Chinese who took up jobs in Bangkok and elsewhere in Southeast Asia in the latter part of the nineteenth century and early part of the twentieth century. Of such subordinated minorities Weber wrote: "national or religious minorities which are in a position of subordination to a group of rulers are likely, through their voluntary or involuntary exclusion from positions of political influence, to be driven with peculiar force into economic activity" (Weber 1958: 39). For a discussion of the "work ethic" of the Chinese in Thailand and of the contrast between Chinese and Central Thai values regarding work, see Deyo 1974, 1975, and Tobias 1973.

9. ETHICS, WEALTH, AND ESCHATOLOGY

1. See Troeltsch (1922). Here Troeltsch's historical description of development within the Christian tradition is far more helpful as a basis for comparative study than direct application of the Weber-Troeltsch types of ascetic and mystic

(cf. Weber 1946: 294). The quotations from Troeltsch's essay in this chapter are from an unpublished translation by Ernest B. Koenker.

2. At times, however, bishops have organized their clergy into monastic communities, and abbots have received episcopal honors.

3. Of course, Theravāda Buddhism has not lacked millennial movements, especially in times of crisis and widespread social change (Tambiah 1984). The call to abandon the present order of things and put one's hopes in the appearance of Maitreya Buddha echoes familiar themes in Christian millennialism. The point, however, is that this is not the approach to change that has been fostered by the major, established tradition of the Theravāda *sangha*. Their strategy has been instead a selective legitimation that assures ruler and people alike that the society is ordered in accord with the fundamental requirements of *dhamma*. The ruler and the leaders of lay society may play important roles in initiating and implementing the purification, but they never can claim legitimacy for their reforms simply on the basis of common wisdom or material success. Christian monasticism, by contrast, brought into the main currents of Christian social thought the eschatological emphasis that the Theravāda *sangha* generally sought to exclude.

INTRODUCTION TO PART V

1. For a historical treatment and critical analysis of these developments and their implications for moral theory, see Stout (1981) and MacIntyre (1981).

2. A helpful elaboration of these two competing conceptions of equality may be found in Ronald Dworkin's chapter, "Liberalism," in Hampshire (1978).

10. BUDDHIST ECONOMIC ETHICS

1. For an application of this approach to the basic tenets of a variety of religious traditions, see Green (1978).

2. The issue of entitlement and the "deservedness" of ownership is at the heart of the dispute between Rawls and his libertarian critics. For one such critical view, see Nozick (1974). For a Rawlsian response to this libertarian view, see the essays by Daniels and La Follette in Arthur and Shaw (1978).

3. For a fuller discussion of this problem, see Olson (1965.)

4. For a discussion of this aspect of Buddhist monasticism, see the essay by Rājavaramuni, Chapter 1 in this volume.

5. Telapatta-Jātaka and Pañcagaru-Jātaka in Cowell (1973: I, 236, 289); Sarkisyanz (1965: 15).

6. Acts 2 – 5. For a fuller discussion of Christian social teachings about property, see Troeltsch (1960: I, 58 – 64, 321ff., 343ff).

7. Winston L. King (1964: 186) characterizes the Buddhist monastic community as "the nearest possible approximation to the ideal social order possible to approximate in time and space, which all men ought to approximate as nearly as possible in their social relations to each other."

11. INDIVIDUALISM, COMMUNITARIANISM, AND THEORIES OF JUSTICE

1. Dumont sees his 1965 essay as having to do with the differentiation of politics from religion and the new concept of the individual this involved; the 1977 book demonstrates how politics gave birth to economics (1977: 15–16). I take it he is saying that, although the genesis of the modern individual begins before the economic ideology, the latter gives it definitive form. Cf. Dumont (1982) and Eisenstadt's critique (1983).

2. T. M. Scanlon makes a distinction between ''subjective'' and ''objective'' criteria of well-being (1975: 656–58); the former evaluates ''the level of well-being . . . or the importance . . . of a . . . benefit or sacrifice solely from the point of view'' of an individual's ''tastes or interests''; the latter ''provides a basis for appraisal of a person's level of well-being which is independent of that person's tastes and interests, thus allowing for the possibility that such an appraisal could be correct even though it conflicted with the preferences of the individual in question.'' Scanlon's sense of objectivity does not require, however, an essentialist theory of the good; the point is that for the ''interpersonal measure of benefit and sacrifice'' (663) we do and should assume that the malleability and hence the strength and weakness of individual preferences lie in the area of ''interests which are peripheral rather than central'' in a ''normal life'' (665). For normative theory, in other words, we do and should make a distinction between types of concerns; where concerns are central, we will not allow strength of preference to be the criterion of importance or urgency. Such a notion of objectivity could be justified, says Scanlon, either by dropping the idea of consensus and defending it as the ''objective truth about which interests are more important and which are less so'' or by understanding relative importance as a matter of consensus, a useful ''construct'' that is the ''best available standard of justification that is mutually acceptable to people whose preferences diverge'' (668). Rawls (1971) uses objective criteria in Scanlon's sense but takes the second option of an appeal to consensus as a construct that ultimately still rests on the strengths of the desires of the individuals who make up the consensus.

3. Rawls holds that ''good'' has a constant descriptive sense: ''something's being good is its having the properties that it is rational to want in things of its kind'' given one's ''interests and aims'' (1971: 405, 407; cf. sections 61, 62, 63); if certain things are good for persons ''generally,'' they are ''human goods'' (1971: 399). The prescriptive or elocutionary force is given in the context (1971: 406). Compare Gewirth, who holds that ''good'' has the common elocutionary force of expressing a favorable, positive evaluation of the objects or purposes to which it is attributed'' (1978: 51). Gewirth sees a common evaluative meaning, with the descriptive criteria varying according to context, whereas Rawls puts things the other way around (cf. Richards's Rawlsian view, 1971). This is a dispute in the theory of meaning or language; substantively, Rawls and Gewirth are very close.

4. Cf. Charles Taylor (1985: 266) on "strong evaluation." Intrinsic goods are not merely objects of choice or desire, but ends we *should* seek.

5. I believe that MacIntyre and Sandel propose what R. P. Wolff called a "social value," which makes an "essential reference to reciprocal states of consciousness among two or more persons" (1968: 181); communal values are a type of social value (184 – 85).

6. Adina Schwartz argues that Rawls's formal "thin" definition of the good does not support a preference for the primary goods (1973: 299ff.), even with the help of general facts about human nature. One can specify very general notions of the primary goods (which are instrumental to any life plan), but they (wealth, for example) will be too vague to be of use in formulating principles of justice; to define them more specifically is to commit oneself to a nonneutral concept of the good. For example, a socialist would define liberty differently—more stress on nonalienation of labor—and would prefer less rather than more of the primary good of wealth. For a response to this criticism see Rawls 1975b.

7. It is important to distinguish Hume's claim that because of the weakness of benevolence humans need justice, from his own theory of what justice is, namely, an agreement or convention about "property" between self-interested agents. The importance of self-interest in Hume's theory, however, does not necessarily mean that he was a "possessive individualist" in Macpherson's sense (1962); see David Miller (1980) to the contrary. On Hume, see MacIntyre (1988: 312; cf. 337).

8. The history and nature of this socialization could also be variously explained. See, for example, Nancy Chodorow 1978; cf. Gilligan 1982, 1986; and Keller 1986.

9. See Brian Barry's (1978) objections to Hume's theory. Barry agrees that justice would have no application in situations of extreme abundance, because "the subject-matter of justice is the distribution of things in short supply . . . (relative to total demand)" (1978: 209ff.). But Barry argues, contrary to Hume, that justice would apply to situations of extreme scarcity, for example, famines or the distribution of medical equipment. Barry also agrees with Hume that if there were perfect benevolence, there would be no conflicting claims and hence no need for justice; but the opposite of total benevolence is not total self-interest, as Hume suggests, but unenlightened self-interest; what Hume wants to insist on is the capacity for self-interested agreement, his own notion of justice (1978: 214ff.). As for the approximate equality of agents, Barry also thinks this reflects Hume's theory of justice as an agreement between those in a position to harm one another; Barry, in contrast, thinks that justice would apply to situations in which power is disproportionate (1978: 220ff.). In short, Barry is prepared to accept some of what Hume says about the circumstances of justice but rejects Hume's theory of justice as a convention for mutual advantage.

10. I am not convinced that the "Kantianism" of the later essays displaces the rational choice model in Rawls's thought. On the purported shift in Rawls's later work, see Tom Beauchamp (1980: 150 – 51). On the role of contract in

Rawls's thought, see Barry (1978: 228ff.) and Hampton (1980). On both rational deduction and the notion of an agreement for mutual advantage, see Rawls (1985). See Rawls 1988: 268ff.; 274 n. 32 on justice as a final end.

11. The society formed by the principles of justice Rawls argues for would not resemble the circumstances of justice. In addition to the affirmation of principles of justice, individuals would come to value their justice-based institutions as intrinsic interpersonal goods (1971: 521–23, 528–29); cf. Proudfoot (1974: 113) and Delaney (1983: 116ff.). I think Rawls intends to say this, although his remark that the "successes and enjoyments of others are necessary for and complimentary to our own good" (1971: 522–30) could be read instrumentally; see Werpehowski (1982).

12. Rawls early on speaks of "society" as a cooperative venture (1971: 4) when he is delineating the circumstances of justice. But this usage should not confuse us; society in this sense is a technical concept that must be seen within his more general concept of the "social nature of mankind." Cf. Sandel (1982) on the meanings of social union.

13. The freedom of the self to choose ends is a metaphysical belief; the contractors have a highest-order interest in structuring society so as to protect and promote that capacity (Rawls 1982: 169; cf. 1985). The other highest-order interest is in exercising the capacity for justice, and Rawls also identifies a higher-order interest, namely, to realize a particular conception of the good, whatever that may be. This is a third major interest of "moral persons," but it is only higher-order, not highest, because it is "subordinate" to the other two (1980: 525, 547–49; cf. 1982). I am uncertain whether by "interests" Rawls means (*a*) the aims and purposes one has once committed to the moral point of view expressed in the original position or (*b*) one's view of the good which directs one to take up that point of view. I favor (*a*); see Rawls 1988. Cf. Jeffrey Stout on a "self-limiting consensus" on the good (1988) and MacIntyre on the "good" of a liberal social order (1988: 336, 345). Nancy Rosenblum (1987: 165ff.) discusses several theorists who argue that there is a "latent communitarianism" in American society, a set of "shared meanings" and "affective attachments," for example, Walzer (1983). Cf. also Bellah's response (1986) to Stout and other critics.

14. Schneewind (1986: 71) argues that for Rawls benevolence is to be ignored in the original position not because it is absent or weak, but because its role in individual psyches is dependent on the natural and social lottery. I think the Rawls of 1971 assumes the preference theory of the good and the variability of benevolence as part of the "circumstances" of justice. One's actual benevolence or lack of it is bracketed, however, by the moral stance of the original position (the veil of ignorance).

15. See Tambiah (1976: 45, 54; cf. 38–49, 58, 60, 62).

16. I am uncertain whether to view *karma* (there are various conceptions in Buddhist traditions, of course) as distributive or retributive justice; some interpreters apparently take it only as a causal law.

17. Dumont seems to hold normatively that both "equality" and hierarchy" are valid perspectives, but his comments on equality and its false sociological underpinnings seem to undermine this stance. He needs to argue for a view of equality which is not simply the "valorization" of a sociologically false, atomistic individualism. He would still presumably want equality qualified by a recognition of some form of "hierarchy" reflecting our social nature.

18. I think that Dumont (1980: 8) confuses two assertions: (1) we learn to speak and think in the categories of our society (the sociological apperception); (2) each person is only the expression of a metaphysical or moral collectivity (holism). In regard to (1), a crucial question is whether and how I can think of myself differently than others think of me (see Outka 1980: 111–12). In regard to (2), Dumont is right to say that in many societies people do not conceive of themselves as individuals with a right to equal consideration. Nonetheless, it may not be the case that holism is characteristic of all "traditional" societies. The concept of holism should not be projected back onto all nonmodern societies or philosophies. Cf. Dumont 1980: 5, 9–10.

19. Lukes (1973) does think that the abstract individual (the presocial individual of the atomistic model) is at the heart of other sorts of individualism—for example, the political individualism according to which self-sufficient individuals consent to form governments in order to protect their interests and the economic individualism in which agents with a presocial right to private property seek to maximize their interests; Nozick (1974) would be a modern example. Cf. Macpherson (1962) on the possessive individual of a full market society in contrast to the notion of the person in a customary or simple market society.

20. Rawls in "Fairness to Goodness" (1975b) tries to meet the charge that his theory rests on "abstract individualism," the theory that aims and interests are formed independent of social arrangements (547). Cf. Rapaport (1977) and Delaney (1983), who criticize earlier attacks on Rawls's individualism, for example, Teitelman (1972), Schwartz (1973), and Eschete (1974).

21. Other authors would refer to theses about the social nature of the self as "metaphysical." Keller (1986) adduces the "social" nature of the self as part of a metaphysical theory of personal identity. Some critics of individualism, such as Sandel (1982), however, distinguish purely sociological theses (for example, one's consciousness is shaped by one's social relations) from metaphysical assertions about the nature of personhood or personal identity. Sociological claims may be stated so that they can be compatible with various theories of personal identity, but I think Keller is correct that a "social" view of the self can be part of a metaphysical position.

22. Rawls's basic intention is to do just what Lukes's persons do, or Lukes does in their name, namely, determine what will protect and promote their common capacities, no matter what other differences of natural or social circumstances may characterize them. Lukes apparently thinks that having capacities *grounds* respect for capacities. That we are to bargain as Lukes's persons and not as specific individuals is the moral equality of the original position for Rawls.

As part of a coherentist justification, Rawls posits the equal right to choose, that is, to bargain freely. Gewirth (1978), in contrast, thinks that given certain facts about agency the constraint of consistency—the principle of universalizability—will require human agents, his version of Lukes's persons, to accord to others the rights they claim for themselves.

23. In opposition to the notion that "political community [is] entirely produced by choice or agreement," Galston (1980: 45) argues as follows: "As human beings, our separate existences are linked in important ways prior to our application of reason and will to the construction of common life. If this is so, then it is necessary to explore the ways in which justice, the chief virtue of communities, expresses these links." Galston is calling for a neo-Aristotelian notion of justice based on a theory of human good.

24. The Rawls of 1971 held the thesis that persons qua persons do not have essential ends; this metaphysical view was a crucial premise in his moral reasoning. In certain essays after 1971, however, Rawls seems to deny that he requires his contractors to hold a preference theory of the good. Now he seems to say that the contractors, on the basis of whatever comprehensive moral view they hold, will merely *assume* a preference theory for the purpose of devising principles of justice (see 1985: 238, 239n.21, 240n.22, 241, 249n.32). It is a historical fact, says Rawls, that since the Reformation there are "conflicting and incommensurable" conceptions of the good (1985: 230, 248). But the nature of the good is a philosophical question, which moral and political philosophy need not debate. Thus the moral assumption made by the contractors not only calls for them to disregard their actual conceptions of the good (sensual bliss, *nibbāna*, communion with God), but they are to disregard their views about the metaphysical status of their ends. Some will hold the preference view of the Rawls of 1971 and some will hold, say, a MacIntyre view, but they will bracket these metaphysical views about persons and their ends. They will hold on some moral grounds or other that selves have a highest-order interest in forming and revising conceptions of the good; they will assume this in order to give expression to their moral commitment to "toleration" (Rawls 1985). But those who hold that a communal good is essential to persons will not be prepared to bracket their conviction. They can admit that actual views of the good are influenced to some degree by natural and social conditioning, but they will insist that their view of the good specifies what to a considerable extent is truly good for persons. They do not have to hold some version of epistemic foundationalism, namely, that their beliefs about the good are self-evident or otherwise self-justifying and immutable; but they will claim that their view of the good for persons is warranted by their beliefs about the nature of persons. Patrick Neal (1987: 571ff.) makes a similar point: those who view the good as essential to their view of themselves will not be willing to act as if their "meta-theory" were simply one other preferential conception of the good.

25. Williams (1985: 223n.16; cf. 205n.6) notes that there are arguments for and against the notion that, had I been brought up differently and had different ends, I would not have been the same person. He distinguishes this question of

''metaphysical necessity'' from the ''practical necessity'' of what is ''possible'' for me given my ''ideals and character''; here he wants to ''resist the Kantian idea that the truly ethical subject is one for whom nothing is necessary except agency itself.'' For a Kantian such as Rawls, it is practically possible for persons to govern their ideals and character by what they believe is acceptable to anyone; the ethical subject is the subject who acknowledges such governance. Whether one should so conceive *morally* of the ethical subject is the substantive issue, in my view, not whether such a conception is practically possible.

26. Schneewind (1986: 72), in a discussion of the Butler-Kant-Rawls tradition of moral autonomy, also claims that

> metaphysical, epistemological, sociological, psychological, or language-based theories of the self's nature and formation have no bearing on the validity of the idea of autonomy. The defender of autonomy need have no view about the existence of an enduring substantial self, the immortal soul, the Cartesian subject, or the transcendental ego. The autonomist need not deny that the self is a cultural product, rather than a divine or natural one. Her claim is that the culture itself [the moral tradition in question] requires us to think of ourselves as able to look at our lives and actions from, among many others, the point of view of a self-legislator. . . . To have a relevant objection to autonomy-centered views of morality and to the self as portrayed in them, it is necessary to object to them on moral grounds.

Schneewind is not denying that a theory of the good, taken as a metaphysical position about the nature of persons, can function as a crucial assumption (as I argue here) on which a liberal theory is based. He is saying that the ''autonomist'' need not be committed to a broader range of metaphysical views, for example, a view of personal identity. Schneewind could also admit that notions of personal identity do play a role in the moral reasoning of other traditions (cf. Kirkpatrick 1986). For example, the Theravāda Buddhist doctrine of no-self (*anatta*) (of which there are various interpretations) seems to play a role in Buddhist accounts of compassion and benevolence, but Rawls's theory of justice is compatible with several theories of personal identity. Steven Collins (1982: 193–94) argues, for example, that ''the rationale for action which acceptance of Buddhism furnished provides neither for simple self-interest nor for self-denying altruism. The attitude to all 'individualities,' whether past and future 'selves,' past, future, or contemporary 'others' is the same—loving-kindness, compassion, sympathetic joy, and equanimity.'' Collins (1982: 94n.22) refers to Parfit and Nagel, saying that ''any given individual cannot know'' which self it is (its own past or future ''individualities'' or others). But does *anatta* teach this? Is it not that I am aware of being a particular being (even though I may have no memory of past lives)? *Anatta* teaches me the true account of personal identitiy (over karmic lives), but once I grasp what personal identity really is, I will no longer conceive of the world in terms of discrete individualities? In any case we should expect to find not a single sort of relation of ethics and metaphysics, but various sorts of relations, depending on which metaphysical beliefs and which moral notions are involved.

27. The later Rawls does not claim that his theory of the good, the basic moral position modeled in the veil of ignorance, or the principles of justice are descriptively universal or even common, nor does he argue for a foundationalist epistemology on the basis of which to claim that all humans should adopt his theory. See 1980: 518–19 and 1985: 225. MacIntyre in the Postscript to *After Virtue* (1984a) indicates that he also is operating as a coherentist (neopragmatist or holist) seeking the best explanation and justification (cf. 1988). I take him to say that we are justified in believing that some communal good(s) is constitutive of personhood; communities justify their particular conceptions holistically by reference to their webs of beliefs. MacIntyre seems to reject the idea that anyone would be excluded from "new forms of community," but his notion of tradition-relative justification would seem to allow, for example, for patriarchal communities in which women are included, yet in inferior roles (see Bernstein 1984: 25 on what MacIntyre owes to the Enlightenment; see MacIntyre's reply, 1984b: 40). His proposal, moreover, for an alternative to Rawlsian liberalism seems incomplete. If the search itself is the good, it is unclear exactly which vision of justice, etc., it requires (cf. Schneewind 1982, and MacIntyre's reply, 1982). MacIntyre intended to say that various neo-Aristotelian communities will profess to know enough about the good to constitute themselves politically; each group will continue to search for full knowledge of the good in dialogue with other communities. But if so, communities even with partial knowledge of the good will not be prepared to bracket their conceptions. See Amy Gutman (1985: 313–14; cf. 312n.18), who puts this point in "contextualist" or "constructivist" form: if selves were "radically situated" in terms of "commonally given ends," they could not "appreciate the value of justice," that is, they would not appreciate the value of justice in *Rawls's* sense. As for MacIntyre's argument that the "Enlightenment Project" or "liberal individualism" is dead, none of the grounds he suggests seems at all decisive. First, MacIntyre (1988: 334ff., 399–400, 345 passim) says that Enlightenment liberalism tried to establish tradition-free standards of rationality and justice but that subsequently its advocates have understood it as a historical tradition; his major argument against the continued viability of the liberal tradition is the "fragmentation" it has produced. But the current "fragmentation," for example, the fissure between Rawls's and Nozick's views of justice, is no more intractable than the conflict between two versions of MacIntyre's neo-Aristotelianism (cf. Bernstein 1984: 9). Second, the putative failure of quasi-foundationalist arguments does not mean there are no other suitable modes of justification for an Enlightenment-liberal view (cf. Stout 1988, III). Third, it is not at all clear why Enlightenment premises (taken nonfoundationally) cannot justify common rules and virtues (as opposed to the thesis that only a neo-Aristotelian view of the "good for man" can suffice). In fact, the major question left unanswered is this: if we are not to resuscitate Aristotle's metaphysical biology, how do we ground a vision of the "good for man"? Is human nature

sufficiently determinate that we can argue from what we are to what is good for us? Or is it too ''plastic'' to posit an ideal of human fulfillment or flourishing on which a ''virtue-centered'' ethic would rest (Wong 1984)? (Cf. Stout 1988: 223.)

28. Ronald Green suggests in this volume that the consent to a king in the *Aggañña Suttānta* suggests the acceptable-to-any rational agent model. I am not certain whether this interpretation constitutes sufficient evidence to attribute the model to Buddhist tradition. One could accept *because* of one's ''thick'' view of the good.

29. I am grateful to a number of readers for helpful suggestions, in particular Harlan Beckley, Paul Lauritzen, Russell Sizemore, and Donald Swearer.

References

INTRODUCTION

Buddhadhāsa Bhikku.

1986 *Dhammic Socialism*. Edited by Donald K. Swearer. Bangkok: Interreligious Committee for Development.

Geertz, Clifford

1968 *Islam Observed*. Chicago: University of Chicago Press.

1973 *The Interpretation of Cultures*. New York: Basic Books.

Little, David, and Sumner B. Twiss

1978 *Comparative Religious Ethics: A New Method*. New York: Harper and Row.

Weber, Max

1958 *The Religion of India: The Sociology of Hinduism and Buddhism*. Trans. H. H. Gerth and Don Martindale. Chicago: Free Press.

2. ETHICS AND WEALTH IN THERAVĀDA BUDDHISM

1971 *Dika Malai Deva Sut*. Bangkok: Thambanakhan Press.

Lovin, Robin W., and Frank E. Reynolds, eds.

1985 *Cosmogony and Ethical Order: New Essays in Comparative Ethics*. Chicago: University of Chicago Press.

Macy, Joanna

1983 *Dharma and Development: Religion as a Resource in the Sarvodaya Self-help Movement* West Hartford, Conn.: Kumarian Press.

Reynolds, Frank E.

1979 Four Modes of Theravāda Action. *Journal of Religious Ethics* 7:1 (Spring): 12–27.

Reynolds, Frank E., and Regina T. Clifford

1980 Sangha, Society and the Struggle for National Integration: Burma and Thailand. In *Transitions and Transformations in the History of Religion*, edited by Reynolds and Ludwig. Leiden: E. J. Brill.

Reynolds, Frank E., and Mani B. Reynolds, eds. and trans.

1982 *Three Worlds According to King Ruang*. University of California Research Series No. 4. Berkeley: Asian Humanities Press.

Swearer, Donald K.

1978 A New Look at Prince Vessantara. *Journal of the National Research Council of Thailand* 10:1 (January-June): 1–9.

3. ETHICAL ANALYSIS AND WEALTH IN THERAVĀDA BUDDHISM

Aronson, Harvey B.
1980 *Love and Sympathy in Theravāda Buddhism.* Delhi: Motilal Banarsidass.

Gombrich, Richard F.
1971 *Precept and Practice: Traditional Buddhism in the Rural Highlands of Ceylon.* Oxford: Clarendon Press.

Gunawardana, R. A. L. H.
1979 *Robe and Plough: Monasticism and Economic Interest in Early Medieval Sri Lanka.* Tucson: University of Arizona Press.

Ladd, John
1957 *Structure of a Moral Code: A Philosophical Analysis of Ethical Discourse Applied to the Ethics of the Navaho Indians.* Cambridge, Mass.: Harvard University Press.

Little, David
1982 The Present State of the Comparative Study of Religious Ethics. *Journal of Religious Ethics* (March).

Little, David, and Sumner B. Twiss
1978 *Comparative Religious Ethics: A New Method.* New York: Harper and Row.

Müller, Max, ed.
1965 *Sacred Books of the East.* Volume 10. Delhi: Motilal Banarsidass.

Phillips, D. C.
1976 *Holistic Thought in Social Science.* Stanford: Stanford University Press.

Reynolds, Frank E.
1980 Contrasting Modes of Action: A Comparative Study of Buddhist and Christian Ethics. *History of Religions* 20:1, 2 (August and November).

Reynolds, Frank E., and Regina T. Clifford
1980 Sangha, Society and the Struggle for National Integration: Burma and Thailand. In *Transitions and Transformations in the History of Religions*, edited by Reynolds and Ludwig. Leiden: E. J. Brill.

Spiro, Melford E.
1970 *Buddhism and Society.* New York: Harper and Row.

4. COMPARATIVE RELIGIOUS ETHICS AS A FIELD

Green, Ronald M.
1978 *Religious Reason: The Rational and Moral Basis of Religious Belief.* New York: Oxford University Press.

Gustafson, James M.
1965 Context Versus Principles: A Misplaced Debate in Christian Ethics. *Harvard Theological Review* 58:2 (April). Reprinted in *New Theology*

No. 3, edited by Martin E. Marty and Dean G. Peerman (New York: Macmillan, 1966).

Little, David

1974 Max Weber and the Comparative Study of Religious Ethics. *Journal of Religious Ethics* 2:2 (Fall): 5–40.

Little, David, and Sumner B. Twiss

1978 *Comparative Religious Ethics: A New Method.* New York: Harper and Row.

Reeder, John P.

1978 Religious Ethics as a Field and a Discipline. *Journal of Religious Ethics* 6:1 (Spring): 32–53.

Saddhatissa, H.

1970 *Buddhist Ethics: Essence of Buddhism.* New York: George Braziller.

Stout, Jeffrey

1981 *The Flight from Authority: Religion, Morality, and the Quest for Autonomy.* Notre Dame: University of Notre Dame Press.

Troeltsch, Ernst

1976 *The Social Teaching of the Christian Churches.* Chicago: University of Chicago Press. [German edition 1911]

5. RICH MAN, POOR MAN, *BHIKKHU*, KING

Aronson, Harvey B.

1979 The Relationship of the Karmic to the Nirvanic in Theravada Buddhism. *Journal of Religious Ethics* 7:28–36.

Bloch, Jules

1950 *Les inscriptions d'Aśoka.* Paris: Les Belles Lettres.

Burlingame, Eugene Watson, trans.

1921 *Buddhist Legends.* Vol. 1. Harvard Oriental Series, vol. 28. Cambridge, Mass.: Harvard University Press.

Ch'en, Kenneth K. S.

1964 *Buddhism in China.* Princeton: Princeton University Press.

Cone, Margaret, and Richard F. Gombrich

1977 *The Perfect Generosity of Prince Vessantara.* Oxford: Clarendon Press.

Denis, Eugene, ed. and trans.

1977 *La Lokapannatti et les idées cosmologiques du bouddhisme ancien.* Vol. 2. Lille: Atelier Reproduction des Thèses.

Fausbøll, V., ed.

1896 *The Jātaka.* Vol. 6. London: Pāli Text Society.

Feer, Leon, trans.

1891 *Avadāna-cataka: cent légendes (bouddhiques).* Annales du Musée Guimet, vol. 18. Paris: E. Leroux.

References

Filliozat, Jean
1967 The Devas of Aśoka: ''Gods'' or ''Divine Majesties"? In *Studies in Aśokan Inscriptions*, trans. Mrs. R. K. Menon. Calcutta: Indian Studies Past and Present.

Geiger, Wilhelm, ed.
1958 *The Mahāvamṣa*. London: Pāli Text Society.

Geiger, Wilhelm, trans.
1960 *The Mahāvamṣa or The Great Chronicle of Ceylon*. Colombo: Ceylon Government Information Department.
1973 *Cūḷavamṣa*. Parts I and II. London: Pāli Text Society.

Gombrich, Richard F.
1971 *Precept and Practice*. London: Oxford University Press.

Grousset, René
1971 *In the Footsteps of the Buddha*. Translated by J. A. Underwood. New York: Orion Press.

Htin Aung, Maung
1962 *Folk Elements in Burmese Buddhism*. London: Oxford University Press.

Irwin, John
1983 The Ancient Pillar-Cult at Prayāga (Allahabad). *Journal of the Royal Asiatic Society* :253–80.

Lamotte, Etienne
1958 *Histoire du bouddhisme indien*. Louvain: Institut Orientaliste.

Lévi, Sylvain, and Edouard Chavannes
1916 Les seize arhat protecteurs de la loi. *Journal Asiatique* 8: 5–48, 189–304.

Mookerji, Radha Kumud
1965 *Harsha*. Delhi: Motilal Banarsidass.

Morris, Richard, ed.
1885 *The Anguttara-Nikāya*. Vol. 1. London: Pāli Text Society.

Mukhopadhyaya, Sujitkumar, ed.
1963 *The Aśokāvadāna*. New Delhi: Sahitya Akademi.

Mus, Paul
1935 *Barabuḍur*. Vol. 1. Hanoi: Imprimerie d'Extreme-Orient.

Nikam, N. A., and Richard McKeon, eds. and trans.
1959 *The Edicts of Aśoka*. Chicago: University of Chicago Press.

Norman, H. C., ed.
1906 *The Commentary on the Dhammapada*. Vol. 1. London: Pāli Text Society.

Przyluski, Jean
1923 *La legende de l'empereur Acoka*. Paris: Paul Geuthner.

Rhys Davids, T. W., trans.
1894 *The Questions of King Milinda*, Part II. Sacred Books of the East, vol. 36. Oxford: Clarendon Press.

Rhys Davids, T. W., and Hermann Oldenberg, trans.
1885 *Vinaya Texts*, Part III. Sacred Books of the East, vol. 20. Oxford: Clarendon Press.
Spiro, Melford
1970 *Buddhism and Society*. New York: Harper and Row.
Strong, John
1979 The Transforming Gift: An Analysis of Devotional Acts of Offering in Buddhist Avadāna Literature. *History of Religions* 18: 221 – 37.
1983 *The Legend of King Aśoka*. Princeton: Princeton University Press.
Swearer, Donald K.
1976 *Wat Haripunjaya*. Missoula, Mont.: Scholars Press.
Trenckner, V., ed.
1880 *The Milindapanho*. London: Williams and Norgate.
Vaidya, P. L., ed.
1958 *Avadāna-śataka*. Buddhist Sanskrit Texts, No. 19. Darbhanga: Mithila Institute.
Watters, Thomas
1961 *On Yuan Chwang's Travels in India*. Vol. 1. Delhi: Munshi Ram Manohar Lal.
Woodward, F. L., trans.
1932 *The Book of the Gradual Sayings*. Vol. 1. Pāli Text Society Translation Series, no. 22. London: Pāli Text Society.

6. EXEMPLARY DONORS OF THE PĀLI TRADITION

Beal, Samuel
1884 *Si-yu-Ki: Buddhist Records of the Western World*. Vol. 2. London: Trubner.
Cone, Margaret, and Richard F. Gombrich
1977 *The Perfect Generosity of Prince Vessantara*. Oxford: Clarendon Press.
Dutt, Sukumar
1962 *Buddhist Monks and Monasteries of India*. London: George Allen and Unwin.
Foucher, A.
1963 *The Life of the Buddha*. Middletown, Conn.: Wesleyan University Press.
Geiger, Wilhem
1956 *Pāli Literature and Language*. Translated by Batakrishna Ghosh. 2nd ed. Calcutta: University of Calcutta.
Gombrich, Richard F.
1971 *Precept and Practice*. Oxford: Clarendon Press.
Law, Bimala Charan
1925 *Heaven and Hell in Buddhist Perspective*. Calcutta and Simla: Thacker, Spink.

Malalasekera, G. P.
1928 *The Pāli Literature of Ceylon*. Colombo: M. D. Gunasena.
Rhys Davids, C. A. F., trans.
1964 *Psalms of the Brethren; Psalms of the Early Buddhists*. Part II. London: Luzac.
Schopen, Gregory
1984 Filial Piety and the Monk in the Practice of Indian Buddhism: A Question of "Sinicization" Viewed from the Other Side. *T'oung Pao* 70: 110–26.
Strong, John
1977 Making Merit in the Asokāvadāna: A Study of Buddhist Acts of Offering in the Post Parinirvāṇa Age. Ph.D. diss., University of Chicago.

7. WEALTH AND REFORMATION IN SINHALESE BUDDHIST MONASTICISM

Aung Thwin, Michael
1979 The Role of Sasana Reform in Burmese History: Economic Dimensions of a Religious Purification. *Journal of Asian Studies* 38: 671–88.
Carrithers, Michael
1979 The Modern Ascetics of Lanka and the Pattern of Change in Buddhism. *Man* 14: 294–310.
Dissanayaka, T. B., and A. B. de Soysa
1963 *Kandyan Law and Buddhist Ecclesiastical Law*. Maradana.
Geiger, Wilhelm
1953 *The Culavamsa*. 2 vols. Colombo: Ceylon Government Information Department.
1960a *The Mahavamsa*. Colombo: Ceylon Government Information Department.
1960b *Culture of Ceylon in Medieval Times*. Wiesbaden: Otto Harrassowitz.
George, K., and C. H. George
1966 Roman Catholic Sainthood and Social Structure. In *Class, Status, and Power*, edited by R. Bendix and S.M. Lipset, 394–401. New York: Free Press.
Gombrich, Richard F.
1971 *Precept and Practice*. Oxford: Clarendon Press.
Gunawardana, R. A. L. H.
1979 *Robe and Plough: Monasticism and Economic Interest in Early Medieval Sri Lanka*. Tucson: University of Arizona Press.
Jayatilaka, D. B.
1934 *Saranankara, The Last Sangha-Raja of Ceylon*. Colombo: Lankabhinava Vissruta Press.
Kemper, Steven
1984 The Buddhist Monkhood, the Law, and the State in Colonial Sri Lanka. *Comparative Studies in Society and History* 26: 401–27.

Lawrie, A. C.
1896 *A Gazetteer of the Central Province of Ceylon.* 2 vols. London: John Murray.
Levy, Paul
1951 *Buddhism: A "Mystery Religion"?* London: University of London Press.
MacIntyre, Alasdair
1981 *After Virtue: A Study in Moral Theory.* Notre Dame: Notre Dame University Press.
Malalasekera, G. P., ed.
1935 *Vaṃsatthapakāsinī.* London: Pāli Text Society.
Rahula, Walpola
1956 *History of Buddhism in Ceylon.* Colombo: M. D. Gunasena.
Ratanapala, Nandasena.
1971 *The Katikavatas: Laws of the Buddhist Order of Ceylon from the Twelfth Century to the Eighteenth Century.* Munich: Kitzinger.
[n.d.] *Sannas of the Central Provinces.* Colombo: Ceylon Government typescript, vol. 1.
Saram, P. A. S.
1976 Weberian Buddhism and Sinhalese Buddhism. *Social Compass* 23: 355–82.
Smith, Bardwell
1978 Kingship, the *Sangha*, and the Process of Legitimation in Anuradhapura Ceylon. In *Religion and Legitimation of Power in Sri Lanka*, edited by Bardwell Smith, 96–106. Chambersburg, Penn.: Anima Books.
Tambiah, H. W.
1962 Buddhist Ecclesiastical Law. *Journal of the Ceylon Branch of Royal Asiatic Society*: 71–107. Colombo: Colombo Apothecaries' Co.
Tambiah, S. J.
1976 *World Conqueror and World Renouncer.* Cambridge: Cambridge University Press.
Weber, Max
1958 *The Religion of India: The Sociology of Hinduism and Buddhism.* Translated by H. H. Gerth and Don Martindale. Chicago: Free Press.
Wickremaratne, L. A.
1969 Religion, Nationalism, and Social Change in Ceylon 1865–1885. *Journal of the Royal Asiatic Society* (Great Britain): 123–50.
Woodhouse, G. W.
1917–18 "Sissiyanu Sissiya Paramparava," and Other Laws Relating to Buddhist Priests in Ceylon. *Ceylon Antiquary and Literary Register* 3: 174–85, 281–90.
Yalman, Nur
1962 The Ascetic Buddhist Monks of Ceylon. *Ethnology* 1: 315–28.

8. BUDDHIST PRACTICAL MORALITY IN A CHANGING AGRARIAN WORLD

Blofeld, John

1960 *People of the Sun*. London: Hutchinson.

Burns, Douglas

1971 Silent Heritage: Thailand's Meditating Monks. *Visakha Puja* (Annual Publication of Buddhist Association of Thailand, Bangkok): 20–26.

Deyo, Frederic C.

1974 Ethnicity, Organization, and Work Values: A Comparative Study of Thai and Chinese Industry. Ph.D diss., University of Chicago.

1975 Ethnicity and Work Culture in Thailand: A Comparison of Thai and Thai-Chinese White-Collar Workers. *Journal of Asian Studies* 34.4: 995–1015.

Geertz, Clifford

1973 *The Interpretation of Cultures*. New York: Basic Books.

Golomb, Louis

1978 *Brokers of Morality: Thai Ethnic Adaptation in a Rural Malaysian Setting*. Asian Studies at Hawaii, no. 23. Honolulu: University Press of Hawaii.

Holt, John

1981 *Bhikkhu Discipline: The Canonical Buddhism of the Vinayapiṭaka*. Delhi: Motilal Banarsidass.

Keyes, Charles F.

1966 Peasant and Nation: A Thai-Lao Village in a Thai State. Ph.D. diss., Cornell University.

1967 *Isan: Regionalism in Northeastern Thailand*. Ithaca, N.Y.: Cornell University, Southeast Asia Program, Data Paper No. 65.

1981 Death of Two Buddhist Saints. In *Charisma and Sacred Biography*, edited by Michael Williams. Chico, Cal.: Scholars Press.

1984 Mother or Mistress but Never a Monk: Culture of Gender and Rural Women in Buddhist Thailand. *American Ethnologist* 11.2: 223–41.

1986 Ambiguous Gender: Male Initiation in a Buddhist Society. In *Rural Education and Cultural Change in Southeast Asia*, edited by Charles F. Keyes.

1987 *Thailand: A Profile of a Changing Buddhist Kingdom*. Boulder, Col.: Westview Press.

In Press The Proposed World of the School: Thai Villagers' Entry into a Bureaucratic State System. In *Reshaping Local Worlds: Rural Education and Cultural Change in Southeast Asia*, ed. by Charles F. Keyes. New Haven: Yale University Southeast Asia Studies.

Little, David, and Sumner B. Twiss

1978 *Comparative Religious Ethics: A New Method*. New York: Harper and Row.

MacIntyre, Alasdair

1981 *After Virtue: A Study in Moral Theory.* Notre Dame: University of Notre Dame Press.

1978 *Nangsų̄phāp chīwaprawat lae pathipatthā khōng phra ācān Fan Ācārō* [Photographic Essay of the Life and Practice of Phra Ācān Fan Ācārō]. Bangkok: Committee Responsible for Compiling the Work.

1972 *Phācananukrom phāk īsān-phāk klāng* [Northeastern Thai-Central Thai Dictionary]. Bangkok: Thai Watthanāphānit.

Phillips, Herbert P.

1958 The Election Ritual in a Thai Village. *Journal of Social Issues* 14.4: 36–50.

Placzek, Jim

1979 International Aspects of the Thai "Forest Temple" Tradition. Paper presented to the ninth annual conference of the Canadian Council for South East Asian Studies, University of British Columbia, Vancouver, B.C., November.

Spiro, Melford E.

1966 Buddhism and Economic Action in Burma. *American Anthropologist* 68.5: 1163–73.

Tambiah, Stanley J.

1984 *The Buddhist Saints of the Forest and the Cult of the Amulets.* Cambridge: Cambridge University Press.

Thak Chaloemtiarana

1979 *Thailand: The Politics of Despotic Paternalism.* Bangkok: Social Sciences Association Press.

Tobias, Stephen F.

1973 Chinese Religion in a Thai Market Town. Ph.D. diss., University of Chicago.

Weber, Max

1958 *The Protestant Ethic and the Spirit of Capitalism.* Translated by Talcott Parsons. New York: Charles Scribners Sons.

World Bank

1978 *Thailand: Toward a Development Strategy of Full Participation—A Basic Economic Report.* Washington, D.C.: International Bank for Reconstruction and Development.

9. ETHICS, WEALTH, AND ESCHATOLOGY

Arendt, Hannah

1958 *The Human Condition.* Chicago: University of Chicago Press.

Berman, Harold

1983 *Law and Revolution.* Cambridge, Mass.: Harvard University Press.

Bouyer, Louis

1955 *The Meaning of Monastic Life.* New York: P. J. Kennedy and Sons.

Holt, John
1981 *Discipline: The Canonical Buddhism of the Vinayapitaka.* Delhi: Motilal Banarsidass.

Knowles, David
1969 *Christian Monasticism.* New York: McGraw-Hill.

Maritain, Jacques
1966 *The Person and the Common Good.* Notre Dame: University of Notre Dame Press.

Merton, Thomas
1949 *The Waters of Siloe.* New York: Harcourt, Brace.

Reynolds, Frank
1985 Multiple Cosmogonies and Ethics. In *Cosmogony and Ethical Order: New Studies in Comparative Ethics*, edited by Robin W. Lovin and Frank E. Reynolds. Chicago: University of Chicago Press.

Spiro, Melford
1982 *Buddhism and Society.* 2nd. ed. Berkeley: University of California Press.

Tambiah, Stanley J.
1976 *World Conqueror and World Renouncer.* Cambridge: Cambridge University Press.
1984 *The Buddhist Saints of the Forest and the Cult of Amulets.* Cambridge: Cambridge University Press.

Troeltsch, Ernst
1922 *Die Sozialphilosophie des Christentums.* Zurich: Verlag Seldwyla.
1976 *The Social Teaching of the Christian Churches.* Chicago: University of Chicago Press, Midway Reprints.

Weber, Max
1946 *From Max Weber: Essays in Sociology.* Translated and edited by Hans Gerth and C. Wright Mills. New York: Oxford University Press.
1958a *The Protestant Ethic and the Spirit of Capitalism.* New York: Scribner's.
1958b *The Religions of India.* Glencoe, Ill.: Free Press.

INTRODUCTION TO PART V

Hampshire, Stuart, ed.
1978 *Public and Private Morality.* Cambridge: Cambridge University Press.

MacIntyre, Alasdair
1981 *After Virtue: A Study in Moral Theory.* Notre Dame: University of Notre Dame Press.

Stout, Jeffrey
1981 *The Flight from Authority: Religion, Morality, and the Quest for Autonomy.* Notre Dame: University of Notre Dame Press.

10. BUDDHIST ECONOMIC ETHICS

Arthur, John, and William H. Shaw, eds.
1978 *Justice and Economic Distribution.* Englewood Cliffs, N.J.: Prentice-Hall.

Cone, Margaret, and Richard Gombrich, trans.
1977 *The Perfect Generosity of Prince Vessantara.* Oxford: Clarendon Press.

Cowell, E. B., ed.
1973 *The Jātakas or Stories of the Buddha's Former Births.* London: Pāli Text Society.

Green, Ronald M.
1978 *Religious Reason.* New York: Oxford University Press.

King, Winston
1964 *In Hope of Nibbana.* LaSalle, Ill.: Open Court.

Little, David, and Sumner B. Twiss
1978 *Comparative Religious Ethics: A New Method.* New York: Harper and Row.

Narada, Tera, ed. and trans.
1972 *The Dhammapada.* New Delhi: Sagar Publications.

Nozick, Robert
1974 *Anarchy, State and Utopia.* New York: Basic Books.

Olson, Mancur
1965 *The Logic of Collective Action.* Cambridge, Mass.: Harvard University Press.

Rawls, John
1971 *A Theory of Justice.* Cambridge, Mass.: Harvard University Press.

Rhys Davids, T. W.
1921 *Sacred Books of the Buddhists. Digha Nikaya,* Part III. Aggañña Suttanta. London: Humphrey Milford.

Sarkisyanz, E.
1965 *Buddhist Backgrounds of the Burmese Revolution.* The Hague: Martinus Nijhoff.

Tambiah, Stanley J.
1976 *World Conqueror and World Renouncer.* Cambridge, Mass.: Harvard University Press.

Troeltsch, Ernst
1960 *The Social Teachings of the Christian Churches.* New York: Harper Torchbooks.

Weber, Max
1958 *The Religion of India.* New York: Free Press.

11. INDIVIDUALISM, COMMUNITARIANISM, AND THEORIES OF JUSTICE

Aronson, Harvey B.
1980 *Love and Sympathy in Theravāda Buddhism.* Delhi: Motilal Banarsidass.

References

Barry, Brian

1974 *The Liberal Theory of Justice*. Oxford: Clarendon Press.

1978 Circumstances of Justice and Future Generations. In *Obligations to Future Generations*, edited by R. I. Sikora and Brian Barry. Philadelphia: Temple University Press.

1984 Review of Sandel, *Liberalism and the Limits of Justice*. *Ethics* 94: 523–25.

Beauchamp, Tom L.

1980 Distributive Justice and the Difference Principle. In *John Rawls' Theory of Social Justice*, edited by H. Gene Block and Elizabeth H. Smith. Athens: Ohio University Press.

Beckley, Harlan

1985 A Christian Affirmation of Rawls's Idea of Justice as Fairness.

1988 "The Priority of Right and Ideas of the Good." *Philosophy and Public Affairs* 17 (Fall): 251–76.

1986 *Journal of Religious Ethics* Vols. 13: 210–42; 14: 229–46.

Bellah, Robert N., Richard Madsen, William S. Sullivan, Ann Swidler and Steven M. Tipton

1985 *Habits of the Heart: Individualism and Commitment in American Life*. Berkeley: University of California Press.

1986 "A Response: The Idea of Practices in *Habits*." *Soundings* Vol. 69: 181–87.

Bernstein, Richard

1983 *Beyond Objectivism and Relativism*. Philadelphia: University of Pennsylvania Press.

1984 Nietzsche or Aristotle: Reflections on Alasdair MacIntyre's "After Virtue." *Soundings* Vol. 67: 6–29.

Brandt, Richard B.

1979 *A Theory of the Good and the Right*. Oxford: Clarendon Press.

Chodorow, Nancy

1978 *The Reproduction of Mothering: Psychoanalysis and the Sociology of Gender*. Berkeley: University of California Press.

Collins, Steven

1982 *Selfless Persons: Imagery and Thought in Theravāda Buddhism*. Cambridge: Cambridge University Press.

Delaney, C. F.

1983 Rawls and Individualism. *Modern Schoolman* 60.2 (January): 112–22.

Dumont, Louis

1965 The Modern Conception of the Individual: Notes on Its Genesis and That of Concomitant Institutions. *Contributions to Indian Sociology* 8:13–61.

1977 *From Mandeville to Marx*. Chicago: University of Chicago Press.

1980 *Homo Hierarchicus*. Chicago: University of Chicago Press.

1982 A Modified View of Our Origins: The Christian Beginnings of Modern Individualism. *Religion* 12: 1 – 27.

Dworkin, Ronald

1974 The Original Position. In *Reading Rawls*, edited by Norman Daniels. New York: Basic Books.

1978 Liberalism. In *Public and Private Morality*, edited by Stuart Hampshire. Cambridge: Cambridge University Press.

Eisenstadt, S. N.

1983 Transcendental Visions—Otherworldliness—And Its Transformations. *Religion* 13:1 – 17.

Eschete, Andreas

1974 Contractarianism and the Scope of Justice. *Ethics* 85 (October): 38 – 49.

Galston, William A.

1980 *Justice and Human Good*. Chicago: University of Chicago Press.

Gauthier, David

1977 The Social Contract as Ideology. *Philosophy and Public Affairs* 6 (Winter): 130 – 64.

1979 Thomas Hobbes: Moral Theorist. *Journal of Philosophy* 76 (October): 547 – 59.

1986 *Morals by Agreement*. Oxford: Clarendon Press.

Gewirth, Alan

1978 *Reason and Morality*. Chicago: University of Chicago Press.

Gilligan, Carol

1982 *In a Different Voice*. Cambridge, Mass.: Harvard University Press.

1986 Remapping the Moral Domain: New Images of the Self in Relationship. In *Reconstructing Individualism: Autonomy, Individuality, and the Self in Western Thought*, edited by Thomas C. Heller, Morton Sosna, and David E. Wellbery. Stanford: Stanford University Press.

Gould, Carol

1978 *Marx's Social Ontology: Individuality and Community in Marx's Theory of Social Reality*. Cambridge, Mass.: MIT Press.

Gutman, Amy

1985 Communitarian Critics of Liberalism. *Philosophy and Public Affairs* 14 (Summer): 308 – 22.

Hampton, Jean

1980 Contracts and Choices: Does Rawls Have a Social Contract Theory? *Journal of Philosophy* 77 (June): 315 – 38.

Hare, R. M.

1981 *Moral Thinking: Its Limits, Method, and Point*. Oxford: Clarendon Press.

Hume, David

1957 *An Inquiry Concerning the Principles of Morals*. Edited by Charles W. Hendel. New York: Liberal Arts Press.

Johann, Robert
1979 Rationality, Justice and Dominant Ends. In *The Value of Justice: Essays on the Theory and Practice of Social Justice*, edited by Charles A. Kelbley. New York: Fordham.

Keller, Catherine
1986 *From a Broken Web: Sex, Separatism and the Self.* Boston: Beacon Press.

Kirkpatrick, Frank G.
1986 *Community: A Trinity of Models.* Washington, D.C.: Georgetown University Press.

Lukes, Steven
1973 *Individualism.* New York: Harper.
1974 Relativism: Cognitive and Moral. *Proceedings of the Aristotelian Society* 48 (1974): 165–89.

MacIntyre, Alasdair
1982 Intelligibility, Goods, and Rules. *Journal of Philosophy* Vol. 79 (November): 663–65.
1984a *After Virtue: A Study in Moral Theory.* 2nd ed. Notre Dame: University of Notre Dame Press.
1984b Bernstein's Distorting Mirrors: A Rejoinder. *Soundings*: 30–41.
1988 *Whose Justice? Which Rationality?* Notre Dame: University of Notre Dame Press.

Macpherson, C. B.
1962 *The Political Theory of Possessive Individualism.* New York: Oxford.

Miller, David
1976 *Social Justice.* Oxford: Clarendon Press.
1980 Hume and Possessive Individualism. *History of Political Thought* 1 (Summer, June): 261–78.

Nagel, Thomas
1973 Rawls on Justice. *Philosophical Review* 82 (April): 220–34.

Narveson, Jan
1987 Review of Sandel, *Liberalism and the Limits of Justice. Canadian Journal of Philosophy* 17: 227–34.

Neal, Patrick
1987 A Liberal Theory of the Good? *Canadian Journal of Philosophy* 17 (September): 567–82.

Nozick, Robert
1974 *Anarchy, State and Utopia.* New York: Basic Books.

Outka, Gene
1980 Character, Vision, and Narrative. *Religious Studies Review* 6: 110–18.
1982 Equality and Individuality: Thoughts on Two Themes in Kierkegaard. *Journal of Religious Ethics* 10 (Fall): 171–203.

Proudfoot, Wayne
1974 Rawls on the Individual and the Social. *Journal of Religious Ethics* 2 (Fall): 107–27.

Rapaport, Elizabeth
1977 Classical Liberalism and Rawlsian Revisionism. In *New Essays on Contract Theory. Canadian Journal of Philosophy*, Supplementary Vol. 3: 95–119, edited by Kai Nielsen and Roger A. Shiner. Guelph, Ontario: Canadian Association for Publishing in Philosophy.

Rawls, John
1971 *A Theory of Justice*. Cambridge, Mass.: Harvard University Press.
1975a A Kantian Conception of Equality. *Cambridge Review* Feb.: 94–99.
1975b Fairness to Goodness. *Philosophical Review* 84 (October): 536–54.
1980 Kantian Constructivism in Moral Theory. *Journal of Philosophy* 77: 515–72.
1982 Social Unity and Primary Goods. In *Utilitarianism and Beyond*, edited by Amartya Sen and Bernard Williams. Cambridge: Cambridge University Press.
1985 Justice as Fairness: Political not Metaphysical. *Philosophy and Public Affairs* 14 (Summer): 223–57.
1988 "The Priority of Right and Ideas of the Good." *Philosophy and Public Affairs* 17 (Fall): 251–76.

Reeder, John P., Jr.
1989 Visions of Community. *Religious Studies Review*. 15.4.

Richards, David
1971 *A Theory of Reasons for Action* . Oxford: Oxford University Press.

Rorty, Richard
1988 "The Priority of Democracy to Philosophy." In *The Virginia Statute for Religious Freedom*, edited by Merrill D. Patterson and Robert C. Vaughan. Cambridge: Cambridge University Press: 257–82.

Rosenblum, Nancy L.
1987 *Another Liberalism: Romanticism and the Reconstruction of Liberal Thought*. Cambridge, Mass.: Harvard University Press.

Sandel, Michael
1982 *Liberalism and the Limits of Justice*. Cambridge: Cambridge University Press.
1984 The Procedural Republic and the Unencumbered Self. *Political Theory* 12: 81–96.

Scanlon, T. M.
1975 Preference and Urgency. *Journal of Philosophy* 72 (November): 655–70

Schneewind, J. B.
1982 Virtue, Narrative, and Community: MacIntyre and Morality. *Journal of Philosophy* Vol. 79 (November): 653–63.

1986 The Use of Autonomy in Ethical Theory. In *Reconstructing Individualism: Autonomy, Individuality, and the Self in Western Thought*, edited by Thomas C. Heller, Morton Sosna, and David E. Wellbery. Stanford: Stanford University Press.

Schwartz, Adina
1973 Moral Neutrality and Primary Goods. *Ethics* 83 (July): 294–307.

Smith, Ruth L.
1985 Feminism and the Moral Subject. In *Women's Consciousness, Women's Conscience: A Reader in Feminist Ethics*. Edited by Barbara Hilkert Andolsen, Christine E. Gudorf, and Mary D. Pellaver. San Francisco: Harper and Row.

Stout, Jeffrey
1988 *Ethics after Babel: The Languages of Morals and Their Discontents*. Boston: Beacon Press.

Swearer, Donald
forthcoming *Buddhist Ethics*.

Tambiah, S. J.
1976 *World Conqueror and World Renouncer: A Study of Buddhism and Polity in Thailand against a Historical Background*. Cambridge: Cambridge University Press.

Taylor, Charles
1985 The Person. In *The Category of the Person: Anthropology, Philosophy, History*, edited by Michael Carrithers, Steven Collins, and Steven Lukes. Cambridge: Cambridge University Press.

Teitelman, Michael
1972 The Limits of Individualism. *Journal of Philosophy* 69:18 (October): 545–55.

Walzer, Michael
1983 *Spheres of Justice*. New York: Basic Books.

Werpehowski, William
1982 Rawls and Christian Ethics. Ph.D. diss., Yale University.

Williams, Bernard
1985 *Ethics and the Limits of Philosophy*. Cambridge, Mass.: Harvard University Press.

Wolff, R. P.
1968 *The Poverty of Liberalism*. Boston: Beacon Press.
1977 *Understanding Rawls*. Princeton: Princeton University Press.

Wolgast, Elizabeth
1980 *Equality and the Rights of Women*. Ithaca: Cornell University Press.

Woodward, F. L.
1932–36 *The Book of the Gradual Sayings*. Vols. 1–5. London: Pāli Text Society.

Wong, David B.
1984 *Moral Relativity*. Berkeley: University of California Press.

Glossary of Pāli Terms

Abhidhamma. Higher teaching. The third division of the canonical teachings of Theravāda Buddhism.
Adhicitta. Higher thought. Contemplation.
  Adhicitta-sikkhā. Mental training.
Adhipaññā. Higher wisdom.
  Adhipaññā-sikkhā. Training in higher wisdom.
Adhisīla. Higher morality.
  Adhisīla-sikkhā. Training in higher morality.
Ājivakā. An ascetic movement contemporaneous with early Buddhism.
Āmisadāna. Giving of material goods, usually by lay persons to the monastic order.
Anattā. Not-self; the doctrine of no-soul.
Anicca. Impermanence; transience.
Añjali. Paying obeisance or respect.
Appamāda. Heedfulness, diligence, earnestness.
Appicchatā. Contentment, frugality.
Arahant. A venerable or holy person; the final stage of sanctification.
Ārāma. A park or pleasure garden; the enclosure surrounding a monastic dwelling place.
Attattha. One's own good or interest.
Attanātha. Being a refuge to oneself; self-reliance.
Atthacariyā. Acts of help or service.

Bhāvanā. Meditation.
Bhikkhu. One who depends on alms; an almsman; a monk.
  Bhikkhu-saṅgha. The Buddhist monastic establishment or order.
Bodhisatta (Sanskrit: bodhisattva). A wisdom-being; one destined to attain Buddhahood.
Brahma-vihāra. A perfected state. The exercise of exceptional states of consciousness—love, compassion, sympathetic joy, equanimity.

Cakkavatti. Wheel-turner; world-ruler. An epithet applied to a mythological monarch in such Theravāda texts as the *Cakkavatti-Sutta*.
Chanda. Wish, intention, resolve.

Daliddiya. Poverty.
Dama. Taming, training, educating.
Dāna. Giving, charity, generosity.
Dasa-kusala-karma. Ten good deeds of which the foremost is charity.

Glossary

Deva. A male god, celestial being.
  Devatā. Same meaning as *deva*.
  Devi. A female god, celestial being.
Dhamma. Truth, reality, natural and moral order; teachings of the Buddha.
  Dhamma-vinaya. The doctrine-and-discipline of the Buddha.
  Dhammādhipateyya. One who holds the *dhamma* as supreme; one who relies on the supremacy of righteousness.
  Dhamma-dāna. Giving the gift of the *dhamma*.
  Dhamma-kamena. Codes of conduct.
  Dhamma-chanda. Desire to be good.
Dhammapada. A *sutta* text summarizing the lofty ethical ideals of the Theravāda tradition.
Dīgha Nikāya. The long-discourses; one of the divisions of the Sutta Piṭaka.
Diṭṭhadhammikattha. The goals of the here and now; temporal welfare.
Dukkha. Suffering; the sense of the basic unsatisfactory nature of worldly life or mundane existence.

Gahaṭṭha. Householder; the laity.
Gāthā. Verse; stanza.
Gantha-dhura (Sanskrit: Grantha-dhura). The study of texts. Contrasted in the Theravāda tradition with *vipassanā dhura*, the practice of meditation.
Guṇa. Quality, characteristic.

Jātaka. Stories purporting to relate previous lives of the Buddha.

Kalyāṇamitta. A good friend; one who teaches the dhamma; a meditation teacher.
Kamma (Sanskrit: Karma). Act; moral law of cause and effect—"As ye reap so shall ye sow."
Karuṇā. Compassion.
  Karuṇāyantakama. The intention of kindness or compassion.
Karikāvata. Codes of monastic regulations.
Khattiyabala. The Five Strengths of a Ruler—arms, wealth, ministers, royal ancestry, wisdom.
Khettan. Field; field of merit.
Koṭi. Summit, extremity; excess, ten-millions; measurement of mythic time.
Kusala-chanda. Desire to do good.
  Akusala-chanda. Desire to do evil.

Loka. Realm; world.
Lokiya. Worldly; of the mundane world.
Lokuttara. Trans-mundane.

Magga. Path, way.
Mettā. Love. The first of the stages of infinite consciousness or the supreme abodes.
Muditā. Sympathetic joy. The third of the stages of infinite consciousness or the supreme abodes.

Nāyaka. Chief, lord. Head of a monastic order.
Nibbāna. The supreme realization of the Buddhist path; to have overcome ignorance and extinguished all sense attachments.
Nikāya. Multitude; assemblage; association; fraternity; sectarian tradition.

Pabbajita. One who has gone forth; a mendicant; a monk.
Paccayadāyaka. A giver of material things to the monastic community.
Paccekabuddha. A "solitary Buddha." One who has attained Buddhahood unaided and does not preach the *dhamma*.
Pañcavārṣika. Quinquennial Festival of *dana*.
Paññā. Wisdom.
Paramattha. Final goal; the supreme peace of *nibbana*.
Parattha. The welfare of others.
Paṭicca-samuppāda. Dependent-co-arising; interdependent origination.
Pātimokkha. The title given to various precepts in the *vinaya* recited twice monthly by fully ordained Theravāda monks.
Patta-nikkujjana. Inverting the alms-bowl; refusing alms.
Peta (Sanskrit: Preta). Dead; departed; spirit of a dead person. Inhabitants of one of the states of punishments of hells (*naraka*).
Pita (Sanskrit: Pitṛ). Father; parents; deceased parents.
Piyavācā. Kindly and beneficial speech.
Paṇidhāna (Sanskrit: Pranidhana). Earnest resolve; vow.
  Paṇidhi. Wish, resolve.
  Patthanā (Sanskrit: Prārthanā). Earnest wish; prayer.
Puñña. Good, virtuous, just, righteous, meritorious.
  Puñña-kiriyāvatthu. The Three Bases of Meritorious Action.
  Puñña-sikkhā. Training in the good.
Purisamedha. Shrewdness in the encouragement of government officials. One of the four royal virtues promoting the integration of the state.

Rājadhamma. Kingly or royal *dhamma*. Ruling justly.
  Rāja-saṅgahavatthu. Royal virtues promoting the integration and well-being of the state.

Samaṇa. An ascetic; a Buddhist monk.
Samānattatā. Impartiality; equality.
Sāmaṇera. A novice monk.
Sammā-diṭṭhi. Right-view.
  Samma-saṅkappa. Right-thought.
  Samma-vācā. Right-speech.
  Samma-kammanta. Right-action.
  Samma-ajīva. Right-vocation.
  Samma-vāyāma. Right-effort.
  Samma-sati. Right-mindfulness.
  Samma-samādhi. Right-concentration.
Samparāyikattha. Benefits of spiritual welfare.
Saṁsāra. Rebirth.
Saṅgha. Association; fraternity; monastic order.
  Sanghika. Belonging to or of the monastic order.

Santuṭṭhi. Contentment.
Sassamedha. Shrewedness in promoting agriculture. One of the four royal virtues promoting national integration.
Sati. Mindfulness.
Seṭṭhi. A wealthy merchant.
Sigālovāda Sutta. A Pāli text often referred to as containing a code of ethics for the laity.
Sikkhā. Training; training in virtue.
Sīla. Ethics; morality.
Sīmā. Markers consecrating a sacred precinct, e.g. an ordination hall.
Sissa-paramparā (Sanskrit: Siṣyā-paramparāva). Student-lineage.
Sutta (Sanskrit: Sutra). Pāli texts often in dialogue format.

Taṇhā. Desire, passion, grasping.
Tāpasa. Ascetic; ascetic practice.
Tathāgata. Thus-gone. An epithet for the Buddha.
Thera. Elder. Buddhist monk.
Thūpa (Sanskrit: Stūpa). A conical mound; a reliquary.

Ubhayattha. Welfare of oneself and others.
Uposatha. The Buddhist sabbath or fast day; monastic ceremony of reading the *patimokkha*.
Uppekkhā. Equanimity.

Vājapeyya. Kindly and beneficial words.
Vana. A grove of trees, forest.
Vassa. Rain; rainy season; monastic rains-retreat.
Vihāra. A monastic dwelling place.
Vinaya. Training, discipline; especially the discipline of monks and nuns.
Vinaya-piṭaka. The Book of Monastic Discipline.
Viriya. Energy, effort.
Visuddhimagga. The Path of Purification, a famed Theravāda text written by Buddhaghosa.

Yogi. An ascetic; one who practices yogic disciplines.
Yonisomanisikāra. Systematic reflection or attention.

Contributors

Nancy Auer Falk is Professor of Religion at Western Michigan University. She was trained in history of religions at the University of Chicago (Ph.D. 1972), with special concentration on Indian Buddhism. She has published articles on aspects of popular Buddhism in India and on the study of women in religion. She has also edited, with Rita M. Gross, *Unspoken Worlds: Women's Religious Lives* (Harper and Row, 1981; 2nd ed., Wadsworth, 1988).

Ronald M. Green is the John Phillips Professor of Religion at Dartmouth College. He has published many articles in the fields of ethical history, applied ethics, and comparative ethics. His books include *Population Growth and Justice* (Scholars Press, 1976), *Religious Reason* (Oxford University Press, 1978), and *Religion and Moral Reason* (Oxford University Press, 1988). He is a contributor to the new *Encyclopedia of Religion* (Macmillan, 1987), associate editor of the *Journal of Religious Ethics*, and a member of the editorial board of the *Journal of the American Academy of Religion.*

Steven Kemper is Professor of Anthropology at Bates College. In 1985 and 1986 he was a Rockefeller Foundation scholar in Sri Lanka, where he carried out an anthropological study of the Mahāvaṃsa, the Sinhalese national chronicle. The project resulted in a manuscript entitled, "A History of Representations: The Sinhalese National Chronicle and Its Social Context." His published articles include "The Buddhist Monkhood, the Law, and the State in Colonial Sri Lanka" (*Comparative Studies in Society and History* 26:3 [1984]:401–27).

Charles F. Keyes is Professor and Chairman of the Department of Anthropology at the University of Washington, and has chaired the Joint Social Science Research Council/American Council of Learned Societies Committee on Southeast Asia and Indochina Studies Program. His publications include *The Golden Peninsula: Culture and Adaptation in Mainland Southeast Asia, Thailand: Buddhist Kingdom as Modern Nation-State, Reshaping Local Worlds: Rural Education and Cultural Change in Southeast Asia* (editor, forthcoming), "Millenialism, Theravāda Buddhism, and Thai Society," "Mother or Mistress but Never a Monk: Culture of Gender and Rural Women in Buddhist Thailand," and "Buddhist Politics and Their Revolutionary Origins in Thailand."

David Little is Professor of Religious Studies at the University of Virginia and a Distinguished Fellow at the United States Institute of Peace, where he is writing a book on human rights and public emergencies. He has taught at Harvard and

Yale universities and held distinguished posts at the University of Colorado, Haverford College, and Amherst College. In addition to numerous articles he has coauthored *Comparative Religious Ethics* (with Sumner B. Twiss, Harper and Row, 1978) and *Human Rights and the Conflict of Values: Freedom of Religion and Conscience in the West and Islam* (with Abdulaziz Sachedina and John Kelsay, University of South Carolina Press).

Robin W. Lovin is Associate Professor of ethics and society at the Divinity School of the University of Chicago. He is the author of *Christian Faith and Public Choices* and coeditor, with Frank E. Reynolds, of *Cosmogony and Ethical Order*.

Phra Rājavaramuni, recently elevated to the rank of Chao Khun Thēpwēthi completed his monastic studies exams (*naktham*) in 1953, and in 1961, the year of his higher ordination (*upasampadā*), passed the ninth and final level of Pāli studies. A year later he received his B.A. in Buddhist Studies at Mahāchulalongkorn Buddhist University, where in 1982 he was awarded an honorary doctorate. In 1986 he received honorary doctorates from Thammasat and Silapakorn universities in Bangkok.

Rājavaramuni was abbot of Wat Phra Phirain monastery in Bangkok from 1972 to 1976 and was Assistant Deputy Secretary and Secretary General of Mahāchulalongkorn University from 1964 to 1974. He has held visiting appointments at Swarthmore College (1976) and Harvard University (1981). Among his best-known publications in Thai are *A Dictionary of Buddhism* (rev. ed. 1985) and *Buddhadhamma* (rev. ed. 1982), a systematic exposition of Theravāda doctrine. His published work in English includes *Thai Buddhism in the Modern World* (1986) and *Looking at America to Solve Thailand's Problems* (1987, trans. Grant A. Olson).

John P. Reeder, Jr. is Professor of Religious Studies and chair of the Department of Religious Studies at Brown University. He is the co-editor, with Gene Outka, of *Religion and Morality*, and is the author of *Source, Sanction, and Salvation: Religion and Morality in Judaic and Christian Traditions*. His principle fields of interests are ethics and religious thought.

Frank E. Reynolds is Professor of History of Religions and Buddhist Studies at the University of Chicago, where he holds appointments in the Divinity School, the Department of South Asian Languages and Civilizations, and the College. He is coeditor and translator, with Mani Reynolds, of *Three Worlds According to King Ruang: A Thai Buddhist Cosmology* (Asian Humanities Press, 1981) and is coeditor with Robin Lovin of *Cosmology and Ethical Order: New Essays in Comparative Ethics* (University of Chicago Press, 1985). He is a contributor to the *Encyclopedia of Religion* (Macmillan, 1987) and to *Religions of the World* (2nd ed., New York: St. Martin's Press, 1988).

Russell F. Sizemore is Assistant Professor of Religion in the Humanities Division of New College of Sarasota, Florida. He was trained in religious ethics at Harvard University and teaches courses in religion and society, Christian ethics, and ethics and international relations. He is a contributor to *A Bibliographic Guide to the Comparative Study of Ethics* (Cambridge University Press, forthcoming), a joint project of the Berkeley-Harvard Program in Comparative Religion that contains annotated bibliographies of the religious ethics of diverse traditions. Most recently he has published "The Prudent Cold Warrior" (*Ethics and International Affairs*, 1988).

John S. Strong is Associate Professor of Religion at Bates College. He is the author of *The Legend of King Aśoka* (Princeton, 1983) and coauthor (with Frank Reynolds and John Holt) of a *Guide to Buddhist Religion* (G.K. Hall, 1981). His articles include "A Post-Cultural Revolution Look at Buddhism" (*China Quarterly*, 1973), "The Transforming Gift: An Analysis of Devotional Acts of Offering in Buddhist Avadāna Literature" (*History of Religions*, 1979), and "Filial Piety and Buddhism: The Indian Antecedents to a Chinese Problem" (*Traditions in Contact and Change*, 1982). He has just finished a book on the legend and cult of the Buddhist saint Upagupta.

Donald K. Swearer teaches courses in Asian and comparative religion as the Eugene M. Lang Professor and Chair of the Department of Religion at Swarthmore College and Adjunct Professor in the Department of Religious Studies at the University of Pennsylvania. He has pursued research in Thailand, Sri Lanka, and Japan and has published numerous articles and books, including *Dialogue: The Key to Understanding Other Religions* (1977), *Buddhism and Society in Southeast Asia* (1981), *The Dhammic Socialism of Bhikkhu Buddhadasa* (1986), *For the Sake of the World: The Spirit of Buddhist and Christian Monasticism* (with Patrick Henry, 1988), and *Me-and-Mine: Selected Essays of Bhikkhu Buddhadasa* (forthcoming).

Index

Action, 79, 96, 103, 105
Adhipañña, *see* Wisdom
Agañña Suttanta, 21, 22, 79, 222, 226, 227–234, 280n.28
Age, 167
Ajatasattu, 5, 67, 78, 113
Ājīvikas, 132, 134
Alcohol, *see* Intoxicants
Alms, 33, 38, 41, 42, 113, 136, 138, 140, 159, 186, 196, 263n.5;
  Festival of Alms-Giving, 116
  Plain of Alms-giving, 115
  Unparalleled Almsgiving, 140
Alut Vihāra, inscription of, 162
Ambapalī of Vesali, 126
Ananda, 111, 138
Anāthapiṇḍika, 14, 119, 127–131, 133–134, 257–258n.10, 263n.10, 264n.11
  and the household spirit, 5, 136–137, 263n.9
  as model of giving, 40, 44, 71, 104, 106, 109, 263n.5
  and Visākhā, 135, 139
Anatta, *see* Not-self
Aṅga, 134
Anuradhapura, 160, 267n.8
Appamāda, 51
Ariyan, 42, 43, 45, 46
Aristotle, 81, 236, 239, 243, 277n.23, 279n.27
Aronson, Harvey B., 259n.3
Asceticism, ascetics, 1, 29, 129, 132, 155, 157, 174, 201, 204
  "inner-worldly," 149, 188
Aśoka, 14, 18, 114, 118, 154, 266n.5
  Quinquennial Festival of, 109–112, 114
  as model giver, 15, 72, 104, 105, 106, 120
  and the myrobalan, 118–121, 122
  rock inscriptions of, 46, 114, 245
Aśokāvadāna, 104–105, 110, 119
Association, *see* Friends
Attanātha, 37
Augustine, Saint, 6
Auspicious(ness), 133, 134, 167
Avadānaśataka, 113

Ban Nọng Tụn, 171–189 *passim*
Barry, Brian, 274n.9
Beauty, 167–168, 227, 231, 262n.11
Benedict, Saint, Rule of, 195, 200
Benedictine monks, *see* Monks, Christian
Bentham, Jeremy, 81
Bhikku(s), *see* Monk(s), Buddhist
Bible, 230
Bimbisāra of Magadha, 125
Bodhi tree, 135, 158
Bodhisatta, 232
Book of Discipline, 80
Book of Gradual Sayings, 245
Brahmāyusutta, 258n.13
Brandt, R. B., 238
Buddha, the, 20, 29, 44, 53, 71, 104, 116, 166–167, 224
  stories about, 113, 127, 134, 135, 264n.14, 267n.7
  teachings of, 33–34, 35–36, 40, 41, 46, 50, 51, 127, 133, 140, 191, 196
  See also Gotama Buddha
Buddhadhamma, 27
Buddhaghosa, 30, 35, 114
Buddhism, 1, 8, 10, 23, 31–32, 96, 257n.1
  and Christianity, 6, 17, 207
  criticisms of, 10, 16–17, 19, 75, 157, 190, 223
  and economics 58, 222; *see also* Economic(s)
  ethical system of, 28, 30, 46–53
  ethics of, 1, 17, 35–36, 45, 57–58, 60–62, 95, 97, 147, 232
  fundamentalist, 150
  and politics, 22, 159
  Sinhalese, 147; *see also* Sri Lanka
  social concerns of, 7–8, 15, 16, 19
  social ethics of, 191, 194, 203–204, 207

Index

Indra, 113–115
Inequality, *see* Equality
Initiation,
lay, 16, 20
monastic, 20, 117–118, 122
Intoxicants, drinking, 35, 71, 135, 176, 180, 185, 187, 229
Islam, 8

Jain(s), 195
Jambudīpa, 119, 140, 155
Jātakas, 35, 36, 104, 107, 197, 258n.12, 262n.1
Commentaries, 133–139
Jeta, Prince, 106, 128, 264n.12
See also Monasteries, Buddhist
Jīvaka of Rajagāha, 126
Johann, Robert, 237, 238, 239
Jotika, 5, 67, 78
Judaism, 190, 201, 225, 247
Jūkaka, 108
Justice, 244, 245–246, 275n.14
distributive, 20, 82, 97–98, 211, 212, 222, 236, 241–243
norms of, 247
principles of, 248, 249, 250, 274n.6, 277n.24, 279n.27
social, 74–75, 224–226, 233, 239, 244, 250–251, 277n.23
theories of, 213, 243, 252, 274n.9
Kamma, Karma, 103, 168, 223, 251–252, 256n.9, 275n.16
good, *see* Merit
law of, 4, 7, 11, 14, 57, 58, 66–67, 82, 175, 224
See also Laity

Kammic system, 3, 11
Kant, Immanuel, 59, 247, 274n.10, 277n.25, 278n.26
Katikāvatas, 160, 164, 165–166
See also Monastic regulation, codes of
Keller, Catherine, 276n.21
Ketumati, 262n.10
Khattiya, 229
King, kingship
and *dāna*, 112, 116
duties of, 38–39, 64–65, 154
impersonation of, 118
as mediator, 9, 259n.6
and reformation, 160, 198
and rulership, 20, 21–22
and the *sangha*, 17, 18, 110–111, 114, 153, 155, 156, 159, 160, 197, 267n.8
and society, 63, 118, 177–178, 197, 232, 234, 245
See also Cakkavatti; State, the
Kosala, 51, 136
Kirti Sri Rājasinha, 162, 164, 166
Kunāla, Prince, 110–111
Kuncanaga, 269n.11
Kūṭadanta-Sutta, 257n.7

Labor, 200
See also Ethic, work
Laity, layman, 2, 34–36, 79
life of, 63, 66
and monks, 15, 16, 28, 103, 160, 167; *see also* Unity
and society, 49
and wealth, 43, 44, 70–71, 73, 223
See also Dhamma; Individual, the; Monks, Buddhist; Ordination, temporary
Land ownership, 16, 148, 183, 266n.5
See also Sangha, as landowner
Laos, 75, 172
See also Merchant(s), Thai-Lao
Layman's Code of Discipline, 35
Liang Wu-ti, 116, 117
Liberation, 192, 193, 196, 203, 233
See also Enlightenment; Salvation
Little, David, 261n.8,
See also Little and Twiss
Little and Twiss, 77, 78, 80, 82, 91, 95, 170, 215
Lokapaññatti, 112
Love, 34, 64, 252
Lukes, Steven, 248, 276nn.19, 22
MacIntyre, Alasdair, 152, 170, 236, 239, 243, 245, 248, 249, 250, 251, 252, 279n.27

Macpherson, C. B., 276n.19
Magga, 28, 46–47, 51
pre-*magga*, 28, 46–47, 52
Mahā Sammata, 63, 228, 232
Mahasena, King, 159
Mahasiva, 159
Mahāvagga, 134, 265n.16
Mahāvaṃsa, 111, 114, 147, 153, 160, 198
See also Sacred histories
Mahinda, Prince, 111, 158, 267n.8
Mahinda IV, inscription of, 159
Maitreya, *see* Metteya
Mapitigama Buddharakhita, 162
Maritain, Jacques, 194
Marx, Karl, 235
Meditation, 63, 165, 176, 193, 229, 271n.6

Index

Index